EVERYBODY
HAD AN OCEAN

EVERYBODY HAD AN OCEAN

MUSIC AND MAYHEM IN 1960S LOS ANGELES

WILLIAM McKEEN

CHICAGO
REVIEW
PRESS

The Library of Congress has cataloged the hardcover edition as follows:

Names: McKeen, William, 1954– author.
Title: Everybody had an ocean : music and mayhem in 1960s Los Angeles / William McKeen.
Description: Chicago, IL : Chicago Review Press, 2017. | Includes bibliographical references and index.
Identifiers: LCCN 2016029172 (print) | LCCN 2016030065 (ebook) | ISBN 9781613734919 (cloth : alk. paper) | ISBN 9781613734926 (pdf) | ISBN 9781613734940 (epub) | ISBN 9781613734933 (kindle)
Subjects: LCSH: Rock music—California—Los Angeles—1961–1970—History and criticism.
Classification: LCC ML3534.3 .M4 2017 (print) | LCC ML3534.3 (ebook) | DDC 781.6609794/9409046—dc23
LC record available at https://lccn.loc.gov/2016029172

Cover design: Marc Whitaker/MTWdesign.net
Cover images: Photofest
Typesetting: Nord Compo

Printed in the United States of America

For those friends who share my affliction:
Bill DeYoung, Wayne Garcia, Sarah Kess,
Neil Sharrow, Steve Webb, and John Young

For my children, who share this music with me:
Sarah, Graham, Mary, Savannah, Jack, Travis, and Charley

CONTENTS

CONTENTS

AUTHOR'S NOTE

I was sitting on the spare bed in Dennis Wilson's hotel suite. We had a few more minutes before the Beach Boys would take the stage at Cincinnati's Riverfront Coliseum. I was on a magazine assignment and had spent most of the day interviewing Carl Wilson and Alan Jardine and having dinner with Mike Love. Dennis didn't want an interview. He invited me to his room to drink a beer, watch television, and bullshit before the concert.

I asked about his old roommate, Charles Manson. "Some things," he said, "I don't talk about."

He didn't throw me out or berate me for asking about his friend, the mass murderer. Instead, he offered me a ride to the show in his limousine. When we got to the coliseum, where a couple of years later eleven fans would be trampled to death at a concert by the Who, we got out at the stage door. Inside the hall, he shook hands and clutched my shoulder, then walked up the riser to his drum kit. I'll never forget the crowd's thunder as he took the stage. That was as close as *I'll* ever get to being a rock star.

I talked to Dennis several times in those years but never got out the Manson question before he'd cut me off. I was persistent because I wanted to know what it was like to wake on that morning when everybody finally knew about Manson and connected him with the Tate and LaBianca murders.

Imagine one of your best friends lived in that house on Cielo Drive. You'd been there for parties. You'd sipped vodka in that living room where Sharon Tate and Jay Sebring were butchered. You'd played football on the lawn where Abigail Folger was killed, stabbed twenty-eight times.

And you knew this guy, the man responsible. When you couldn't turn him into the rock star he so desperately wanted to be, he threatened to kidnap your five-year-old son. He left a bullet with a friend of yours and said, "Tell Dennis there's more where that came from."

So what was it like, Dennis? How did it feel that morning when you woke up and Manson was in all the papers? We'll never know.

Long before reality television shows made hoarders into celebrities, I'd begun stockpiling stories about the artists in that time and place—Los Angeles rock 'n' roll in the sixties. Some of the most joyous music of my life was made there and then, but the trajectory of that decade led to a season of dread. Over the years, interviewing other artists from that era, I'd always have to ask a Manson question. Few wanted to talk about it. *Bad vibrations*, they said.

When I was diagnosed with cancer, I figured it was time to finally do this book, which I'd been thinking about for years. My illness rendered me sedentary, but I still wanted to tell the story, not knowing if I'd ever have another chance. Carl and Dennis Wilson are gone, as are so many others I'd interviewed, as well as others gone before I could speak to them. I've done my best to tell their stories.

William McKeen
Boston, Massachusetts

INTRODUCTION

BROTHERS

From the world of darkness I did loose demons and devils in the power of scorpions to torment.

—Charles Manson

It was there in his face, loss and doubt behind hollow eyes. Once, he'd been unstoppable, one of the most successful young men of his generation. He was the reclusive king of California rock 'n' roll, ruling from the background as a music industry was transformed around him and, in some ways, because of him. But at the key moment, when the whole world was watching, he abdicated and withdrew into his cocoon.

That was last year. Now it had reached the point where Brian couldn't *let go* of anything. He was intimidated, gun-shy, pathologically apprehensive, and much too afraid to let his songs out into the world, where they would be played and heard and judged by others.

No matter how great the songs, no matter how much everyone told him he was a genius, Brian Wilson was afraid of the criticism that came after he shared the music in his soul. So he kept adding superfluous fractions of melody to the recordings until he worked the musicians, and especially his brothers, up to a plateau of exhaustion and impatience. *As long as we are all working*, he thought, *then we never have to finish*. Thus was the state of Brian's mental illness in the spring of 1968.

Difficult as it was now, in the middle of the night, and bleary at the end of a long recording session, Dennis Wilson still couldn't help but admire his big brother. At that point in their history, the Wilson brothers (including younger brother Carl) had spent five golden years as America's preeminent rock 'n' roll band, the Beach Boys. They'd begun recording in 1961, when Carl was just fifteen. Brian, nineteen then, was responsible for writing, producing, and arranging all of the group's recordings. It was a lot of responsibility for a guy not yet old enough to vote.

The Wilson brothers came from modest beginnings in Hawthorne, California, cheek by jowl with Los Angeles, but, as they bragged in one of their hit songs, they'd "been all around this great big world." Not bad for five boys from the suburbs.

Most rock 'n' roll artists, up to that point, had been subject to the whims of Svengali-like record producers or music business executives serving as masterminds behind the scenes, telling the young artists what to record, how to record it, and what musicians to use on the recording.

The Beach Boys were among the first to have its Svengali as a member of the band. Dennis once said of his older brother, "Brian Wilson is the Beach Boys. He is the band. We're his fucking messengers. He is all of it. Period. We're nothing. He's everything."

Brian's "messages" had sold millions of copies and made the Beach Boys famous. But now detractors were stepping forward to knock the great Brian Wilson off his pedestal.

All evening and into the cracks of morning, Dennis had watched Brian, in his home studio, go through more than twenty takes of a new song called (for the moment) "Even Steven." Instruments had been recorded the week before, and the track had a vague sort of bossa nova sound that would have been hot stuff ten years ago but that seemed monstrously out of place in the überhip late spring of 1968.

The lyrical highlight of "Even Steven" was the verse in which Brian Wilson, famous American rock star, gave listeners directions to his house. In another verse, he sang of sharpening a pencil.

Dennis didn't agree with it, but he understood where the criticism was coming from. The year before, after months of buildup in the press, Brian had decided not to release the experimental album he'd written and recorded for the group. *Smile* was full of odd and delightful musical ideas, but Brian began tinkering incessantly. He was afraid to let go of the tracks, to share the music with the world.

Brian had become monumentally nervous. When he was nineteen and twenty, churning out the band's hits about surfing and hot rods,

Brian was invincible. The hits kept on coming: "I Get Around," "Fun, Fun, Fun," "California Girls," and a dozen others. He'd capped off that era in 1966 with the *Pet Sounds* album, a relatively somber meditation on lost love and aging, and then tied everything up with "Good Vibrations," a number-one record that seemed at once as sweet and innocent as anything else in the Beach Boys' candy-striped all-American canon and, at the same time, very hip.

"Good Vibrations" was also when the not-letting-go began to be a problem. It took him six months and three recording studios to finish the record, and at the end of all that frustrating studio time, the finished record didn't sound that much different from the first take.

"Good Vibrations" was such a wondrous, worldwide success that expectations were high for what was to be the follow-up album, a work to be called *Smile*. Brian referred to it as his "teenage symphony to God." Magazine writers and admiring musicians made the pilgrimage to Brian's home or to Western Recorders studio to see where the world of music was going next. New York Philharmonic maestro Leonard Bernstein put Brian on one of his television specials. Brian sat alone at a piano, playing an oblique, severely intellectual song called "Surf's Up," which, of course, had nothing to do with surfing:

> *A blind class aristocracy*
> *Back through the opera glass you see*
> *The pit and the pendulum drawn*
> *Columnated ruins domino*

But then, nothing. Brian couldn't or wouldn't finish *Smile*, so the other members of the group intervened to produce an album—long overdue under their contract with Capitol Records—made out of salvaged fragments and quickly recorded and innocuous ditties. *Smiley Smile* was lightweight, "a bunt instead of a grand slam," as Carl Wilson so eloquently put it. Significantly, the credit "Produced by BRIAN WILSON" was replaced with "Produced by THE BEACH BOYS."

In the dragging months he had tinkered with the album under relentless media scrutiny, Brian had been passed by. Before he could finish *Smile* to his satisfaction, his cross-Atlantic rivals, the Beatles, had released *Sgt. Pepper's Lonely Hearts Club Band*. The world anointed the British group as the undisputed heavyweight champs, and the world soon forgot Brian Wilson. The *Smiley Smile* release was another nail in the coffin of Brian Wilson, Musical Visionary.

He's a fool, the critics said, thinking he can compete with the Beatles. Despite his gentle exterior, Brian was enormously competitive, and the criticism stung.

What hurt worse was that some of the criticism came from within his group. His older cousin, Mike Love, was lead singer and often the lyricist for Brian's lavish melodies. Mike liked the recipe that had worked so well a few years ago: benign songs about summer, cars, girls, and young love. Mike had hated the turn Brian made with *Pet Sounds.* "Don't fuck with the formula," he told Brian during the vocal tracking for that album. Grudgingly, Mike recorded his parts, feeling vindicated when the album did not become a huge hit. Furthermore, Mike was irritated that Brian had gone outside the group and employed lyricists Tony Asher for *Pet Sounds* and wunderkind Van Dyke Parks for *Smile.* In addition to the rebuff, Mike knew he'd lose the significant songwriter royalties that boosted his income above others in the band.

A month after *Pet Sounds,* Capitol Records released a greatest-hits anthology called *Best of the Beach Boys,* which went to the top of the *Billboard* album charts. *That's what they want,* Mike told Brian. But when "Good Vibrations" became a huge hit later that year, it was Brian's season of vindication.

Then came the *Smile* catastrophe, and now, a year after that ambitious project imploded, the group put out two pleasant but aggressively insignificant albums, *Smiley Smile* and *Wild Honey.* It was the era when each single or album from rock 'n' roll heavyweights—the Beatles, Bob Dylan, the Rolling Stones, the Byrds, and, up to now, the Beach Boys—was supposed to be infused with great meaning and offer clues to deciphering the mystery of life.

Now here was Brian, looking broken and confused, doing twenty-two takes of a song about sharpening a pencil.

Dennis and Carl were loyal to Brian, though they recognized he was losing what remained of his tenuous grip on reality. He'd turned the dining room of his Bel-Air mansion into a sandbox and moved his piano into the room so he could wiggle his toes in the sand when he composed. "He wanted a sandbox, so he got a sandbox," said his wife, Marilyn. "I mean, who am I to tell a creator what he can do? He said, 'I want to play in the sand, I want to feel like a little kid. When I'm writing these songs, I want to feel what I'm writing, all the happiness.'" A carpenter built a wall two and a half feet tall, and a work crew emptied eight tons of sand into it.

Additionally, the living room was draped with canvas and stuffed with pillows so he could have friends over to his Bedouin tent. That proved impractical because the fabric blocked the air-conditioning vents, making the tent stifling. Through it all, Marilyn Wilson could teach patience to a time bomb.

Brian *amused*. Because he was deaf in one ear and not suited for travel, he had retired from touring with his group at the beginning of 1965. He promised to stay home, write songs, and make records (using an immensely talented group of session musicians) while the remaining members of the group kept a rigorous concert schedule. When the group came off the road, Brian would steer them to the studio with a score of songs needing only to be finished with the Beach Boys' lush harmonies.

Away from the group, at home or in the studio, Brian's eccentricities multiplied. He went beyond *amusing* and fell into a chasm of paranoia. Marilyn, his patient young wife, could handle the sandbox, though she hated that the family cats shat there. She put up with the tent and the meetings held in the drained swimming pool. She even thought it was kind of funny when Brian refused to speak at a meeting with Capitol Records executives, instead playing recorded tape loops with such sayings as "That's a great idea," "No, let's *not* do that," or "I think we should think about that."

But then he began to fear the outside world. He once bolted from a movie theater when one of the onscreen characters addressed a "Mister Wilson." *They're after me*, he thought. So he became a recluse, a rock 'n' roll Howard Hughes. The other members of the group, which also included friends Al Jardine and Bruce Johnston, were fine composers and singers in their own right. But they needed Brian for the extra touch of magic. He was the goose with the golden ear. "That ear," tough-to-please Bob Dylan once said. "Jesus, he's got to will that to the Smithsonian."

So the group had built a recording studio in Brian's Bel-Air home. It didn't have the sonics of Gold Star or Western, where he had recorded the Beach Boys' classics. It was small, with a well-worn beige sculptured carpet and a pink door with STUDIO spray-painted on it in green in Brian's balloonish script. Engineer Jim Lockert handled the nuts and bolts of building the mixing board and outfitting the room. It was homey, and it would do, the group figured, since rock 'n' roll was on a back-to-basics movement in the summer of 1968.

Young Marilyn gamely went along with having a recording studio directly below her bedroom. It meant constant traffic at odd hours, but it also meant that Brian, her lumbering beast of a husband, the tortured artist of rock 'n' roll, had a reason to get out of bed. Work, she knew, might be his salvation. In the weeks since the carpenters had finished, though, she discovered that the studio's existence did not always lure Brian from his room or out of his bathrobe.

But tonight, the studio held his attention. Marilyn heard the thumping of bass and drums from the room below, a monotonous unfurling of melody. So here they were, working on the song about sharpening a pencil, while Marilyn struggled through a fitful sleep upstairs.

During the golden days, no one questioned Brian or his judgments. If they did, they were immediately shot down.

"This sounds like shit, Brian," Carl told his brother while recording "Little Honda" in 1964. Brian had instructed him to play a distorted guitar line to open the song. "Brian, I hate this."

"Would you fucking do it?" Brian said. "Just do it."

Later, Carl would tell this story as a way of saying he learned never to doubt his big brother. "When I heard it, I felt like an asshole," he said. "It sounded really hot."

But that was on-top-of-the-world Brian, at twenty-two. Now he was an insecure, frightened twenty-six-year-old. Dennis still believed in him but knew his brother's issues would not be easily solved, which is why he was at the session, supporting him.

Though he was, in the words of writer Ben Edmonds, the "primary architect of their early sun-tanned masculine image," Dennis was the embodiment of the group's surfer persona, but he was not integral to the great harmonic blend of the Beach Boys. His voice was rougher, sometimes lurching toward off-key. When the performing group did "Their Hearts Were Full of Spring" onstage—a cappella, of course—Dennis sat behind his drum kit, silent, arms crossed. His presence was not urgent in the vocal tracking tonight, but he knew that Mike would try to work the room into some expression of disaffection with Brian and the scattered, unsure ways he labored these days in the studio. Dennis was there to support his big brother and help tamp down a rebellion, should one occur. It had been a quiet session, though, and now discontent was yawning in the wee hours.

Brian had lived for years under pressure to make the records that lit up the radio. A lot of people depended on him: the Beach Boys, their families, their accountants and road managers. A lot of people needed Brian to write, produce, and arrange two or three albums of material each year.

Don't fuck with the formula.

But now his productivity had slipped and the pressure was doubled. At the home studio, at least he wasn't tying up thousands of hours of expensive time at Gold Star or Western Recorders. The session musicians enjoyed working with Brian, but they were paid an hourly rate, so if he demanded unending takes of a song or wasn't sure how he really wanted to do the song, it became an onerous expense. They had an on-call engineer and contracted with individual outside musicians on an as-needed basis.

Dennis and Carl both had grown up in Brian's shadow. They had shared a room and, as the eldest, Brian was the natural leader, though he lacked Dennis's sexual magnetism and Carl's precocious diplomacy.

In childhood and adolescence, Brian had been particularly close with Carl, and the two brothers and their parents spent hours harmonizing around the piano. Dennis, the extrovert, usually missed the family sessions in favor of hitching a ride to the ocean for a day of surfing. He was the handsome golden-boy athlete, the opposite of shy Brian and overweight and insecure Carl. But when Brian and Carl decided to start a musical group with their cousin Mike and a friend, it was Audree Wilson who told her sons they had to include the middle brother in the group. Thus did Dennis Wilson become the drummer of the Beach Boys. He did not take lessons and never became revered as a rock 'n' roll drummer. But he attacked his drums the way he attacked everything in his life: he pounded them with fury.

Hands down the best looking of the band, Dennis gave the group a sex appeal it sorely lacked. He also gave the group its identity. He was the only member of the group who actually surfed, and he came up with the idea to write songs about surfing. He even supplied Brian with the language of the sport and the names of the best surfing spots up and down the coast. In one of their first hits, a Chuck Berry rewrite called "Surfin' USA," Brian name-checked some of the spots Dennis had mentioned:

At Haggerty's and Swami's, Pacific Palisades, San Onofre and Sunset, Redondo Beach, L.A.

Brian and the others ran with Dennis's idea, even though it was false advertising. They weren't surfers, and Brian, the composer, was not the confident, strutting character embodied in his songs. They weren't even the first artists to produce surf music. Guitarist Dick Dale, who recorded piercing instrumentals heavy on reverberation, had carved out that musical territory on the beach. But what Brian did with his songs and with his recordings with the group was to take the music beyond the beach-rat subculture of Los Angeles and bring it to teenagers in Des Moines, Columbus, and Topeka. Kids in Omaha, taking the Beach Boys' cue, strapped makeshift surfboards to the roofs of their old Impalas and pretended they were heading to the beach. "Surfin' USA" even opened with Brian's benevolent wish for his landlocked friends:

If everybody had an ocean across the USA
Then everybody'd be surfin' like Californ-I-A

The Beach Boys were not a one-trick pony, despite their name (which was selected by a promotion man at their first record company). They did not confine themselves to surfing but instead moved on to songs about cars, school, love, and the joys of summertime. Again, it was Dennis Wilson who lived the life the Beach Boys sang about, but because his voice didn't always fit in the harmonic blend, he was excluded.

But now, as Brian's star was beginning its descent to uncertainty, Dennis stepped forward. For the new album, he'd written and produced two songs. Brian guided him through these maiden compositions, which were as idiosyncratic as anything Brian had ever written. Dennis inherited Brian's fascination with celebrating small moments of joy (such as pencil sharpening). With "Little Bird," Dennis exulted in the sensuality of nature, imagining that he had a bond with a bird he'd seen singing in a tree. Filled with strong images ("the trout in the shiny brook") and arranged with chugging cellos, it was clearly a standout track. His other composition, "Be Still," was a delicate lover's prayer arranged for organ and Dennis's voice, which barely rose above a choked whisper. But the track was as deeply affecting as the more complex "Little Bird."

Still—no way in hell would either of those songs become a concert sing-along like "Fun, Fun, Fun" or "California Girls."

Brian was proud of Dennis's accomplishments, but there was still much to do if they were to complete an album. Brian was still writing but now needed help from Mike, Carl, and Alan, as well as Bruce, who'd stepped into the group when Brian had quit touring. Brian was no longer the confident mastermind. Now the others held their breath in an unconscious effort to help get him through a session. He'd become so fragile.

Again, Brian said.

Take 22, Lockert said, and the tape rolled.

Though a lightweight confection, "Even Steven" was a window into Brian's state of mind. This was his life: an unanswered phone call, sharpening a pencil, a lonely young man asking for someone to come visit.

The session ended at three in the morning, not unusually late, but Dennis decided to go home rather than hit a club. It was a fifteen-minute winding drive down Sunset Boulevard between Dennis's home and Brian's studio, but in the middle of the night, in his Ferrari GTB, Dennis could easily make the drive in twelve.

Depressed and somewhat disturbed by the sight of his awkward and unsure big brother stumbling through a session, Dennis decided to seek respite in his usual manner. He'd spend the rest of the night sport fucking.

The other members of the band called Dennis "the Wood" because he claimed he was always hard. Mike Love, the only real competitor for heartthrob in the group, was the front man who picked girls out of the audience and, unknown to the young women, signaled the road manager to make sure the prettiest ones got backstage. Despite a receding hairline and the inconvenience of marriage, Mike rarely had problems finding a woman for a one-nighter while on tour. He was handsome, looking much like actor James MacArthur, the young swain of Disney's *Swiss Family Robinson*. Gifted with athletic stamina and, by all reports, a significant sexual organ, he gave Dennis a run for the money with the prettiest of the girls.

There was a natural and not entirely good-spirited rivalry between Mike and Dennis. Mike often saw himself as the leader of the band and, as commanding officer, looked upon Dennis as a surly buck private who was there only because of the insistence of his mother.

And it also aggravated Mike when Dennis took the best-looking of the backstage girls to his room.

Dennis had his share of backstage girls and young starlets. He nightly pleasured himself at the trough of Hollywood's most beautiful young actresses. He had been married and truly loved Carole, his wife, but he was addicted to sex. "Dennis was the bane of the rest of the band, thanks to his lack of self-discipline," journalist Jeff Guinn wrote. "Dennis knew no limits in his fondness for alcohol, drugs and sex." An interviewer once asked him where he would like to go on a dream date. "The ovaries," Dennis responded.

While his love for Carole was genuine—he adopted her son, Scott, and together they had a daughter, named Jennifer—he could not stop doing the forbidden polka with other women, taking drugs, drinking booze, and reveling in danger. He was reckless; his record of maimed cars spoke to that. He was fearless when he surfed. He seemed to live at only one speed: full throttle.

Carole had finally had enough of his serial adultery and moved out, filing divorce papers. Though they would always love each other, they could not live together.

So now Dennis was one of Southern California's most eligible and sought-after bachelors. The record sales of the Beach Boys might have been in eclipse, but that didn't make Dennis Wilson any less handsome or charming.

He'd leased an impressive estate befitting a good-looking rock star with voracious appetites, and he'd lost track of how many young women he'd brought back to the log-cabin mansion with its swimming pool in the shape of California. Humorist and film star Will Rogers had built the home back in the thirties as his hunting lodge, and though it had a Sunset Boulevard address, it was at the end of a long driveway, somewhat isolated by deep woods and adjacent to Will Rogers State Historic Park. Here, Dennis could revel in his bacchanals with young women, and they could luxuriate nude by the pool, hidden from prying eyes of neighbors.

Dennis figured that when he got home, the two girls he'd met would still be there. He'd seen them hitchhiking a few days before on the Pacific Coast Highway and stopped to pick them up. He showed off the silver Ferrari, bragged about being Dennis Wilson, laughed and joked and let them off at their destination. They said their names were Yellerstone and Patty.

Then he ran into them again, in the hours before the night's recording session. They were hitchhiking on Sunset, and Dennis pulled over when he recognized them. He had time before the session. *Would you like to come back to my place for milk and cookies?* This was no lame pick-up line; it was a genuine Dennis Wilson offer. The girls giggled. *It's raw milk, the only kind I drink.* How could the girls resist?

He took them back to his home and showed off his gold records, the rustic mansion, and the pool. Yellerstone and Patty liked Dennis but didn't care too much about his celebrity or his music. The Beach Boys were already passé and not the kind of stuff they listened to. But Dennis was genuinely nice and deeply generous. He'd be a soft touch.

It was a beautiful, clear California day. Dennis slipped out of his clothes, and the girls followed. He fucked both of them, then excused himself for the recording session.

He'd be back late, he'd said. *Make yourself at home.*

They were both tall, with long hair parted down the middle. He was a rock star and had dated doe-eyed starlets and ingénues, and though these girls didn't have movie star genes, they were attractive enough for what he wanted. He asked the polite questions but got only vague answers, oblique references to where they came from, their home now out in the desert, and the man who ran their commune, a man they called the Wizard.

Yellerstone and Patty liked Dennis because he was handsome and athletic and friendly and solicitous. They were not beautiful, and Dennis knew he could do much better. Hell, he'd *always* done much better. But these girls giggled, enjoying his jokes, fawning respectfully as if everything he said was some insight to Holy Writ. They were willing. He was an addict, and so he went after any fuck in a storm.

As he dressed for the session, Dennis noticed that the women were in no hurry to cover up. He liked that. Their bodies weren't what he was used to either. They were both modestly built, thick through the middle, and not groomed like some of the starlets he'd dated. But he found a lot of those starlets to be tedious. He'd once had a date with actress Yvette Mimieux, but she was brittle and tiresome. He didn't even try to fuck her. He left her at the door of her apartment with a thunderous explosion of gas in place of good-bye. He loved to tell that story.

Yellerstone and Patty didn't come with the bullshit that came with show business girls. Some of those types had dated him, he figured, because they thought it was good for their careers to go out with a rock 'n' roll drummer. These girls wouldn't be like that. Hell, they'd be grateful.

He'd been doing seventy-five down Sunset and didn't slow for the turn into his long driveway. As he drove up, he worried that the girls might have gotten bored and left. Instead, it looked like someone was throwing a party at his house.

Dennis pulled up the lane and turned to park on the concrete driveway adjacent to the pool. There was a school bus in the driveway. The home's outside spotlights were on; Dennis was certain he hadn't turned them on before leaving. He looked to the house, glowing with electricity; he hadn't left those lights on either.

He warily got out of the car. Judging from the noise, there was a hell of a blowout going at his place. Through the windows, he could see a half dozen, maybe more, people in silhouette, and they all appeared to be girls. He walked slowly toward the house, uncharacteristically nervous. He was a few yards from the back door when it opened and a man emerged. Dennis stopped, taken aback.

The man was short—a half foot shorter than Dennis—with long hair to his shoulders and a patchy, unkempt beard. In the yellow glow of the porch light, Dennis could see that his clothes—a work shirt, blue jeans, and moccasins—were well worn and filthy. He waved Dennis toward the house, toward his own house. The little man was acting as if he was lord of the manor.

Though he was small, to Dennis, the man looked dangerous. Dennis stood still, but the man continued coming toward him, getting so close that Dennis took a step back. The craziness jellied in the man's eyes frightened Dennis.

"Are you going to hurt me?" Dennis asked suddenly. He had no idea where that came from. It was unlike him to show fear.

The man beamed, flashing yellowed teeth. "Do I look like I'm going to hurt you, brother?"

Suddenly the man dropped to his knees, leaned over, and kissed Dennis's tennis shoes. When he stood up, he again grinned at Dennis.

"Who are you?" Dennis asked.

"I'm a friend," the man said.

Come on in, brother. The women await.

The man's smile was welcoming, though his eyes held menace. But as Dennis walked into his house, he saw that there were several nude young women walking around, comfortable and friendly in their nakedness. His stereo was turned up to maximum volume and was blasting *Magical Mystery Tour*, the latest album from the Beatles.

Dennis saw Yellerstone and Patty, who came to greet him like a long-lost friend. They tugged at his shirt, urging him to join them in the orgy that was imminent. Patty unbuttoned Dennis and nodded toward the strange man. "This is the guy we were telling you about," she said.

Dennis turned and looked at the man again, who smiled, baring his teeth.

"This is Charlie," Patty said.

And that was how the friendship of Dennis Wilson and Charles Manson began.

1

DREAMERS OF THE GOLDEN DREAM

> California is a place in which a boom mentality and a
> sense of Chekhovian loss meet in uneasy suspension;
> in which the mind is troubled by some buried but
> ineradicable suspicion that things better work here,
> because here, beneath the immense bleached sky, is
> where we run out of continent.
>
> —Joan Didion

Like the rest of the country it bookended, California was a place of
contradiction: site of spectacular sunsets and lonely dead ends; land
of dreams, home of nightmares; and happy endings alongside wither-
ing tragedies.

As the twentieth century dawned, the East Coast attained its
adulthood. New York, Boston, and Philadelphia were civilized, intellectual, and economic centers, and the nineteenth century disappeared into vapor. Not so in Los Angeles. Even as starched Arrow
Collar men strode around New York City, Los Angeles was still the
Wild West.

The film industry preceded the music business in California by
several decades, but parallel experiences prove the maxim that those
who do not remember history get stuck on repeat.

The motion picture industry began in New York, where early filmmakers saw themselves as adjuncts of the theater business. Films were
three-minute novelty pictures—a kiss, a scandalous dance exposing a
woman's ankle, waves on the beach. Soon, films grew in length. In
1903, Edwin S. Porter made the ten-minute *Great Train Robbery* at
Edison Studios in New York, with location work in New Jersey, Wild

West enough at the time. Audiences recoiled when a bandit fired at the screen in the film's last moments.

Enter boosters from the infant city of Los Angeles. They went after the nascent movie business, hoping to turn it into a dominant California industry. They had some good arguments: the weather was perfect year-round and the terrain was varied and could pass for most other parts of the world. There were forests, deserts, oceans, flatlands, and jagged peaks. Jersey couldn't compete with the San Gabriel Mountains.

The westward migration began around 1910. Pioneer filmmaker D. W. Griffith tired of the unpredictable and often insufferable winters back east. Moving to California, he found all the landscapes he'd need to film his Civil War epic (and racist diatribe) *The Birth of a Nation* in 1915. It was the first modern narrative film, with a running time of two hours and thirty-five minutes. Griffith was sold on Los Angeles as his new base. Soon the majority of film companies made the move to Southern California, and those stubbornly remaining back east, such as the Edison Studios, went bankrupt.

Most film companies settled in the just-annexed section of Los Angeles known as Hollywood. The village was incorporated in 1887, and when filmmakers arrived it was still a town of orange groves and a single trolley.

The entertainment business and scandal went hand in glove. The film industry established a pattern of crime and shame soon to be replicated by music moguls, record producers, and naive artists and performers.

Hollywood's hundred years of scandal included murdered movie stars, anti-Semitic tirades, and drug overdoses. A century after it happened, the story of silent-film star Roscoe Arbuckle still made most lists of show business infamy. Arbuckle, a portly fellow known as Fatty to his fans, costarred with Charles Chaplin in one- and two-reelers. His real life and habits would have been the grist of a horror film to audiences. He was a junkie, his drug of choice being morphine, which he injected into the track-filmed arm he carefully covered on filming days.

Arbuckle had finished a harrowing withdrawal when he decided to stage a colossal party. He had signed a lucrative new Warner Bros. contract and booked a floor of the St. Francis Hotel in San Francisco for a bacchanal with a few score friends. A near orgy ensued. Witnesses said on September 6, 1921, actress Virginia Rappe ran from Arbuckle's room in the middle of the night. Other guests assumed she was drunk or sick, but when she died three days later, Arbuckle was charged with manslaughter. Word was that Arbuckle raped the young woman with a champagne bottle, rupturing her bladder. She died of peritonitis.

Arbuckle's first two trials ended in hung juries, and the third acquitted him. But the damage was done, and his career never recovered. He died destitute at forty-six.

Scandals kept on coming. Film director Thomas Ince died aboard a yacht owned by newspaper tycoon William Randolph Hearst. His death was attributed to heart failure, but his corpse was cremated before the coroner could perform an autopsy. The story on the down low was that Hearst had shot Ince while aiming for Chaplin. Hearst suspected Chaplin was *shtupping* actress Marion Davies, Hearst's girl-friend. (If true, behold Chaplin's *cojones* for carrying on with Hearst's woman while on the man's yacht.) Though the Hearst-shooting story was oft repeated, no additional inquiry was launched into Ince's death.

By many accounts, Chaplin was a penis with a small man attached. Chaplin proudly referred to his organ as "the eighth wonder of the world," and the two of them kept Hollywood gossip fires stoked. His first divorce yielded assertions from his spurned wife that he had "abnormal, unnatural, and perverted sexual desires." Through pater-nity suits, multiple marriages, political persecution, and his eventual deportation in 1952, he was a one-man scandal machine.

Los Angeles was fecund with corruption. As it became the American capital of crazy, it also became a reliable source of ghastly crimes, often found on the fringes of the entertainment business. One of the most horrific was the 1947 murder of Elizabeth Short, a Boston girl who went west to make it big in the movies. She was found sawed in half, body washed and neatly bleached, in the Leimert Park neigh-borhood. The press dubbed her the Black Dahlia, after the noir film from a few years before, *The Blue Dahlia*.

California had sunshine and the Pacific, but it also had a dank underbelly of stunningly bizarre murders. As Woody Allen said of California in *Annie Hall*, "There's no economic crime, but there's ritual, religious cult murders, you know there's wheat-germ killers out here." Reporters loved to name the spectacular murders—hence the Black Dahlia—and a body of literature grew from the tales of Southern California's horrific violence and the historically corrupt Los Angeles Police Department.

Novelists James M. Cain and Raymond Chandler explored the milieu of dirty cops and double-crossing broads in such remarkable books as *The Postman Always Rings Twice* and *Double Indemnity* (Cain) and *The Big Sleep* and *The Long Goodbye* (Chandler). Chandler was one of the great and underappreciated literary figures laboring in the movie studio vineyards. His only original screenplay produced was *The Blue Dahlia*, and he adapted Cain's *Double Indemnity*. Cain wrote as if being charged by the word. He could teach an egg to be hard-boiled.

Los Angeles was the promised land and a pathetic and brutal place. Nathanael West wrote screenplays for low-rent Hollywood pot-boilers, but he also wrote the best novel about corruption and tragedy in Tinseltown. He picked up the rock and studied its underside in *The Day of the Locust*, offering a grim vision of the dreamers of the golden dream:

> They realize that they've been tricked and burn with resentment. Every day of their lives they read the newspapers and went to the movies. Both fed them on lynchings, murder, sex crimes, explosions, wrecks, love nests, fires, miracles, revolutions, war. This daily diet made sophisticates of them. The sun is a joke. Oranges can't titillate their jaded palates. Nothing can ever be violent enough to make taut their slack minds and bodies. They have been cheated and betrayed. They have slaved and saved for nothing.

Charles Chaplin built his film studios at the corner of LaBrea and Sunset in 1917, and, long after his deportation from America during the McCarthy era, those studios became home to the hugely successful A&M Records. The film industry bequeathed its property and its propensity for scandal to the music business.

The American music industry had been centered in New York as long as it had existed. In the days before recording, music publishers supplied performers and families gathered round the family upright with the sheet music needed in order to play.

In the late nineteenth century, several music publishers located to a row on Twenty-Eighth Street, between Fifth and Sixth Avenues. This became Tin Pan Alley, and those music publishers dominated the industry. Recording was introduced in 1877, but it took thirty years for music to be readily available to the general public on disc.

The recording industry evolved from the New York music publishers. Columbia was founded in the 1880s, and the Victor Talking Machine Company (later known as RCA Victor) began in 1901. Those two giants duked it out for well over a century, along with other majors—Decca, a British company whose American division opened in New York in 1934, and Mercury, which started in Chicago in 1946.

The first West Coast label to become a major player was Capitol Records, founded in Los Angeles in 1942. Songwriter Johnny Mercer ("Moon River," "Days of Wine and Roses," "Summer Wind," and scores of other standards) decided he wanted to start a record company and mused about the prospects to Glenn Wallichs, owner of the massive retailer Music City on Sunset Boulevard. They looked for investors and approached Buddy DeSylva, a sometime–songwriting partner of Mercer's and film producer for Paramount. When Mercer asked if Paramount might want to invest, DeSylva said no but that he did. He handed over a personal check for $15,000.

Within just a few years, Capitol was competing with Columbia, RCA, and Decca, giving the world such recording stars as Nat "King" Cole, the first African American superstar to cross over to the mass market. The company's diverse catalog of pop, jazz, and country featured Tennessee Ernie Ford, Miles Davis, and Jackie Gleason. Crooner Frank Sinatra's career came back from the dead when he signed to Capitol in 1953, re-creating himself as a mature saloon singer providing the soundtrack for a million conceptions. The revenue from Sinatra and other Capitol artists helped the company build its distinctive headquarters, the Capitol Tower, across the street from Wallichs Music City. The building resembled a thirteen-story stack of records and was soon a major Los Angeles landmark.

Though Capitol was the only major label in Los Angeles, the city had given birth to a number of significant independent labels.

Historian Frederick Jackson Turner's "frontier thesis" suggested that because America was a young nation with challenges, it constantly required innovation.

Adapt that concept to rock 'n' roll. The major labels aimed for the middle ground, which is why they were slow to respond to the music embraced by teenagers, who began to assume prominence as consumers in the fifties. On the frontier of the music industry, small, independent record companies—often run by lunatics—ended up reaching these new, adolescent consumers with disposable income.

The principal lunatic was Sam Phillips in Memphis. Though a poor white sharecropper's son from Florence, Alabama, his greatest love was the blues music he heard from African American musicians in Memphis. He and business partner Marion Keisker opened the Memphis Recording Service in 1950. The slogan on the business cards said, WE RECORD ANYTHING—ANYWHERE—ANYTIME. Among the first artists Phillips recorded were B. B. King, Rufus Thomas, and a group of convicts known as the Prisonaires. It was an exclusively black group.

Phillips had a great ear for talent, but he had no record label. He sold his master recordings to Jules and Saul Bihari, two Hungarian Jews who'd set up Modern Records with a Beverly Hills address in 1945. Phillips got a flat fee for recordings he sent to Los Angeles, and he grumbled about doing all the heavy lifting while the Bihari brothers built their label with King and other artists.

Phillips also got credit for discovering Howlin' Wolf, a massive, growling blues singer born as Chester Arthur Burnett in 1910. After recording Wolf, he sold the master tapes to another set of brothers, Leonard and Phil Chess in Chicago, whose Chess Records made significant contributions to the birthing of rock 'n' roll.

In March 1951, nineteen-year-old bandleader Ike Turner from Clarksdale, Mississippi, set a recording date with Phillips for his band, the Kings of Rhythm. Band and equipment were shoehorned into a car for the hour-long drive from Clarksdale, up Highway 61. As Turner and his sardines neared Phillips's studio on Union Avenue, the car hit a pothole and guitarist Willie Kizart's amplifier came loose from the trunk and smacked down on the asphalt. *That's that. We won't be recording today.* The dejected band drove on to the studio to tell Phillips the bad news.

Sam Phillips wasn't worried. *Well hell. Let's plug it in and hear what it sounds like.*

Only a lunatic would record with a broken amplifier, but Sam Phillips did, and critics will still wrestle nude in creamed corn to argue that the result was the first rock 'n' roll record. Phillips sold the recording—"Rocket 88," credited to Jackie Brenston and His Delta Cats; Brenston was Turner's sax player and singer—to the Chess brothers, and they reaped the benefits of Sam Phillips's madness.

Investing every farthing he could find, Sam Phillips founded Sun Records in 1953, continuing to record the black artists he admired and musing about what would happen if he found a white singer with the naked emotion of the black artists he loved. In the segregated world of 1953, it was unlikely any black artists would ever cross over to the mass market, unless they were nonthreatening crooners such as Nat King Cole or the Mills Brothers.

That summer, Sam Phillips's savior walked through the door. New high school graduate Elvis Presley was a truck driver for Crown Electric Company when he came by the studio to make a vanity recording for his mother. Marion Keisker ran the shop that day, and when Presley started singing, she heard something she liked and turned on the tape recorder—the vanity recordings were cut direct to disc, not taped—so she could later share Presley's voice with Phillips.

Phillips released five Presley singles on Sun, music that provided much of the DNA of rock 'n' roll: "That's All Right, Mama," "Good Rockin' Tonight," "Milkcow Blues Boogie," "Baby, Let's Play House," and "Mystery Train." After a year and a half, Phillips sold Presley's contract to a major label (RCA) and used that money to continue his discoveries of new and singularly American talent, including Carl Perkins, Johnny Cash, Jerry Lee Lewis, Roy Orbison, and Charlie Rich.

By the time Phillips sold Presley's contract, the young singer had already defined his style. Some argue that he never made a great record again after leaving Phillips. RCA called in Phillips as a consultant, but the label insisted on recording at its studios in Nashville, and there was no way to re-create the magic of the cracker box in Memphis.

RCA would have no interest in Presley—or any other young and untrained singer—if Phillips had not found genius lurking inside the pimpled truck driver. That's why it took independent labels, such as Sun in Memphis and Chess in Chicago, to mine and refine the talent. Chess gave the world blues greats such as Muddy Waters, Little Walter, and Willie Dixon, as well as early rock 'n' roll stars Chuck Berry and Bo Diddley.

Modern (and its subsidiary, RPM) was not the only independent label in Los Angeles. There were small labels operating from offices behind a Laundromat or out of a camper truck. The craziness of the label owners made them willing to try just about anything, and some of those L.A.-based labels ended up producing significant recordings, even if they didn't make much money.

Arthur Rupe (real name Arthur Goldberg) established Specialty Records in 1946 and was picky about what he recorded. In the late forties and early fifties, he favored rhythm and blues and spirituals. He had one of the great gospel groups of the era, the Soul Stirrers featuring Sam Cooke. His secular discoveries included Lloyd Price and Guitar Slim; Rupe discovered them while in New Orleans scouting talent. He also had an excellent artists and repertoire (A&R) staff, led by Robert "Bumps" Blackwell.

One day in 1955, Rupe got a delivery at his office on Sunset Boulevard, a reel of recording tape with human bite marks on the packaging. The sender was Richard Penniman, a dishwasher at the Greyhound bus station diner in Macon, Georgia. Rupe heard something he liked and sent Blackwell to New Orleans to meet Penniman and see what he could get on tape at Cosimo Matassa's J&M Recording Studios in the French Quarter.

"There's this cat in this loud shirt," Blackwell said, "with hair waived up six inches above his head. He was talking wild, thinking up stuff just to be different." Penniman ran through his songs in the studio, and Blackwell was profoundly unimpressed. He heard nothing unique.

He'd heard that Little Richard—Penniman's onstage nom de plume—was wild, but behind a studio microphone he was a milquetoast.

"The problem was that what he looked like and what he sounded like did not come together," Blackwell remembered. "If you look like Tarzan and sound like Mickey Mouse, it just doesn't work out."

Blackwell called a break, and he and Penniman went to the Dew Drop Inn. There was a crowd there, and when they walked through the door, Penniman's eyes lit up. Within a couple of minutes he was onstage banging on the piano.

> *Awop-bop-a-loo-bop a good goddam!*
> *Tutti frutti—good booty!*

When the impromptu performance ended, Blackwell told Penniman that *that* was what he wanted on tape. Sure, the song was about anal intercourse, but the lyrics could be changed and the energy left intact. Back at the studio, Blackwell developed new lyrics. Three takes and fifteen minutes later, Little Richard had come up with the first of his rock 'n' roll classics, "Tutti Frutti."

Had Blackwell been working for a major label, that would have never happened. Like Sam Phillips, Bumps Blackwell (and Leonard Chess and Art Rupe and several others) worked on the fringes, on the frontiers of the music industry.

That didn't mean that larger labels didn't take notice. As soon as "Tutti Frutti," on tiny Specialty Records, began selling, producer Randy Wood, owner of Dot Records of Gallatin, Tennessee, decided to record and rush release a cover version by a white artist. He set up a session with whiter-than-white singer Pat Boone—who, no doubt, had no idea of the song's origin story—and his bland, Velveeta-like version outsold Little Richard's.

"At first I was mad," Penniman recalled decades later. "I thought he was stopping my progress. I wanted to go to Hollywood and find him. The thing was, the kids would go out and buy my version because it was rough and raw and had a *gut* to it. But they'd buy Pat Boone's version and put his record on top of the dresser for their parents to see, and they'd put mine in a drawer. But I was in the same house."

Little Richard's experience was typical for black artists. Fats Domino, who also recorded at Matassa's New Orleans studio (his work was released on Imperial Records, another Los Angeles independent label), found his sales undercut by the white-bucks-wearing Pat Boone.

———————

Rock 'n' roll enfranchised a huge new audience of teenagers, freeing them from the musical tyranny of their parents. By the midfifties, the goofy "How Much Is That Doggie in the Window" and the overly sentimental "Tennessee Waltz" gave way to a rawer music rooted in African American culture. Even Boone's sanitized versions carried core elements of the original artists and made millions of teenagers—compulsive consumers with disposable income—shove coins into jukeboxes, badger disc jockeys, and buy 45 RPMs from their local record stores.

It was a strange time for kids to take center stage. Their parents were kicked in the gut, first with the Great Depression and then with the Second World War. They sucked it up; they dealt with it. But their postwar babies found themselves in a mobile, affluent culture such as the nation had never seen.

Radio and the automobile presented America in the late fifties with a volatile cultural mix. The greatest generation was defined by its times, but the baby boomers, growing up in an era of affluence and peace—Cold War be damned—had choices.

Technology divided the family. We can picture Mom, Pop, Sis, and Baby Boy Phil in the living room, gathered round a massive radio for a fireside chat with President Roosevelt or hunkering down, listening to war news together. But by the dawn of the fifties, radio's format was usurped by television. Left without its programming—who would want to *hear* Amos and Andy when you could *see* them?—radio reverted to its original format of platters and chatter.

All music, all the time catered to teenagers who didn't sit around the new box in the living room but instead went upstairs to the radio in their bedroom sanctuaries. Elvis Presley, the "Hillbilly Cat," invaded the airwaves in 1956–57 with his battery of hits ("Hound Dog," "Don't Be Cruel," "Jailhouse Rock") that turned the music industry upside down and sent record executives scattering for new Elvises. Radio was the youth medium, loosening the belt on a nation's culture.

America went mobile in the fifties. The post office awarded mail contracts to airlines, shutting out the railroads that had counted on that steady income for decades. Personal travel in the family car kept America on the road.

Thus was a revolution in love born. Teenagers had once courted under the scrutiny of parents; now cars freed them from stolen kisses in the parlor and took them to drive-in movie theaters, the Tastee Freez, or even Lovers' Lane.

Teenagers were free to define themselves in a way no other generation had before. Jack Kerouac spoke to this in his electric prose: "The only people for me are the mad ones, the ones who are mad to live, mad to talk, mad to be saved, desirous of everything at the same time, the ones who never yawn or say a commonplace thing, but burn, burn, burn, like fabulous yellow roman candles exploding like spiders across the stars."

With the sublime, of course, came the ridiculous. Sophisticated advertising agencies targeted teenagers' disposable incomes. Music, books, television shows, and films were aimed at this youth audience, giving the world, for good or ill, *Gidget*, the idealized surfer girl, and the Ricky Nelson rock tune at the end of *The Adventures of Ozzie and Harriet*. Nearly simultaneous with *On the Road*'s publication was the debut of *American Bandstand*, a successful televised effort to lure teens into the marketplace disguised as a daily after-school program that the kids could watch before Dad came home.

A generation rose from the ass end of the fifties and carried itself through the sixties, perhaps the first generation to consider itself relevant without earning its place at the table.

Radio was as revolutionary socially as it was technologically. For the first two-thirds of the twentieth century, we were an apartheid nation with separate water fountains, separate bathrooms, separate schools. The US Supreme Court said it was OK for the races to be separate, as long as they were treated equally.

A separate but equal society was easy to maintain. Different schools. Don't rent to black people in this neighborhood. Write ordinances telling black people where to sit on the bus. . . . Those were Jim Crow laws. But the air didn't obey the law.

Air wasn't legislated, and radio traveled through it. At night, that weird thing happened. After dark, suddenly voices from around the nation were on the radio dial, voices too faint to hear during the day. WLAC in Nashville was audible all the way from Tallahassee to the Canadian border.

Black America met White America through music, through the music played on radio. Once we were all dancing to the same beat, Jim Crow didn't have a chance and walls came tumbling down. *Separate* was inherently unequal. Two things separate began to merge, and when they did, something better resulted.

And so independent labels sprang up to serve these new consumers. There was Sun in Memphis and Chess in Chicago. King Records in Cincinnati gave the world "the hardest-working man in show business," James Brown. New York had Atlantic, Jubilee, Gee, Roulette, and Gone. Peacock Records was in Houston, and Ace's headquarters was in Jackson, Mississippi. Los Angeles was home to Era, Candix, Specialty, Aladdin, Imperial, and Modern, among many others.

The frontier ethos of the independent label with madmen owners produced an impressive and revolutionary blending of black and white American music in the fifties. By 1960, major labels had taken notice now that the independents had done the heavy lifting, and they were willing to put their corporate toes in the waters of the youth market.

But that market was unlike that of earlier generations. The music business began to change from a trickle-down enterprise to a from-the-ground-up movement led by kids in their parents' garages, banging away on drums and guitars. As the industry began slowly migrating to Los Angeles at the beginning of the sixties, the business model changed, and the industry relocation was led, in large part, by a shy, emotionally fractured musical savant named Brian Wilson.

2

MAGIC TRANSISTOR RADIO

Music is God's voice on Earth.

—Brian Wilson

Murry Wilson's voice carried. All the way down 119th Street in Hawthorne, neighbors heard him screaming at his boys, telling them they weren't good enough, didn't try hard enough, would never be as good as their old man.

Murry was tightly wound, with a chip the size of Kansas on his shoulder. He'd grown up abused, once beaten so badly by his father that part of his ear was torn off by the steel pipe his pop used as a weapon. Buddy Wilson drank to get drunk nearly every night, and when he was deep in the sauce, he'd start in on his children with his usual armament of choice, a broomstick. Murry was one of seven children, and none were spared the father's brutal anger.

Buddy Wilson was a plumber, and the family moved often, eventually arriving in Southern California. They began their lives there like the transplanted Okies of John Steinbeck's *Grapes of Wrath*, their first home a tent on Huntington Beach. Eventually Buddy Wilson was able to buy a small house, affording him the privacy he needed to beat his wife and children. Murry—second-oldest boy in the Wilson herd— intervened when his parents battled, trying to protect his mother. Buddy backed off but would go to Murry's attic bedroom in the middle of the night and beat his son senseless.

Murry Wilson moved out of the hell house as soon as he could after high school, securing a clerk's job at the gas company. At twenty-one, he married his high school girlfriend, Audree Korthof. Like Murry's family, Audree's family had come to California from the

Midwest. Murry and Audree began their life together in Inglewood, eventually moving to Hawthorne.

Murry and Audree loved playing piano and singing together. Music had been the one pleasure of Murry's childhood, and he considered himself a musician, though he did factory work. Though their house trembled with his rage most hours of the day, the time that he sat at the upright and sang along with his wife was the one time the man was at rest.

Murry worked in a low-level semimanagement position at Goodyear Tire's Southern California plant. One day, he was instructing new hires in the art of manufacturing, lost patience with a slow-to-cotton student, and angrily shut off the machine he was demonstrating. A stabilizing pole came loose. "Flying free of the wheel rack, the stick hurtled like a harpoon, straight into Murry's left eye," journalist Timothy White wrote. "The awful jolt of the projectile knocked Murry back on his heels for an instant, and then he crumpled to the concrete floor in shock, the stick slipping away as blood poured from the pulverized eye."

As if the abusive childhood had not been enough to turn Murry Wilson into coiled venom, the accident deepened his rage. He resented the world for what life handed him.

Children learn what they live (goes the modern proverb), and so Murry followed in his father's footsteps and took out his anger on his family, especially his three sons: Brian, born in 1942; Dennis, born in 1944; and Carl, born in 1946.

After his recovery from the accident, Murry left Goodyear and opened a modest machine shop called ABLE (for Always Better Lasting Equipment), and he roused his boys early on weekends and made them scrub-brush the shop's floors. Murry kept his boys in line by beating them with two-by-fours. Brian and Carl learned ways to placate and steer clear of their father, but middle child Dennis, the most rebellious—and the one who shared his father's volatile temperament—often played chicken with his pop, coming right at him to see who would turn away first. "We had a shitty childhood," Dennis recalled.

Owing to size, Murry won his battles with Dennis. At one extended-family gathering, Murry saw Dennis sneaking sips of alcohol. He picked up his son and hurled him into a wall. He didn't hesitate to smack his sons across their faces with his open hand, and he whipped them on their behinds with a doubled-over leather belt.

"You think the world owes you a living?" he'd rage. "You think the world is going to be fair?"

A neighbor across the street, David Marks, a couple years younger than Carl, remembered hearing Murry's screaming, from *inside* the Marks home. The fights were constant. "I saw a fistfight between Murry and Dennis," Marks said. "My dad had to break them up."

Years later, Dennis recalled, "My father resented the fucking kids to death. It's that fucking simple. The asshole beat the shit out of us."

No one in the family, not even Audree, was spared the wrath of this "overbearing Cyclops." Unable to stop her husband from beating the boys, she withdrew into a haze of highballs.

When Brian was six, his pediatrician discovered the boy was deaf in one ear. The cause was never determined, but Brian always assumed it was from one of his father's beatings.

The Hawthorne house had only two bedrooms, so the three boys shared, and if they committed the sin of making the noises young boys make, their father would charge in from the adjacent room, fists flying.

Brian loved listening to music but hid his transistor radio under the sheets, playing it at a mere murmur for fear of Murry. Middle brother Dennis was the most aggressive of the boys and the one most willing to cause trouble. He tried to deflect his father's anger to his brothers. Both Brian and Carl had bedwetting issues, so while they slept, Dennis would urinate on their beds, hoping to get them into deep shit with their dad. It usually worked.

Murry tormented his sons by removing his glass eye and forcing them to look into his scarred, empty socket. He used it to guilt his sons: *Look what happened to me when I was out earning money to support you.* Ed Roach, a close friend of Dennis, recalled one of the stories he'd heard: "Murry had made him stand nose-to-nose and stare into his empty eye socket. Dennis said he flinched once out of fear, and his father knocked him across the room and into the wall. He began to cry, which caused Murry to be on him like a bat out of hell, just whacking the shit out of him, screaming, 'Stop your fucking crying—stop being a baby.' After that beating, Dennis swore he'd never cry in front of his father again. No matter how much it hurt, and how much more it hurt not to cry, he was never going to give Murry the satisfaction of thinking he'd broken him down."

Dennis got the worst of it, but no one was spared. "He yelled so loud that you could have sworn the devil was in the room," Brian said. Brian and Carl withdrew, but Murry's fury turned Dennis Wilson into an unpredictable and violent force in the house. "If you walked by Dennis on a normal day," Brian recalled, "just try to get past him to the other side of the room, there was a good chance that you'd end up involved in a wrestling match."

The boys knew they could stem the brutality with music. The one thing that made their father melt was their singing. They turned back his fury with harmony. Music dispersed the blizzard of profanity and anger coming from the driver's seat when the whole gang was shoehorned into the family car. "We used to sing three-part harmony in the back seat," Dennis said. "My dad used to really like that."

Carl's earliest memories are of his father at the piano. "Music was always present," he said. "My dad was a part-time songwriter, and we always had a couple of pianos in the house and a jukebox. We had a garage that my dad fixed up into a den. We'd all get around the piano. My mom would play, and later Brian started to play."

History was repeating itself. The one thing that Murry remembered from his childhood, the one thing that did not cause him pain, was the memory of his family singing. Even brutal Buddy Wilson liked to sing and watched with awe and his own twisted version of love as his wife and children sang together. His anger apparently spent by Saturday night, Buddy presided over family concerts. Murry and his brothers accompanied the family choir on guitars. As writer Peter Ames Carlin described it, "Weaving his voice together with those of his wife and kids was as close as Buddy could get to actual emotional intimacy with his family. And perhaps this was why Murry, the son who had come to be the family's last line of defense against their drunk, vicious father, came to love music so very much."

Murry considered himself a songwriter. His tunes were relentlessly mediocre, yet he was able to get a couple songs published and one recorded. His "Two-Step Side-Step" had been played on television by Lawrence Welk's orchestra. This was enough success for Murry to justify renovating the garage and enclosing it as a music room. The upright was rolled inside, along with guitars and framed covers of Murry Wilson sheet music. "The Wilson Boys have always heard music in their home from my writing songs and friends of ours who came over," Murry told an interviewer. "We were all so poor we'd just sit around singing and on occasion drinking a glass of brew. Not the children, the adults. We'd play duets, my wife and I. And then Brian would get in the act and sing. All they ever heard was music in their house. And, on occasion, family arguments."

An understatement, of course. "My dad was an asshole," Dennis said. "He treated us like shit and his punishments were sick. But you played a tune for him and he was a marshmallow. This mean motherfucker would cry with bliss, like the lion in *The Wizard of Oz*, when he heard the music."

Wilson family lore held that Brian nearly exited the womb singing. He hummed along with the "Marine's Hymn" before he could walk. "By age 10, he already played great boogie-woogie piano," younger brother Carl remembered.

In an odd way, Brian looked up to his father. "I used to wish I could play like my dad could," he recalled. "That's what got me going. My dad was the most inspirational person in my life, though he was also the worst person I ever met." On another occasion, Brian said of his father, "He was like our coach. He scared me so much I actually got scared into making good records."

By the time Brian was entering his senior year in high school, he was something of a musical prodigy. He was tall (six foot three) and lanky, with a crew cut and a drawn, yet handsome, face. His blue eyes were sharp and reacted immediately with emotion. He could never hide his feelings. Dennis, two years younger, was known in the neighborhood as Dennis the Menace. Blessed with a breathtaking handsomeness, he charmed girls and intimidated boys. Carl, the youngest, was chubby and shy, the most likely to hide behind his mother's skirt when trouble began. He was an observer, which granted him the precocious maturity and tactfulness to navigate his life and career. "Carl was born thirty," his mother said.

Brian began to think of the music room as *his* in those hours before his father came home from work. After school and his team practice—quarterback in football, center fielder in baseball for the Hawthorne High Cougars—he raced home and stationed himself at the piano, calling it "my refuge from the uncertainty that plagued our home." Music represented peace and salvation for Brian. "Music was a compulsion, as necessary to my health and well-being as food and sleep," he recalled. "It provided harmony in my life. It nourished me with everything I lacked, like love, care, and stability."

Uncertainty. Murry was badger one minute, puppy dog the next.

Brian was drawn to the music of the Four Freshmen, a vocal group formed in 1948 at Butler University in Indianapolis. The group began as a barbershop quartet but then merged that vocal style with jazz. Discovered by bandleader Stan Kenton during a midwestern tour, he insisted that his label, Capitol Records, sign the group. By the midfifties, the Freshmen were bridging the gap between parents and kids, starting with their first national hit, "It's a Blue World," in 1952. Mom and dad liked the smooth blend of the singers, and the kids recognized the Freshmen as cousins of the new rock 'n' roll vocal groups, such as the Platters, the Spaniels, and the Flamingos.

Audree bought her son *The Four Freshmen and Five Trombones*, the group's 1955 album, and for a full week, Brian spent nearly every waking moment huddled with the record on the hi-fi in the music room. At the end of that week, he announced that he had come up with a vocal arrangement for Carl, Audree, and Murry to back him. The family was stunned by the way Brian had parsed the vocal parts to fit their voices.

When Brian heard the Freshmen were appearing at the nearby Cocoanut Grove, he begged to go, and, in a rare moment of parental bonding, Murry took his oldest son as his date. Brian sat in awe during the concert, and afterward Murry bullshit his way backstage for his son to meet the singers.

"They were in varying states of undress, changing out of their stage clothes," Brian recalled. Murry introduced himself to the group and said, "This is my son, Brian. He's a big fan."

"You got our records, man?" one of the members asked.

"All of them," he said.

For months, the Four Freshmen were all that Brian could talk or think about. Their lush harmonies caromed around his noggin, and he drew in his parents and brother Carl into a near cult of Freshmen worship. He listened to the record "months at a time, days on end," Carl remembered. He said his brother would pull up a chair in front of the hi-fi and bend down, his one good ear cocked toward the speaker, absorbing the vocal blend.

Murry's younger sister, Emily—known to family and friends as Glee—married a native Californian, Milton Love. After flunking out of UCLA, he joined his father's business, Love Sheet Metal. Business was good and got even better after the Second World War. It allowed Milton and Glee a comfortable life in their suburban hacienda at the corner of Mount Vernon and Fairway in the View Park neighborhood.

The Wilsons and the Loves gathered at the holidays and sang. Even though Murry and Glee grew up in a house of parental abuse, music had always been the salve on the wounds. History repeated itself in Hawthorne. The gatherings at the Loves' convinced the Wilson boys they had allies in their cousins: Michael, the eldest, was born in 1941, a year and change older than Brian. He had two younger brothers, Stephen and Stanley, and two little sisters, Maureen and Stephanie. They all sang together.

Murry's modest little machine shop was nothing compared to Love Sheet Metal, and the two-bedroom in Hawthorne could be lost in the cavernous home of the Loves. Murry swallowed his resentment when the music started as the two families sat around the piano and married voices. Brian showcased his Four Freshmen arrangements, and Mike, who loved rhythm and blues, tried to steer his cousins toward the style of the black vocal groups he liked, such as the Drifters, from Atlantic Records, the great independent label in New York run by two Turkish brothers in love with American black culture.

Mike also told Brian where to tune his under-the-covers transistor to hear those sounds of black America. Brian listened as rhythm and blues murmured from his palm-sized transistor, and added the beautiful voices of black America to the music library in his head. Years later, during one of the darker periods of his mental illness, Brian wrote about those musical pockets of his childhood in "Mount Vernon and Fairway (A Fairy Tale)." It was a half-spoken, half-sung tale of a prince—with two brothers, of course—who discovered music on his magic transistor radio and who learned to sing and play and find the golden chords of God.

The Wilson-Love musical throw-downs were the highlights of the year for the boys. Mike and Brian were navigating high school. Despite his success in athletics, Brian felt on edge most of the time. "High school was confusing," he recalled, "a struggle to fit in and seem normal. I might've looked like anyone else in my V-neck sweaters and polished shoes, but inside I was always on edge, trying to balance the fear I'd grown up with against my desire to fit in."

Though tall and delicately handsome, Brian was disinclined to approach girls. His unrequited love for cheerleader Carol Mountain tormented him and ended up inspiring several of his finest songs. (Years later, as he worked on *Pet Sounds* with lyricist Tony Asher, he wrote a monumentally sad end-of-love song he called

"Carol, I Know," which Asher heard as—and eventually titled—"Caroline, No.")

Brian's love for Carol was an open secret. He rhapsodized about her beauty to friends, but he and she had only one (uneventful) date. Somehow, though Carol liked Brian—*who didn't?*—she was unaware of the torch he carried, which made the Statue of Liberty look like an Ohio Blue Tip. "I really had no idea until 25 years later," she told one of Brian's biographers. "He was just a really nice guy, someone you wanted to protect."

Mike attended the mostly black Dorsey High, named for the first woman who served as superintendent of the Los Angeles School District. Though intelligent and funny, Mike had no interest in academics and limped to the graduation finish line in 1959. His teachers said he put his energy into being a smart-ass or staying after school to reign as locker room superjock. Teammates said he lingered in the shower because he liked the echo it gave his singing voice.

"Most of his classmates were black," Carl recalled. "He was the only white guy on his track team. He was really immersed in doo-wop and that music, and I think he influenced Brian to listen to it. The black artists were so much better in terms of rock records in those days that the white records sounded like put-ons."

Adult life was getting off to a bad start for the Dorsey class clown. He'd worked briefly at Love Sheet Metal, but the company's fortunes plummeted at the end of the fifties, due to bad management. By 1959, Milton Love wore the scarlet B of bankruptcy. Mike had to seek other employment. In later years, during his onstage banter, he'd often say that he started off in the "oil business," but that meant he pumped gas, which he hated, especially after he was robbed at gunpoint.

On top of the dead-end job, Mike faced another crisis when he found out his girlfriend was pregnant. He briefly considered a then illegal abortion across the border in Mexico, but Glee wouldn't hear of it, so the young couple was married by shotgun in the home of the bride's parents.

High school graduation was better for Brian Wilson the following year. That fall, he started at El Camino Junior College in Torrance, intending to study psychology. "People confuse me," Brian shrugged when a counselor asked him why. "I'd like to understand them better."

Another Hawthorne High classmate, Al Jardine, attended El Camino, and he and Brian rekindled their friendship there. They had both played football for the Cougars, but Brian's mistake caused

Jardine injury. As Carl recalled, "Brian got Al's leg busted in a game, for fucking up on a play. He was quarterback, and the ball went the wrong way and Al got his leg broken."

Jardine was also a fledgling musician and was particularly fond of folk music. "Tom Dooley," the recent hit by the well-scrubbed Kingston Trio, had taken folk music from smoky clubs with unhygienic singers to national television. The trio of Bob Shane, Nick Reynolds, and Dave Guard was spirited and handsomely outfitted in candy-striped shirts.

Brian liked so many different kinds of music and was willing to try some folk tunes, even though Jardine already had a trio of his own called the Islanders. Brian once described Jardine's voice as being clear as a ringing bell, so they practiced singing together and talked daily between classes. They sounded good, Brian told Al.

Al liked Brian's voice and his musical knowledge, so he suggested that maybe they should form a group, maybe a *Hawthorne* Trio. He wanted to build this new venture around Brian instead of his Islander partners.

In his gruff way, Murry encouraged his sons to develop their musical talent. He'd bought a fairly pricey Wollensak reel-to-reel for Brian on his eighteenth birthday, and the boy carried the cumbersome tape recorder everywhere and even recorded some of the song sessions at the Loves' house. That same year, Murry lavished Carl, just fourteen, with a Rickenbacker twelve-string guitar. Dennis, though he would take part in family sing-alongs, didn't seem to have the drive to make music that his brothers and his parents had. For his special present, Murry bought his second son a surfboard, which he stored in the corner of the boys' shared bedroom.

Dennis was the outlier in the family. When everyone else gathered at the piano, he was out the front door, trying to find a ride to the beach. It was a twenty-minute drive, and if he couldn't hitch, he'd carry his surf board the seven miles to Dockweiler State Beach. Manhattan Beach, a prime surfing spot, was seven miles farther south.

The boys decided to go public with their singing, scheduling an appearance at a Hawthorne High School assembly. Even Dennis, the incorrigible student, planned to perform at the school he rarely attended. Brian and Al Jardine had graduated, so they were happy to return to the alma mater in glory. Mike Love was also part of the quickly assembled group, and singing, even at a high school, beat pumping gas.

The sole reluctant participant was Carl. Shy and overweight, he didn't think he was ready for the scrutiny that would come with a public performance. Brian argued that they needed his voice and guitar. To convince him to take part, Brian said they would call themselves Carl and the Passions.

The performance was a success, and Dennis had liked being on the inside for once. Maybe he could combine his other life, the one at the beach, with the musical life of his family. "He'd disappear every Saturday and Sunday he could, without cutting the lawn," Murry complained. "He loved the sport."

Late one Saturday afternoon, Dennis came home, propped his surfboard against the house, went inside, and walked up to brother Brian. *Why don't you write a song about surfing?*

As the Beach Boys, the group that started life as Carl and the Passions became the most famous of all artists associated with surf music. But Dennis and Mike were the only ones who ever surfed. Brian, in fact, was afraid of water.

"Dennis was really living it," Carl said. "This was his life. I remember everyone was bleaching their hair; Brian tried it and it turned out a very unnatural orange—very funny. But Brian drew on Dennis' experiences. I remember Brian would drill Dennis on what was going on, really pump him for the terminology and the newest thing. Dennis was the embodiment of the group; he lived what we were singing about. If it hadn't been for Dennis, the group wouldn't have happened in the same way. I mean, we could have gotten it from magazines like everyone else did, but Dennis was out there doing it. He made it true."

Surf music was in existence before the boys ever walked into a recording studio. It probably began in the eighteenth century in the form of Hawaiian chants (or *mele*) that celebrated history and surfing skill and presented surfing not as mere sport but as a significant determinant of social status. These chants evolved into *hapa haole* (meaning "part white") songs that emanated from Hawaiian composers as well as the slick pros of Tin Pan Alley. The songwriters used surfing in the lyrics to draw people to the islands and to this mysterious and unique practice. The songs often dealt with exploits of surfers—many of whom were women—and focused on geography. *What waves and where.* That's an essential element of the original surf music that carried over to the Beach Boys and the other groups of the sixties: the constant shout-out of names and places in song.

"Geography is key to surfing," said historian Timothy J. Cooley. "The size of the wave, the direction the swell approaches—these become central to a surfer's knowledge. That's a fascinatingly consistent part of the *mele* and it also shows up in interesting ways in some of the [modern] surfing songs."

When surfing started to become hugely popular in California in the late fifties, the first music it inspired was mostly instrumental and mysterious. The gut rumble of Dick Dale's heavily reverbed Fender Stratocaster matched the ominous beauty of the mammoth waves rolling in on Southern California's beaches. Dale called it "the wet, splashy sound of reverb," and his frenzied pick work on the strings conveyed urgency and danger.

Dale—born Richard Monsour in Boston—grew up south of the city in Quincy, Massachusetts, until his family moved to Southern California during his senior year in high school. He was already adept as a guitarist, and once he discovered surfing, he merged those interests, playing his odes to the perfect wave at perilous volume. He pushed his Fender amplifiers so hard in performance that sometimes they caught fire. Movie-star handsome and skilled as a surfer, he began his recording career in 1959, and within a couple of years, he'd moved from the small Deltone label (his band was Dick Dale and the Deltones) to Capitol Records, which proclaimed him king of the surf guitar. His most celebrated songs followed: "Let's Go Trippin'" in 1961 and "Misirlou" in 1962. (The latter song had a second life as a hit in 1994, when it was used as the theme for the film *Pulp Fiction*.)

Up north in Washington State, the Ventures were an instrumental guitar-driven group whose heavy reverb and vibrato shared Dale's sound, though the group never considered itself part of the surf music world. Still, the heavy twang of the group's "Walk Don't Run" (number two on the *Billboard* chart) made it seem part of this new musical movement. Other instrumental groups—the Chantays, the Surfaris, the Marketts—began appearing in 1961 and 1962.

Murry and Audree Wilson planned to spend the long Labor Day weekend of 1961 visiting Mexico with another couple. They decided to leave the boys at home alone—Brian *was* in junior college, after all—and left one hundred dollars for each boy. "When we left," Audree recalled, "the refrigerator was completely stocked and we gave the boys enough money to buy whatever else they needed."

As soon as the elder Wilsons were out of the driveway, the boys began spending the money. Carl already had his Ricky, so they bought a small drum kit (just a bass, snare, and cymbals) for Dennis. Brian played the family piano. Al Jardine borrowed money from his mother and rented a stand-up bass. Mike showed up to sing. They spent the holiday weekend rehearsing songs—mostly folk songs that Al suggested—and Brian recorded the tunes on his Wollensak with rented microphones.

Murry and Audree returned to their house full of hungry boys, but before Murry could blow a gasket over the squandered money, Brian set up the Wollensak and said, "We have something we want to play for you." Hearing the boys' voices on tape had the desired effect. Angry Dad turned marshmallow.

In the waning days of summer, the five boys showed up at the offices of Guild Music, a mom-and-pop music publishing company run by Hite and Dorinda Morgan. The Morgans already knew Al Jardine because he'd tried and failed to interest them in the Islanders. The Morgans had published a couple of Murry's songs, so his was the other foot in the door.

The boys played the tape for the couple, which featured a stab at the folk song "Sloop John B," and although the Morgans thought the voices sounded just fine, they didn't really smell anything original. At that point, the boys were calling themselves the Pendletones. Dorinda Morgan scoffed at their name and said they could sing like angels, but if they didn't have an angle or an original approach, they were doomed to fail. Then Dennis spoke up and lied, telling Mrs. Morgan that Brian and Mike had written a song about surfing. *What's surfing?* Though they'd lived in Southern California for years, the Morgans were ignorant of this new part of youth culture. Dennis's enthusiasm was infectious. They made an appointment to follow up.

A week later, at the Morgans' home studio, the boys debuted "Surfin'," the hastily written song with music by Brian and lyrics by

Mike. The primitive song was certainly memorable, with "bop-bop-dip-de-dip-dip-dip" backing vocals and verses that extolled surfing as a way of life. "Drop everything," Dorinda Morgan said. "We're going to record your song." The Morgans booked World Pacific Studios on October 3, 1961, to get a clean master recording.

Murry took it upon himself to manage that session, immediately angering his middle son, Dennis, by telling him he wasn't a good enough drummer to play on the record.

"It was my guitar," Carl said. "Alan had the upright bass, and Brian played a single snare drum with a pencil, and that was it. Brian took his shirt off and put it over the drum because it was too loud. We did it all at once, with Michael on one microphone and the rest of us on another."

It took eight attempts to get a satisfactory recording of "Surfin'," and they did twelve takes of a song called "Luau," written by the Morgans' son, to use on the B-side of a possible single. The sound was rudimentary and high on the treble, in a nascent style that was the essence of garage-band music.

The Morgans had a few connections with local labels. Candix Records was formed in 1960 by twins Robert and Richard Dix and their partner, William Canady Silva, who contracted Canady and Dix for the label's name. When the Morgans played the recordings for the Candix brain trust, they immediately decided to release the record. But they hated the group's name.

It wasn't until the first carton of singles arrived at the Wilson house that the group realized they had a new name: *Beach Boys*. There had been a lot of debate at Candix about the name. There already was a group with a name similar to Pendletones, and the company briefly considered renaming the boys the Surfers. Russ Regan, the director of record distribution (and part-time recording artist), said that name would limit their appeal to record buyers on the coasts. Regan came up with the new name.

Within a day, the record was played on KFWB, then the most popular AM station in Los Angeles, featuring an impressive list of on-air personalities, including disc jockey B. Mitchell Reed. The first time the boys heard it on the radio, the reaction was immediate.

"We got so excited hearing it on the radio that Carl threw up," Dennis said. "I ran down the street screaming, 'Listen! We're on the radio!'"

Even though he had not played a large role in the recording, Dennis took particular pride in the record. "Dennis was so thrilled, because he was living it," Carl said. "He went to school and his friends said, 'We were on our way home from the beach, totally exhausted from riding the waves all day. We heard your record come on, and it turned us on so much that we went back to the beach.'"

———————

The record earned heavy play on KFWB and KRLA, eventually rising as high as number three on one of the local charts. It even began to make some noise nationally, getting as high as the seventies on the *Billboard* chart. This was enough momentum to get the band a booking at the Rendezvous Ballroom in Newport Beach. This venerable showcase had opened in the twenties, but its great days were long past until 1959, when Dick Dale played his first show there and thought it was the perfect venue for his music. Two years later, Dale had nearly singlehandedly revived the old hall and the Beach Boys were signed to play two songs during the intermission of Dale's pre-Christmas show. Two other bands were on the bill—the Surfaris and the Challengers—and it was clear that the boys from Hawthorne were there simply to help the promoters avoid dead air during the bathroom break. To Brian, the short, rushed performance was a disaster.

Brian pushed the band to work harder, grinding them through a week of relentless rehearsals. Murry bought Brian a bass, and Al switched to electric guitar. On New Year's Eve, they played three songs at a show in Long Beach promoted as a tribute to Ritchie Valens, the young Chicano rock 'n' roll star killed in a 1959 plane crash with fellow rocker Buddy Holly. The Beach Boys followed the Ike and Tina Turner Revue on the bill, and the hours of rehearsal paid off—they were all happy with their performance. Even Murry praised the boys.

"Although we were still raw recruits in the music business, the producer of the show dug our performance enough to book us for other shows," Carl told *Tiger Beat*, the bible of American teenagers. "Our first trip took us to San Diego, where we played during the intermission of a surfing movie."

And then . . . *nothing*. The record was a regional hit, but when the boys got their first royalty checks, they were horrified. *Eight-hundred bucks*—that was it . . . *for a hit*. Murry kicked in 200 zorts, which meant he had $1,000 to divide, giving each boy $200 for their efforts.

Al Jardine was disgusted. *If this is the music business, then the hell with it.* He told Brian he was quitting the band and going back to college. The microscopic royalty discouraged the other boys, but they decided to stick it out and look for another guitarist.

Brian had written a few new songs, "Surfer Girl" and "Surfin' Safari" among them, and recorded them, again with the Morgans, at World Pacific Studios, and the group continued on as a quartet until they could find a replacement.

"Surfin'" made the Wilson boys local celebrities, and one of their neighbors, Benny Jones, urged his nephew to drop in on the boys when he was visiting one Sunday. Gary Usher had also dipped his toes in the music business, with a single on the tiny Titan label, "Driven Insane." Usher wasn't a surfer, but he was nuts about cars.

He could hear the Wilsons from his uncle's house and could tell someone was playing music in the converted garage. He ambled over and introduced himself to Brian.

"I've heard you guys on the radio," Usher said.

"Yeah?" Brian asked. "What'd you think?"

"Cool. Really cool. Can I listen to what you're doing?"

Despite the age difference (Brian was nineteen, Gary was twenty-four), they hit it off immediately. For the next several days, they practiced together: Gary played guitar, and Brian ad-libbed on piano. Almost immediately, they began writing songs.

They quickly became friends, and for the first time, Brian had reached outside his family. "We became almost platonic lovers," Usher said. "Brian isn't gay, and neither am I, but there was a really deep attraction."

Gary reeked of confidence, and that fascinated the pathologically insecure Brian. "Gary and I spent all that afternoon and evening exchanging thoughts about music and life," Brian said. "We told things to each other that we wouldn't share with our families or our girlfriends, secrets we wouldn't discuss with anyone else. We understood each other without having to explain."

Lyrics had always been difficult for Brian, so he longed for a good, clever collaborator. Mike Love would prove to be a memorable lyricist, but Brian felt that Gary could bring a lot to the party, especially with his love of automobiles.

They wrote their first song that night, a hypnotic little ballad called "The Lonely Sea," but then they began to expand the scope of their writing. They realized they shared an admiration for the songs of Goffin and King, the young songwriting team from New York's Brill Building. Gerry Goffin and Carole King were married and had just written a dance song called "The Loco-Motion," which their babysitter recorded and turned into a number-one hit. Brian and Gary decided to replicate that success, writing a dance song that wouldn't work for the Beach Boys, since it had a rhythm and blues feel. When they finished the song, "Revo-lution," they decided it needed a young black woman's voice. Brian suggested they drive to Watts, the largest black community in L.A., to find a singer.

"Shit, we'll get killed for sure," Usher said. "You don't walk up to some black girl and proposition her to sing."

But that's what they did. After stopping strangers on the street and knocking on doors (*Excuse me, sir. Do you have a daughter who sings?*), they found a girl named Betty Willis, though when Brian produced a finished record of the song late in the summer, it was credited to Rachel and the Revolvers. Brian was single-minded when it came to music. When he hatched an idea, he *had* to follow it through.

Though Brian loved collaborating with his new friend, Murry worked overtime to make Gary feel ill at ease. Gary pushed Brian to cast a wider net, and they began pairing Brian's melodies with Gary's paeans to muscle cars, drag racing, and all things automotive. He had an encyclopedic knowledge of anything related to internal combustion engines. They wrote a song about Gary's dream car, "409," and when Brian talked about his need for refuge in the Wilson house of pain, he came up with the lyrics of "In My Room." Jealous of the collaboration, Murry insisted that Gary and Brian write a song about yellow roses. Usher jeered.

"That's really old-fashioned," Usher said.

Murry was apoplectic. "It is *not* old-fashioned," he roared.

"You don't have to write with him," Gary told Brian. "He's doing Lawrence Welk stuff. Let's do Goffin and King."

That's when Murry told Gary to get out of the house. The Brian Wilson–Gary Usher collaborations would continue on Usher's turf or as they drove around with a six-pack and a couple of girls. Brian wasn't about to give up his new collaborator just because his father said so.

Murry was shopping around some of the recordings the Morgans had made of Brian's new songs, without much luck. Candix had been unable to keep up with the demand for "Surfin'," and was headed toward bankruptcy that spring. The recordings tucked under Murry's arm were owned by the Morgans, but he had decided the couple was no longer necessary. He felt he knew as much about the music business as Hite and Dorinda.

Murry worked his way through the reception rooms of other record labels—Dot, Liberty, Decca—with no luck. Years before, he had sent demos of his songs to Ken Nelson, who ran the country-and-western division of Capitol Records. Nelson had passed on Murry's songs, but at least he'd been nice about it. The Beach Boys weren't country and western, but Murry felt certain that Nelson would like their old-fashioned harmonies, suburban cousins to those of the Sons of the Pioneers. Ken brushed Murry off to the youngest producer on the Capitol staff, twenty-three-year-old Nick Venet.

By the time he was twenty, Venet had produced jazz artists such as Chet Baker, Peggy Lee, and Stan Kenton. He joined Capitol at twenty-one and produced the smoothie harmonies of the Lettermen, getting them to the top of the charts with "When I Fall in Love" and "The Way You Look Tonight" in 1961.

Murry nearly blew his audience with the Capitol whiz kid. He wouldn't shut up, telling Venet how great his kids were. Finally, Venet got him to play the demo of one of the new songs, "Surfin' Safari."

"Before eight bars had spun around, I knew it was a hit record," Venet said. "I knew the song was going to change West Coast music."

Venet got the attention of the Capitol head honcho, Voyle Gilmore, and they agreed to buy the master recordings. Murry had brought the label a ready-made single: "Surfin' Safari" backed with "409." Brian had wanted to give Gary's car-love song a special touch, so he carried his Wollensak to the curb in front of the Wilsons' house—stretching an extension cord to its limit—and recorded the sound of Gary revving his engine and driving back and forth in front of the house.

Murry screwed over the Morgans, who recorded and owned some of the master recordings, and later gloated that he had cost them $2.5 million. When they learned what Murry had done, the Morgans could have successfully sued. But getting Murry Wilson out of their lives? *Priceless*.

Capitol issued the single on June 4, 1962, initially pushing "409" because the company figured it would have national appeal. Disc jockeys didn't take the bait, but when they flipped over the record and played "Surfin' Safari," there was an immediate response. It became a Top Twenty song nationally, and it was time for an album.

Brian didn't look very far to replace Alan Jardine. The Wilsons' neighbor across the street, twelve-year-old David Marks, played rudimentary guitar and was tall for his age. With sun-bleached blond hair, he could be mistaken for Dennis in a squint. He easily followed Carl's lead on guitar.

As their single lurched up the charts, the group convened at Capitol Records studio in August to begin recording the songs they'd need to fill an album. Brian had written four songs with Mike Love and five with Gary Usher. There were a few covers, including Eddie Cochran's "Summertime Blues" and "Little Miss America" by a trumpeter named Herb Alpert.

Venet was the official producer, sitting in the control booth elbow to elbow with Murry Wilson, who puffed his pipe and barked orders. But Brian ran things inside the studio, pushing the group with their vocals and charting arrangements that masked the fact that they were still novices on their instruments.

Murry drove Nick crazy, and the young producer set up an early warning system with the Capitol receptionist. She buzzed an intercom warning when Murry was marching toward Nick's office, and Nick dove under his desk and hid until Murry left. But he put up with it all because he thought the Beach Boys were worth it.

And they were. Within six months, the group had scored a number-three national hit, "Surfin' USA," based on Chuck Berry's "Sweet Little Sixteen," followed by the *Surfin' USA* album, which rose to number two on the *Billboard* chart.

Suddenly surf music was everywhere. Kids in Kentucky fashioned surfboards from plywood to put atop their cars. Surf bands sprang up in such nonsurf locales as Minneapolis. Bands played surf music in Winnipeg and El Paso. The sound, the style, and the language of surf music suddenly spread over the country.

3

THEY PUT THE BOMP

When I was young I had all the advantages. My father worked for Howard Hughes, we lived in Bel Air. I went to the best schools, and got the best girls. My intelligence quotient was well above average; and yet I could be a rebellious, troublesome punk who brought more than a little anxiety to my parents.

—Jan Berry

The locker room had the best echo. After practice, some of the guys on the team liked to linger in the showers and sing, to bounce voices off the tiles until they sounded like those guys on the radio.

Bomp bomp bomp ba do wah do wah do wah do wah wah

Anyone could sing along. They just needed someone to take the lead, which Jan Berry usually did. Jan had it all: good looks, wealth, and talent.

University High School opened in West Los Angeles 1924, at first named for President Warren G. Harding. But Harding's role in the Teapot Dome scandal became common knowledge that year, the late president's name was an embarrassment, and the school was renamed when UCLA moved its main campus to nearby Westwood four years later.

Uni was a formidable structure, two stories of blond brick under a Spanish tile roof, looking more like a California version of a small, elite college campus than the typical bunker-like high schools erected in the fifties, that era of nuclear fear. A half block off Santa Monica Boulevard, it was a twelve-minute drive—or a one-hour walk—to the beach.

45

Jan Berry met Dean Torrence when they attended Jefferson Junior High together, and by their last season as members of the Uni Wildcats football team, they'd grown into close friends. Jan was a tight end and Dean, lanky and athletic, was a wide receiver on offense and a free safety on defense. Their lockers were side by side during the 1957 season, and they became even closer, sharing interests in cars, girls, and music.

Both boys had gone nuts when Elvis Presley came along, and now, a year later, both Jan and Dean—and most of their other friends— were steeped in the rock 'n' roll music blasting from the radio: Chuck Berry, Bo Diddley, Buddy Holly, Little Richard, Eddie Cochran, Fats Domino . . .

Presley's blend of white and black music had opened the door for African American artists and also inspired a lot of young white artists with country music leanings to goose their style with a dose of rhythm and blues. Uni was like a finishing school for young musicians. Nancy Sinatra, daughter of the chairman of the board, was a classmate. Randy Newman, the future Oscar-winning composer, was a couple years behind.

But the boys in the shower had a particular affinity for doo-wop music. This style didn't depend so much on guitars or pounding pianos or honking saxophones. The primary element of doo-wop was the oldest instrument on the planet: the human voice. Doo-wop depended on nonsense sounds that accompanied a heartfelt profession of unceasing love.

Dun dun dun da-da-dun-dun duh dun dun

That was the opening of "I Wonder Why" by Dion and the Belmonts, one of the biggest hits of the era. This new vocal style began to emerge around the same time as Presley's hybrid country-and-blues style, and was characteristic of street-corner singing groups. You needed a bass voice, a tenor, a falsetto (if possible), and a few others in between. Nonsense was essential:

Dum dum dum dum dum-de-do-dum dum dum dum dum

Rama lama lama lama lama ding dong

Show dote un showbie doe show dote un showbie doe

The term *doo-wop* wasn't even in common use then, but California was beginning to compete with Philadelphia and Brooklyn street corners as the petri dish for the new style. L.A. had a different urban culture, so the spontaneous singing groups gathered in showers, not on street corners.

After practice, Jan Berry, Dean Torrence, Arnie Ginsburg, James Brolin (yes, the actor), Barry Keenan, and other Wildcats bounced voices off the shower wall:

Bop du baw bah do wah do wah do wah wah

For their soggy repertoire, they chose the best doo-wop songs of the era: "Get Job" by the Silhouettes (*dip-dip-dip-dip sha na na na sha na na na na*), "Why Do Fools Fall in Love?" by Frankie Lymon and the Teenagers (*oom bop zoom bop zoo do duh duh*), "Whispering Bells" by the Del-Vikings (*ding-ding-ding-a-ding dong-dong-dong-a-dong*), and "Rock 'n' Roll Is Here to Stay" by Danny and the Juniors (*raw raw raw rah oh baby raw raw raw rah*).

When the annual University High School talent show was announced, Jan Berry took charge. *We need to take this act from the showers to the stage. Come over to my house and we'll rehearse in the garage.*

Ah, but which one, Jan? Jan Berry's father, William, was an electrical engineer who worked for Howard Hughes and helped Hughes build his monstrous Hercules H-4 aircraft, known as the Spruce Goose. The seaplane was a project conceived during the Second World War, but Hughes's ambitious design and his endless tinkering meant the Goose, which had the longest wingspan of any aircraft in history, was not ready until 1947. William Berry was onboard for the only flight of the plane, piloted by Hughes. After a successful test flight—seventy feet in the air for a mile off the California coast—Hughes put the plane in dry dock, and it never flew again.

Working for a madcap multibillionaire made William Berry a wealthy man, affording him a comfortable house in Bel-Air with a *four*-car garage. But no cars were stored there when Jan Berry was a senior at Uni. Because his eldest son (*of ten children!*) was serious about music, William Berry had the garages turned into a music studio for Jan, with a piano and two Ampex tape recorders.

It was time to get serious about their music, Jan told his friends. And so they convened in the massive garage and began rehearsing the locker room repertoire. Jan took the bass vocal, and Dean handled the falsetto. Chuck Steele was the lead singer, and John Seligman, Arnie Ginsburg, and Wally Agi filled out the sound.

They rehearsed each song several times before Jan was satisfied. Then he recorded each song three times on his two tape recorders. Then he merged the recordings, one played slightly behind the other, to give the song an echo. Then he spliced together the best parts of the three takes of each song to create one, finished recording. Most of the other singers, save Dean, had long been dismissed, but Jan invited over his classmate from next door, Bruce Johnston, to record a piano track for the songs. Dean called up his friend Sandy Nelson and asked him to come over to Bel-Air to play drums.

The songs sounded good. Not bad for a seventeen-year-old kid working in a garage—even if it *was* a four-car garage. The group was called the Barons, after Jan Berry's car club.

The vocal group, augmented by Johnston and Nelson, performed at the talent show, but rather than it being the start of something—as Jan Berry had hoped—it was the end of the singing Barons. Most of the guys wanted to concentrate on girls and teenage carnalities for the last semester of high school. So it came down to Jan . . . and Dean.

"One night, while Jan and I were trying to write our own song to record," Dean recalled, "Arnie Ginsburg showed up. Arnie had an idea for a song called 'Jennie Lee.'" The inspiration was Arnie's new inamorata, an exotic dancer. He had just broken up with his high school girlfriend and took solace at the Burbank Theater in downtown Los Angeles. The theater offered "New Follies Burlesk" and featured one of the reigning exotic dancers of the day, Jennie Lee.

It was just a stage name. She was born in Kansas City in 1928 as Virginia Hicks and began working as a chorus girl while still in high school. Within a year, she was stripping in Missouri, in Kansas City and Joplin, and Chicago, provocatively disrobing before the crowned heads of the American Midwest. She came to Los Angeles in the midfifties, already with a reputation as "the Bazoom Girl." Her body was athletic, and her large, awe-inspiring breasts defied gravity. Like many strippers, she wore tassels (more like propellers) over her nipples and was adept at swishing them at her front-row customers. Her body was sleek and smooth, like the long, finned cars of the era, and her athleticism set her apart from other exotic dancers. She was known to cartwheel across the stage and perform acrobatics. Her bust measurement was 42D, though she was often billed as "Miss 44 and Plenty More."

Also something of an activist, she had organized a strippers' union, the Exotique Dancers League, soon after moving to Los Angeles in 1955, feeling that she and her colleagues were being systematically underpaid by theater owners. Later, when her dancing career ended, she ran a club (the Sassy Lassy in San Pedro) and collected artifacts for a striptease museum that eventually became the Burlesque Hall of Fame in Las Vegas.

But all Arnie Ginsburg cared about that night in January 1958 was Jennie Lee and her magnificent bazooms.

Jan and Dean were in the garage working on a song they'd written called "Sally She Lived upon the Hill." Soon bored, they gave over to try to work up a cover version of "She Say" by the Diamonds.

She say ah oom dooby doom ooby dooby doom

And that's when Arnie Ginsburg walked in with the news that he'd broken up with his girl and had fallen in love with an older woman who had the biggest *you-know-whats* he'd ever seen. He showed Jan and Dean the ad he'd ripped from the newspaper advertising the Bazoom Girl. Parking was free after six, and for only one dollar they could get a copy of Jennie Lee's "art book."

The three boys crammed into Arnie's car and showed up at the Burbank, sitting in the theater's dark recesses, leaving the best seats for the regulars—older men holding raincoats on their laps to mask erections. As Jennie Lee began her act, Jan admitted she had the biggest *you-know-whats* he'd ever seen. Dean concurred, even though he'd never seen any *you-know-whats* before. The old men puffed on cigars and studied Jennie Lee as if they were zoologists and she was a new, exotic species. As her magnificent breasts bounced and her propellers twirled, the regulars chanted along with each rise and fall of the majestic bosom:

Bom bom bomp! Bom bom bomp!

The boys were impressed, and on the way home in the car, they replicated the old men's *bom-bom-bomp* chant. Arnie told Jan and Dean to ditch that song they were working on and write a song about the new love of his life, Jennie Lee. With the *bom-bom-bomp*, they already had a good start. Jan decided he wanted the Barons to sing the song and debut it at an upcoming car-club party. But he wanted to do what he'd done before the talent show: make recordings of the song and splice together the best of three versions, only this time he wanted to have the song cut to disc so he'd have authentic-looking 45 RPMs to give away at the party.

When the time came to record the song, though, no one was available. Even Dean couldn't come over to Jan's garage. Dean was a half year ahead of his friends in school and was graduating in January and would be spending the spring of 1958 on active duty as part of his commitment to the army reserves. He was leaving the next day, and he had to pack.

Two months later, at Fort Ord on Monterey Bay, Dean was cleaning his rifle when he heard "Jennie Lee" on the radio. When the song was over, the disc jockey said the song was by Jan and Arnie.

Bom-bom-bom ba ba ba baba bom

Turns out that when Jan took his tape in to have his discs cut, a fellow in another room at the recording studio heard the song and came down the hall from his office.

What's that song, kid?

It's just a home recording. I'm going to give these singles away at a party next week.

The man introduced himself as Joe Lubin, and he said he was a producer for Arwin Records, an independent label on North Canon Drive in Hollywood, owned by Marty Melcher, husband of singing movie star Doris Day. Lubin said he wanted to take the tape, add some instruments to it, and put it out on Arwin. He vowed he would make Jan and his partner into bigger stars than the Everly Brothers. As soon as he got home that night, Jan had called Dean, who was packing for his move to Fort Ord.

Drop everything. We're going to be bigger than the Everly Brothers.

But what about the army?

Call them up and tell them you've changed your mind.

Dean hung up and thought no more of it until he was cleaning his M-1 one day that summer and heard the song on the radio. When the disc jockey announced "Jan and Arnie," his heart sunk. Now Jan and *Arnie* would be as big as the Everly Brothers and he would be . . . *what?*

> *Who put the bomp in the bomp bah bomp bah bomp?*
> *Who put the ram in the rama lama ding dong?*
> *Who put the bop in the bop shoo bop shoo bop?*
> *Who put the dip in the dip da dip da dip?*
> *Who was that man? I'd like to shake his hand*
> *He made my baby fall in love with me*
>
> —"Who Put the Bomp?" by Barry Mann

By July, "Jennie Lee" was number three on the national chart. It was kept out of the top spot by the Everly Brothers' "All I Have to Do Is Dream" and "The Purple People Eater," a novelty song by Sheb Wooley. Dean's military obligation dragged on and he was depressed, fearing he'd missed his chance at stardom. "I had to accept the fact that I blew it," Dean said. "I spent many after-duty hours at the base Dairy Queen and drowned my sorrows in a bottomless vanilla malt."

Once, during Dean's tour of duty, Jan called his friend's house to see if he could get an address or phone number for Dean. But Dean's mother told Jan not to bother him, assuring him that if his planned postarmy career pumping gas at Dick Martin's Chevron didn't work out, he'd consider making music with Jan as his fallback plan.

In Dean's absence, Jan and Arnie basked in their lucky break, getting a Top Five hit on their first try. They toured as part of rock 'n' roll package shows and made several appearances on television. Jan should have been readying a follow-up single as "Jennie Lee" reached its peak, but nothing was happening. Plus, Arnie Ginsburg wasn't thrilled with life on the road.

By the end of the summer, Dean was back home, stewing about his missed opportunity and contemplating whether to start his career in the oil business at the corner Chevron. One weekend, some of his old Uni teammates were having a flag football game and invited him. Jan also showed up, and when the game was over, he asked Dean if he wanted to come by his garage studio and work on a song. Dean hesitated. He desperately wanted to work with Jan again but didn't want to step on Arnie's toes. Jan shrugged. Arnie wasn't interested in being a rock 'n' roll star, he said.

"I am stunned," Dean said. "What was there not to like about making lots of money, performing on *American Bandstand*, rubbing shoulders with Elvis, Frankie Avalon, Sam Cooke, flirting with Annette Funicello, buying a new car right off the showroom floor, having dinner at Dick Clark's house, having chicks scream at you. What am I missing? What's there not to like?"

Jan and Dean worked together for several months, and Dean held his breath the whole time, expecting Arnie to return and for him to be booted from the duo. He desperately wanted to make an impression on Jan so he'd be seen as a valuable partner. But he couldn't tell if Jan was truly committed to their musical partnership.

Then Jan suggested that they get in touch with two young guys he'd met during his and Arnie's time at the top of the charts. They had appeared on those late fifties package shows that allowed them to perform "Jennie Lee" and a couple of other songs and hustle off stage. They shared the bill with a lot of young rhythm and blues singers, but none of them could hold a candle to the singer who topped the bill, Sam Cooke.

———————

Sam Cooke was gospel music royalty. When Aretha Franklin was a young girl, Cooke and his fellow Soul Stirrers would show up at her father's church and stun parishioners with their powerful singing. C. L. Franklin was a minister whose national celebrity brought the Soul Stirrers and other great performers to his parish in Detroit. As a young teenager, Aretha Franklin remembered being among the swooning crowd of young girls who nearly fainted in the presence of Cooke, who was blessed with movie-star good looks and a voice from God.

Cooke was born in Clarksdale, Mississippi, ground zero for American blues music. The town was home to Ike Turner, John Lee Hooker, Sir Mack Rice, Jackie Brenston, and scores of others. Muddy Waters lived on Stovall's plantation outside town and Robert Johnson was said to have sold his soul to the devil at the crossroads of highways 49 and 61 on Clarksdale's outskirts.

Cooke grew up in the church—his father was a minister—and, at nineteen, he was invited to join the hugely popular gospel group the Soul Stirrers. As lead singer, Cooke sang with a mixture of vigor and delicacy on such spiritual classics as "Free at Last" and "Touch the Hem of His Garment."

The Soul Stirrers were signed to Specialty Records, the Los Angeles label owned by Art Rupe. Itching to start a career in secular music by the time he reached his midtwenties, Cooke released his first non-gospel side ("Lovable," his rewrite of the spiritual "Wonderful") on Specialty, under the name Dale Cook. Afraid of offending his gospel fans, Cooke thought he should mask his identity. But he could not mask his unforgettable voice. Rupe encouraged him to record more secular music, as he hoped Cooke could fill the void left by the retirement of his label's biggest star, Little Richard, who had just renounced rock 'n' roll, quitting show business and becoming a minister.

But Cooke's secular recordings were nothing like Little Richard's blistering records. When Rupe heard Cooke recording George Gershwin's "Summertime" in the studio, he began arguing with his A&R man, Bumps Blackwell. After a shouting match, Rupe kicked Blackwell and Cooke off Specialty.

By the next year, Blackwell and Cooke had landed at Keen Records, another small L.A. independent. Founded by Bob Keane early in 1957, the label would launch not only Cooke's secular career but also that of two doomed young rock 'n' roll stars. Hispanic singer Ritchie Valens was on Keane's subsidiary label, Del-Fi, and had the number-one song in the country—a double-sided single of "Donna" and "La Bamba"—not long before his death at seventeen in the same plane crash that killed Buddy Holly in 1959. Keane also helped Texas singer Bobby Fuller to the top of the charts a half decade later with "I Fought the Law," not long before Fuller died under mysterious circumstances in 1966. Keane also produced a lot of surf music on Del-Fi, which was home to the Surfaris, the Centurions, and the Lively Ones.

Cooke's first release for Keen was under his real name, and, though written by Cooke, he named his brother L. C. Cook as the composer, to control songwriter royalties. The simple tune—almost a vamp—repeated variations on the title phrase, "You Send Me," and was an ideal evocation of teenage love. Recorded June 1, 1957, at Radio Recorders in Hollywood, it entered the national charts that October and spent two weeks at number one in December. It was the beginning of a long string of hit records for Cooke, who provided a template for the soul singers who would become so popular within the decade.

As Blackwell said, "Anybody with soul, anybody with blood in their veins, when they hear Sam Cooke, they're gonna like it."

Cooke found a happy home at Keen. Bob Keane was a benevolent overlord, Bumps Blackwell was taking charge of A&R, and Cooke himself was maturing as a singer, beginning on a run of modern classics such as "Chain Gang," "Twistin' the Night Away," "Only Sixteen," "Another Saturday Night," and "Bring It on Home to Me."

Should Cooke's muse fail him, Keen had a safety net in place. Two young songwriters, Herb Alpert and Lou Adler, were on the company payroll and charged with finding and producing material. Keane was pushing forty and Blackwell was already there, so Cooke gravitated toward Alpert and Adler, who were hungry young guys around his age.

Alpert came from a musical family. His father had emigrated from Ukraine and played both balalaika and mandolin. In New York, he met the woman he married, a talented violin player. The family relocated to Los Angeles, where their son, Herbert, was born.

The boy began playing trumpet before he was ten and was drawn to show business. He tried his hand at acting but didn't get much more than extra work. His greatest film performance was in *The Ten Commandments*, the 1956 Cecil B. DeMille spectacle. Alpert played the back of a guy at the foot of Mount Sinai when Charlton Heston, as Moses, came down the mountain with his stone tablets and got pissed off.

Lou Adler was born in Chicago but, like Alpert, was raised in Southern California. Though not a musician, he loved music and wanted to be part of that business. Alpert married Adler's former girlfriend in 1956, and Adler, who still had feelings for his ex, suggested that Alpert, then twenty-one, buy a life insurance policy. They soon became friends and decided to join forces and make an assault on the record business. Two heads were better than one.

Adler called himself a poet, and he thought he was the perfect partner for the musically sophisticated Alpert. They wrote songs and recorded demos, making the rounds of L.A. record companies. After the departure of Bumps Blackwell, Specialty hired a new head of A&R, twenty-four-year-old Sonny Bono. Prematurely worldly-wise, Bono listened to the Alpert-Adler demo and encouraged Alpert and Adler to look for a new line of work.

Alpert and Adler were thrown together at Keen in 1957. Blackwell gave them their marching orders: listen to every tape that comes in over the transom and let us know if you hear anything good. They each earned seventy-eight dollars per week, even then not enough to live on. Alpert supplemented his income by being a weekend trumpet for hire. "I was making more money playing brises than at the record company," he said.

In addition to their daily duties, Alpert and Adler accompanied Keen artists when they went on tour. On one such tour, all of the acts were signed to Keen except for these two crew-cut boys straight out of high school who had a hit with a song about a stripper.

Stuck for material, Jan suggested to Dean that they call "a couple of very talented guys" he'd met while on tour. He set up a meeting that night with Herb Alpert and Lou Adler. They were not much older than Jan and Dean but were intensely focused and ambitious. Adler took himself seriously and arched his critical eyebrow when he showed up at Jan's garage and saw that neither of these young guys was wearing shoes. Not a good first impression.

But as Alpert and Adler listened to Jan and Dean, their minds began working. A lot of the teen idols then flooding the market—Dion, of Dion and the Belmonts, Paul Anka, Fabian, Frankie Avalon, those kinds of guys—were all Italian, dark, and from back east. Here were two tall, blond white guys who were goofballs—goofballs with talent, but goofballs nonetheless.

Alpert and Adler had collaborated on a song with Cooke, the immaculate "Wonderful World." The song was one of Cooke's greatest successes and enjoyed a long shelf life, recorded by hundreds of singers. With the success of that song, the two young men decided to take their earnings and look for more satisfying work. They landed at Doré Records, a small label that had had a number-one hit a couple years before, "To Know Him Is to Love Him," by a trio of high school kids calling themselves the Teddy Bears.

As the two young record men listened to Jan and Dean spin their stories and their demos, they thought they found an act they could work with. They thought they had the perfect tune for them, a novelty song by Melvin Schwartz. Stylistically, "Baby Talk" wasn't much of a stretch for Jan and Dean:

> *Bom ba ba bom bab um dab um dab um wa wa wa*
> *Bom ba ba bom bab um dad um dab um wa wa wa*

With Alpert and Adler supervising, they cut the song in Jan's garage and a flipside by Jan, Dean, and Jan's friend Don Altfeld, "Jeanette, Get Your Hair Done." "Baby Talk" went to number one in Los Angeles, which got the boys a spot on *American Bandstand*, the weekday show out of Philadelphia hosted by eternally youthful disc jockey Dick Clark. The national television exposure gave the record a boost, and it started up the *Billboard* charts. Clark liked Jan and Dean a lot and had them back to sing the song five times on the air during "Baby Talk"'s life on the charts. Within a few months, the song cracked the national Top Ten.

There were a few more follow-ups on Doré, including a clever rock 'n' roll version of the classic American ballad "Oh My Darling Clementine" (shortened to "Clementine" for the young audience).

Alpert and Adler decided it was time to start their own company, Herb B. Lou, and released a string of novelty tunes on the Arch Records label. Six months later, with no success, Alpert cashed in and decided to leave the recording business. (He would be back in a couple of years and launch another label, A&M Records, which became one of the great success stories in the American recording industry.)

For his part, Lou Adler hung on to Jan and Dean and made them building blocks of his musical empire. He steered them through several more record releases, all of which stiffed. It was time to move on. Jan and Dean thought they were ready for prime time.

"We were determined to sign with a *major* company," Dean said, "and never . . . deal anymore with record companies that carried on business out of a tent in an empty lot." Their next single, the chestnut "Heart and Soul," was released on Challenge Records. "At least they didn't carry on business out of a tent," Dean said. "They had an almost new camper with decals of trout on the sides and 'Challenge Records' painted on the door."

Dean was being a little too hard on Challenge. Founded by Gene Autry, cowboy singing star of the movies, the label had a number-one hit in 1958 with "Tequila" by the Champs. The recording was a one-off intended to be a B-side of a single, but it became a hit. Unfortunately, there were no genuine Champs. It had been put together by a group of studio musicians. Later, various touring bands of Champs were formed, featuring Glen Campbell and the seventies soft-rock duo Seals and Crofts (Jim Seals and Dash Crofts).

And there were others on Challenge Records during its decade-long existence: Baker Knight, composer of "Lonesome Town"; Marty Balin, who would found Jefferson Airplane; seminal rocker Gene Vincent; and the Peanut Butter Conspiracy.

Challenge did all right by Jan and Dean, promoting "Heart and Soul" enough to get it into the national Top Twenty. (It was number one on KFWB, L.A.'s leading rock 'n' roll station.) Jan and Dean had issued one album with Doré in 1960, and after the success of "Heart and Soul," Adler was determined to get the boys an album deal, and he eventually settled on Liberty Records, another L.A.-based independent, founded in 1955 and with a strong artist roster, including rhythm and blues singers Gene McDaniels and Billy Ward and His Dominoes. Liberty also had the great young star Eddie Cochran ("Summertime Blues," "C'mon Everybody"), who'd been killed in a 1960 automobile accident while on tour in England. It was also the label of the novelty act the Chipmunks. In fact, the three shrill chipmunk singers were named after Liberty executives Alvin Bennett, Theodore Keep, and Simon Waronker. Dean liked the Chipmunk namesakes, saying they were "a new breed of young men who were working in the music industry for the first time and were raised on rock 'n' roll. We were a perfect fit on the Liberty artists roster."

Like Jan and Dean, Adler had been frustrated by the minor league Doré and Challenge, so he looked at Liberty as the big time. He was dressing the boys in suits now, which they abhorred. Their first Liberty album, *Golden Hits*, collected all of their singles thus far ("Jennie Lee," "Baby Talk," "Heart and Soul") and was filled out with rock standards "Barbara Ann" and "Who Put the Bomp." Decked out in shiny gray suits on the cover, they looked like the goofballs they were. Jan balanced on one foot while Dean fiddled with his tie, wearing a *Can't wait to get this shit off* expression.

The album didn't chart, but Adler and his charges pressed on and Liberty showed both patience and faith. With Jan and Dean's sixth single release on Liberty, they finally had a hit with "Linda." The song was written by a soldier named Jack Lawrence in the early days of the Second World War and had been recorded by a number of artists, and Jan and Dean turned it into doo-wop:

Li-li-li-lili Li-li-la-Linda!

The song was a big enough hit for Liberty to contract for another Jan and Dean album. "Surfing music had just arrived," Dean recalled, "and Jan and I were physically involved in surfing, so it was just natural that we became involved with the music."

Jan and Dean used studio musicians when they recorded and did not have a band for their concert appearances. Their contracts with promoters required an opening band that would stick around and provide backing for Jan and Dean's set. The pickup band had to know three or four key Jan and Dean songs and a couple of standards in the rock 'n' roll repertoire.

They were signed to headline the Valentine's Day dance at Hermosa High School, in Los Angeles's South Bay area. The opening band was a new local group, the Beach Boys. In the classroom set aside as a green room for the show, Jan and Dean met Brian and Carl Wilson, Mike Love, and David Marks. Dennis Wilson was out of commission, having crashed his Corvair the week before. His good pal, Mark Groseclose, sat behind the drum kit.

The Beach Boys had rehearsed three or four Jan and Dean songs, "Louie Louie," and a few other crowd-pleasers. They figured they'd still need a couple more songs to fill out the set, and Jan and Dean asked if they could sing the two Beach Boys hits to that date, "Surfin'" and "Surfin' Safari." Brian Wilson was flattered, and Jan and Dean loved singing the surf songs. The audience went bonkers.

A couple of days later, Jan Berry called Brian Wilson at home to tell him how much they'd enjoyed sharing the bill. "He said that he had talked it over with our producer Lou and me and we had decided to try our hand at making surf music, if that was okay with him," Dean recalled.

Brian was ecstatic and offered the services of the band at the recording session at the end of the month. They assembled at Western Recorders, and the Beach Boys cut backing tracks for "Surfin'" and "Surfin' Safari." Jan and Brian circled each other, but when the sniffing period was over, they began sharing secrets and becoming friends.

Brian felt musically limited by two major factors: Since signing with Capitol Records, he felt he had to record at the company studios. He also felt that his bandmates were limited musically and that the records suffered because of their amateurish sound.

Jan was barely a year older yet spoke with the weight of an industry veteran. He told Brian he should break away from the Capitol Tower and experiment with independent studios, like Western Recorders. He also suggested that when it came to record making, he should rely on that army of talented and dedicated studio musicians who produced hits for all of the major labels. Save his brothers and bandmates for concert appearances, where audiences didn't expect perfection. Both suggestions impressed Brian and opened his eyes to greater possibilities.

Then, at the end of the session, Brian sat down at the studio piano and asked Jan and Dean if they'd like to hear the new Beach

Boys single. He began pounding the keys, but the song that came out sounded a lot like Chuck Berry's "Sweet Little Sixteen."

It was, Brian said. He had changed all the words to be about surfing.

Enchanted, Jan immediately asked if he could record the song. Brian demurred. *No, it's our song.* Jan also told Brian to be careful. He couldn't just appropriate Berry's melody and structure. He might get sued. "My dad said it would be OK," Brian said, somewhat taken aback.

One of Brian's most endearing qualities was his generosity. He knew he'd disappointed Jan and Dean by not giving them "Surfin' USA," so he offered them something else.

"He said he had another song that wasn't finished," Dean said, "but if we wanted to finish it, we could have it."

Again at the piano, Brian began singing his ode to hedonism:

Two girls for every boy!

Brian had the melody and a lyrical concept, but the song was far from finished. Jan said he'd love to have it.

First things first. The two Beach Boys songs were the last two tracks needed for the next Jan and Dean album, the one featuring their old hit "Linda." To capitalize on that hit and indicate their new direction, Lou Adler suggested the album be titled *Jan and Dean Take Linda Surfin'*. Elegant it was not; successful it was. Instead of the lame gray suits, this time Jan and Dean wore swim trunks and sweaters on the cover, posing with a girl and a surfboard in front of a dune buggy. They were the picture of California Cool. Finally, Jan and Dean had an album that hit the national charts.

Adler told them not to stop. *You're just getting started.*

Jan set to work finishing that song Brian had given them. Because they were part of the surfing world, it wasn't much of a challenge for Jan and Dean to fill out the lyrics with the requisite references to the surfer's preferred mode of land transportation, the woodie—station wagons with wood exteriors—and big waves, wipeouts, and the general joy of life at the beach.

Jan came up with the lyrical idea of a magic place for surfing—"Surf City," as he called it in the song. Just as Brian Wilson had done with "Surfin' USA," Jan was trying to make this West Coast phenomenon accessible to the kids in Kansas City and Keokuk. And what red-blooded American male couldn't respond to the song's rallying cry of "two girls for every boy"?

Brian attended the recording session for "Surf City," which now shared the Wilson-Berry credit, and was impressed by the way Jan commanded the studio. The musicians were the cream of L.A.'s session crop: Hal Blaine and Earl Palmer on drums and Billy Strange, Bill Pitman, and Glen Campbell on guitars.

The real magic, though, was Jan's vocal arrangement. "Jan and Brian sang the lead together," Dean recalled. "Then Brian and I sang some of the background parts, plus a falsetto part that Brian and I had written. Brian then suggested that he and I sing the very same vocal part a second time and see what that sounded like, so we did. Now we had four vocals all singing the same melody. Everybody in the studio loved the final result."

So did the rest of the world. By July 1963, "Surf City" was the number-one record in the country, and Murry Wilson burned his biscuits. "You have recorded on Jan and Dean's record, which was an absolutely treacherous act," he wrote his son.

Watching Jan Berry at work on "Surf City" opened Brian's eyes. Though pathologically shy, Brian asserted authority in the studio. It's almost as if another personality emerged when he sat down behind the control panel. He instructed his brothers exactly what to play and forbade David Marks from singing. Brian vowed that he would never have David Marks's voice on a Beach Boys record. Even Cousin Mike, older and physically intimidating, marched to the beat of Brian's drummer. They were all smart enough to realize that Brian had the vision.

Alas, the other Beach Boys did not live up to Brian's vision. The first three albums—*Surfin' Safari*, *Surfin' USA*, and *Surfer Girl*—were all recorded by the basic band members—Carl on lead guitar, Alan or David on rhythm, Brian on bass, and Dennis on drums. Brian played piano on "Boogie Woodie" and overdubbed strings on a romantic composition called "The Surfer Moon."

He was doing all right with the band in the studio, but he wanted to do better. The Beach Boys were average musicians, and Brian knew their real contribution was their vocals. Why make do with average musicians just because they were great singers? "Surfer Girl" was one of the best early examples of the group's astonishing vocal blend.

"'Surfer Girl' has a real spiritual quality to it," Carl Wilson said. "There's a real heart attached to that. The chords are just so filling. For its time, the record was so advanced. It was really beautiful to be alive when that record was playing. The way our voices sounded on that, the melody Brian wrote, the way he put the arrangement together—that might be the perfect melding of all the elements."

Brian excelled at his ballads, including his moody and introspective "In My Room," a song he wrote with Gary Usher. "'In My Room' is a tune we've learned to appreciate more as the years go by," Carl said. "You can tell it's getting pretty close to home for Brian, and all those tender, vulnerable things are coming out."

Brian—now living out of the house, sharing a small apartment with Gary—recalled the old days at the Wilson House of Pain, when he shared a room with his brothers and they'd sing before falling asleep. It was a nightly ritual. "It brought peace to us," Brian said. "When we recorded 'In My Room,' there was just Dennis and Carl and me on the first verse and we sounded just like we did in our bedroom all those nights."

During his turbulent childhood, Brian's room was his only sanctuary from his father—whether it was a bedroom or the garage-turned-music-room, where Brian often slept after playing piano all evening. He needed "somewhere where you could lock out the world, go to a secret little place, think, be, do whatever you have to do."

Brian's ballads were complemented by his song that eschewed surfing in favor of the teenage fascination with cars. He'd been creating asphalt dramas from the start, with "Shut Down," a tense saga of boulevard competition crammed with automotive lingo and braggadocio, clocking in under two minutes. His collaborator this time was the prime-time voice of KFWB, disc jockey Roger Christian. Roger was a part-time poet whose muse was the internal combustion engine.

Now Brian added a few more car songs to the repertoire. The flip side of "Surfer Girl" was Christian's ode to the 1932 Ford, "Little Deuce Coupe." Brian's up-tempo songs, driven by Dennis's much-improved drumming, matched the confidence in Christian's lyrics.

> *She's got a competition clutch with the four on the floor*
> *And she purrs like a kitten till the lake pipes roar*

So things were great for the Beach Boys in 1963. The "Surfer Girl"/"Little Deuce Coupe" single was released on July 22, with the

A-side reaching number seven and the B-side number fifteen. Sensing a change of direction, Capitol Records urged the band to put out two albums back-to-back that fall.

Surfer Girl, released September 16, was the first album over which Brian had complete production control. Nick Venet's name was nowhere on the album jacket. Unfortunately, there was an uncredited shadow producer: when Brian was in the studio, Murry would scoot behind the microphone in the booth and begin barking orders at his son. But Brian was able to more or less run the show, from start to finish.

Less than a month later, Capitol issued *Little Deuce Coupe*, which included four songs that had already been released (including the title track and "Our Car Club," which had just appeared on the *Surfer Girl* album). It held together as an album and included a stunning a cappella song, "A Young Man Is Gone," an ode to James Dean to the tune of "Their Hearts Were Full of Spring." Brian continued to grow as a producer. But the quick repackaging was done with negligible consultation with the group.

Brian began to experiment with using outside musicians on his non–Beach Boys productions. He also stopped using the Capitol Studios, where he felt corporate eyes watching his every move. He branched out to independent studios, including Western Recorders and Gold Star, a mere hole-in-the-wall storefront at 6252 Santa Monica Boulevard, and only a four-minute drive down Vine Street from the Capitol Tower.

The studio, founded by Dave Gold and Stan Ross in 1950, was popular with early rock 'n' rollers such as Ritchie Valens, Eddie Cochran, and Bobby Darin and was an early haunt of high school student and rock star wannabe, Phil Spector. When Spector became a hugely successful producer in the sixties, he did almost all of his work at Gold Star, because of the studio's unique sound and its brilliant engineer, Larry Levine.

By the end of the year, Brian was emulating both Jan Berry and his new infatuation, Phil Spector, by challenging them on their own turf—Gold Star—with the same players—the Wrecking Crew.

4

THE SECOND JESUS

I'm dealing in rock 'n' roll. I'm, like, I'm not a bona
fide human being.

—Phil Spector

It's not like they had membership cards or anything. It was just something that happened gradually . . . organically. A changing of the
guard. *The sun also rises, the sun also sets.*

Hal Blaine's first big break, at the end of the fifties, was playing
drums behind teen heartthrob Tommy Sands. Sands had emerged
as one of many Elvis Lites in 1957, and for three years Hal Blaine,
former jazz drummer, anchored the touring band and made a pretty
good living. Sands was signed to Capitol, and he used Blaine as his
studio drummer. Hanging around the Capitol Tower allowed Blaine
to meet some of the studio regulars, including Earl Palmer.

Palmer was a New Orleans transplant who began his career at
Cosimo Matassa's J&M Studios in the French Quarter, laying down
the beat on a score of rock 'n' roll classics from the Crescent City. He
grew up in New Orleans's Treme neighborhood, too poor as a child to
buy a drum kit. "I got with a bunch of guys and they needed somebody
to play the drums," Palmer said. "I said, 'I play the drums,' but I had
no drums. So we made drums out of an orange crate and had lard-can
covers for cymbals, and a piece of inner tube for a foot-pedal spring."
Using a pencil as his drumstick, Palmer's career was under way.

His résumé was impressive: "Lawdy Miss Clawdy" by Lloyd Price,
"I Hear You Knocking" by Smiley Lewis, and nearly all of the hits
by Little Richard and Fats Domino, including "Tutti Frutti," "Keep
a-Knockin'," "Blueberry Hill," and "I'm Walkin'."

Palmer headed to Los Angeles in 1957, hoping to land more session gigs. He worked with two R&B labels, Specialty and Aladdin, but began getting called for recording dates from a diverse set of clients from Frank Sinatra to Eddie Cochran to Sam Cooke.

"Earl Palmer was really the only guy in Hollywood who was playing what they called 'rock 'n' roll,'" Blaine said. "It was impossible for Earl to handle everything, so he started recommending me, God bless him. Before you know it, every producer in Hollywood knew who I was and wanted me."

Palmer and Blaine became the anchors of a group of studio musicians that became known as the Wrecking Crew. No one called them that back then. It was a name bestowed by time, and Blaine gets the credit for coining the phrase.

During the sixties, the Crew included such future recording stars as pianist Leon Russell (under his real name, Claude Russell Bridges) and guitarist Glen Campbell. But within the recording world of Los Angeles, any member of this particular tribe was a superstar: guitarists Tommy Tedesco, Billy Strange, James Burton, Al Casey, and Bill Pitman; bassists Carol Kaye, Lyle Ritz, and Ray Pohlman; keyboardists Larry Knechtel, Al De Lory, and Don Randi; and horn players Steve Douglas, Plas Johnson, Jay Migliori, and Nino Tempo.

They had come from all over. Glen Campbell grew up dust-poor in Delight, Arkansas. Leon Russell came from Tulsa, where he'd been playing in nightclubs since age fourteen. Blaine (real name Harold Belsky) grew up in Hartford, Connecticut, and Carol Kaye came from Washington State.

The group came together informally, and membership, such as it was, was determined by who showed up at the studio. That decision was usually made by the producer contracting the session or simply by availability.

The session musicians made enormous contributions to the arrangements of the songs. Kaye came up with distinctive bass lines that defined "The Beat Goes On" by Sonny and Cher and "California Girls" by the Beach Boys but didn't get composer credit or royalties. Often it didn't matter. "I was making more money than the president of the United States," Kaye shrugged.

Like a lot of her colleagues, Kaye's real love was jazz, and her career playing in clubs led her to Los Angeles, where she settled. Relying on music alone would accelerate a headlong dive into poverty, so she worked as a daytime typist at the Bendix Corporation in North Hollywood and spent several evenings a week feeding her music addiction at a series of seedy nightclubs.

She was playing lead guitar in a jazz combo at the Beverly Caverns when a man from the audience approached her at break.

"I'm a producer," Bumps Blackwell said by way of introduction. "I've been watching you play tonight and I like your style. I could use you on some record dates. Interested?"

Kaye's first session was with Sam Cooke, and it opened the door for a number of other dates. She played the trills on Cooke's "Wonderful World" and the ping-pong guitar on "La Bamba" by Ritchie Valens. Before long, she was doing well enough to quit her day job.

When Jan Berry told him about the Wrecking Crew, Brian Wilson thought he'd been let in on a great industry secret. Jan was just a year older than Brian, but in studio years he was much wiser. Since he'd always taken an active role in producing, dating from "Jennie Lee" days, Jan was too busy working on vocals and technical details to worry about being adept enough to play instruments on recordings. He went to the usual session-player well, but the producer who had the greatest success with the Wrecking Crew was Phil Spector.

Spector played guitar and piano, but his real instrument was the recording studio. No one had done it quite like Phil Spector before. He brought the group together—the best players: Blaine, Palmer, Kaye, Campbell, Tedesco, Russell, and the others—and changed the way records were made.

Harvey Philip Spector was born in New York City in 1939 or 1940 (he was never really clear about the year of his birth), on December 26. His mother liked to lie and say he was born on Christmas, and that she had "given birth to the second Jesus."

Father Ben, a Russian Jewish immigrant, was thirty-six. Mother Bertha, born in Paris, was twenty-eight. The Spectors were a devoted couple; Ben labored in an ironworks factory, and Bertha was a housewife. Ben was beefy faced, with spectacles that strained at his temples. Bertha was handsome, and Harvey's older sister Shirley was quite attractive. Young Harvey, however, was the star of the show. With impish eyes and a cunning smile, he was favored by everyone in the family.

He grew up in the Soundview section of the Bronx, a bastion of bricked-front respectability, but didn't put in hours of stickball like the other boys in the neighborhood. He was allergic to sunlight and was often wheezing from asthma. Bertha was a helicopter mother before the term existed. She'd hyperventilate at the thought of her golden boy out in the sun or skinning his knees during some street games with local ruffians. Early on, the boy tended toward pudgy, so he was teased by the neighbor kids and spent most of his childhood indoors, watching the other kids in the street while his mother hovered over him, keeping him safe from harm, and from life.

The world changed when the boy turned ten. Ben Spector got up one morning, drove to Brooklyn, ran a garden hose from his car's exhaust pipe to the interior, and asphyxiated. There was no note and few suggestions about why he'd shitcan himself. He was not rich but was doing OK. He suffered from diabetes, but he didn't moan about it incessantly. Then again, he might have suffered from chronic depression. That would become a family tradition.

He was buried in a Jewish cemetery in Queens, a hefty drive from the Spector home. Eventually the family placed a tombstone at his grave. The inscription read, "To Know Him Was to Love Him."

Too many bad memories, so Bertha Spector packed up her two children and headed to California in 1950. They settled in a small apartment in the Jewish-dominated Fairfax area in Los Angeles. If she hadn't been an overprotective mother before, Bertha now became obsessive in coddling her son. She saw danger lurking around every corner for her frail little boy. He'd lost weight after his father's suicide, becoming drawn, kind of a self-made invalid. Bertha had help in mother-henning from daughter Shirley, who both doted on her little brother and protected him from the dangers of teenage life, such as having fun and making friends.

High school is hell for a shy kid too sickly for sports and not blessed with good looks. Spector withdrew to his room and worshipped at the altar of radio. He loved it all: rhythm and blues, bebop, classical music. He joined the school band and took up French horn. Bertha wanted to please and encourage her son—who now insisted on being called Phillip (he added another L to his name)—and so she got him a guitar for his bar mitzvah. Now Phil leaned close to the radio, guitar across his knees, and tried to mimic the sounds he heard.

Again, encouraging mother Bertha arranged for her son to have lessons from the great session guitarist Bill Pitman. Pitman didn't do lessons with snot-nosed schoolboys, but giving up his Saturday mornings was preferable to having to deal with Bertha on the phone.

Phil was a diligent student and obviously loved music, but Pitman thought he was a lost cause. Before Pitman had to figure out how to gently break it to the kid though, Phil brought up the subject himself.

"Do you think I have a future as a jazz guitarist?" Phil asked.

"No, Phil," Pitman said. "In truth, I don't see that for you. You're lacking one thing that a musician has to have. And that's meter. You don't feel when one musical phrase ends and another begins."

Phil sighed. "I know."

"I'm sorry," Pitman said, feeling he'd broken the kid's heart. "But I can't teach you that. I don't know anyone who can."

But rather than being crushed by Pitman's pronouncement, Phil took it in stride. He discovered the music of one of Pitman's colleagues, Barney Kessel. Like Pitman, Kessel was a sought-after session guitarist. His jazz guitar recordings were breathtaking and a precursor to hipster lounge music.

When Phil read an article in *DownBeat* naming the best guitarists in the world, he sent off an indignant letter to the editor to note Kessel's omission. When it was printed as the lead letter in the next issue, Phil's sister, Shirley, tracked down Kessel, showed him the letter, and said he should meet and thank her brother. A meeting was arranged at a coffee shop near the Capitol Tower—a place where the studio musicians hung out between sessions—and Kessel was a little stunned to find out his stalwart defender was a wimpy-looking, chinless kid. Yet he was charmed by the boy and also became a mentor to young Phil Spector. Kessel would play a major role in Phil's career.

Music helped Phil create a bond with a classmate, and they became an unlikely duo. Phil, the shy weakling butt of jokes, made friends with chisel-chinned Marshall Leib (shortened from Leibovitz, for showbiz), as handsome as Phil was homely. They discovered they both loved to sit by their radios at night, teaching themselves chords on their guitars. Leib didn't mind being seen with the Spector kid, even though it might gnaw away at his cool-guy status. He kept watch on Phil, intervening when he felt someone was taking the teasing too far with his puny friend.

Marshall was Phil's entree to high school society. Through his new friend, Phil met Harvey Goldstein and a beautiful and popular girl, Annette Kleinbard. Soon the quartet was harmonizing after school, and Phil emerged as the guiding musical force. In his hours of loneliness, he had dedicated himself to music and was the most literate in that realm. "Phil was definitely the leader," said one school friend. "He would sing all the different parts, showing us what he wanted us to do."

He was determined to have a career in music, but Bertha wanted to make sure her son had something more practical on which he could fall back. She pushed him to begin training as a court stenographer, since he had an interest in crime stories. As part of an internship in the year after his high school graduation, he covered an appeal for death row inmate Caryl Chessman. He also got involved with a couple of political campaigns.

But the dream was always music. In early 1958, nearly a full year after his graduation from Fairfax High, he gathered Leib and Goldstein and began rehearsing some of the songs he'd written in his bedroom solitude. When he felt they were ready, Spector walked into nondescript Gold Star Studio and approached co-owner Stan Ross with the news that they were fellow Fairfax High alumni and that should mean a reduced recording rate.

Ross was unmoved but admired the kid's dedication and suggested he hang around the studio to see how recordings were made. Spector kept telling Ross he was going to make hit records and intimating he should get a discount. Ross said he'd need forty dollars to pay for studio time.

Forty bucks was a lot for young Spector. Money was tight at home, but Bertha kicked in ten dollars. Leib had another ten, and Goldstein had a few bucks. One day at school, Phil approached Annette Kleinbard and asked her if she had ten dollars. Heck no, she said. But when Phil told her that he needed the money to make a record—and that Annette could sing on it—she scrounged the dough.

He finally got the money together and got his three friends into the studio to record his song, "Don't You Worry My Little Pet." It was a pleasant, if unremarkable, tune, and even though she sang on it, Kleinbard thought it was "dreadful." It was up-tempo, and in his fantasies, Phil thought it would make it to the top of the charts.

For the flip side, he'd crafted a ballad inspired by his father's tombstone. He turned the inscription into a testament of teenage devotion, "To Know Him Is to Love Him," with a memorable, simple lead vocal from Kleinbard, and syncopated backing by Phil and Leib. Goldstein was not there for the recording.

The songs were released in September 1958 as a single on Doré Records, one of the proliferating independent labels in Los Angeles. The singers called themselves the Teddy Bears, after the Elvis Presley song of the year before, "(Let Me Be Your) Teddy Bear."

The record company pushed the A-side of the single, "Don't You Worry My Little Pet," on disc jockeys, but the song did not inspire much airplay. Since Kleinbard had the lead vocal on the B-side, her friends began dialing into the nightly request shows on L.A. radio stations and asking to hear "To Know Him Is to Love Him." After a lackluster month—and through some kind of karmic, magical, serendipitous hocus pocus—disc jockeys elsewhere began to flip over the disc.

The song took off in Fargo, North Dakota . . . and then in Minneapolis, Minnesota, where Kleinbard's breathy vocal got a disc jockey there all hot and bothered. The song began inching up the *Billboard* Hot 100 chart, and the record company (Doré was a subsidiary label of Era Records) got a call from Philadelphia disc jockey Dick Clark, host of ABC's daily rock 'n' roll dance show *American Bandstand*. Clark played the song on the air, and the exposure accelerated its rise up the charts. When it hit the Top Ten, Clark invited the Teddy Bears to the studio to lip sync in front of *Bandstand*'s squirming adolescents. Spector and Leib wore matching monogrammed sweaters, and Kleinbard was the embodiment of the teenage dream in her daring spaghetti straps. Harvey Goldstein was not along for the ride. He'd gone off to do his duty to the army reserves and missed the "To Know Him" recording session. He wasn't needed to lip sync a song he didn't sing on, and wasn't really needed at all, Phil told him.

For three weeks in the late autumn of 1958, "To Know Him Is to Love Him" was the number-one record in the country. Phil Spector would never craft a successful Teddy Bears follow-up, and the group disbanded within the year. (Leib moved behind the scenes for a long career in music, and Kleinbard, under the name Carol Connors, became a successful songwriter, Oscar-nominated for "Gonna Fly Now," the theme from *Rocky*. She lost to "Evergreen" from *A Star is Born*.)

Phil Spector was determined to avoid the ash heap of one-hit wonders and began methodically plotting career moves. He told Bertha he wouldn't need the fallback career as a court stenographer, because he knew how to make a number-one record. The "duh-duh-duh-duh" backing vocal wasn't what gave him his jollies. It was the actual *making* of the record that tingled his glands. Stan Ross had amused himself watching little Phil running back and forth from the booth to the studio as he simultaneously tried to sing *and* produce the record. He had to admit—it worked.

Phil came under the wing of Lester Sill, a recording executive who had helped launch the careers of songwriters Jerry Leiber and Mike Stoller. With them, he formed a small L.A. independent called Spark Records and released seminal R&B hits "Riot in Cell Block #9" and "Smokey Joe's Cafe" with a vocal group called the Robins. Demand for the records was so great that Sill ended up selling the master recordings to Atlantic Records in New York, and the Robins morphed into the Coasters.

As a thank-you from Atlantic, Sill got seed money from the New York label to start Trey Records in Los Angeles, with independent producer Lee Hazlewood. Still searching for a follow-up to "To Know Him Is to Love Him," Spector showed up at Sill's door. With Leib and Kleinbard, Spector released two singles as the Spectors Three (Doré owned the Teddy Bears name), and both flopped. But Spector had ingratiated himself to Sill and got to produce a couple of other records for Trey. Even though the records flopped, Spector felt that he really was, finally, part of the music business. He was smart enough to know he had a lot to learn.

He'd lived in California for nearly a decade, but Spector considered himself a New Yorker, so—with Sill's advice and assistance—he returned to the East Coast to see what he could learn there from the record men he most admired.

He was naturally drawn to Atlantic Records, home to the best rhythm and blues records in America. Started by two sons of a Turkish diplomat in 1948, Atlantic forged impressive legacies in the worlds of jazz and R&B. Older brother Nesuhi Ertegun supervised the jazz catalog, and younger brother Ahmet took charge of R&B. Atlantic became the label with the blackest sound and a pioneer of what would become known as soul music in the sixties. Ahmet Ertegun benefited from the genius and (for a while) partnership of Jerry Wexler, who produced many of Atlantic's greatest hits. Wexler had worked at *Billboard* magazine, where he was instrumental in changing the very categories of popular music. He saw that "hillbilly" was changed to "country and western" and that "race" records became "rhythm and blues."

Phil Spector approached Wexler and Ahmet Ertegun asking them to mentor him. He wanted to know everything that they knew. At first amused by the kid, the Atlantic brass eventually began to recognize that Spector not only was willing to do anything but also actually had a good set of ears.

In the fifties, Atlantic had given the world the genre-defying Ray Charles as well as a number of black vocal groups, including the Drifters, arguably the best of the doo-wop lot. There was natural resentment from some of the artists, who felt a couple of white guys were getting rich off of their efforts.

As Spector summarized the attitude, "'We bought your home, goddamn, and don't you forget it, boy.'" The record business was corrupt in many ways, with record companies signing artists to cheap-ass contracts, withholding royalties, and paying off disc jockeys to get the records played. Some disc jockeys got songwriting credits or music publishing shares to create a new and semisecret revenue stream. "All the Drifters were gettin' was $150 a week and they never got any royalties," Spector recalled. "It wasn't that Atlantic didn't pay them; it was that everybody screwed everybody in those days. I mean, I was in the Teddy Bears and what did we get—one penny a record royalties!"

Nevertheless, Spector put his nose to the musical grindstone (and up the asses of Ertegun and Wexler), absorbing their secrets like a kitchen sponge. He also—thanks to a long-distance introduction from Leonard Sill—glommed onto the greatest songwriting team of the era, Jerry Leiber and Mike Stoller. In addition to writing songs for Elvis Presley, they wrote and produced seminal recordings for the Coasters. The renamed Robins had a talent for telling Leiber and Stoller's musical stories:

> *He walks in the classroom cool and slow*
> *Who calls the English teacher "Daddy-O"?*

Leiber and Stoller had written "Hound Dog" for Big Mama Thornton, but the song had its biggest success a couple of years later when Presley took it to number one. At first dubious, the songwriting team discovered they actually liked Presley and began writing for him.

Like Wexler and Ertegun, Leiber and Stoller didn't need this *kid* hanging around. But he was so eager, and they had to admit, somewhat grudgingly, that he did have some good ideas.

During his New York apprenticeship from 1960 to 1962, Spector made some classic recordings. He romanticized the subdued domesticity of his childhood in the Bronx, roughening up his neighborhood and turning it into "Spanish Harlem," where an idealized and lovely young woman awaited him.

I'm going to pick that rose
And watch her as she grows in my garden

Spector wrote the song with Jerry Leiber (another fellow Fairfax High grad!), and when they presented the song to Ahmet Ertegun, Phil played guitar, Jerry sang, and Mike Stoller accompanied them on piano. Stoller improvised on the piano. "Since then, I've never heard the song played without that musical figure," Stoller said. "I presumed my contribution was seminal to the composition, but I also knew that Phil didn't want to share credit with anyone but Jerry, so I kept quiet."

"Spanish Harlem," recorded by Ben E. King, made the *Billboard* Top Ten and was King's first hit since leaving his job as lead singer for the Drifters. Leiber and Stoller gave King his next hit, "Stand by Me," which hit number one in 1961 *and* 1986.

In addition to Leiber and Stoller, Spector felt into the gravitational pull of the so-called Brill Building songwriters. *Brill Building* was used loosely to describe a tribe of young songwriters. Leiber and Stoller were actually in the Brill Building at 1619 Broadway. But many of the other songwriters worked for Aldon Music, which was at 1650 Broadway. The music of those songwriters became known as the Brill Building sound. Aldon was a contraction of the two owners' names: Al Nevins, guitarist and composer for the middle-of-the-road instrumental group the Three Suns, and young Don Kirshner, who, like Spector, didn't want a lack of musical talent to keep him from a career in the industry. Kirshner was a genius at knowing what kinds of songs kids wanted, and he found the best young talent to write them.

Several of these songwriters were young, far from being Tin Pan Alley pros. They were kids writing for their peer group. Consider "Will You Love Me Tomorrow?" by the Shirelles, the first number-one record by an all-female group. It's a classic *Will you respect me in the morning?* song, written by a newlywed couple, Gerry Goffin (then twenty-one) and Carole King (then eighteen). Goffin and King became the gold standard. (In the infancy of the Beatles, Paul McCartney proposed to John Lennon that they should have a songwriting partnership. He argued, persuasively, that they could be England's Goffin and King.) Goffin and King wrote such classics as

"Up on the Roof," "One Fine Day," and "Take Good Care of My Baby".

Goffin and King worked in a loft space at 1650 Broadway, in a small cubicle with a piano and a couple of chairs. There were others working in these spartan conditions, including two other young couples: Barry Mann and Cynthia Weil ("On Broadway," "You've Lost That Lovin' Feelin'," "Who Put the Bomp (in the Bomp, Bomp, Bomp)," and "Walking in the Rain") and Jeff Barry and Ellie Greenwich ("Chapel of Love," "Be My Baby," "Da Doo Ron Ron," and "Do Wah Diddy Diddy").

Then there was Doc Pomus, the songwriting alias of Jerome Felder. He'd wanted to be a blues singer and had modest success as a young man. But polio crippled him, and fans did not respond to a man on crutches, no matter how impassioned his singing. Instead he became one of the country's best songwriters, providing Ray Charles with "Lonely Avenue" and the Coasters with "Young Blood." It was with younger songwriting partner Mort Shuman that Pomus tapped into the soul of young America with some of the most heartfelt songs of the era: "This Magic Moment," "I Count the Tears," and "Save the Last Dance for Me."

Pomus became another mentor to Phil Spector. "This man was more than a songwriter," Spector said years later, eulogizing Pomus, "He was a poet, for I need not remind you that while he wrote 'Save the Last Dance for Me,' he never experienced the thrill or the emotion of that wonderful feeling."

Spector studied at the feet of these songwriters and later drew from them their best material for his recordings. But in addition to songwriting, he was eager to study record production and try out some of his ideas. He had success with solo productions for Dunes Records, a label owned by singer Ray Peterson, famous for the tragic teen weeper "Tell Laura I Love Her." Spector produced Peterson's hit version of the traditional "Corrina, Corrina" ("Corrine, Corrina," as printed on the label) and Curtis Lee's "Pretty Little Angel Eyes." Both songs made the Top Ten.

Spector made an impression on the New York star-making machinery. Label owners and music publishers recognized his talent but considered him pushy and professionally selfish. "Phil had quirks that nobody liked," Don Kirshner recalled. "He was a practical joker. He would work at being different and eccentric. I'm sitting with some fairly normal Jewish kids who were going to go home, get married, this and that. And he was walking in with capes, shoes up to your eyeballs or whatever, which stand out in any crowd. Phil had to compensate for his size, his looks, by being different."

By the end of 1961, Spector was back in the L.A. bosom of Lester Sill. Sill and Hazlewood had folded Trey Records and created a new label called Gregmark. Spector brought back from New York a Barry Mann–Larry Kolber song called "I Love How You Love Me." It was pure schmaltz but also perfect for the Paris Sisters, a new group Sill was pushing. Spector accentuated lead singer Priscilla Paris's breathy voice with a lush string section and Priscilla's older sisters added appropriate *ooohs.*

Boom! Spector had given Lester Sill a Top Five record on his new label.

Now, after young Phil Spector's badgering, Sill was partnering with the twenty-one-year-old on a new venture, Philles Records. Spector got first billing as they contracted their names.

He was back in familiar territory. Gold Star was always the standard by which Phil Spector measured recording studios. Studio A had the acoustics he wanted, and the homemade echo chambers were unsurpassed. "The pure tone of the echo chambers was due to their trapezoid-shaped rooms," said writer Gareth Murphy. They were "about twenty feet long, built in a specially formulated cement plaster. Incoming sounds entered though a two-foot-square trap door and were miked back into the control room."

The room, the echo chambers, the mixing board, even the Gold Star secretary—everything combined to make Spector feel *comfortable.* It was as if recording engineer Larry Levine could read Spector's mind. To other producers, Gold Star was a slag heap. "Most regarded it as a dump," biographer Mick Brown wrote. "But for Spector it provided an environment where he was totally at ease, totally in command. He became the studio's most ubiquitous client and would wrangle with Stan Ross to have it available whenever he required."

But it was that core group of musicians, the ones that came to be known as the Wrecking Crew, who led Spector to return to the studio time and time again. The sound of those musicians in that small studio was exactly what he'd been looking for.

He'd begun to articulate that sound in New York. He'd already made a couple of major hits with his preferred girl group of the moment, the Crystals. "There's No Other (Like My Baby)" was a Top Twenty song Spector based on the gospel song "There's No Other Like My Jesus." And then came "Uptown," a Barry Mann–Cynthia Weil tune that subtly addressed racism and poverty in a way that popular songs rarely, if ever, did. Full of drama and pseudo-Spanish tinges, including castanets (soon to become a Phil Spector staple) and a thrilling pizzicato plucking of violin strings, it had stretched-tight drama and intensity, all in two minutes and eighteen seconds.

Back in L.A., Spector entered the familiar landscape of Gold Star to record "He's a Rebel" with the Crystals. It *had* to be a Crystals record. It was the perfect follow-up to "Uptown" (an intervening record, "He Hit Me (and It Felt Like a Kiss)" was pulled from release when mainstream radio program directors found it too controversial). He needed a strong follow-up to the one-two punch of "There's No Other (Like My Baby)" and "Uptown."

Unfortunately, the Crystals were in New York, and here was Spector, in Los Angeles, with his Gold Star engineer and a cadre of brilliant musicians. He needed to make a record immediately, so he called Steve Douglas (*another Fairfax High grad!*), now an in-demand sax player, and asked him to contract the session. His mission was to round up the usual suspects for a recording date on October 6, 1962. It was Phil Spector's first big West Coast gig since his days as the chinless wonder of the Spectors Three. When they all arrived at the studio, Douglas took him around to meet the musicians. He met guitarist Tommy Tedesco and pianist Al De Lory for the first time. There were a few familiar faces—he'd already worked with guitarist Howard Roberts and Lyle Ritz, who played electric bass—and, of course, there was Larry Levine, who had engineered "To Know Him Is to Love Him."

The tour stopped in front of the drum kit.

"I'm Phil."

The drummer extended his hand. "Nice to meet you, Phil. I'm Hal Blaine."

Everyone was ready to make the next Crystals record, except the Crystals. Rather than have his session scuttled by this inconvenience, Spector hired another girl group. Jack Nitzsche, a musical arranger and one of Spector's right-hand men, suggested the Blossoms. The quartet, led by Darlene Wright, had backed up Doris Day, Ray Charles, Jan and Dean, and many others. They were the ones to chant the "shoop shoop" on Betty Everett's hit "The Shoop Shoop Song (It's in His Kiss)." Nitzsche had worked with them before and vouched for them, so Spector brought them in for the session. He taught them the song and had them stand behind the microphones and belt it out. Wright's lead vocal gave the tune a soaring drama that took it to number one. A classic tale of the misunderstood bad boy and his loving, nurturing girlfriend, "He's a Rebel" struck a chord with teen America.

Nearly everyone loved the song except the Crystals. The group was unaware that the song existed until they heard it on the radio and had to quickly copy the Blossoms' recording, since they were expected to sing it in their nightly shows.

Though the Crystals' star began to rise with this new hit, they began to realize how expendable and replaceable they were. The record label said "The Crystals," but that was a lie. It was really a Phil Spector record. It didn't matter who sang it. The producer was the force behind it. He was, to borrow that term used to describe French New Wave cinema, the *auteur*.

With the Crystals releases and on subsequent records, Spector defined his approach. Instead of one bass player, he'd use two—one with a stand-up, one with an electric Fender. Maybe he'd hire two pianists, joined by a couple organists. *Two guitars? Hell, let's go for five. Why settle for one drummer when we can have three?*

The standard configuration for a rock 'n' roll band dated from the midfifties: two guitars, a bass, and drums; Buddy Holly and the Crickets were a perfect prototype for a rock group. But now, not even a decade later, Phil Spector was redefining what rock 'n' roll sounded like. He went over the top. He crammed all of these musicians into cozy Gold Star and had them play live. Mistakes were inevitable, but that's what he wanted. He wanted the combined sound of all of these musicians *going for it*.

Eventually his technique was described as "the wall of sound." At the turn of the twentieth century, American journalists used that term to describe the "sonic totalitarianism" of Richard Wagner. Think "The Ride of the Valkyries" and "*The Flying Dutchman* Overture"— powerful . . . commanding . . . *overwhelming*. Spector had spent those adolescent evenings in his bedroom listening to Wagner and now, in his mind, he was making minioperas for American teenagers.

What the Crystals and other singers, including Darlene Wright, would learn was that they were merely bricks in Spector's wall of sound. They were interchangeable.

Music historian Bob Stanley described the wall of sound this way: "The sound was all-consuming, left no room for anything else in your head, and tore at your heart with tympani and an exuberant rush of noise." The drama of teenage life was fertile soil for Phil Spector. "He gave the subject matter the backdrop it deserved," Stanley wrote. "This was the stuff of life itself."

The musicians heard themselves in the studio, but when they went into the control room, after the recording had been rocketed through an echo chamber, they heard the music in a different way, the way Spector had heard it in his head and the way teenage America would hear it thundering from car radios and transistors.

"The control room at Gold Star was the greatest listening environment imaginable," Spector said. "It just consumed you, enveloped you—all of the sound coming out of these three speakers. It was more than being in the record. See, it was not truthful at all. What everybody strives for in studio speakers is truth; this didn't in any way duplicate what you heard in the studio; it was just exciting and thrilling and full-bodied. The musicians would come in the control room for the playback and just be blown away. They simply couldn't believe that what they were hearing was the way they'd been playing, and it made them excited."

Spector demanded total control over his recordings, and after the success of "He's a Rebel," he decided he wanted to have total control of his record company. Though Philles Records was not even a year old, Spector had tired of having Lester Sill as his business partner. He put pressure on two minority investors to buy out their shares, then went after his benefactor, harassing him so much that eventually Lester caved. He sold his shares for $60,000 and was promised all the royalties on the next Crystals record, which seemed like a good severance package. The Crystals—whether the genuine article or the Blossoms in disguise—were on a roll.

But Spector had a cruel streak, and he hurt both Sill and the Crystals. He wrote and recorded a song called "(Let's Dance) The Screw—Part 1." No radio program director would go near a record with such blatantly suggestive language, and they'd certainly not program a song that lasted five minutes. Radio had a three-minute limit, and that barrier had not yet been breached.

"He wanted to get me," Sill said. "That was him saying, 'Fuck you, buddy.'"

The real Crystals sang on the record. Recording a dirty song was a mark against their good name. Though "(Let's Dance) The Screw—Part 1" was given a catalog number (Philles 111), it's unclear if the song was ever commercially released. The only surviving copies are marked as promotional recordings for disc jockeys.

Still, Spector achieved his goal of jettisoning the man who had helped him build his career. "I sold out for a pittance," Sill recalled. "It was shit, ridiculous, around $60,000. I didn't want to but I had to. Let me tell you, I couldn't live with Phillip. . . . I just wanted the fuck out of there. If I wouldn't have, I would have killed him. It wasn't worth the aggravation. No matter how important it was, it wasn't that important."

That was the Phil Spector modus operandi: glom on to a mentor, suck out his knowledge, then move on. "Philly was a user and pretty manipulative," Don Kirshner recalled. "To me, Philly was not an overwhelming friend, but a business associate we made a lot of money with."

———————

Jeff Barry and Ellie Greenwich, two of Kirshner's staff songwriters at Aldon, were plugged into the Phil Spector audience. In 1963, they teamed with Spector to create two teen classics that were prime examples of the wall of sound technique. (There is speculation that the songs came to Spector fully formed but that he took a cowriter's credit for his musical arrangement.)

The first collaboration, released in April 1963, was "Da Doo Ron Ron," a simple girl-meets-boy song with some nonsense syllables thrown in for good measure. It could be viewed as prime goofiness or maybe a stand-in phrase for sexual intercourse.

Session pianist Don Randi knew it was a hit from the first run-through. "The minute I heard the title was 'Da Doo Ron Ron' I knew this was going to go Top 10 so fuckin' fast your hair'll fall out," he said. "It was so silly, but so great. That record had every hook in the book to make it a hit."

Spector planned to do the usual: have Darlene Wright and the Blossoms record the song but then release it under the Crystals' name. The instrumental track was great—Blaine's drumming sounded like rat-a-tat-tatting machine guns, and the Wrecking Crew played with a crazed frenzy, as if Gold Star was on fire but they couldn't evacuate until they finished recording. "That's gold," Spector told his studio gofer, Sonny Bono. "That's solid gold coming out of that speaker."

Everything about the song was good—except the vocal. Darlene Wright's voice was magnificent, but it just didn't seem to go with the adolescent longing in the song. After all, she was a worldly woman, soon to be twenty-three years old. Spector decided it needed a younger voice.

The youngest member of the Crystals was fifteen-year-old LaLa Brooks. She was summoned from a concert tour back east—just her, none of the other Crystals—and flown to Los Angeles (her first plane ride). She had a powerful voice. At earlier sessions, Spector had instructed her to stand farther from the microphone than the other Crystals because she overpowered them. She also had the freshness and innocence the song needed.

Spector erased Darlene Wright's vocal and used LaLa Brooks. Two minutes and eighteen seconds of exploding teenage hormones, "Da Doo Ron Ron" went to number three on the *Billboard* charts.

Lightning struck again when Spector took another Greenwich-Barry song into the studio, "Then He Kissed Me." Again he used LaLa and built high drama for a song about a first kiss. *Billboard*, number six.

He eventually gave Darlene Wright her moment in the sun. He'd promised her a solo record, but ended up releasing it ("He's Sure the Boy I Love") under the Crystals' name. He had her team with Bobby Sheen to be a faux group named Bob B. Soxx and the Blue Jeans on the old Disney song "Zip-a-Dee-Doo-Dah," which became an unlikely hit. She finally got her solo moment with "(Today I Met) The Boy I'm Gonna Marry," but it was credited to Darlene Love. Phil Spector had chosen a new name for his go-to singer.

He was a fickle man. Just as the Crystals had recovered from the twin debacles of "He Hit Me (and It Felt Like a Kiss)" and "(Let's Dance) The Screw" with the back-to-back monsters of "Da Doo Ron Ron" and "Then He Kissed Me," Spector lost interest in the group.

Something else had come along that caught his eye and ear: three girls called the Ronettes from New York's Spanish Harlem.

Spector had dated Annette Merar for three years. She'd been a few years behind him at Fairfax High and was beginning her schooling at Berkeley when Spector insisted she come be with him in Los Angeles. As 1963 dawned, they decided to get married, but the marriage was over nearly the moment it began.

The Ronettes were a trio—two sisters, Veronica and Estelle Bennett, and their cousin Nedra Talley. They'd been in the business for a couple of years and had a record deal with Colpix, a label run by Don Kirshner of Aldon Music. The Ronettes were going nowhere and were considering cashing it all in when they met Phil Spector.

The young producer was immediately taken with the group. In a rock 'n' roll world that revered wholesome boy-worshipping female singers (see Shelley Fabares, "Johnny Angel"), the Ronettes were a marked departure. They weren't the girls next door, unless you lived next door to a strip club. With their bodies barely concealed under tight dresses and their lethal hair piled high like nuclear weapons, they were both a visual and sonic assault.

Newlywed Phil fell hard and fast for Veronica, the lead singer, who went by the nickname Ronnie. When he heard her voice, he was a goner.

Hoping to re-create the formula that worked with the Crystals, Spector got a couple more songs from Jeff Barry and Ellie Greenwich and took the Ronettes into Gold Star in July 1963. With Hal Blaine's thunder-hammer drumming and Ronnie's primal voice, the productions showed the maturation of Phil Spector's wall of sound technique. "Be My Baby" was two and a half minutes, yet melded into the grooves of the seven-inch single were all the power and elements of an opera. Rich with strings and the frenetic energy of a guitar army, the songs built to a peak, fell into a momentary silence, then built again to a higher peak.

It was unforgettable.

Brian Wilson was driving down Sunset Boulevard with his girlfriend in his new turquoise Pontiac Grand Prix when the new Phil Spector song came on KFWB. Hal Blaine's drum, augmented by the outrageous Gold Star echo announced the arrival: *Dum-dum-dum dum / Dum-dum-dum dum—BAM*. Then the pianos—Don Randi, Leon Russell, and Al De Lory, all reading the same charts . . . and then castanets . . . and then Carol Kaye's bass supporting the foundation, topped by the chiming guitars of Tommy Tedesco and Bill Pitman. And then, soaring above it all, that *voice*, that great rock 'n' roll voice of Veronica Bennett, offering the kind of love and devotion articulated only in the cry of a teenage girl.

The night we met I knew I needed you so

Brian pulled to the curb, unable to concentrate on driving while the song was playing. He couldn't breathe. "Oh my God," he said to Marilyn Rovell, grabbing her forearm. "This is the best song I've ever heard." He turned the radio up all the way. The song was exhilarating—but as it ended, Brian grew depressed. "I can't do that," he muttered. "Not that great. Not ever."

"Don't worry, Baby," Marilyn said, reaching over the seat to rub his neck. "You will."

5

EVERYBODY HAD AN OCEAN

In their matching candy-stripe shirts, the Beach
Boys were America's biggest band of the early '60s,
transmitting utopian bulletins of summer without end
to a cold and overcast nation.

—Stephen Michael Erickson

The third Capitol single by the Beach Boys, "Surfin' USA," was an
attempt to make inroads with the landlocked audience in America.
Surf music was largely a Southern California phenomenon until Brian
Wilson voiced his wish for the masses out there in flyover country:

If everybody had an ocean across the USA
Then everybody'd be surfin', like Californ-I-A

The vocal blend and Carl Wilson's sharp faux Chuck Berry guitar
brought the song a national audience and made fans crave more songs
with such unchained joy. "I combined that surf style with a white
approach to the Chuck Berry style," Carl Wilson recalled. "I would
mute the strings a bit to get that clipped surf sound. I'd just hit the
strings lightly with the palm of my picking hand to give it more of
a percussive sound. It was a style that became popular in Southern
California with a lot of surf bands. Most of them were guitar bands,
though, and we surfaced because we had the vocals."

Dick Dale had been playing surf music in California for a couple
of years by then and, since he was picked up by the Beach Boys' label,
he started getting the national push. His first Capitol album was *King
of the Surf Guitar*. Few could twang as well as Dale, with hits such as

"Misirlou" and "Let's Go Trippin'," both of which the Beach Boys recorded on their *Surfin' USA* album and became set-list staples for any self-respecting surf band.

And such bands were legion. Los Angeles independent labels, such as Bob Keane's Del-Fi, tried to cash in on the craze, producing twangy instrumental surf music by the Lively Ones ("Surf Rider") and the Centurions ("Bullwinkle, Part II"). Liberty gave the world the Marketts and "Surfer's Stomp." The Chantays (often listed on record labels as the Chantay's) from Orange County, just south of L.A., had recorded a spooky instrumental called "Liberty's Whip." But after band members saw a film about surfing, they decided to cash in on the Beach Boys' momentum and retitled the song "Pipeline," a surfing term for what happened when a surfer rode through a near tunnel of water as huge waves broke overhead, creating a tube. The instrumental combined toes-on-the-noise guitar with a menacing organ, conveying the beauty and peril of surfing. It was number four on the *Billboard* charts in 1963, proving that surf music was no longer a regional phenomenon.

Indeed. Ronny and the Daytonas were a surf group from Nashville, Tennessee. The Trashmen, the frenetic band responsible for the howling jibber of "Surfin' Bird," came from Minneapolis. Winnipeg, Manitoba, had a band called the Squires, who recorded "The Sultan," a surf instrumental augmented with a gong. The lead guitarist was a fifteen-year-old prodigy named Neil Young.

Later, far-flung surf bands arose in Croatia and Finland and Russia. Apparently everybody *did* have an ocean, and the music industry wanted to make some money off it.

Philip Gary Schlein made his bones as a songwriter extolling Southern California's surfing culture, but he wasn't a beach baby. He was born back east, in Queens, at the end of the summer the Second World War ended. He was the second of two children from a family that would always have little regard for their son or his accomplishments. His father was a druggist and expected his son to follow in his pharmacological footsteps or, even better, become a doctor. His mother was the house disciplinarian, beating her son with a leather strap. His crime was serial shoplifting, which he performed with a gaggle of neighborhood boys who called themselves the Rooftop Gang. They'd rip off stores in the neighborhood, then retreat to the rooftops to divide the spoils. Philip was six when he started running with the crew.

His stern, Romanian-born mother routinely beat her son. "To expect love and understanding from your mother is not to expect too much," Philip wrote in his autobiography. Finally, while still in single digits, the boy could no longer stand the ritual beatings. One day, as his mother prepared for the daily whipping, Philip ran to a kitchen drawer and withdrew a paring knife. As his mother watched, he jabbed the knife into the meat of his thumb and began peeling back skin, exposing bone. He told his mother that if she ever beat him again, he would cut off his thumb and then his other fingers until the abuse stopped. He knew how to hit her where it hurt: "You'll have to explain to everybody why this is." *What will the neighbors say?*

She backed off and promised never to hit her son again, a promise she kept.

"To not receive the love you need is to leave a hole in your soul that only Divine love can heal," Schlein said.

When Philip was nine, he fell under the spell of Elvis Presley. Even the waist-up-only Elvis of television was enough to entrance the boy. In his first attempt at musical performance, Schlein painted on sideburns and patted his wingtips white with powder and thrust his hips into an Elvis impersonation. Neighborhood girls—even his older sister—squealed.

Such moments were rare for him. Of he and his sister, Philip was the neglected child of the family. The Schleins were Jews in a Gentile neighborhood, and the boy was bullied mercilessly at school, and when he fought back, he was the one who got in trouble. There were other issues: his father's pharmacy in Forest Hills was being squeezed by competition, and near-arctic winters didn't help his mother's arthritis.

Mother and children packed themselves into the family Buick and took off for California. Father stayed behind to finish up with his business before relocating.

The cross-country trip was one of Philip's most vivid memories of childhood. They took the southern route and therefore saw the bone-grinding poverty of the Deep South, something he could not have imagined. In New Orleans, they ate catfish while serenaded by trumpet players and saw real live cowboys racing horses along highways in Texas and New Mexico.

All the way across the country, the car radio blasted the rock 'n' roll hits of 1957. Philip was still in the throes of Elvis admiration, and music was quickly becoming his main preoccupation. Both his mother and sister were enraptured by Elvis. Mrs. Schlein called him "my boy." Philip began to see that in show business, he might find an avenue to discover love he did not get from his family.

Settled into a small Los Angeles apartment a block off Sunset Boulevard, the reunited family changed its name. As the father tried to establish his new business, he discovered that a man named Schlein had trouble obtaining a liquor license. They became the Sloan family.

The Sloans all pitched in to help arrange a smooth financial landing in California. For his part, Philip sold newspapers at the corner of Sunset Boulevard and Crescent Heights, in front of Schwab's Pharmacy. Philip stood in the median hawking *Herald Examiner*s to Clark Gable, William Holden, and other movie stars waiting at the red light. When he could, he also worked as a babysitter. One client offered to pay him not in cash but with a ukulele. Philip was thrilled with the new instrument and played it continuously, plucking along with the radio's steady output of rock 'n' roll.

The family was soon established enough to buy a house with double-peaked roofs at the corner of Fairfax Avenue and Del Valle Drive. They hired a cleaning woman named Freddy, who lavished young Philip with attention he didn't get from his family. She also shared her love of rhythm and blues music, and the boy began hiding out in the listening booths at Wallichs Music City, across the street from the newly opened Capitol Records stack-of-platters building at Hollywood and Vine. He didn't have the disposable income to actually buy many records, but if there wasn't a line at the door, he could sit in the booth and listen until closing time. At the kitchen table, he talked to Freddy about the new music he heard, and she suggested other records he might like.

Philip continued to plunk away at his ukulele and wrote his first song, "The Outsider." Though just a teenager, he was prone to depression and lived in solitude, even in the family home. His sister did her job, harassing her younger sibling mercilessly, calling him Flip, though the morose young man was anything but flip. "For the most part, what I was experiencing in life, I was experiencing alone," he said. "I could not find anyone more on the outside than me."

His father wanted to both reward his son's diligence and also get the high-note irritant of the ukulele out of his life. He took his son to Wallichs and bought the boy a Kay acoustic guitar. The monster was unleashed. The guitar had more strings than the ukulele, was much larger, and was painful for the pads on his fingers, making it frustrating for Philip to play. Still, he was determined to learn.

Phil carried the guitar everywhere and played it wherever and whenever he could. One day, when he was twelve, he took the bus to Wallichs and was stunned to find hundreds of hyperventilating teenage girls in front of the store. Guitar under his arm, he worked his way to the door, guarded by two policemen. They saw the guitar and figured since he was a musician, they could let him in. Inside, the store was empty and mostly dark. He moved toward a lighted room off of the main showroom and plunked his guitar down in front of the young man behind the counter.

Philip started describing his troubles with the guitar, and the clerk did what music clerks have done since the days when Moses first struck a power chord: he urged him to buy a Mel Bay guitar instruction book. Philip leafed through the book and suddenly realized the clerk was silent, mute as a toad, fixed on something awe inspiring behind the boy.

When Philip Sloan turned around, he faced Elvis Presley—the thief of hearts, the man his mother loved more than her son. But Sloan was in awe of the young man's presence and at that moment felt reverence, not resentment.

Presley took the guitar from Sloan and said, "I bet you'd like to learn how to play this, son."

Sloan gulped. "Yes, sir, I would," he said. It was the first time he'd used the word "sir" in his life.

Presley showed the boy how to hold the guitar, then stood behind him, moving his fingers with his own. He sang the opening of "Love Me Tender" and strummed the guitar with Sloan's fingers. Because the boy's hands were so small, Presley showed him some chording shortcuts.

Turns out the king of rock 'n' roll was at Wallichs that day on orders from his manager, Colonel Tom Parker. Parker decided that Elvis Presley needed a gold-plated guitar. Presley knew it would make the guitar impractical, much too heavy to play, but he told Sloan he'd learned not to tangle with his manager.

The brief music lesson concluded, Presley told Sloan he'd be happy to sign an autograph for his sister. That comment placed the whole encounter squarely in the realm of the mystic, because Philip Sloan hadn't mentioned having a sister.

Back at home, Philip showed the autograph to his family. They didn't believe he'd actually met the king. "Anybody can sign Elvis's name," his sister said. "If you carry on making up stories, you're going to wind up in a mental hospital."

The Mel Bay Guitar Primer for the Early Beginner became the boy's new bible. The instruction book was a godsend, and Philip Sloan was a quick study. He woke in the middle of the night to finger the chords and softly strum in his room. It became his obsession, and he listened to the radio after school with Freddy, trying to keep up with the guitarists he heard on the rhythm and blues stations.

Los Angeles was home to two key R&B record labels—Specialty, which had given the world Little Richard and Sam Cooke (among others), and Aladdin. After school one day, Freddy greeted thirteen-year-old Philip with the news that Aladdin was auditioning new talent and that several kids from her neighborhood were going to try out.

"Aladdin is all R&B guys, Freddy," he said.

"So?"

"So I'm white."

"What's your color have to do with rhythm and blues?" she asked. "You've got more soul than you know. You go in there and sing. Belt it out loud and true and you'll be OK."

The Aladdin artist roster would have intimidated most novice musicians. Consider those who had recorded for the label: Louis Jordan, Wynonie Harris, Lightnin' Hopkins, Charles Brown, Johnny Ace, Billie Holiday, Shirley and Lee, and Nat King Cole, before he joined the larger and more generic Capitol. A thirteen-year-old Jewish kid had every right to be petrified at the thought of auditioning.

With his guitar stashed in a pillowcase, Philip took the bus down to Pico Boulevard and joined the line waiting to get into the studio. He arrived at 10:00 but did not get in front of the Aladdin executives until 4:00. He was the only white kid in the long line.

Like a lot of record companies that catered to a largely black audience (Chess and Specialty being good examples) Aladdin was run by a couple of white guys—in this case, brothers Leo and Eddie Mesner. Philip stepped up to the microphone, Eddie (the bald brother) nodded, and as the red recording light came on, he opened his mouth and the deep voice of his guitar tutor came out:

I don't care if the sun don't shine
I get my lovin' in the evening time

When he finished, Philip quickly slipped his guitar back into the pillowcase and was hotfooting out of the studio when Leo Mesner's voice barked out of the talkback speaker.

"Do you write any songs?" Leo asked.

"No, but I can," Philip said.

The Mesners packed Philip onto the bus with a contract to show his parents. The boy was high as a kite, but his parents were horrified. What about UCLA and medical school and all these plans they'd made for their son? He couldn't throw that away for some musical pie in the sky.

Freddy took him aside. "I want you to know that I am just so proud of you," she told him. "I knew you had it in you and I want you to keep it in you, no matter what."

The Mesners thought enough of young Philip to come to the Sloans' house to plead their case. The parents put their heads together and figured the sooner their son failed at this music business, the sooner he'd move on to a normal life.

His sister had been calling him Flip for years, so he adopted that as his performing name. It was a more welcoming name than the starchy "Philip," and there was a precedent: "It Was I" was a hit that year by a duo known as Skip and Flip.

Flip Sloan had the A-team on board for his first recording. He came into RCA Studios with Bumps Blackwell behind the console. Three members of L.A. recording royalty backed up the kid: Earl Palmer (drums), Plas Johnson (bass), and Mike Deasy (guitar). The Elvis-like single, "All I Want Is Loving," backed by "Little Girl in the Cabin," both Flip Sloan compositions, was tagged as a "best pick" by *Billboard* magazine, but it died on the vine. Aladdin Records died not long after.

His parents thought this might be the end of their son's dream, but it was just the beginning. Flip Sloan carried the thought around the halls of Fairfax High School: *I'm in the music business.*

Freddy died a year after the Sloans moved to California. "It was the first time I lost someone I loved," Philip said. "She was the one in my life who nurtured my dreams."

Aladdin's closing didn't kill Flip's career. After school, he kept hustling his songs around to music publishers and record labels. Arwin Records was near home and had some impressive lineage. The owner was Marty Melcher, husband and manager of eternal virgin Doris Day. He even had a subsidiary label he'd named after himself: Mart.

Arwin obviously liked rock 'n' roll aimed at white kids. In 1958, Jan and Arnie scored with "Jennie Lee." Another duo, comprised of Melcher and Day's son, Terry, and his University High School pal, Bruce Johnston, recorded hot-rod songs under the name the Rip Chords.

Flip was older now—fifteen—so he reverted to the more mature *Philip*. After one quick audition, he was signed to Arwin Records. Excited to get another break in the music business, he ran home to tell his parents he was signed to a record label run by Doris Day's husband. Mrs. Sloan was not impressed, pronouncing Doris Day too goy for her tastes.

He recorded two more original compositions—"She's My Girl" and "If You Believe in Me"—which he had structured in the style of then current teen idols. Again he was backed by musical gods in the studio, and again he earned a pick hit from *Billboard*. Again the record stiffed, but Philip was not deterred.

He continued haunting the offices of publishers and record producers, hauling around an eighty-five-pound Webcor tape recorder and playing his résumé tape of nearly two dozen original songs he'd recorded—some professionally but mostly in his bedroom.

Word got to Steve Venet, a producer at United Artists, to listen to the Sloan kid. Venet—whose brother Nick was in the process of signing the Beach Boys to Capitol Records—arranged for Philip to audition for Screen Gems, the music publishing subsidiary of Columbia Pictures. Philip's ass had been wearing out the couch in the Screen Gems lobby for months, but now, thanks to Steve Venet, he had an audience.

The Los Angeles office was affiliated with the New York songwriting arm of Columbia, Aldon Music. As the sixties dawned, there was no greater concentration of songwriting talent than those who worked in the cubbyholes of Aldon's offices in New York's Brill Building, including Goffin and King, Mann and Weil, and Barry and Greenwich. They were married couples as well, though in most cases the marriages did not last as long as their professional partnerships. Aldon turned out some of the best rock 'n' roll songs of the Tin Pan Alley tradition: "Will You Love Me Tomorrow?," "Be My Baby," "One Fine Day," and "He's a Rebel."

Venet played the audition reel for Lou Adler, manager of Aldon West. He immediately turned down the kid. But the walls in the offices were thin, and the sound of Flip Sloan's songs bled through the partition. Al Nevins, the Al of Aldon (the Don was Don Kirshner), was in the next office, visiting from New York. He came in and told Adler to sign Sloan to a songwriter contract and hire Venet as a finder's fee for bringing in the kid.

Nevins was more of a musician than a businessman, and as one-third of the easy-listening instrumental trio the Three Suns ("Twilight Time" and "Peg O' My Heart"), he made a lot of money. Investing nearly all of it in music publishing, he built a hit songwriting factory with Kirshner. He had Adler sign the Sloan kid to a ten-dollar-a-week contract.

A few weeks later, Adler and Venet sparred, and Adler fired him and installed Sloan, all of sixteen, as the head of A&R. His job was not only writing songs and looking for talent but also keeping his ear to the ground for all that was appealing to teenagers, Aldon's prime audience.

One day, Adler brought a young man named Steve Barri into the office where Sloan worked after school. Barri was a few years older, with a wife and child and mortgage at home, and Adler offered him ten dollars a week to work part time writing songs with the kid. Their mission was to do the impossible: understand the American teenager.

For the new songwriting team of Sloan and Barri, it was obvious that surf music was the next big thing.

The Beach Boys made a smooth transition from surf to turf. The flip side of the "Surfin' Safari" single was "409," that Brian Wilson–Gary Usher ode to a dream car. Brian continued to collaborate with Gary, but he also brought car freak Roger Christian into the mix. Christian had no shortage of mash notes he'd written to cars. Brian supplied the music for Roger's words for "Cherry, Cherry Coupe," "Custom Machine," "Car Crazy Cutie," and "No-Go Showboat."

Brian was getting ready to move on. Surfing songs were in the (relatively) distant past, and now he felt he was ready to leave cars behind for more important themes. He was obsessed with Phil Spector's "Be My Baby," sometimes playing the single a hundred times a day. That's what he wanted to do: create a lush production about something other than a superstock Dodge, something that might expand his audience beyond sun-bleached kids and gearheads.

He had a lyrical idea. He remembered what Marilyn Rovell had told him that day they were driving and first heard "Be My Baby." "Don't worry, baby," she told him when he expressed doubt about his talents and abilities.

At first, he thought it would be a perfect follow-up for the Ronettes and that it might be his way to impress Phil Spector. "I started out with the verse idea and then wrote the chorus," Brian said. "It was a very simple and beautiful song."

Though he was traveling in the same circles as Phil Spector, Brian still contemplated him from a distance with great awe.

Brian remembered their first meeting. He was in Lou Adler's office waiting for Jan and Dean. "Spector walked in unexpectedly," Brian recalled. "I didn't know what to say. He was short and scrawny, much less of a physical presence than I imagined by listening to his immense Wall of Sound. Scared to speak, I told him I thought he was a genius. He said thank you. Neither one of us looked the other in the eye."

Spector knew that Wilson idolized him, and so he toyed with Brian by asking him to attend a session in the late summer of 1963. Spector was recording *A Christmas Gift for You from Phil Spector* with several of his artists. He asked Wilson to sit in on piano. At first, Wilson demurred, drawing the stink eye from Spector and looks of stone horror from the session musicians. *You don't say no to Phil.* A few minutes later, Spector asked again and Brian complied. They were recording Spector's rearrangement of "Santa Claus Is Coming to Town," performed by the Ronettes. Brian could read music but not as well and as fluidly as members of the Wrecking Crew. After a couple of clumsy takes, Spector indicated to Wilson that he could sit out. The whole purpose of the exercise had been to humiliate Brian.

It didn't matter. Brian took no offense, and he still loved Phil Spector. "His aberrant personality was perhaps his best tool in making records," Brian wrote in his memoir. "He didn't bend to the world; it bent for him." He was a master manipulator and was used to getting what he wanted, inside the recording studio and out.

Brian had tentatively begun to use members of the Wrecking Crew on his sessions for other artists. He recorded several singles with a girl group called the Honeys, which included his girlfriend Marilyn Rovell, her sister Diane, and her cousin Ginger Blake. He'd also produced sessions for a singer named Sharon Marie and for actor Paul Petersen, star of *The Donna Reed Show*. He had experimented on a couple of sessions with having the tracks played entirely by Wrecking Crew personnel while he stayed in the booth as producer. He had begun staying home from concert tours and cajoled Alan Jardine into returning to the group to replace him onstage. For a few weeks, Jardine was in the group with David Marks, who had replaced *him*. But the volatile Marks was constantly bickering with Murry Wilson.

"I quit!" Marks said after one argument.

"You heard that," Murry said, turning to the others for confirmation. "David quit."

The other Beach Boys thought it would blow over, but Murry and Marks, both stubborn, stood firm.

The tours that Brian made were often disastrous. He hated flying and convinced himself that he had suffered a nervous breakdown during one trip. He stayed home as often as he could get away with it. Murry viewed his eldest son's stage fright as cowardice.

Now, in early 1964, he was still ping-ponging between recording studios—Gold Star and Western Recorders—and, more and more, using outside musicians. On January 7, he gathered some of the cream of the Crew (Blaine, Pitman, Tedesco, and Russell) for an invigorating new recording of "Why Do Fools Fall in Love?," the old hit by Frankie Lymon and the Teenagers. None of the other Beach Boys was present.

Unable to make a complete break, Brian alternated not only studios but also bands. He worked with the Wrecking Crew one day and the self-contained Beach Boys the next.

He knew that "Don't Worry Baby" was perhaps the best song he'd written. Roger Christian took Brian's idea of a doubt-filled man reassured by a loving woman and turned it into a car song—sort of. Turns out that the narrator is having such doubt because he's challenged some local ruffian to a drag race and now he's come to think it's not such a good idea. By the end of the song, we're not sure if our man has won the race, but he was encouraged to try.

Phil Spector passed on the song. Brian was disappointed but not crushed, because he thought *he* might be able to do the song justice. After the Beach Boys' first foreign concert tour (Australia and New Zealand), the group convened at Western Recorders on February 20 to finish the album they had started in early January. "Don't Worry Baby" was on the docket, with a spare instrumental lineup: Brian on piano, Al on bass, Carl on guitar, and Dennis on drums. Brian had intended to mimic Hal Blaine's dramatic drum opening on "Be My Baby," but instead of hiring the man himself, he instead used his brother.

Although Dennis was not a technically skilled drummer, Brian thought he could handle the introduction, a distinctive and stately prelude. Fed through Western's echo chamber, it sounded like the second coming of Hal Blaine. Dennis, often considered—even by others in the band—as the one who didn't carry his musical weight, acquitted himself spectacularly on that session. He knew how to rise to an occasion.

The finished production of "Don't Worry Baby" showed how well the apprentice had learned from the master. Playing "Be My Baby" a hundred times a day paid off. Brian was inside the song, creating a car radio masterpiece of singing and storytelling.

Musicologist Philip Lambert said of the similarities between this song and "Be My Baby," "They're in the same key—E Major—and they start the same. The phrase structure is the same, the chord progressions are almost the same, the melodies are almost the same." Lambert points out what set Wilson's composition apart: the song's key change, which was an unexpected touch that made the song memorable.

Decades later, Al Jardine recalled the importance of that recording: "Just about everything about it was an era-change for us."

By the time "Don't Worry Baby" was released, the Beach Boys had been riding high for nearly three years. They were the preeminent rock 'n' roll band in America, but that might be faint praise considering the anemic state of the music industry. There were bright spots, such as the teenage symphonies of Phil Spector and the irresistible music coming from Motown Records, but there was a lot of garbage as well. Perhaps the vilest example of that era's musical excreta was "Sugar Shack" by Jimmy Gilmer and the Fireballs. Despite being recorded

by Buddy Holly's old producer, Norman Petty, and in Buddy's old
Clovis, New Mexico, studio, and with the Fireballs, a reputable surf
music band, the song was anathema to rock 'n' roll. Yet it was the
bestselling song of 1963. Other rivals in the 1963 music hall of lame
were "Go Away Little Girl" by Steve Lawrence, "Blue Velvet" by
poodle-haired Bobby Vinton, and "Dominique" by the Singing Nun.

By contrast, the Beach Boys—and their imitators—produced a
more vigorous and virile music, something with a strong connection
to rock 'n' roll's origins. Carl Wilson had obviously stolen the key
chapters from the Chuck Berry playbook, and Brian's vocal arrangements blended the influence of the Four Freshmen and the great
black harmony groups of the 1950s.

The Beach Boys made great rock 'n' roll, but the group might
be just as important in music history for providing a working model
that generations of bands have followed since. Before Brian Wilson's
arrival, few artists had taken such control of their careers. There was
always a Svengali: Norman Petty for Buddy Holly; Sam Phillips for
Elvis, Jerry Lee Lewis, Johnny Cash, and Carl Perkins; Leonard Chess
for Chuck Berry and Bo Diddley; and scores of music-biz sharpies
who manufactured careers for modestly talented kids with looks that
made teenage girls swoon.

But the Beach Boys had their own Svengali. Brian was nineteen
when the group began its recording career, and though the credits
might read "Hite Morgan" or "Nick Venet" on their early releases—
and though Murry Wilson thought of himself as the group mastermind—it was clear, watching the group in the studio, who was in
charge and who had the vision.

The first two Capitol albums, credited to Venet, overcame the
crudeness of the band's playing and the thinness of some of the material largely due to Brian's vision. *Surfin' Safari*, released on October
1, 1962, had twelve songs, nine of which were cowritten by Brian, in
partnership with Gary Usher ("County Fair," "Ten Little Indians,"
"Chug-A-Lug," "409," "Heads You Win, Tails I Lose," and "Cuckoo
Clock") and Mike Love ("Surfin'," "Surfin' Safari," and "The Shift").

"I went into the songwriting aspect of it with gusto," Brian recalled.
"I worked off youthful energy and my head was full of needs to get
a bad childhood off my chest."

Lyrically the songs were simple stuff—about root beer, tight skirts,
boys trying to impress girls. The songs were also modest musically,
with competent playing and the occasional addition of a Farfisa organ.

But when it came to the production, Brian was laying down some style right from the start.

Nick Venet was present, but clearly Brian was in charge. "Brian would [make] all the settings on the control board and go out into the studio and Murry would change everything," David Marks said. "Then Brian would come back [into the booth] and go, 'What the fuck happened? It sounds different.' They were fighting all the time, I guess Murry was trying to live through his sons. It was finally agreed that Murry wouldn't try to produce anymore."

Carl concurred. "Brian was really the one making the records. Nick would call out the take numbers, but he wasn't part of making the music. When Brian said he wouldn't work with Nick anymore, Capitol sent over this other guy. Then it became clear to Brian, and he said, 'Look, I'm not cutting with these guys, and what's more, I'm not going to use your studio. We'll send you the next record.' Now, this was a big thing in those days, because record companies were used to having absolute control over their artists. It was especially nervy, because Brian was a twenty-one-year-old kid with just two albums notched on his belt. It was unheard of. But what could they say? Brian made good records. He wouldn't work at Capitol, because it was a crappy-sounding studio. It had a fabulous string sound, and that was great for those records that Nat King Cole made, but not for rock 'n' roll guitar. So we recorded at Western Recorders, which was really our home."

Venet's major contribution, other than being the Capitol executive on duty and a seasoned sounding board, was to allow Brian the space to learn how to work the studio. Venet supplied the voice of a carnival barker in an audio skit dropped in the middle of "County Fair" and howled along with the others during the surf instrumental "Moon Dawg," one of the album's four cover songs.

"Brian did everything," Marks said. "He didn't need any help. You listen to those first albums and they sound campy and corny but Brian was dead serious."

The bulk of the *Surfin' Safari* album was recorded in three three-hour sessions at Capitol Studios, remarkably efficient for a novice producer. Within a month, Brian was producing records for other artists, including Bob Norberg, with whom he shared an apartment.

By early January, Brian broke away from Capitol Studios and booked time at Western Recorders. "I could get a ballsier sound at Western," he said. Capitol agreed to the move because its executives had faith in the kid and also because there had been some friction during the *Surfin' Safari* album sessions. As the producer in name, Nick Venet had rushed Brian through some of the sessions because he had other projects on the docket. Brian wanted more time to fuss with the recordings.

So as the New Year began, Brian was firmly in charge and in an independent studio. Western allowed for three-track recording, and Brian decided that the group should double track all of its vocals, boosting the virility of the voices and giving their records much more punch.

Brian had been an avid listener as he hunkered under the covers in his room, hiding from his father and listening to his magic transistor radio. He knew song structure, and he knew what kids liked to hear. One day, he was humming the old Chuck Berry tune "Sweet Little Sixteen." Berry's song was a travelogue, mentioning a geographically dispersed group of cities, perhaps hoping listeners in those cities would rush out and buy the record. "The concept was about 'they're doing this in this city and they're doing that in that city,'" Wilson said. "I thought to myself, 'God! What about trying to put surf lyrics to 'Sweet Little Sixteen's melody?" He cornered a friend who was a devoted surfer. "I want to do a song mentioning all the surf spots. So he gave me a list."

The subliminal goal of the song was to be inclusive, to draw in envious teenagers from the landlocked world. Brian bequeathed to them an ocean and surfing and friends and fun, fun, fun. To be young and Californian became that new American ideal.

What made Brian's records truly memorable was the vocal blend. As a musical and vocal arranger, Brian was without equal. Other young artists ceded those tasks to Svengali or Svengali assistants. Brian took control of the total package: songwriting, arranging, producing.

Yet Nick Venet stood in his way. Though essentially marginalized, Venet still had control of the final project. When it came time to do the mixing of the album—the vital final step before the record was manufactured—Venet set appointments with Brian to supervise the mastering but had everything finished by the time Brian arrived. Though Wilson had a generally good relationship with Venet, this was intolerable and required Brian to humble himself by asking his father for help.

"I realized that with Nick Venet out as producer, my dad clearly planned to take over the job himself," Brian said. And that, he knew, was one definition of hell.

6

SACRED AND PROFANE

The road has taken some of the great ones: Hank
Williams . . . Buddy Holly . . . Otis Redding . . . Janis . . .
Jimi Hendrix . . . Elvis. It's a goddamn impossible way
of life. I mean, *16 years* on the road . . . the numbers
start to scare you.

—Robbie Robertson

The ancestors of rock 'n' roll are blues, hillbilly music, and gospel.
Think about blues . . . *rhythm and blues* . . . whatever you want to call
it. *Its* ancestor was the field holler, sung by black farm workers of the
nineteenth century. They sang for each other. The back and forth of
the field holler was carried over to the gospel-flavored call-and-response
incorporated as part of rhythm and blues.

The music wasn't left in the fields. At Dockery Plantation in
central Mississippi, owner Will Dockery held Saturday night fish fries
for his workers, to mark the end of a hard week and to entertain the
laborers. This is the land where the blues began. Charley Patton, who
some call the father of the Delta blues, worked on Dockery and sang
on Saturday nights. Roebuck Staples—known as Pops Staples later
in life when he led his performing family, the Staple Singers—was
a young boy in the audience. In the fields that radiate through the
Delta, there were laborer-performers such as Robert Johnson and
Muddy Waters. That small button of America also produced John
Lee Hooker, Ike Turner, Son House, and Sam Cooke.

Those owner-sponsored fish fries gave way to house parties—
field hand Muddy Waters was known to throw a good party over on
Stovall's plantation, featuring his glorious collection of 78s. And soon
those house parties begat juke joints.

Juke . . . jook—a great word, however you spell it. Writer Zora Neale Hurston defined it thusly: "Jook is a word for a Negro pleasure house. It may mean a bawdy house. It may mean the house set apart on public works where the men and women dance, drink, and gamble. Often, it is a combination of all these."

Maybe you thought they were called "juke joints" because they had jukeboxes. The jook/juke predates that money-eating music player. *Jook* is a derivative of a word brought from Africa, along with men and women bound in chains.

Blues music took root in house parties and then in these juke joints that stood forlorn at rural crossroads in the Delta. Similarly, hillbilly music—the yodeling, primitive form of country—found its audience at county fairs and barn dances and standing alongside the flatbed where the band played.

Jazz made its way into the nightclubs of the major cities—New Orleans, Memphis, and Chicago—and there was pop music ensconced at the sophisticated clubs in New York and Los Angeles. At the end of the thirties, blues and hillbilly music was still working its way from the country to the city.

What became rock 'n' roll in the fifties arose from twin subcultures. The music industry's official term for black music was *race,* and for white country music it was *hillbilly.* They appeared so different on the surface, but they had much in common, both forms being born of poverty and the blues.

And though there might be some truth to the claim that rock 'n' roll is just black folks' music played by white guys, the road did go both ways. Standing on a flatbed with his fiddle and his trombone players, Bob Wills and His Texas Playboys introduced a poor white audience to his interpretations of blues, his versions of the songs he heard on those Negro radio stations.

It took a while, but the musical revolution that led to a social revolution began to occur in those juke joints and roadhouses, and on those flatbeds.

You hear a lot of the vocabulary of rock 'n' roll in the primitive recordings of Charley Patton and Robert Johnson. Both men made the juke joint and house party circuit. That music remained a secret shared by African Americans, although a rare spot of radio play for something like Johnson's "Terraplane Blues" would send a ripple through the collective ear of white America.

If John Hammond had to list his occupation on an employment application in 1938, it might have been "talent scout," though that title isn't magnificent enough to describe his contributions to American music. He found—and shared with the world—Bessie Smith, Benny Goodman, Count Basie, Bob Dylan, Aretha Franklin, Bruce Springsteen, and Stevie Ray Vaughan. But in 1938, he was the scion of the Vanderbilt family, a young man dissatisfied with wealth and affluence, dabbling in the world of Negro music. He chose to showcase the music of the disaffected and disenfranchised in the palace of white America, Carnegie Hall.

Hammond began to put together a roster of entertainers to show off the diversity of African American music. He booked the Count Basie Orchestra, gospel singer Sister Rosetta Tharpe, and boogie-woogie master Albert Ammons. Hammond had heard one of Robert Johnson's 78 RPMs but had never met the man. He enlisted the aid of music scholar and song finder Alan Lomax. Lomax and his father, John Lomax, gave their lives to preserving American music in all of its rich forms. Hammond had found a good agent.

But even the best agent was not a magician. As Lomax traveled rural Mississippi, he asked after Johnson. One tip led to another, and that led to a blind alley. He retraced his steps and started again. Eventually the path led him to Johnson's mother, still aching with grief months after her son's death. "Little Robert, he dead," she told Lomax, and then began wailing and dancing in a private ceremony of grief.

Robert Johnson's last gig was at a house party at Three Forks, Mississippi. He had been romancing a married woman, and the jealous husband passed him an open bottle of whiskey laced with strychnine. The first time the bottle was passed, Sonny Boy Williamson—also playing at the party—took it out of Johnson's hands. "Man, don't ever take a drink from a [sic] open bottle," he said. Johnson spat back that Sonny Boy should mind his own business. When the next bottle came around, Johnson responded with a defiant swig. Within days, he was dead. In his last hours—so says the Johnson legend—he was in such agony that he crawled on the floor, baying like a hellhound.

Much folklore and superstition follow life on "The Road," and though Johnson's early death was not the first of a performing musician, it makes a suitable reference point for all of the tragedies that followed in the history of the insane life of an itinerant minstrel—from Johnny Ace through Buddy Holly and Ritchie Valens, Eddie Cochran, Lynyrd Skynyrd, Stevie Ray Vaughan, and the others on rock's death roll.

Hammond got the news about Johnson and booked Big Bill Broonzy for Johnson's slot on the bill. *The show must go on.*

The Spirituals to Swing concert at Carnegie Hall wasn't rock 'n' roll, but it was a giant step down that road.

The crystallizing event that began the rock concert as industry was kicked off in Cleveland fifteen years after Carnegie Hall was rocked by Hammond's show. The casual fan may wonder why the Rock and Roll Hall of Fame is there by the lake, and not in Memphis, where logic would locate it. But Cleveland was the site of the first rock 'n' roll concert.

Alan Freed was a disc jockey at WJW, and in 1952, he played rhythm and blues on his show. Billy Ward and His Dominoes, the group with the risqué "Sixty Minute Man," came by the studio to chat on-air with Freed while in town for a gig. After the interview ended, Freed put on a record and started walking Billy Ward out of the studio.

He asked Ward where he was going now.

Ward smiled lasciviously. *I'm gonna go rock 'n' roll.*

Rock 'n' roll. Freed liked the way it sounded. "Rhythm and blues," the new industry term for black music, still bore the stigma of "race records" and Freed saw it as his sad duty to push his particular boulder uphill, trying to introduce the masses (mostly white kids) to this music he loved. Then Billy Ward showed up and planted that phrase squarely in Freed's cerebrum.

Rock 'n' roll. The rest of the night was full of Freed's howling about this music that he had suddenly decided to call rock 'n' roll. The next day, Billy Ward called. He'd heard the show and couldn't believe that Freed said that on the air.

What?

You know . . . . Rock 'n' roll. *Don't you know what it means?*

Apparently not. The rock 'n' rolling Billy Ward had in mind was of a sexual nature. "Rock 'n' roll" meant *fucking.*

Oops. But for Freed, there was no going back. He'd get the kids to listen to this music, he'd get them into the tent like a carnival barker with "rock 'n' roll" as his sales pitch. Soon his radio show was renamed *The Moondog Rock 'n' Roll Party* (he was known on the air as Moondog), and as the music grew in popularity, he decided it was time to call a meeting of the young minds.

The Moondog Coronation Ball at Cleveland Arena on March 21, 1952, was the first rock 'n' roll concert. A little bit of the genetic material from that show can be found any place where guitar, bass, drums, and fans gather. That concert featured an all-star bill (including Billy Ward and His Dominoes, Tiny Grimes, and Danny Cobb). It also featured mayhem, essential to any good rock concert: twenty-five thousand fans showed up for ten thousand seats. If you couldn't sit down, you had to dance. Considering all the hip grinding going on, it was like rock 'n' roll in the Billy Ward sense. Still, the riotous nature of the show—the sort of thing that had parents shaking their heads and preachers thumping their pulpits—made national news. Cleveland could no longer contain Freed, who took his act and his go-man-go white boy jive and left for New York, where he sat behind a WINS microphone and promoted a series of Brooklyn Paramount Theatre shows that made the Cleveland Arena show look like the Cuyahoga Falls Glee Club rehearsals.

Starting in 1955, Freed promoted some of the best examples of early rock concerts, with the Drifters, the Clovers, Fats Domino, and Big Joe Turner. The rock concert juggernaut started rolling, thanks in large part to Freed. What had once been the province of house parties and juke joints had moved into theaters and concert halls. But it was about to take the larger stage of television.

Elvis Presley burst out of Memphis in 1954, but remained a regional phenomenon until his new manager, Colonel Tom Parker, took him to the next level. He signed Elvis to RCA Victor and got him bookings on national television.

Still an oddity itself, television was drawn to weirdness, and the thing called Elvis Presley seemed weird enough to draw viewers. Milton Berle, the man known as Mr. Television, invited Elvis onto his variety show at the beginning of April 1956. But it was Elvis's second visit on June 5 that really caught the nation's attention. Elvis sang and swiveled, and the lascivious bump and grind was more than the television audience could reasonably stand. It was the talk of the watercooler the next day: He was *vulgar*. He was an *animal*. He was *evil*.

Voices from the pulpit lashed out, guaranteeing that the curious folks who were in front of their televisions when Elvis showed up on the top-rated *Ed Sullivan Show* would burn in the everlasting fires of hell. Ed Sullivan wasn't even on the *Ed Sullivan Show* on September 9, 1956. He'd been injured in an automobile accident a month before, and so it was portly English actor Charles Laughton who introduced Elvis to Sullivan's huge audience.

From the waist up, that is. The CBS Standards and Practices Office said Elvis was fine above the waist, but the movement in his hips was deemed to be too much. Elvis sang "Don't Be Cruel," "Hound Dog," "Reddy Teddy," and "Love Me Tender."

A month later, he came back—again from the waist up, but this time with a healed Ed Sullivan to introduce him—and sang, "Don't Be Cruel," "Love Me Tender," and "Hound Dog." The TV appearances, though toned down by the camera angle, built more anticipation for Elvis's shows as he barnstormed the country—for the first time, finding an audience outside the Deep South—and prepared for his third Sullivan show appearance. This time, Elvis got the full-body treatment.

On January 6, 1957, Elvis—all of him—showed up alongside Ed Sullivan and sang, "Hound Dog," "Love Me Tender," "Heartbreak Hotel," "Don't Be Cruel," "Peace in the Valley," "Too Much," and "When My Blue Moon Turns to Gold Again." In the eight months since Elvis's debut on the Berle show, the world had changed. The world was finally ready for Elvis's hips, and from that point, there was no looking back. Kids could buy records. Singles were only fifty-nine cents. But getting money to see a package tour of rock 'n' rollers might be a little harder.

Television was the only way to actually see what these people looked like, and the *Ed Sullivan Show* became a weekly glimpse into the development of rock 'n' roll. Buddy Holly and his chirping Crickets. Jackie Wilson. The Everly Brothers.

"Tonight . . . on our stage . . . we're proud to bring you . . ."

Ed Sullivan could teach sequoias to be wooden. But he was a great showman; he knew what people wanted. Alan Freed was a great showman too, and after his move to New York, he began a series of three or four shows a year at the Paramount Theatre in Brooklyn. On September 1, 1957, Freed hosted The Biggest Show of Stars, and then sent it out on tour for two months—Philadelphia, Pittsburgh, Akron, Cincinnati, Norfolk. . . . Not a bad show: Buddy Holly and the Crickets, the Everly Brothers, Chuck Berry, Paul Anka, Jimmy Bowen, Sam "the Man" Taylor, and Clyde McPhatter.

These were wild shows. Rock concerts took well to this package-show mentality: lots of acts, three songs each, back on the bus for the next stop. The Crickets, out of Lubbock, Texas, had a good year in 1957, hitting the charts with "That'll Be the Day," a title pinched from a line in John Wayne's new movie, *The Searchers*. The next year was even better for the Crickets, but leader Buddy Holly—singer, lead guitarist, principal songwriter—was more infatuated by New York and his new life as a semi-Bohemian in Greenwich Village. He'd just gotten married to a beautiful young woman and in early 1959 learned that they would become parents that summer.

The other Crickets, J. I. Allison and Joe B. Mauldin, disliked New York life and went home to Lubbock. Rock 'n' roll had its first major divorce.

With a new bride and a child on the way, Holly needed cash, and so he joined the Winter Dance Party package tour. He hired a couple of new musicians—Tommy Allsup on guitar and Waylon Jennings on bass—billed as the Crickets by the promoter. They were joined on the tour by Dion and the Belmonts, Frankie Sardo, Ritchie Valens, and disc jockey J. P. Richardson, who recorded as the Big Bopper.

The Winter Dance Party tour hit all the hot spots of the upper Midwest: *Milwaukee . . . Kenosha . . . Mankato*. It was ass-numbingly cold on the bus, and the heater kept breaking down. *Eau Claire . . . Montevideo . . . St. Paul*. They all huddled together on the bus, but it wasn't enough to protect them from the cold. *Davenport . . . Fort Dodge . . . Duluth . . . Green Bay*.

Finally, the Surf Ballroom in landlocked Clear Lake, Iowa, equidistant from the oceans and void of surf. After the show, Holly chartered a small plane to take him on to Moorhead, Minnesota, site of the next night's show.

Sioux City . . . Des Moines . . . Cedar Rapids—in all, twenty-four dates in twenty-four days. No break, and in the dead of winter.

There was enough room for him to bring Tommy Allsup and Waylon Jennings along for the plane ride. Valens and Richardson heard that Holly had chartered a plane and asked to go along. No room, but headliners had prerogatives. Ritchie Valens was seventeen. It was his first big trip away from home. He just wanted a warm bed. Coins were flipped. Richardson and Valens joined Holly on the plane. Allsup and Jennings got on the bus. And so the road got its first rock 'n' roll tragedy on February 3, 1959.

Every night brought the same relentless dream. María Elena went to sleep, knowing he waited, still her husband, forever young, with his life spread before him. Then she imagined it: what he saw and what he thought in those last moments.

A small charter plane crashed in a cornfield in the wee hours, extinguishing three of rock 'n' roll's brightest stars. Their young pilot, Roger Peterson, also was killed.

It's likely Buddy Holly and his passengers didn't know what was happening until they saw the frozen Iowa tundra racing up at them through the windshield. This was the image that haunted María Elena Holly, Buddy's widow. She was home in New York when the news came. Barely six months wed, she collapsed, losing the baby she carried.

The plane crash ended the first chapter of the world's love affair with rock 'n' roll, the music that blended the plaint of white country with the beat of black rhythm and blues. Few young artists were better at creating this chemical mixture than Holly, the gawky, bespectacled kid from Lubbock. He was twenty-two.

Ritchie Valens, a pioneer of Latin rock from Southern California, had recently burst onto the charts with a double-sided smash: "Donna," a slow dancing/heavy petting number about a real-life girl-friend, paired with "La Bamba," a Spanish-language romp.

J. P. Richardson was a charismatic voice on Texas radio who'd christened himself the "Big Bopper" and parlayed that persona into the hit record "Chantilly Lace," supposedly the Bopper's end of a phone conversation with a sultry woman. He was twenty-eight.

Each night of the Winter Dance Party tour, teenagers turned up at warm cocoon-like ballrooms to greet the stars who'd made the four-hundred-mile trips between venues on a bus with no heat.

Holly told Tommy Allsup and Waylon Jennings he'd given their seats on the plane to Valens and the Bopper. Jennings was pissed.

"Well, I hope your ol' bus freezes up," Buddy told Jennings.

"Well, I hope your ol' plane crashes," Jennings joked.

When the plane crashed just after takeoff, a generation that had danced and swooned to the sounds of early rock 'n' roll was left to wonder, if the best and the brightest are susceptible, aren't we all?

Ten years later, singer Don McLean would call it "the day the music died." It didn't, of course. Other artists continued to mine the Buddy Holly song catalog. Ritchie Valens joined him as a staple of oldies radio, and both artists were introduced to new generations through the films *The Buddy Holly Story* and *La Bamba*. The Big Bopper still awaits his close-up.

The year following the Clear Lake tragedy, rock 'n' roll suffered another devastating loss. Eddie Cochran, a vibrant young singer-songwriter, was on tour in England with Gene Vincent. Both Cochran and Vincent were rough-hewn rockers, and Cochran was an especially appealing young voice, merging the middle-American simplicity of his upbringing (Minnesota, then Oklahoma) with the cool of his adopted home, Los Angeles. His party invitation "C'mon Everybody" was a conspiratorial wink at all of the other young partiers beating back the rising tide of conformity, partying while mom and pop were out of town.

The house'll be shakin' from the bare feet slapping on the floor

Vincent wore black leather and was not as well scrubbed as Cochran. His US Navy service spoke of a worldliness young kids envied. He was also the quavering menace behind the poetic "Be-Bop-a-Lula," one of the early benchmarks of rock 'n' roll.

Cochran had invited his girlfriend, songwriter Sharon Sheeley, to come celebrate her twentieth birthday in England. They were in a taxicab with Vincent, on the way to London, when the car skidded, slamming into a lamppost. The front-seat passengers—the driver and Cochran's manager—were both wearing seatbelts (not yet standard equipment) and were unhurt. The backseat passengers, all unbuckled, were not so lucky. Sheeley broke her pelvis in the crash, Vincent broke his rib and collarbones, and Cochran was thrown through the windshield and suffered major injuries. He died in a hospital sixteen hours later.

Within fourteen months, rock 'n' roll had suffered two tragedies. Though Vincent survived, he never fully recovered and performed in pain the rest of his life, often needing support to stand at the microphone.

Danny and the Juniors had sung "Rock 'n' Roll Is Here to Stay," and, a half decade after Elvis, it appeared that the music did have some staying power.

By 1960, a full five years after it had been decried from pulpits as the devil's music, it still filled auditoriums with package tours from the likes of genial television host Dick Clark. But some of the edge was gone. To many, it was rock 'n' roll in name only.

A lot of the major players were gone.

Elvis was drafted in 1958, and instead of seeking a deferment, he did what any other young American man would do: he went off to serve. A backlog of recordings kept him in the public eye, but he stopped performing in public. And when he returned to the States in 1960, he was different. The danger of young Elvis was gone. It was as if some space alien had sucked the brains from his head.

Chuck Berry, long a staple of Alan Freed's package shows—along with his chief rival, Jerry Lee Lewis—had run afoul of the law. During a gig in El Paso, Berry met a young prostitute named Janice Escalante and invited her back to St. Louis to work in his nightclub. When that relationship soured, he gave her bus fare and sent her back to Texas. She instead went to the authorities. She was fourteen, not nineteen as she had told Berry, and the authorities pounced. They had been looking for a way to neutralize this popular black entertainer—a man particularly popular with young white women. Berry was charged under the Mann Act, which decreed it was unlawful to take a minor across state lines for immoral purposes, and he was convicted. The arrest, trial, and eventual jail term kept him out of action for three years.

Little Richard, the architect of rock 'n' roll, was one of the first wild men in the new music's early days. His performances—also part of the Alan Freed package shows—were frenetic and crazed. It was while on tour in Australia that Richard dreamed of the apocalypse and decided what they were saying about him back in the States was true: he *was* playing the devil's music. He forsook his career and returned home to study for the ministry.

What a festival of loss: Buddy Holly, Eddie Cochran, Ritchie Valens, and the Big Bopper were dead. Chuck Berry was in prison. Jerry Lee Lewis was in disgrace following the revelation that he married his thirteen-year-old cousin. Little Richard was in the ministry. Elvis was in the military.

As American rock 'n' roll became less rock 'n' roll and more pop, the Dick Clark package tours took on a teen idol aroma. Fabian, Frankie Avalon, and Paul Anka (Lord help us!) dominated the stages and the charts. Good things were happening, but not on America's main stage. For the African American artists who had yet to cross over to the mainstream, there remained the chitlin circuit—a series of black-owned, black-dominated nightclubs.

Every night these artists perfected their acts—somewhere in the Deep South . . . or on the South Side of Chicago . . . or in the underbelly of L.A. . . . . or perhaps on the stage of the Apollo Theater in Harlem.

For a decade, James Brown worked out his sobbing, begging-his-woman onstage shtick, but it remained a secret of black culture until Brown's crossover to the mainstream in the midsixties.

There were others who refused to smooth the rough edges—Hank Ballard and the Midnighters, Little Willie John, some of the rockabilly gods. In roadhouses and nightclubs, the mayhem continued while the kids, en masse, got a dose of the Brylcreem teen idol set, courtesy of Dick Clark and his Caravan of Stars.

Buddy Holly and the Crickets had been the model of a rock 'n' roll band: two guitars, a bass, and drums. By the early sixties, teen idol types were blending a homogenized version of rock with schlocky elements of pop music. The music industry had reluctantly embraced rock 'n' roll and begun to bland it. Though Phil Spector added Wagnerian epic touches, his music still spoke to that teenage audience, with songs that chronicled the agonies of adolescence. The schlockmeisters with their assembly line pop were cynically trying to bag the prized discretionary income of the new teenage consumer.

There were *still* rock 'n' roll bands. America's best exemplar of the drums-bass-guitar ideal in the early sixties was the Beach Boys.

––––––––––––

Rock stars had died in plane crashes, automobile accidents, and in backstage games of Russian roulette (Johnny Ace, 1955). But in the midsixties, some artists met even more gruesome ends.

At the dawn of the sixties, Los Angeles was a huge, sprawling city and was still growing, spreading like an oil spill. But the music community was like a common backyard shared by a diverse neighborhood.

Lou Adler had his foot in the white rock 'n' roll arena with Jan and Dean and the various identities of Phil Sloan—as himself, as seer-philosopher P. F. Sloan, and as the phantom surf and hot rod studio group the Fantastic Baggys. Adler eventually would launch the folk-rock careers of Barry McGuire, the Mamas and the Papas, and Carole King. But he was also there at the launch of Sam Cooke's secular career. Cooke was already the matinee idol of gospel music when he scored his first rock 'n' roll hit in 1957. Adler helped Cooke get started on tiny Keen Records, with a number-one record as its first release, Cooke's "You Send Me."

Cooke became the prototype of a soul singer and a symbol of the new black capitalist, arising from the world of gospel to stardom as sort of a black Elvis. To his huge and somewhat fanatical gospel audience, he betrayed God when he began singing love songs for teenagers, and he further blasphemed when he used gospel structures, the very melodies even, to construct his pop paeans to young love. Gospel zealots believed singer Ray Charles would burn for all eternity for taking a staple of black spirituals—the call-and-response—and incorporating it as a groan-and-moan simulating sex in his 1959 hit "What'd I Say." They might've believed in God, but gospel fans weren't a forgiving crowd.

Cooke was born in Clarksdale, Mississippi, a town steeped in gospel and the blues, a down-home Julliard for generations of song-writers, guitar players, and singers. But Cooke did not stay there long. His father felt called to join the great migration as African Americans left the South in those years between world wars and headed north, where bigotry was not as overt and institutionalized. The family landed in the South Side of Chicago, a black neighbor-hood known as Bronzeville.

His father was a preacher, so Cooke was raised in the church and sang from nearly the moment of birth. He became gospel roy-alty when, in 1952 at age twenty-one, he was brought into the preeminent gospel quintet, the Soul Stirrers. He was soon the lead singer and sex symbol. He was like a perfect man assembled from parts manufactured in heaven: gorgeous smile, beautiful eyes, and a stunning voice that floated through the air like falling leaves on a blustery day.

Being a gospel star was not enough for the ambitious Cooke. During one of his Soul Stirrers tours, he was passing time in a hotel room with fellow singer Paul Foster. He leafed through a magazine and paused when he saw a picture of Harry Belafonte, then a huge recording artist with his calypso-by-way-of-Harlem hits. Nat King Cole, who'd attended the same elementary school as Cooke in Chi-cago, was another role model.

Cooke pointed at the picture of Belafonte. "I gone just as far as I can go on this side," he told Foster. "I'd like to change over and try some other field."

The Soul Stirrers were signed to Specialty Records, the home of Little Richard. Label owner Art Rupe was not opposed to Cooke switching to secular music, but he wanted the second coming of Little Richard. Richard was heading the other direction, transitioning to the ministry.

For so many African American artists raised in the church, their music reflected a struggle between the sacred and the profane. Little Richard came to believe his music was wicked and renounced Long Tall Sally and Miss Molly for a half decade while he dwelled in the spiritual world. Sam was going the other way, but in the eyes of some, committing the greater sin of adapting elements of gospel into his teenybopper tunes. (Writer David Ritz titled his book about the similar struggles of brilliant but troubled singer Marvin Gaye *Divided Soul*. That sums up the state of Sam Cooke's mind in the late fifties.)

Rupe wanted lightning to strike twice, so he sent Cooke to New Orleans to inaugurate his secular career where Bumps Blackwell had found the magic with Little Richard, but the resulting record stiffed. Sam continued to perform with the Soul Stirrers but was determined to make the move to the mainstream market. Cooke took charge of his material and sent Blackwell a tape of songs in advance of their rendezvous at Radio Recorders in Los Angeles. Earl Palmer had also relocated to L.A., hoping for more lucrative session work. Blackwell booked him for the date with Cooke.

Blackwell was convinced the smart money was on a cover of "Summertime" by George and Ira Gershwin. Unfortunately, he figured the *Porgy and Bess* showstopper would be the centerpiece of the session on June 1, 1957. But when Rupe saw that Blackwell had hired three white backing singers, he blew a gasket. He didn't want ballads. He didn't want pop. He didn't want a bunch of talentless white hacks messing with his record company. He wanted Sam Cooke to be Little Richard.

Sam Cooke wanted to be Sam Cooke and shouted back at Rupe, "If . . . that's the way you want me to record, then I quit your label." Blackwell stepped in to back up Cooke, and Rupe promptly fired him. He turned to a session hanger-on, a sort of Blackwell apprentice, wannabe songwriter, and full-time truck driver. "You're hired!" Rupe shouted at Sonny Bono, installing him as Blackwell's replacement as head of Specialty's A&R department.

Blackwell had already been looking for another deal and promptly landed with Cooke at Keen Records, a brand-new label yet to release its first 45. A wealthy manufacturer named John Siamas wanted to invest in music. He met Bob Keane, a clarinet player hoping to keep alive the hope that he could somehow make enough in the music business to sustain life. When Blackwell played them the songs he'd recorded at the tumultuous session at Radio Recorders, they flipped over an innocuous piece of fluff that Cooke had tossed off. It wasn't much of a song, just a phrase repeated in a series of swoops and swallows in Sam's blowing-leaf voice.

Blackwell thought it was a piece of shit. "I thought it was the most ridiculous song I ever heard in my life," he said. "He just kept singing, 'You send me,' and I thought he was out of his fucking mind." But there was something to it, the newly minted record executives said.

For newbies, their instincts were acute. "You Send Me" was number one on the pop and rhythm and blues charts. Sam needed the beginner's luck. He didn't even have a home and was sleeping on Blackwell's living room davenport when the record was released.

Make a little money, and all of the parties go to war. Art Rupe decided he'd been deceived by Blackwell and Cooke and began snorting and howling that he was owed a few more Sam Cooke records. Bob Keane and John Siamas began to bicker over their split of the "You Send Me" earnings, and Keane ended up leaving the label built on his name. He started Del-Fi, discovered doomed Latino rock star Ritchie Valens, and became one of the leading purveyors of surf music.

Cooke was the handsome, ever-smiling singer to the public, but there was another side to him. *Divided soul.* He did his best to screw over Art Rupe, who owned publishing rights to his songs, by copyrighting them under the names of family and other associates. "I feel he was a tragic figure," Rupe recalled. "He was arrogant, avaricious, and willing to compromise ethical behavior—qualities which possibly contributed to his untimely demise."

Sam was firmly L.A. based, but back in Chicago, he had a despondent and suicidal ex-wife and another woman who claimed to have borne his child when they were in high school. Even as a gospel star, he had gorged himself at the trough of female lust. He had a stepchild with his first wife, but when they divorced, he saw little of the boy. And when the mother was killed in a drunken one-car accident, slamming into a tree, her parents kept the boy away from Sam. He also had a daughter, Linda, with a longtime Chicago girlfriend, Barbara Campbell. One of his several paternity suits was settled out of court, but Sam was charged with "fornication and bastardy." Judging from the stories about Sam on the road, there was a good chance of other little Cookes out in the world.

Yet none of these rumors or accusations seemed to harm Sam's squeaky-clean image or his reputation as a new teen singing sensation. "Here was a guy who always stepped into a bucket of shit and came out smelling like a rose," Blackwell marveled.

Sam stepped into shit all over Los Angeles, but nothing he did on the party circuit tarnished his image. He bunked with Adler, then one of Keen's young A&R guys (though he could strum a guitar, Siamas knew bupkes about the music business), along with Herb Alpert. A typical night, Adler recalled, started with dinner at ten o'clock and included club hopping until well after sunup. Meanwhile, paternity suits began to stack up, but Cooke continued to smell like a rose. "Sam just seemed to be comfortable within himself," Adler said.

Adler and Alpert were dutiful apprentices. "Bumps was a teacher," Adler said. "He wanted you to learn. He pretty much taught us song structure."

The duo had been sticking their toes into the songwriting waters, and when Cooke heard one of their sketches, he thought it had potential. The song straddled the sacred-and-profane dilemma. Intelligence and wisdom, they wrote, had nothing to do with love. Adler and Alpert were apologetic about the song, which they felt was lame in the extreme, but at every recording session, Cooke kept bringing it up. At that point, Adler recalled, the lyrics went

> *I don't know a good book from another*
> *But I don't have to read a book to be a lover*

Sam liked the contrast of the intellectual with the emotional and thought it might be wise to develop the concept of book learning with love.

> *Don't know much about history*
> *Don't know much biology*

That was the ticket, and the Adler-Alpert-Cooke composition "Wonderful World" became an enduring standard of popular music.

As they recorded the song, Adler stood right behind Cooke, chin over his shoulder, punching the end-of-line words with his bark.

Sam kept moving on and moving up. He bought a luxurious home in Los Angeles and summoned Barbara from Chicago, inviting her to set up a household with their daughter, Linda, at the estate, a triumph of hip early sixties decor, complete with a shamrock-shaped swimming pool. Barbara was pregnant by another man, but after she had the abortion Sam insisted upon, fairy tale life began.

He changed managers, moving from Bumps Blackwell to the most notorious shark in the industry, Allen Klein. He thought it was time for a major label debut.

When Sam had moved on to Keen, Art Rupe continued to issue his recordings from the Specialty Records vault. Sam released five singles and ten albums on Keen before switching to RCA Victor in 1960. Keen continued with the recordings in its vault (including "Wonderful World"), producing singles and albums that competed with the new RCA product.

At RCA, Sam was assigned to the production team of Hugo Peretti and Luigi Creatore, the same duo that had taken on production duties for RCA's biggest star, Elvis Presley. The producers, who were cousins, had started Roulette Records in 1957 with Morris Levy, the mob-connected godfather of early rock 'n' roll. They bought out of that contract and established a production team that made records and sold them to record companies. Sam liked this idea and created a company called Tracey Limited, named after his newborn daughter with Barbara Campbell, now his wife.

Now with one of the major labels and working with a tried-and-true production team, Sam took greater interest in the business side of his career. He decided to form a record label to produce gospel music and take it to a wider audience. He named the company SAR Records—the name stood for Sam, Alex (for J. W. Alexander), and Roy (for S. R. Crain), both longtime associates from Soul Stirrer days.

As cultural historian Craig Werner wrote, "Sam Cooke shared James Brown's belief that success predicated on the goodwill of white Americans could not be trusted. That was why he went out of his way to keep his connections with his original audience." Though he was a major recording artist with significant crossover to the white audience, he was still stung by the comments from gospel fans that he had turned his back on God. Clarence Fountain of the Five Blind Boys of Alabama, a revered gospel group, told a story of Cooke pulling a wad of cash from his pocket and saying, "This is my god now!"

Cooke hoped to do penance by taking God to a mass audience.

Sam's relationships with women were always messy. He was an Adonis, and he knew it. "That man could mess up a whole room full of women," Aretha Franklin recalled. Even during the gospel days, he was always on the prowl. As his audience widened, so did his conquests. Blackwell, in his days as acting manager, had to handle collateral damage. When it came time to deal with the paternity suits, "I was the one," Blackwell said. "The only one I didn't have to pay off was Barbara because he married her." Indeed, Sam was soon the father of a third child with Barbara, a son named Vincent.

Sam wanted a family but was not sure he'd found the right mate. On the road, he continued in his randy ways, in part because he had issues with Barbara's behavior. She was also always on the lookout for a good time and frequently was stoned, which irritated her husband tremendously. Though he was a chain smoker and not averse to marijuana, he didn't indulge on the monumental scale of his wife.

Though he shared Elvis Presley's record label and producers and had appeared on the *Ed Sullivan Show* and other mainstream programs, by the early sixties, he still had not fully crossed over from the chitlin circuit to mainstream audiences. He threatened promoters with a walkout if his audience wasn't integrated, and he risked the disapproval of white fans by being a vocal proponent of civil rights.

From his gospel days, he knew the power of song to unify and to lead. He was stunned, in 1963, to hear the song "Blowin' in the Wind," which was then a pop hit for the well-scrubbed and profoundly white Peter, Paul and Mary. The song was a simple litany of questions about freedom and human rights, punctuated with the refrain that the answers to these questions were obvious, reinforcing eternal verities of justice and truth. Cooke learned that a twenty-one-year-old kid named Bob Dylan had written this masterful and mature work. He shook his head in wonderment and admiration: "A white boy writing a song like that?"

He thought such a song should have been written by a black man. He thought *he* should have written such a song. He began working on what became his masterpiece, "A Change Is Gonna Come," but he fussed with the arrangement and the edit of the song—it ran a bit long, over the semirequired three minutes for radio play—and held back its release for months.

He did, however, work "Blowin' in the Wind" into his set list.

His friendships with boxer Cassius Clay (soon to become Muhammad Ali) and the controversial Malcolm X were further risks to turning off the white crowd. But Sam did not back down or shuck and jive as earlier generations of black entertainers had to do.

He was ringside with Malcolm X for the heavyweight championship bout between Clay and the reigning champ, Sonny Liston. Clay's performance was as acrobatic as it was athletic, and his dancing made the match into a thing of beauty and wonder. When Liston did not answer the bell for the seventh round, the crowd erupted and the new champion danced, this time for joy.

At his moment of glory, surrounded in the ring by reporters and sycophants, Clay called out "Sam Cooke!" and motioned for Sam to join him in the ring. The usually natty Cooke looked bedraggled with tie and shirt askew. He worked his way to Clay's side. With his arm around his buddy, the champ proclaimed, "This is the world's greatest rock 'n' roll singer."

The Cooke home was, by outward appearances, one of domestic bliss. A stunningly beautiful couple and their three children lived in a sprawling house in suburban Los Angeles. All seemed right with the world.

Barbara was home with the children, and when they asked if they could go outside and play, she agreed. Soon she became aware of a silence. She found Tracey in her room, alone. *Where was the baby?* "Mommy, Vincent's in the pool," the little girl said. Barbara found her son at the bottom of the pool, near the rubber duck he'd been trying to retrieve. The ambulance beat Sam home, but he rushed into the house and pushed everyone aside to get to his son and perform mouth-to-mouth, to no avail.

The marriage was already on life support. Though he never accused Barbara directly, Sam felt that her lackadaisical parenting was responsible for Vincent's death. *Was she stoned? Inattentive? On the phone with one of her fancy men? Who would leave a kid that age alone?*

Barbara had been the most unmarried of wives at that time. She
came and went at her own schedule, often staying out all night. She
and Sam were more estranged roommates than partners.

That was the end of Sam Cooke as his friends knew him. Adler
said he changed profoundly. "He was not as quick with a laugh," he
recalled. "Drank more than he had previously." Earl Palmer picked
up on the same thing: Cooke was "starting to drink more than I'd
ever seen him. He was very much grief-stricken." That smile, Adler
said, that beautiful smile, was now forced, not natural.

Sam toyed with the idea of divorce and confided into his young
protégé, Bobby Womack. He did not plan to file a will, he said. "When
a woman start asking about a will, she will kill your ass," Sam said.

Womack, deeply attracted to Barbara Cooke already, told his
mentor that this was no laughing matter. As he recalled, "Sam would
say, 'If I should die before I wake, bury me deep, put two bitches on
either side of me' and he would laugh."

Though such talk made Womack uncomfortable, Cooke was
increasingly crude in the months after his son's death. He advised
Bobby to stay away from his young, adoring fans, most of whom
probably wanted to trap him with a pregnancy. "Now you get you
a high hooker," Sam advised. "You can give her five hundred bucks
and she gone. I'm telling you, man, it save you a lot of grief."

On December 10, 1964, Sam fought with Barbara. He planned to
go out for the evening, and so did she. He asked her to stay home
with the kids for once.

She shot back. *Why don't* you *stay home?* Then the screaming began.

Sam planned to stop off at a bar with friends before meeting J.
W. Alexander and his party at the California Club. Martoni's, just off
Sunset Boulevard, was one of his regular hangouts. He was buzzed and
comfortable, leading the crowd in an impromptu sing-along, including
Lead Belly's "Cotton Fields." Four or five martinis deep in the evening,
Cooke was making the rounds of his fellow drinkers and kept finding
himself drawn to a coffee-with-cream young woman named Elisa Boyer.

At two in the morning, Boyer asked for a ride home. Cooke
escorted her to his red Ferrari and poured himself behind the wheel.
Instead of taking her home, Sam steered the car to Santa Monica
Boulevard. He turned to Boyer. "I'm mad about you, Baby," he said.
"You're a lovely girl, you know that?"

He took her to the Hacienda Motel in south L.A. While she waited in the car, he negotiated with the clerk behind bars of the after-hours window. He got the room key and took Boyer by the hand, leading her into the room. "We're just going to talk," he said, but he quickly pinned her on the bed.

Sam pulled off her sweater, then ripped off her dress. He began taking off his clothes and slipped into the bathroom.

"I knew that he was going to rape me," Boyer said.

While he was in the bathroom, Boyer grabbed her clothes and ran to the manager's office. She beat on the door, but there was no answer for the panicked woman, so she ran around the corner and dressed quickly. That was when she realized she had picked up Sam's clothes as well.

Cooke came out of the bathroom, furious. When Boyer had grabbed his clothes, she'd taken his wallet, fat with money. He went to the after-hours window and yelled until manager Bertha Franklin appeared.

"Is the girl there?" Sam demanded.

"I didn't see no girl." She could see Sam from the waist up only. So far as she could tell, he was wearing only an overcoat.

Sam demanded to be let in, to search the manager's room. Franklin refused and threatened to call police.

Sam began banging on her door and quickly knocked it off its hinges. He rushed past Franklin and into her apartment's kitchen. He came back in the room and accused her of hiding the girl, and they began to fight, rolling on the floor. She bit him, and when he recoiled, she got up and grabbed her handgun off her television set.

She turned, firing three shots point-blank.

"Lady," Sam said in wonderment, "you shot me."

There were two memorial services. For the first one, the body was flown home to Chicago. Sam Cooke lay in state at Leak and Sons Funeral Home. Two-hundred thousand fans lined up to view his body. The body was returned to California at Forest Lawn Memorial Park cemetery in Glendale. Ray Charles sang at the service.

Cooke's last song—the song he wrote in response to Bob Dylan's "Blowin' in the Wind"—was "A Change Is Gonna Come." Twelve days after his death, RCA released the single. It rose to number nine on *Billboard*'s rhythm and blues charts and became an anthem of the civil rights movement.

7

THE BEAUTIFUL FUTURE

I love to be alone. I never found the companion that
was so companionable as solitude.

—Henry David Thoreau

They met at Pandora's Box, a small club on the Sunset Strip, in
November 1962. The Beach Boys released their first album only the
month before. The band had a weeklong engagement at the booze-free
teen cabaret, and Gary Usher showed up with his girlfriend, Ginger
Blake, and two of the Rovell sisters—moody seventeen-year-old Diane
and fifteen-year-old firecracker Marilyn. The girls, sisters and cousins,
were a singing group.

Gary and the girls sat down front, and during the first set, Brian's
fingers fumbled over the bass. He was visibly nervous. It was the girls.
Something about them drew him in. On a break, he stepped down
from the stage to say hello to Gary and smiled at Marilyn. *May I have
a sip of your hot chocolate?* He didn't know what else to say. Passing
it back to her, he spilled it on her legs, burning her. Impressed by
his suavity, Marilyn became friends with Brian, and, within eighteen
months, they were husband and wife.

Brian was twenty-one and Marilyn fifteen, and theirs became an
Elvis and Priscilla type of romance.

When the king of rock 'n' roll was drafted in 1958, Private Presley was
stationed in Germany, where he met Priscilla Beaulieu, fourteen-year-
old stepdaughter of air force captain Paul Beaulieu. Somehow, Presley
was able to convince Captain Beaulieu to sanction a relationship

between his sweet and innocent daughter and the symbol of youth rebellion.

With Presley out of the service and back in the States, Miss Beaulieu moved into Graceland, the king's Memphis home, and lived there until making the relationship legal in 1967. Nine months to the day after the wedding, they had a baby. Mr. and Mrs. Presley were never intimate again after their daughter's birth. "He had mentioned before we were married that he had never been able to make love to a woman who'd had a child," Priscilla recalled. He kept his word. As Presley biographer Joel Williamson wrote, "She tried everything, including a black negligee and cuddling up to him in bed, but her best efforts only ended in her own humiliation."

But at least Elvis didn't have to choose between sisters, as Brian Wilson did. In addition to Diane and Marilyn Rovell, there was a third sister, Barbara, who stayed home from Pandora's Box that first night. When Brian finally saw them all together, he couldn't decide which one he liked most. They were all beautiful, but perhaps Barbara, at fourteen, was the one who most gave him the tingles.

Luckily, Irving and Mae Rovell, the parents, were immediately drawn to Brian. Though confident in his talent, he was still shy and awkward, and the Rovell home became his refuge. The Rovells were the boisterous and affectionate family Brian always wanted. No matter when Brian showed up at their house in the Fairfax neighborhood of Los Angeles, Mae fixed him something to eat.

The Rovells were Jewish, and so Brian's palate was introduced to matzah ball soup, gefilte fish, and Manischewitz. At first, he was just a friend and music mentor to the Rovell sisters, so the parents had no problem letting him crash on the sofa and, eventually, share a bedroom with the two youngest girls. (Barbara and Marilyn slept in one twin bed, Brian in the other.)

As 1963 dawned, the Beach Boys were beginning to find their popularity, and the Rovell home became the group's clubhouse. Mike was (unhappily) married, but Brian, Carl, David, and, to a lesser extent, Dennis, made themselves at home, taking most of their meals at the Rovell table. Irving worked long hours, and though the nocturnal schedule of musicians didn't align with the rest of the working world, he was game. Soon others in the Beach Boys' universe began hanging out, including Gary Usher.

Murry hated the air Gary breathed, but at the Rovells', Gary could sit and sup and spend time with Brian.

Marilyn was besotted with Carl Wilson, closest to her in age. It was assumed since Diane was the eldest that she was the one for Brian. He was attracted to all of them, but at first Brian was simply grateful for having some place to go without his father in it.

Brian rented an apartment with his pal Bob Norberg, but Dennis and Carl still had the 119th Street home as their official residence, though all they did there was sleep. They lived on the road, in the studio, and at the Rovell dining table. Murry Wilson steamed. Audree Wilson was hurt, the injured bystander in the war between a father and his sons.

It wasn't that Murry didn't have his uses. As Brian began to assert himself more in the studio during the recording of the *Surfin' USA* album, he grew more embarrassed with his father's constant interference. Murry was like a demented cheerleader, always exhorting his boys to fight for success, to try harder, to grow up and be men.

But Brian also chafed at the nominal authority of Nick Venet in the studio and asked his father to carry water for him by getting the Capitol brass to get rid of Venet and hand production reins to Brian.

"Dad," Brian asked, "will you go down there and tell Capitol we don't want him anymore?"

Murry was happy to do so, seeing himself as the successor of Venet's authority in the studio. He confronted Capitol vice president Voyle Gilmore.

"You folks don't know how to produce a rock 'n' roll hit in your studios," Murry said. "Leave us alone and we'll make hits for you."

The record executive went red in the face. Gilmore loathed Murry, but since the man's sons were becoming increasingly popular in the summer of 1963—now their ballad "Surfer Girl" was a hit and the B-side, "Little Deuce Coupe," was also in the Top Twenty—he was disposed to keep him happy. Venet was a busy producer, and though he cared deeply for Brian, he took the reassignment with grace. Plus, Murry Wilson was no longer part of his life.

By this point, Brian knew Jan and Dean and the wonders of the Wrecking Crew. He was brother to Carl and Dennis and cousin to Mike, but when he was in the studio, he was a hard-driving producer. He expected the best from the band, and when they didn't deliver, he was on their collective ass and told them to do better. Like father, like son—he could be a tyrant, albeit a younger and not openly violent one.

Brian wanted the best, so he began using the Wrecking Crew on selected recordings and tried out other studios, including Western

Recorders and Gold Star. He also worked outside the group. He talked Marilyn and Diane Rovell and their cousin Ginger Blake into becoming a girl surf group called the Honeys, a name drawn from a reference in "Surfin' Safari."

> *Early in the morning we'll be starting out*
> *Some honeys will be coming along*

With Brian behind the glass and Hal Blaine on drums, Glen Campbell on guitar, and Leon Russell on piano, the Honeys recorded several songs—a surfing rewrite of Stephen Foster's "Swanee River," another surf song called "Shoot the Curl," and a piece called "Raindrops." They all bombed.

But Brian was so enamored of the studio that he began to withdraw from the road. By late April 1963, he felt so overwhelmed by studio obligations that he began to skip concert dates. He called Al Jardine, who was beginning to wish he'd never left the group. Jardine's clear, near-perfect voice would be an excellent replacement on tour.

"I don't want to tour," Brian told the group. "I want to stay at home and make music."

As Carl explained years later, "My dad was so upset at the time. He felt it wasn't fair for him not to go and play for the people, because they had bought the records and wanted to see him."

Brian made hit-and-miss appearances on that spring tour. He saw all the travel between gigs, much of it squished in a station wagon with equipment and flatulent band members, as nothing more than a waste of his valuable time. So the lineup for many of those spring 1963 shows was with Carl and David Marks on guitars, Al on bass, Dennis on drums, and Mike Love as Mike Love—lead singer, stand-up comic, and master of ceremonies.

At home, Brian worked on material for the third Beach Boys album. Firmly in control, he experimented with string arrangements, double-tracked vocals, and elements drawn from classical music, including a breathtaking workout on piano based on Rimsky-Korsakov's "Flight of the Bumblebee." Cousin Maureen Love, Mike's sister, was brought in to play harp on "In My Room" and "Catch a Wave."

By midsummer, the band began another tour, this time of the Great Plains and the Midwest, but again Brian missed several dates in order to stay home and tinker in the studio. Al Jardine again took over on bass and falsetto vocals. Kids in the crowds never knew the difference.

During that tour, Jan and Dean's recording of "Surf City" made it to number one on the *Billboard* charts, infuriating Murry Wilson. He ordered Brian to stop working with Jan Berry and was maddened that Brian had given away such a huge hit.

Brian shrugged it off. "I was proud of the fact that another group had a number-one song with a track that I had written and that this would give me, a young songwriter, just that much more credibility. But dad would hear none of it."

However, once the double whammy of "Surfer Girl" (number seven) and "Little Deuce Coupe" (number five) took over radio in the late summer of 1963, Murry Wilson figured he probably wouldn't have to wait very long for the Beach Boys to hit the top of the charts. Brian was on a roll.

He was also proving to be a relentless taskmaster in the studio. "Sessions on the *Surfer Girl* album lasted nine and ten hours, unheard of periods of time," Brian said. "I let perfectionism born out of my desperate need to be validated and loved, guide me. My reputation as a tyrant spread fast."

He was like a drill sergeant when it came to the vocal arrangements. "Everyone sensed their part," Carl said. "When Brian would present a song to us, we would almost know what our part would be. Michael always sang the bottom; I would sing the one above that, then would come Dennis or Alan, and then Brian on top. We had a feeling for it. It's not widely known, but Michael had a hand in a lot of the arrangements. He would bring out the funkier approaches, whether to go *shoo-boo-bop* or *bom-bom-did-di-did-did*. It makes a big difference, because it can change the whole rhythm, the whole color and tone of it. We're big *oooh*-ers; we love to oooh. It's a big, full sound, that's very pleasing to us; it opens up the heart."

The *Surfer Girl* album, the first to bear the "Produced by BRIAN WILSON" credit, reached number four on the *Billboard* album charts. Three weeks later, Capitol released *Little Deuce Coupe*, with four songs from earlier albums, yet the public didn't mind. The album also peaked at number four. The songs all referenced cars, with the exception of the group's single for the fall, "Be True to Your School." This paean to academic fidelity reached number six in the late fall, and the single version—vastly different from the one on the *Little Deuce Coupe* album—featured the Honeys as cheerleaders and a demented calliope playing "On, Wisconsin!" as the bridge. Not long afterward, Brian reconfigured "Little Deuce Coupe" as a Christmas song called "Little Saint Nick." It got to number three.

Brian's roll continued. By the time the *Little Deuce Coupe* album was nearing its peak, David Marks was no longer a Beach Boy, having reached the mutual blowout point with Murry Wilson. Al Jardine was back in the group full time, but Marks's departure left a hole. So Brian could no longer afford the luxury of skipping concerts.

Concerts were one thing; the time on the road and the time away from writing and from the studio were something else. The other guys in the group began buying cars. Mike was married with a child. Everyone was spending money, and the whole economic engine depended on Brian, who seemed tuned into the cosmic muse. He was providing the soundtrack for the tanned California kids on the New Frontier. The world was on the verge of falling apart, but the music of the Beach Boys provided a veneer that made everything seem young and impossibly beautiful.

By the fall of 1963, the group's popularity moved well beyond the regional level, where it was expected to stall with the surf crowd. But by bequeathing ocean life to *everybody*, the Beach Boys now had rabid listeners not only across the country but also on the other side of the planet. Brian consciously tried to court the landlocked audience, first with the ballad "Farmer's Daughter" on *Surfin' USA* and then "Back Home," about heading back to Ohio for the summer, which he recorded but did not use on *Surfer Girl*. (It eventually showed up on a 1976 album.) Soon Brian had learned he didn't need to pander to flyover audiences. They loved songs about surfing and cars and girls, and he was encouraged to continue to enumerate the virtues of all of the above.

The group was scheduled to play Marysville, California, the night of November 22, 1963. Concert promoter Fred Vail, a kid the same age as the Beach Boys, was destined to become a lifelong friend of the band, and this was their first gig together. Vail listened to the radio that morning to be sure the advertising time he bought for the show was being used. And then the bulletin came.

When he learned that President Kennedy had been assassinated in Dallas, Vail was stunned, like everyone else. But once he regained his wits, he realized he had the Marysville Memorial Auditorium booked that evening and figured a couple thousand teenagers might be gravely disappointed if the Beach Boys didn't show. Vail called Murry Wilson.

"Our president is dead and our country is in turmoil," Murry told him. "We can't come now."

Vail urged Murry not to make a final decision until he had time to sniff around Marysville. Vail called disc jockeys and city officials and tried to gauge whether it would be considered disrespectful to go ahead with a rock 'n' roll concert. The target audience, high school kids, had been sent home early from school, and the radio stations had been deluged with calls about the concert. Ticket sales had actually picked up.

So Vail called Murry and talked him into getting on the rented prop plane. No one's heart seemed to be in the idea of performing, but when the band saw the full auditorium, they began to think they might provide catharsis for the grief-stunned kids. As the group readied itself backstage, the crowd stomped its feet in anticipation.

Vail parted the curtain and walked to the microphone. "It was a tragedy in America today," he told the crowd. "We lost our president, and before we bring out the Beach Boys, I think we should have a moment of silence in honor of the president."

The crowd stilled. Vail was amazed how the throng quieted so quickly. He began to wonder how long was appropriate for a moment of silence. Then he was hit by a towel thrown from the parted curtain, Mike Love's way of saying it was time to get started.

The show was a huge success. The group retreated to the hotel afterward, divided up the money, which was good—the show had set an attendance record—and sat around the room, drinking beer and discussing the day's events.

The pressure to produce never went away. Filled with emotion and a vague sense of spirituality, Brian asked Mike if he wanted to work on a song. The idea was to produce something positive amid loss. Though Brian was overwhelmed by grief, the song did not deal with the president's death. He and Mike focused their music and lyrics on the loss of love. Despite the broken heart, the words spoke of the endurance of hope:

> *Still I have the warmth of the sun*
> *Within me tonight*

"The Warmth of the Sun" became one of the group's most enduring ballads and showed Brian's uncanny capability to discover music in unlikely places.

By the beginning of 1964, the Beach Boys had a good track record of hits, four albums on a major label, and a steady foothold in a business built on sand. Brian Wilson was twenty-two, still suffering anxiety over writing songs, and producing records to help his family maintain its livelihood.

He was out of his hell house, nominally sharing an apartment with Bob Norberg, but spending most of his time with the Rovells. He saw his father primarily at recording sessions, which Murry insisted on attending. Murry was nothing but in the way. To humor him, Chuck Britz, the engineer at Western Recorders, built a special mixing board for him—it was not plugged in. Murry was not in on the joke and assumed that the dials he twirled had some effect on the way the music was being recorded.

Brian was eager to get started and spent New Year's Day recording a song he was sure would be the group's first number-one single: "Fun, Fun, Fun." It told the story of a girl who lied to her father about where she was when she was out cruising in her Thunderbird. She told Pop she was studying, but she was hanging out at a hamburger stand, much like the Foster Freeze in Hawthorne. Both Mike and Dennis would claim the experience that inspired the song. Some stories suggest that Dennis, who was having a secret dalliance with a girl, supplied the hook line, "We'll have fun, fun, fun until her daddy takes her T-Bird away." (For years, the song was credited solely to Brian Wilson, but Mike Love contested this in a lawsuit—saying Murry, as manager of Sea of Tunes music publishing, cut him out of the credit for this and several other Beach Boys songs. He eventually won the case.)

"I suggested that we write a song about a girl who borrows her dad's car and goes cruising, rather than to the library, 'like she told her old man, now,'" Mike said. "I came up with the concept and the lyrics, and Brian went in and recorded the track. And I even told him, it's got to start like a Chuck Berry song with a guitar lead intro, which Carl Wilson supplied." Whatever the case, Murry Wilson thought the song was immoral because it didn't provide stern consequences for lying. The group brushed him off.

During the January 1 recording session, Murry scowled and chomped on his pipe, critical of nearly everything he heard the group playing. He squawked instructions through his talkback mic and twirled knobs on his faux control board.

Brian began working members of the Wrecking Crew into sessions, and both Dennis Wilson and Hal Blaine are credited on "Fun, Fun, Fun," though who played what is still in dispute. Hal said Dennis was never threatened by his presence. He was happy if Hal did a tracking session, because that gave Dennis more time to run around with girls. In addition, Brian used Ray Pohlman on bass and two sax players—Steve Douglas, Phil Spector's Fairfax High classmate, and Jay Migliori.

As they began the session, Mike Love began singing "Fun, Fun, Fun" as if it was a Depression-era relic of the Delta Blues, but once the Chuck Berry–derived riff barked from Carl Wilson's amp, the song took its familiar shape.

When the group finished with "Fun, Fun, Fun," they immediately switched gears and recorded the lush "Warmth of the Sun."

A week later, Brian gathered the Wrecking Crew on Spector's home turf, Gold Star, and cut the track for a cover of the rock 'n' roll chestnut, "Why Do Fools Fall in Love?". If a style could be trademarked, Phil Spector could have sued for infringement. This cover was Brian's best Spector impersonation to date and featured wall of sound loyalists Blaine, Pohlman, Douglas, Leon Russell, Al De Lory, Bill Pitman, Tommy Tedesco, and Plas Johnson. The group recorded its vocals the next day.

Within a week, the Beach Boys left on their first foreign tour—to Australia and New Zealand, where their songs had resonated with the significant surfing culture down under. The day after their return to the States, the double-sided single ("Fun, Fun, Fun" backed with "Why Do Fools Fall in Love?") was released and would climb to the relatively disappointing (to Brian, anyway) number-five spot on the *Billboard* charts.

But by that time, the beginning of February, the Beach Boys had other things to worry about.

The Beatles came together in Liverpool, England, in 1957. John Lennon, a witty but reckless amateur with a skiffle group, met Paul McCartney, another teenager with musical ambition but one who took himself and his work more seriously. Lennon realized that if he asked McCartney to join his group, he would be able to control him rather than have a talented rival. They formed a professional partnership while still teenagers. A year later, McCartney brought a younger boy, George Harrison, into the group. Harrison was a guitar prodigy by Lennon's standards. Thus was the nucleus of the Beatles formed.

Five years later, the group—completed now by Ringo Starr on drums—had risen from playing strip clubs and sleeping in porno theaters to the top of the charts in Great Britain.

British acts rarely translated for an American audience. In England, the Beatles were signed to Parlophone, a small label whose corporate parent was EMI Music, which also owned the formerly independent American label, Capitol. The arrangement gave Capitol first refusal on EMI's musical product, and the company passed. Beatles singles were released in America in 1963 on two small independent labels, Tollie and Swan. Chicago's Vee-Jay, a rhythm and blues label, released an album called *Introducing the Beatles* in mid-1963. All releases stiffed.

By the beginning of 1964, things had changed. National gloom following the president's assassination called for comic relief. The Beatles were hirsute, funny boys created to lift the American public. Capitol Records was stunned by the response to "I Want to Hold Your Hand," a British single played on a Washington, DC, radio station. A flight attendant dating a DC disc jockey brought him the record, which he played on the air even though the product was not available in the States. Reaction was immediate, and Capitol quickly developed second thoughts about the Beatles and began releasing the group's music.

By late January, when their Capitol debut *Meet the Beatles* was released, the group was scheduled for the *Ed Sullivan Show*, and soon the Beatles dominated the charts. Within a couple of months, the Top Five records on the Billboard charts were all singles by the Beatles.

"What I saw impressed the hell out of me," Brian said of the Beatles. "They looked sharp, especially compared to the silly, juvenile striped shirts and white pants the Beach Boys wore onstage. I suddenly felt unhip."

Brian and Mike, at one time inseparable and successful as a song-writing team, began to grow apart. Mike thought the Beach Boys had a good thing going, and he didn't want anything to change. Brian, however, had been deeply affected by the arrival of the Beatles. They had upped the ante of rock 'n' roll records. They also scared the shit out of the Beach Boys.

On February 10, 1964, the day after the Beatles' first appearance on the *Ed Sullivan Show*, Brian and Mike met at an L.A. coffee shop.

"Did you see the Beatles last night?" Brian asked.

Mike nodded. He saw the arrival of the British group as a declaration of war. "Both of us saw them as a threat," Brian said.

"I want to toss the album," Brian said of *Shut Down, Volume 2*, the Beach Boys' work in progress. Suddenly everything he'd done seemed so juvenile. "We'll start over and put out better songs."

"The songs are fine," Mike insisted. "They fit into the Beach Boys' formula."

"That's the point," Brian spat. "We've got to grow, go beyond the formula."

"Brian, if you throw away the album, you're throwing away money in the bank," Mike argued. "The songs have worked so far. They'll keep on working as long as we don't screw with the formula."

"You don't get it, do you, Mike?"

Early January 1964. The Beach Boys were about to embark on a tour of Australia. While waiting in the departure lounge of Los Angeles International with their friends and family, Mike began teasing Brian about all the fun they would be having overseas. *Wink, wink.* Brian picked up on it, but nearby, young Marilyn took offense. Finally, she said, "I hope you guys have a good time because I'm going to have a good time too."

Her comment stung. It was time to get on the plane. While the plane taxied down the runway and prepared for departure, Brian grabbed a stewardess and asked to get off the plane. No way, she said, but she saw the crazy in his eyes and got the captain to call the tower and get a cryptic wire sent from the nervous young man. The telegram was a desperate plea to Marilyn: *Go home and await my call.*

The flight across the Pacific was torture, and as soon as the plane landed, Brian ran to a phone booth and called Marilyn. It was the wee hours back in California, but Irving Rovell woke his middle daughter and put her on the phone.

"I need you so badly," Brian sobbed. "I never want to lose you."

Marilyn recalled Brian precrackup.

> Before he got messed up, he was really pretty funny and a lot of fun. He would do crazy things, like drive a motorcycle into Gold Star studios. And he got away with mostly everything he did, because everybody loved him. He really made people laugh. He was very funny. That's one of the things that attracted me to him. He was also really gorgeous. He had a great body, great hands, great hair; he used to get it done at Sebring.
>
> Brian commands attention, just naturally, because he knows how to get it and he likes it. He gets people to do what he wants, and he liked to have a lot of swimming parties. So when we got the Laurel Way house, it didn't have a yard so we had a pool dug. We would have night parties, and everybody would come and swim. He liked people to get excited about having fun. He liked to do fun things. He was always unpredictable, and you had to go with it.

For his part, Brian saw Marilyn as "the most solicitous of the sisters." Though he would have a complicated and long-lasting personal and professional relationship with Diane Rovell, when it came time for him to make a decision, he chose Marilyn, "the most practical, the most willing to mother me. Marilyn had a warmth the others didn't, and when my soul needed unburdening, I sought her out."

Brian realized he needed someone to help him navigate the world. He'd begun to hear voices—screams, mostly—and he had no control over when and where they would begin. But his head, once so full of beautiful music, was now a cauldron of fear and doubt.

The backing tracks were becoming more complex. If Brian was being held back from changing the "formula" of songs about girls and cars and school and sunshine, the least he could do was change the music.

Mike Love's lyrics for "I Get Around" were full of swagger and male bonding and the frenetic impatience of youth. As Brian wrote in the liner notes to the album they were recording in the spring of 1964, "A sociologist might say I am trying to generate a feeling of social superiority." Yet it was the music that occupied Brian. Beyond the general idea of a song, he was content to let Mike Love exercise his brand of macho in the lyrics.

The backing track for "I Get Around" was a major step forward for Brian and his work with the Wrecking Crew. Both Glen Campbell and Ray Pohlman, on electric six-string basses, played with the intensity of a guitar-cutting contest. Al Jardine also played bass, while Dennis Wilson and Hal Blaine handled the percussion and Carl Wilson provided lead guitar. The sound was rounded out with Brian on a Hammond organ and two saxophone players.

It was a dynamic, superbly played track, sophisticated in its arrangement and performing. Yet it was paired with lyrics about being "bugged driving up and down this same old strip."

Murry Wilson was in the studio and didn't think the track was good enough. Brian called a break and took the band—no Murry—to Denny's for an executive board meeting with cheeseburgers. "Something has to give," Mike said. "The problem is Murry. He's getting in the way of our productivity."

In addition to pushing his boys—his eldest son, especially—in the studio, Murry was a dictator on the road, fining the band (mostly Mike and Dennis) for their swearing and drinking. Mike was over twenty-one, and it chapped him royally that Murry treated him like a child.

As the group talked, they vented about their dictatorial manager/father/uncle who no longer served a purpose. Brian was in charge. Murry was nothing beyond a herculean pain in the ass.

"He has a goddam opinion about everything," Dennis complained, "from where we shit to who we fuck."

"Something has to give," Mike said again.

Back at Western Recorders, Murry began berating Brian, telling him that his arrangement for "I Get Around" was terrible.

"I disagree," Brian said.

Murry shoved Brian, who pushed back. "I'm the producer now," Brian said, "and I don't want you telling me what to do."

Murry shot back, "Remember who you're talking to."

"I know who I'm talking to," Brian screamed. "Tell me what you have done that makes you such an authority."

Brian recalled that his brothers stood by, stunned mute by finally seeing the argument they'd always imagined (and secretly wished for) playing out.

"Something in me snapped," Brian recalled. "I couldn't take any more of his abuse." He screamed it into his father's face. "You're fired! Dad, you're fired. You're fired as manager of the Beach Boys."

Murry stood there a moment, then quietly left the studio. Brian recalled that his father spent most of the next month in bed, incapacitated by depression. Murry also separated from Audree.

Brian finished laying the vocals and hand claps on "I Get Around." By midsummer, it was the number-one song in the country, knocking the Beatles from their perch on the top of the charts.

Obviously there was life after surf music. Jan Berry followed Brian's lead, feeling there was something magical about him. Brian was plugged into something cosmic. His instincts for music and for the marketplace were acute.

Jan studied Brian, watching how he worked. Brian wasn't particularly verbal, so he had to act out what he wanted. Cueing the musicians, he'd offer vague but nonetheless compelling instructions: "OK now, hard and strong all the way!"

Jan tried to hone in on Brian's thought processes and analyze his decision making about musical and vocal arrangements. He and Dean still wore their striped surfer shirts and served as the clown princes of surf music, but Jan began pushing to expand the duo's range and subject matter.

"Surf City" and "Honolulu Lulu" were falling through the lower depths of the chart when he came up with "Drag City," with the help of Brian and his frequent writing partner Roger Christian. "Drag City" was another Top Ten hit and Jan quickly assembled an album of car songs. "Dead Man's Curve" was tucked in at the end of the album's first side, but Jan thought he hadn't gotten the recording quite right.

Jan rerecorded "Dead Man's Curve," adding sound effects of crashing and screeching tires, and gathering a whole chorus of mournful backing vocalists. It was released as a single, backed with "New Girl in School."

> *I got it bad for the new girl in school*
> *The guys are flippin' but I'm playin' it cool*

Jan wrote the song with Brian and Brian's roommate, Bob Norberg, and floated it to the Liberty Records brass under the title "Gonna Hustle You." The record label thought the song was too suggestive and demanded changes. Jan went to collaborator Roger Christian to try to clean up the lyrics.

Jan's productions were nearly as elaborate as Brian's. "Dead Man's Curve" began with honking brass fanfare and an outrageous echo on the voices. It was a straight narrative by Jan, Brian, Roger, and Artie Kornfeld. The song needed four writers to tell its story about an impromptu drag race down Sunset Boulevard, our narrator (Jan) in his Corvette Stingray being challenged by some clown in a Jaguar XKE.

Those intimate with Sunset Boulevard and its geography knew that Berry and Christian had messed with the actual landscape, but it didn't seem to matter, especially to fans in the heartland. The song pinpointed the drag race challenge occurring at Sunset and Vine, but the closest thing to a serious curve was way to the west, where Sunset scooped south into the UCLA campus.

There had been a serious accident there a few years earlier: Mel Blanc, the great voice actor behind Bugs Bunny and Daffy Duck and scores of other cartoon characters, was driving west on Sunset in his customized Aston Martin when he came to the wide turn. An eighteen-year-old college student named Arthur Rolston was in the opposite lane, but when he hit the curve, he lost control and drove right into Blanc's sports car.

Rolston suffered only minor knee injuries. Blanc was another story. "I broke just about everything a guy can break in that wreck," he told reporter Vernon Scott. "I fractured bones in my spine, arm, legs, chest, and even my head. One of the firemen who extricated me from the car said he could have put me in a sack. But I don't remember much about it."

Blanc was in a coma for two weeks but recovered and went on to supply the voice for sidekick Barney Rubble on the first animated prime-time television series, *The Flintstones*. He soon felt well enough to sue Rolston and the City of Los Angeles, which he claimed was

negligent in its design of the curve and for not changing it despite
its well-documented dangers. Six fatalities in the previous year had
been blamed on the curve, so it was a natural for Jan and Dean to
construct a story-song about the fabled site of L.A. danger.

As a disc jockey, Roger Christian admired Mel Blanc, the so-called
man of a thousand voices, and the story of Blanc's wreck caught Christian's interest. Christian took the song idea to Jan Berry. "I thought
someone ought to write a song about Dead Man's Curve," Christian
said. "I said, 'Well, we ought to make it into a race,' because Jan and
I were really into racing. Every Saturday night we'd meet and go to
Sunset and Vine . . . and we'd race. I had a Jaguar XKE, and Jan
had a Stingray—the same cars that are in the song."

That's the way Roger Christian told the story. Artie Kornfeld, then
nineteen, had a different version of events that began with him sitting
with Brian Wilson at the piano. "I always envied Jan's Corvette,"
Kornfeld said. As Brian played on the piano, "I sang to Brian's chords,
'I was crusin' in my Stingray late one night and an XKE pulled upon
the right . . .' Brian repeated what I wrote down with the melody and
I almost finished the lyric in about thirty minutes."

Dean Torrence, who did not have a hand in writing the song,
said that Kornfeld's contribution was at least the equal of Christian's.

Whatever the case, Jan and Dean were hot. After "Surf City" and
"Drag City," they scored the double-sided hit "Dead Man's Curve"
(which rose to number eight) and "New Girl in School." They stayed
on familiar turf for "The Little Old Lady from Pasadena," a Berry and
Christian collaboration with Don Altfeld that rose to number three.
They had their last surfing hit with "Ride the Wild Surf," the title
song of the film of the same name, then scored with the first song
about skateboarding, "Sidewalk Surfin'." Jan had wanted to write
about what was thought to be the new fad, which offered a modicum
of surfing pleasure to those who were landlocked. Unable to come
up with anything satisfactory, he asked Brian Wilson if he could use
the melody of the Beach Boys' "Catch a Wave." Roger Christian
provided the lyrics, and Jan and Dean had another hit.

Life was good if you were Jan and Dean. On television, they
looked cool and confident and performed with a wink and a nod, as
if to say, *This isn't our day job.* They were both still living with their
parents, allowing them to spend their money on fast cars and spoil-
ing their girlfriends. Dean was dating Jackie Miller, and Jan was still
dating Jill Gibson, his girlfriend of six years. Jan and Jill had a few

dates when they were classmates back at University High but began dating seriously around the time Jan and Dean recorded "We Go Together." When Jan and Dean became successful, Jan suggested Jill form a female version of the duo with Dean's girlfriend at the time, Judy Lovejoy. The duo went nowhere, but Gibson stayed in the music business as a backing singer and songwriter. She also worked as a model and studied art at UCLA.

The waves were breaking toward infinity for the golden duo. Crooner Dean Martin had them on the inaugural year of his NBC television variety show. Martin was a member of the easy-listening music establishment, rubbing shoulders with musical pals Sammy Davis Jr. and Frank Sinatra, whose hated of rock 'n' roll was on the record. Martin himself was condescending and rude when introducing the Rolling Stones to an American audience when he hosted *The Hollywood Palace* on ABC.

By the time Martin brought Jan and Dean on his television show, things had changed. For one thing, Martin's beloved son Dino had become a successful rock 'n' roll star with Dino, Desi and Billy. The group scored a Top Twenty hit with "I'm a Fool," and appeared on *Shindig!* and *Hullabaloo*, the major rock 'n' roll television programs, as well as *The Dean Martin Show*. (Desi was another son of Hollywood—the offspring of Desi Arnaz and Lucille Ball; Billy Hinsche, a school pal, later became a Beach Boy in-law when his sister married Carl Wilson.)

So the disdain Dean Martin showed in introducing the Rolling Stones was absent when he welcomed Jan and Dean. "Here's a couple of fellows I think you'll really enjoy," Martin said. "They manage to make some hit records while they're still in college. Dean is majoring in art at USC and Jan is a sophomore at the UCLA medical school. As a matter of fact, Jan is interning right now. He treats the casualties on *Hullabaloo*."

It was hard to not be charmed by Jan and Dean, and Dean Martin obviously liked them. Francis Albert Sinatra, however, was unmoved.

8

THE RANSOM OF JUNIOR SINATRA

[It is] the most brutal, ugly, degenerate, vicious form of expression it has been my displeasure to hear—naturally I refer to the bulk of rock 'n' roll.

—Frank Sinatra

Frank Sinatra was a rock 'n' roll star before there was rock 'n' roll. The Chairman of the Board would bristle at that description, but he provided a working model for rock 'n' roll stars. He was a magnetic presence behind a microphone, with a voice at once so electric and sensual that women screamed, then fell weak in the knees. A decade later, Elvis drove the women wild. And then the Beatles a decade after that. But Sinatra was first.

He loved music and began singing for tips while still in single digits in the early twenties, growing up in Hoboken, New Jersey. He lasted a little over a month in high school before expulsion. In the parlance of the time, he was a hood. As a young man, he was arrested for seduction, for "having sexual intercourse with a single female who was formerly in good repute," something apparently against the law at the time.

His strong-willed mother, Dolly, pushed him into show business as a way to keep him out of trouble. She approached the members of a local singing trio and talked them into becoming a quartet, with the addition of her son. Thus was the Hoboken Four born. The group earned moderate fame after winning the talent contest on the popular radio show *Major Bowes' Amateur Hour*, giving Sinatra his first national exposure. But after the short tour that was the first prize, Sinatra left the group for another gig his mother had arranged. She got him a steady fifteen dollars a week as a singing waiter, with no travel.

A couple years later, bandleader Harry James heard Frank and asked him to front his band. A year after that, megapopular Tommy Dorsey wanted Sinatra for *his* band. James, realizing it would be a great break for the skinny kid to sign on with the swingingest band in the country, released Sinatra from his contract. The rest of his life, Sinatra said nothing would have come of his singing if not for the generosity of Harry James.

Turns out Sinatra didn't like Dorsey and particularly didn't like the onerous contract he'd signed with the bandleader, which awarded Dorsey a percentage of Sinatra's earnings . . . *for life*.

Eventually Dorsey released Sinatra from their business arrangement, but not without rumors swirling about the big hand of the Mafia making Dorsey an offer he couldn't refuse. Though the tales were regularly denied, the stories of Frank's friendships with organized crime figures were widespread. (Later, the bestselling novel *The Godfather* imprinted the story in the public mind as some sort of gospel. A Dorsey-like figure is told to release his young singer from his personal services contract. If not, "either his signature or his brains would rest on that document in exactly one minute.")

Freed, Frank emerged by the early forties as the preferred singer of American teenage girls. While their brothers and boyfriends were fighting evil in Europe and the Pacific, skinny Sinatra with his half-mast eyelids and frail, swaying body was melting their hearts. Though he did not serve in the military, when he started his Hollywood career, he played a sailor in *Anchors Aweigh*, the first of three popular musical films with Gene Kelly (the others were *Take Me Out to the Ball Game* and—again as a sailor—*On the Town*).

He married his hometown sweetheart, Nancy Barbato, and they had three children together: Nancy Jr., Frank Jr., and Tina. At the end of the forties, Frank's career began to slip. Those teenage girls who'd swooned to him—bobby-soxers, they were called—deserted him. As he aged, his hairline receded. He further alienated audiences by deserting his loyal wife and throwing himself at the feet of Ava Gardner, movie star and sexpot du jour at the dawn of the fifties. But as Gardner's star rose, Sinatra's continued to plummet. His marriage to her was a disaster. She was a ball buster par excellence, and Frank realized he'd made a terrible mistake leaving Nancy and the kids. His career bottomed out. Columbia Records didn't renew his contract, and his voice was steadily weakened by the cigarettes and booze he used to soothe his fractured heart.

It was the abyss. But two things happened in 1953 that revived his career and made him a finalist for Entertainer of the Century honors.

First, he secured a part in the film version of James Jones's Second World War novel *From Here to Eternity*. As scrappy Private Angelo Maggio, Sinatra was nearly perfect, holding his own with an excellent cast that included Burt Lancaster, Deborah Kerr, Donna Reed, and Montgomery Clift. (Another *Godfather* rumor persisted about how the washed-up Sinatra got such a plum part. In this story, a film producer was intimidated into casting the Sinatra-like singer in a war movie. All it took was waking up with the severed head of his prized racehorse in his bed to make the movie mogul realize that hiring the skinny singer was a good idea.)

Also, Frank signed with Capitol Records. The work he did for the L.A.-based label would be the best of his career.

Though the überserious rock 'n' roll artists of the late sixties would claim the concept album as their invention (the Who's rock opera *Tommy* being a prime example), it was actually Sinatra who created the form during his tenure at Capitol. *In the Wee Small Hours of the Morning*, from 1955, and *Frank Sinatra Sings for Only the Lonely*, from 1958, explored the postmidnight loneliness of heartbreak. A later album on the same subject, *No One Cares*, from 1959, was a collection so bleak Sinatra himself called the album a compendium of "suicide songs." Music to slit your wrists by.

Not all of his Capitol output was depressing. He made albums of songs on single subjects: travel, flying, dancing, and the usual tunes for swinging lovers. Before, albums had been assembled with little connective tissue. Songs bore no relation to one other. Sinatra's Capitol albums were the musical equivalent of short-story collections.

The Capitol Sinatra was called the new, mature Sinatra, and his albums provided the soundtrack for thousands of baby boomer conceptions. He was an artist of king-hell make-out music, and the sessions at Capitol Studios established it as one of the primo recording venues in town. Across the street from Wallichs Music City and staggering distance to several key coffee shops and taverns, the Capitol Tower at the corner of Hollywood and Vine helped birth the Wrecking Crew. Frank presided in the studio as the old guard retired, and the new guys he recruited, like Hal Blaine, in T-shirts and sneakers, took over for the necktie-wearing professionals. Blaine recalled hearing grumbles about his ilk coming onto the recording scene during the Sinatra era. *They're wrecking the business.* He embraced that role.

Firmly reestablished in music and film by the midfifties, Frank was not amused by the arrival of Elvis Presley, Little Richard, Chuck Berry, and the like. He was vocal in his disapproval of the new artists and saw himself as caretaker of the Great American Songbook.

But then his eldest daughter betrayed him by becoming a fan of Elvis Presley. Nancy Sinatra would go on to a career that straddled rock 'n' roll and pop charts. Dutiful son and namesake Frank Jr. tried to be a dad pleaser by keeping the old man's music alive. (He wasn't really a junior. Dad was Francis Albert Sinatra; son was Francis Wayne Sinatra.) He wore a tailored tux and re-created the teen-sensation version of the old man. The third child, Tina, flirted with acting but ended up behind the scenes in show business.

Whether Old Blue Eyes liked rock 'n' roll or not, Frank had to admit it was a fact of life. By the time Elvis Presley returned from military service in 1960, Sinatra eagerly booked him on his television show. The icons duetted, and ratings went through the roof.

Still, Frank's heart was with the classic American songs of Cole Porter, Johnny Mercer, and Rodgers and Hart. As the sixties began, he created his own record label, Reprise, to keep the good stuff out there in a marketplace filled with rot 'n' roll. He brought his gang along to Reprise, the so-called Rat Pack. Sammy Davis Jr., Peter Lawford, and Dean Martin all left Capitol for the new artist-friendly Reprise Records.

Being artist-friendly would be key to Reprise's success. But the kinds of artists signed to the label changed in the years after its founding, when Frank handed over the management and reins to Warner Bros. (For a hefty stake in the new Warner-Reprise, of course.) Within the decade, Reprise would become a safe haven for exactly the kind of music that Frank hated. In 1968, Reprise released an album by the Fugs called *It Crawled into My Hand, Honest.* One of its songs, "Wide, Wide River," featured these lyrics:

> *Flow on, flow on, river of shit*
> *Right from my toes*
> *On up to my nose*
> *Flow on, flow on, river of shit*

Lord *God*, how Sinatra hated rock 'n' roll. Luckily, the world blessed him with an opportunity to exercise his wrath on a particular rock 'n' roll singing duo.

Jan and Dean had been making records since 1958, nearly a half decade longer than the Beach Boys. Yet by 1963, they were becoming followers rather than leaders. They had goofed around with "Heart and Soul" and "Clementine," but it was that backstage meeting with Brian Wilson that changed the trajectory of their career.

Brian's casual handoff of "Surf City" to Jan Berry led the way to surfing songs and eventually to car songs. Berry was adept at picking up Wilson's morsels, and together they shared credit on a long stream of songs evoking the fun and sun of Southern California. Both acts even wore striped shirts. The Beach Boys' were vertical, and Jan and Dean's horizontal. But no matter which way the stripes ran, the Beach Boys and Jan and Dean were the quintessence of California cool.

Jan Berry was skilled in the studio and working with the Wrecking Crew and was therefore central to Brian Wilson's development as a producer. But then student surpassed teacher, and Brian went off in an orbit by himself, becoming second only to Phil Spector as the gifted auteur of the recording studio.

Perhaps Jan Berry wasn't as serious about making records as Brian Wilson. Jan and Dean's musical career was almost a part-time job, since they were both full-time students who played at being rock stars in their spare time. The easygoing, nearly lackadaisical approach to their music—not to mention their good looks and their laid-back attitude to most things in life—began to attract television and film producers. Doors were opening. Still, the boys in the surfer shirts refused to give music all of their attention. They were smart enough to know that such things didn't last forever.

Jan and Dean remained pretty much the way they had been in high school, and they maintained friendships with the guys from the University High football team and from the Barons car club. Dean, age twenty-two in 1963, still lived with his parents.

Jan and Dean had gone to school with sons and daughters of show business royalty, including the Sinatras. They'd also been friends with the also-rans, kids like Barry Keenan.

Dean Torrence and Barry Keenan had been close in high school, sometimes calling themselves brothers. After high school, as Dean launched his music and academic career, Barry spiraled off in a different direction. He first went into finance, becoming the youngest member of the Los Angeles Stock Exchange. He counseled Dean on how to invest his rock-star money, and his instincts were fairly acute.

He also had good instincts behind the wheel. Driving his year-old Ford Ranchero through Westwood one night in 1961, he spotted a street dog about to tear ass in front of him. He responded quickly and avoided killing the dog, but nearly offed himself. He turned into a row of parked cars and *boom-boom-boomed* down the street before slamming into a wall. He lived, but suffered a near-traumatic back injury. Percodan helped him live with the pain. Soon he was an addict, and addicts generally don't last long in the world of high finance. Keenan was bumped from his perch and lost his place in the moneyed world.

Knocked off the fast track—and, by his own account, mentally ill because of his addiction—Keenan began drifting, visiting those in his social circle. Mostly they were children of wealth, and Keenan was not part of that tribe.

"For the first time in my life, I'd run out of money completely," Keenan said. "By September of '63, I was in desperate straits." His family was in disarray. His father had gone broke, and his mother had failed at committing suicide. He hatched a plan to rescue his family—and perhaps another family as well.

Most of his old Uni classmates closed their doors to him, but good-natured Dean Torrence couldn't say no. He was grateful for his celebrity, even apologetic, so in October 1963, when Barry asked Dean to meet him on the USC campus, he agreed immediately. If his high school pal was in need and wanted to talk, Dean would listen. They met at the statue of Tommy Trojan on campus and ate sack lunches they'd brought. "I was there to listen," Dean said, "kind of like a therapist."

Keenan ranted, but Torrence heard him out. Dean knew that Barry was in a bad patch, so he expected his friend would put the touch on him. "Surf City" had been number one just a few months before, and Jan and Dean were on a roll. Generous to a fault, Dean had no problem giving his friend some cash. He just didn't expect him to describe pulling off the perfect crime.

Keenan was obsessed with their rich contemporaries, the Sinatras in particular. "I went to University High with Nancy," Keenan recalled. "We were friends and when I visited her house and her father was there, I could see how he doted over the girls. But he was distant with Frank Jr., who they sent away to boarding school."

Junior was doing everything he could to please the old man, even turning himself into a virtual clone of Old Blue Eyes, but—to Keenan, at least—it seemed as if the elder Sinatra could care less. At nineteen, Frank Jr. was four years younger than sister Nancy and Barry, and his boarding school education meant Barry didn't really know the kid. The youngest Sinatra, Tina, was also allowed to stay close to her Hollywood home, and followed in Nancy's footsteps at University High.

As they talked in the lengthening shadow of the USC mascot, Barry told Dean he wanted to kidnap someone and invest the ransom to help save his family. He'd also pay back the victim's family, so no one would be hurt. He considered Bob Hope's son and a few others before settling on the Sinatra family.

"I decided on Junior because Frank Sr. was tough," Keenan said. "I had friends whose parents were in show business, and I knew Frank always got his way. It wouldn't be morally wrong to put him through a few hours of grief worrying about his son." Besides, Barry knew the singer from hanging out at his house with Nancy and her other friends. "Frank was always very nice to me," he said. The plan that Barry laid out was to kidnap young Frank, hold him for ransom, and make the father more appreciative of the son. After the payoff from the investment he'd make with the ransom, Keenan would pay his parents' debts and repay Sinatra. He figured if he paid back the ransom, that would wipe the sin off the books in the Catholic Church's ledger. If Sinatra were to refuse the payback, Keenan would donate the money to charity.

Dean listened to Barry unfurl his plan, unfamiliar with the concept of an altruistic kidnapper, one who chose to help his victim, not profit from him. Sure, there'd be a ransom, Barry said, but bringing the family together was the important element of the plan.

"I don't think I ever took him seriously," Dean said. "It was so insane."

Barry, his addled head still in the financial world, presented Dean with a three-ring binder containing the business plan for the kidnapping. "I didn't think he'd say, 'This is a good idea,' but I had to go about rationalizing it so that he might buy into it," Barry said. "So I went about saying we're going to do this kidnapping, only it's not really a kidnapping. I'm just going through this process because I need money to make these investments."

Barry insisted that God—and several others—had spoken to him telepathically and that the kidnap plot had divine blessing.

As his old friend rambled on, Dean waited for the point to arrive. *What's this got to do with me? Is Barry serious? Does Barry want me to kidnap Sinatra? Or is he truly, deeply nuts?*

Finally, Barry asked Dean for money. He needed living expenses and seed money while he worked out the details of the abduction. *You have to spend money to make money,* he argued. He promised to pay Dean back with interest.

"He was my best friend and he didn't have a cent," Dean recalled. "He didn't have any money at all." Dean later said he figured the money would keep his old pal in three squares a day. He certainly didn't give credence to the yammering about snatching a famous kid.

"That all sounds great, Barry," Dean said, "but what happens if you get caught?"

"Well, Dean, I'm not going to get caught. That's not part of the plan."

"I'll tell you what," Dean said. "This is too bizarre for me to even relate to, but I will give you $500 now. You try to get your life together and let me know how things go."

Dean gave Barry the money and promised more if needed, then went home and didn't think much more about the conversation. Surely Barry wasn't serious. *Was he?*

Dean went back to being half of Jan and Dean, making television appearances, promoting their latest single, "Honolulu Lulu," and putting the finishing touches on their first big car song, "Drag City," written by Jan with Brian Wilson and Roger Christian. With its soaring twin falsettos—Dean and Brian, double tracked—it was destined to follow "Honolulu Lulu" to the Top Ten.

He didn't think much about Barry Keenan for a while.

Barry Keenan hooked up with another Uni classmate, Joe Amsler, and they began following Frank Sinatra Jr. around from gig to gig, trying to figure out the perfect time to snatch the kid.

A third kidnapper joined the team around this time. John Irwin was forty-two and a house painter. He had dated Barry's mother, and because Irwin was older and former navy, Keenan thought he sounded tough. He'd be good on the phone as the muscle. Barry was drawn to Irwin's maturity and figured he was old enough and smart enough to see any holes in the plan.

John joined Barry for a reconnaissance mission to the Arizona State Fair in October. Barry told him that it was the famous singer Dean Torrence who had given him the money for the Arizona trip and that Dean was the money behind the Sinatra grab. Irwin had no idea who Dean was, even when Barry said he was half of the Jan and Dean singing group. *OK, singers. Singers kidnapping singers.*

"I always had a paternal feeling about Barry," Irwin said. "He was about 18 when I first met him. Then . . . he called me and said he had an idea for the perfect crime. I laughed and told him I didn't believe there was any such thing as a perfect crime."

Barry asked John to accompany him as he stalked Junior around Hollywood. They saw him leave the Cocoanut Grove nightclub with his dad's pal, crooner Dean Martin. They saw him speeding around the city in his convertible. They even watched his apartment on Beverly Glen Boulevard, picking it out amid the cookie-cutter condos and flats lining the street. It had the added attraction of being a couple blocks from the Torrence home, where Dean lived with his parents.

Barry and Joe decided the abduction would occur on a Friday night, November 22, when young Sinatra was performing at the Ambassador Hotel in Los Angeles. Living large with the Torrence seed money, Barry rented a suite at the hotel, but the president's assassination that afternoon caused the cancellation of young Sinatra's evening performance, and so he scuttled his plan.

John Irwin drifted away and shoved the perfect-crime scenario to the back of his cerebral cortex. Joe Amsler picked up the slack as Barry's confederate. They laid low for a couple of weeks, then Barry suggested they go to Lake Tahoe and see if they could land jobs doing construction.

When they got into town, Joe saw FRANK SINATRA JR. on the marquee of Harrah's casino.

"You're not still thinking about that, are you?" he asked.

"Joe, don't worry about it," Barry told him. It was now or never. After the Harrah's engagement, Junior was booked for a European tour. It took some talking, but Barry got Joe to again embrace his plan.

They settled on Sunday, December 8, to grab Frank Jr. from Harrah's, a scant few feet from the California-Nevada state line. The kidnapping was key to their survival. Barry and Joe had run out of money and couldn't pay their motel bill. They needed to tap into the

Sinatra finances. "Now, we had to kidnap Frank Sinatra Jr. just to get out of the hotel," Barry said. "That's what it boiled down to. I needed to get money from Junior because I didn't have enough gas in the car to get to L.A."

Barry had been stalking Junior for a couple of days and saw that he had established a routine. He was staying in the wing of the motel next to the showroom. He seemed to keep to himself a good deal.

As they stood outside, looking up at young Sinatra's window, Amsler began to have serious doubts. "Let's go back to L.A.," he said. "You're not going to go through with this thing. Let's go to L.A. before we get in trouble."

"No, Joe," Keenan said. "I'm going to do this."

They climbed the stairs and stood outside the second-floor Sinatra suite. Keenan had a box filled with pine cones that was to be part of his ruse. He also had a gun tucked in his waistband, covered by a parka.

He knocked.

"Who is it?" Junior called from inside.

"I have a delivery for Mr. Sinatra—a package."

"Come in," Junior said.

Keenan opened the door and saw that young Sinatra was not alone. The singer was sitting at the end of his bed, eating room service fried chicken off of a tray. He was in his skivvies.

"Put it over there," Junior told Barry Keenan, nodding at the dresser. The other guy, fully dressed, was also eating a chicken dinner. Turned out he was John Foss, a trumpeter in the Tommy Dorsey Band, which accompanied the singer.

Keenan put the package on the dresser and then, with his back to Sinatra and Foss, he pulled out his .38-caliber revolver—only it got stuck in the voluminous folds of his parka. While Keenan tried to free the handgun, Sinatra and Foss continued to enjoy their delicious fried chicken.

Finally, Barry freed the gun. "It sort of flew out," he said. "I cocked it in Junior's face. I could see he was looking at the bullets. I said, 'Don't make any noise and nobody'll get hurt, don't make any noise and nobody'll get hurt,' sort of like a stuck record. Then I started taking charge. I said, 'Both of you get over there and lie on the floor, this is a robbery. Where is your money?'"

Foss handed over his wallet; it was dry. Junior had only twenty bucks.

Joe Amsler entered the room, dazed, unable to believe what he'd gotten himself into. He stood there motionless.

"Joe, get the money!" Barry violated one of the rules set forth in the kidnapping business plan in the three-ring binder at Dean Torrence's house. If they spoke to each other, they were to use the names of dead presidents.

Joe was still too stunned to move. Barry pointed the gun at him, snapping him back to the present. He took the money from Sinatra.

"Let's go," Joe said.

Barry shook his head no. "We're going to have to take one of you guys with us. You in the dark hair, you're going to go with us." For some reason, Barry didn't want Junior to know they knew who he was.

They taped up Foss and told him, "Don't move for 10 minutes," and then allowed Junior to get dressed. He grabbed what was handy: T-shirt, slacks, loafers, and a light coat. No socks. They bound his hands with the tape.

Barry and Joe hustled Junior to the car. They got in, first stuffing Junior in the backseat. Barry got behind the wheel, pulled out the keys, and was ready to start the car and pull away. But he had the nagging feeling he'd left something behind.

Of course! *The gun.*

He went back to the room, where he discovered that Foss had nearly freed himself. Barry was initially pissed that John had not obeyed the ten-minute rule. This time, he said he couldn't move for *five* minutes. That seemed reasonable. He grabbed the gun and left.

Back in the driver's seat, Barry continued to play the role of shovelhead, unaware of his captor's identity. He asked the bound man his name.

"I'm Frank."

"Frank," Barry said, "your friend's going to get up before we get out of Lake Tahoe, and I'm concerned that there's going to be gunplay. There's one way that we can work this out, and that's if you play along with us, and we pretend we're just guys out having a good time."

"You don't have to worry about me," Junior said. "I'll play along. And you better take my signet ring. I'm Frank Sinatra Jr. Somebody might notice the 'FS' ring."

Barry quickly decided on a plan. "Frank, what we should do is make you look like you're drunk, so here, take these sleeping pills and take a swig of this whiskey." He gave Junior two Nembutals.

The kidnappers and their victim headed off toward Los Angeles as a blizzard pounded Tahoe.

Foss had wriggled out of his bindings and called the police. The Nevada Highway Patrol immediately informed the FBI that Frank Sinatra Jr. had been kidnapped. Because of the high profile of the victim and his pop, FBI director J. Edgar Hoover and attorney general Robert Kennedy were told immediately.

Before they could leave the neighborhood of Harrah's, Barry Keenan and Joe Amsler saw the flickering lights of a state police roadblock a quarter mile ahead. They figured it was a checkpoint because of weather—to make sure drivers insane enough to be on the road were equipped to handle the thick snow. Barry turned to Frank Jr. and took off his blindfold. He told young Sinatra to act as if he was asleep. *One word to the police, and you get a bullet in the brain.*

Barry turned to his accomplice. "Joe, you get back to L.A. as best you can. Frank and I will go through the roadblock." Since the word on the radio was that two guys had kidnapped Junior, Barry figured he had a better chance at the roadblock if it was just him and the drunk kid passed out in the backseat. "I'll let Frank go somewhere down the road and we'll meet up later."

Joe wasn't wild about the idea, but he jumped out of the car and scampered up the embankment to the woods.

Barry and Frank made it through the roadblock, but then Junior cautioned his driver that leaving Joe out in the woods could be a death sentence. "You better not leave your friend out here," he said. "I've lived in snow conditions and he could die very quickly."

Barry was impressed by his captor's compassion. "I think Frank was sincerely concerned for the guy."

They picked up Joe when he came bolting from the woods. He'd hit his head on a fence post and was wookety. He slammed the last of the whiskey, and they drove on. "We'd all reassured each other that we weren't going to hurt each other," Keenan said. "We weren't going to hurt Sinatra and he was going to play along if we hit any more roadblocks. We're one big happy family on this drive through the night together."

Word was out. Junior's manager called Nancy Sinatra Sr. in L.A. She told Tina, then a teenager and still at home. Nancy Sr. called Nancy Jr., who was in New Orleans, where her husband, singer Tommy Sands, was performing at the Roosevelt Hotel.

Nancy Sr. then called her ex-husband, who was in Palm Springs. Frantic with worry, the senior Sinatra got to Reno as soon as he could and set up a command post in the Mapes Hotel. Among those who called him to offer advice, counsel, and support: Herbert Hoover, Robert Kennedy, and mafia don Sam Giancana.

"Just keep your mouth shut, Frank," Hoover advised. "Don't talk to anyone but law officers." Sinatra gave his old mob pal, Giancana, a *Thanks but no thanks*. This was the sort of thing probably best left to the FBI.

The kidnappers didn't manage their money well. They stopped for gas on their way to Southern California and realized they didn't have enough cash. They hit up their prisoner for eleven dollars and finally made it to their hideout in Canoga Park, a community in the San Fernando Valley about an hour's drive from downtown L.A.

Junior was becoming belligerent and began baiting Barry. They decided they needed the older guy to come over and show that they weren't afraid to kick some ass. Barry called John Irwin and told him to come over to their safe house.

"Jesus!" John cried when he heard the story. "You actually did it."

Now it was time for him to assume his role. He went over to the Canoga Park house and played wild man for Junior, who was valiant in the face of the macho man.

"Shoot me, beat me up, whatever," Junior said. "I'm not scared of you guys."

It was midafternoon the next day, a Monday, and John got a call through to the Chairman of the Board at his Reno command post.

"Is this Frank Sinatra?" John asked when the singer came on the phone.

"Speaking. This is Frank Sinatra Sr."

"It doesn't sound like Sinatra."

"Well it is. This is Frank Sinatra."

"Can you be available at 9 AM tomorrow morning?" John asked.

"Yes, I can."

"OK. Your son is in good shape, don't worry about him. See if you can do something about the roadblocks."

Aside from making the ransom phone call, John's main job was to watch Frank Jr. in the Canoga Park lair.

Barry needed more cash, so he went to see his money man, Dean Torrence. Dean had been following the story and was stunned. "Dean was a little shaken," Barry said. "I said we needed money. We drove down to the bank, and that was a strange drive. Very quiet. I was disappointed that he wasn't more elated like I was."

"I'm actually going to the bank," Dean recalled, "which made me an accessory. While he was yakking about how he did it, I was trying to figure out why I'm doing what I'm doing." Dean withdrew $500, gave it to Barry, and asked him to drop him back at home and leave. Barry wanted to go back to Harrah's, pay his bill, and get everything out of his room.

By December 10, just two days after the snatch, Sinatra Sr. had pulled together cash for the kidnappers. It was a considerable bundle— twelve thousand individual bills. The FBI photographed the serial numbers, then put the moolah in a satchel.

The kidnappers had gone to the local library, got a phone book for Reno, and looked up the number of a filling station. No chance that the number would be tapped. Irwin called Sinatra and told him his boy was fine and to get to that particular Chevron station in fifteen minutes. Turns out that the phone book served Reno and Carson City. The station they'd selected was in Carson City, and Sinatra was operating on the assumption it was a Reno station.

Getting itchy, John called *his* Chevron station and asked if Frank Sinatra was there.

The busy mechanic said no and hung up. *Damn prank calls.*

John called back fifteen minutes later. "Is Frank Sinatra there?"

The mechanic exploded: "Listen, Buddy: I'm working on a car, and I don't have time to play around. Don't call again."

Again John called back. "Is Frank Sinatra there?"

"Listen, pal. Frank Sinatra is not in the habit of taking his calls at this Chevron station."

Just as the mechanic hung up, a black car tore ass into the parking lot and a man lunged out and ran toward the mechanic.

"I'm Frank Sinatra," the man shouted. "Have I had any calls?"

John Irwin called the station again, and this time he got Frank Sinatra.

"What do you want? Money?"

"Of course," John drawled.

"How much? I'll give you a million dollars if you let my son go."

"We don't need a million dollars," John said. "I'll tell you how much we need tomorrow."

"Can I talk to my son?" Sinatra asked.

John shoved the phone at Junior. "Dad?" the singer croaked.

"Are you all right?"

"Yeah."

John abruptly hung up.

At ten o'clock that night, Irwin called Sinatra back with the demand for $240,000 to be left between two school buses parked at a Texaco station on Sepulveda, about a twenty-minute drive from the house where they'd stashed Junior.

Barry and Joe went to make the pickup, leaving Junior with John. Barry let Joe out of the car to get the money, then circled the block. When Barry came back, he saw the satchel still between the buses and no sign of Joe. He did, however, note the presence of an ice cream truck—odd, since it was the middle of the night—and figured FBI agents were inside, ready to leap out and grab the kidnappers. He pulled up, grabbed the satchel, and split.

Barry stopped to call John Irwin and tell him he had the money. But there was something in the voice on the phone that disturbed John. Barry told him that Joe had gotten the heebie-jeebies and had gotten out of the car and run.

"We got the money but we got a problem," John told Junior when he hung up. "I better not let you go."

Junior had had it by then. "You let me go or I'll kill you," he said. "If you want to stop me, you'll have to kill me. One of us is going to die."

Impressed by Junior's forcefulness, John began pacing and having second thoughts.

Back at his former wife's home in Bel-Air, Frank Sinatra brooded, wondering if he'd seen his son for the last time.

Junior continued his psychological warfare on his kidnapper. John was obviously spooked and hadn't heard anything from Barry since the phone call four hours before. Junior spun off hypotheses, filling his captor's head with doubt.

It worked. John blindfolded Frank Jr., shoved him in the car, drove to a spot near the prearranged drop-off point, pushed his captive from the car, and sped away. Junior pulled off his blindfold and hid in nearby bushes until he was sure John wasn't coming back. He was at the Mulholland Drive exit on the San Diego Freeway.

It was deep into the wee hours. Junior began walking home to his mother's house in Bel-Air. In the relative peace before dawn, every passing car spooked him. He hid again when a car slowed down on its approach, but when he looked in the car, he saw beefy men with big shoulders in black suits, central-casting FBI. But when he tried to hail the car, it was too late. The agents were gone.

He kept walking. Cars sped by on the freeway, not realizing that the guy walking down there at the edge of the frontage road was the number-one news story in the country.

Again a car came slowly up the street. Junior hid again but then ran from cover when he saw it was a Bel-Air Security car. "Hey!" he shouted, and flagged down the officer, George Jones. It so happened that Mrs. Sinatra's house was on Jones's regular patrol.

Jones offered to drive Junior home but then realized it would be difficult to breach the moat of press surrounding the Sinatra estate.

"Suppose I get in the trunk?" Junior suggested.

Brilliant idea. "Nobody knew I had the boy in the trunk," Jones said. "I drove on up to the home, past the cars, the newspaper people, all the officers, into the parking area in front of the house."

He backed the car up to the door, then knocked and told the Sinatras he had their son in the back of his cruiser. "Let's get that trunk open," Frank Sinatra Sr. said.

Junior looked at his father and said, "I'm sorry, Dad," as he pulled himself to his feet.

Barry Keenan returned to the Canoga Park house and found it empty. Things had gotten too scary for his accomplices. Joe Amsler was freaked out by the ice cream truck and took off running to his wife's house. John Irwin had taken off with Junior. Eventually Joe returned to the Canoga Park house. When John came back to the house, he told his coconspirators what he'd done with Junior. It wasn't going all according to plan, but the Sinatras had their boy back and Barry, Joe, and John had the money, which they dumped on the floor. "We laid all the money out," Barry said. "[We] danced on it, lit cigarettes with it, did all the things we'd seen in movies. We had a money war, throwing wads of bills at each other."

Not only did Junior's quick thinking get him home in the early hours of that morning, but he was also instrumental in the FBI's capture of the kidnappers within days. He recalled tiny details that proved telling. He could tell, for example, from the feel of Irwin's rough hands that he was a man who did serious labor. Indeed, he was a house painter.

With forty grand in his pocket, John Irwin took off for New Orleans, planning to blow the wad on wine, women, and whoopee. On the way, though, he decided to stop off and see his brother in San Diego and blabbed of his role in the kidnapping. Tired from the tensions of the previous four days, John took a snooze on his brother's couch. His sister-in-law had heard the whole story and urged her husband to call the cops. The police drove over and interrupted John's nap by arresting him. Down at the station, his interrogators were barely through their first donuts when John squawked, fingering Barry Keenan and Joe Amsler.

The cops picked up Joe while he was playing chess with a friend. They got mastermind Barry at his girlfriend's house.

Dean Torrence waited for another shoe to drop. As 1963 turned into 1964, the three kidnappers were in custody and their rock-star financier was worried that his role—no matter how passive—would soon be exposed.

Two months after the kidnapping, Barry, Joe, and John were on trial. As Dean feared, his name—and Jan Berry's—were on the witness list. Jan had no involvement with Barry Keenan other than being a fellow Uni High grad and having Dean Torrence as a common buddy.

John Irwin was represented by flamboyant defense attorney Gladys Root. A pioneering woman in the previously all-boys club of criminal defense, Root flaunted her womanhood in lavish dresses and vivid, often feathered, hats.

Root's defense suggested that Frank Sinatra Jr. had staged his own kidnapping. There was no evidence to support this, but she knew creating reasonable doubt in the jury's mind was all that really mattered.

Root's colleague on the defense team, George Forde, said, "We intend to show that certain people financed the alleged kidnapping, which I would call an advertising venture." Forde noticed the uptick in Junior's career, including an appearance on the *Ed Sullivan Show*. "If this was a kidnapping," Forde said, "I'll be on the next moon-shot."

Forde also claimed there was a mastermind behind the plot, a "mysterious financier." Root went further, calling him a "mystery singer." The press was in a frenzy about the identity of the unknown collaborator.

Root named Dean Torrence in court, pointing out that he had a safe deposit box at the Century City branch of the California Bank, a box he shared with Barry Keenan. Dean accompanied an FBI agent to the branch bank and was horrified when an envelope stuffed with cash was found.

The show business connection helped boost the defense team's suggestion that the so-called kidnapping was a publicity stunt. The newspapers were drawn in. As one headline screamed: STAGED WITH CONSENT, DEFENSE SAYS—JURY TOLD UNNAMED SINGER FINANCED 'PUBLICITY SCHEME.'

"This was a planned contractual agreement between Frank Sinatra and others connected with him," Root told the court. "Was this the publicity he had been looking for to make ladies swoon over him like poppa?"

Both Junior and Senior Sinatra vigorously denied the concept of a publicity stunt. "It's a terrible experience to go through what I did and then find out I am on trial—and not the defendants," Junior said from the witness stand. "It's a mark on my integrity and guts that will stay with me for the rest of my life."

Dean Torrence was called to testify on February 24 and was immediately attacked by the prosecutor, US attorney Thomas Sheridan: "Did you lend money to defendant Barry Worthington Keenan for the purpose of financing the abduction of Frank Sinatra Jr?"

No, sir.

"Did Mr. Keenan give you $25,000 in a paper sack, hand it to you on the lawn, on December 11?"

No, sir.

"Did Mr. Keenan tell you he went to Tijuana to buy guns?"

No, sir.

It had been an arduous morning, and Torrence began to think he had compounded his trouble. During a break in testimony, he approached Sheridan and asked if he could have another chance on the stand.

Torrence was in the witness box when Sheridan said, "I understand you want to make an amendment to your testimony."

"Yes, I do," Dean said. "I'm afraid I made up some stories. I did know about the so-called kidnapping and did get some money and I gave it back."

Sheridan questioned Torrence about how Keenan described the plan. It was all very methodical, Dean said, and he talked about the three-ring binder with the business plan for a kidnapping.

"At first I loaned him money just as a friend," he testified. Later, he told defense attorney Forde, "When someone comes up to you and tells you he's going to kidnap someone, you don't really believe it." The judge accepted his recanted testimony, and Dean Torrence was not charged with perjury.

The trial lasted twenty days. The three defendants were all found guilty. Keenan, Amsler, and Irwin were sentenced to life plus seventy-five years.

Do not piss off the Chairman of the Board.

It was widely believed in show business circles that Frank Sinatra put out word that Dean Torrence's career must be stymied. The three other guys went to prison, so Torrence was the only tangible target for Sinatra's wrath.

Barely a week after the end of the trial, syndicated columnist Dorothy Kilgallen wrote that Jan and Dean had been given "the chill" by promoters. "So obviously the word is out," Kilgallen wrote. "Not many people in show business want to incur the wrath of Frank Sinatra Sr.—his tentacles reach into too many branches of the industry, from movies, to records and you-name-it."

Jan and Dean had shot a pilot for a television show called *Surf Scene*. Before it could be scheduled by a network, the show was scuttled. The Sinatra affair made Dean Torrence damaged goods. They were also scheduled to appear in a teensploitation film in summer 1964 called *Ride the Wild Surf*. They performed the title song, but their roles in the movie were cut. The following spring, they scored parts in another movie, called *Easy Come, Easy Go*, but the film was canceled after an accident on the first day of shooting. Jan Berry and seventeen crew members were seriously injured when a train that was supposed to stop did not stop. It rammed into a flatcar containing cast and crew, and bodies went flying. Dean escaped without injury, but Jan was injured so seriously that surgeons considered amputating his left leg. They were able to save it, but he was in a cast for much of the next year.

9

FROM ALL OVER THE WORLD

> Los Angeles was the kind of place where everybody
> was from somewhere else and nobody really dropped
> anchor. It was a transient place. People drawn by the
> dream, people running from the nightmare. Twelve
> million people and all of them ready to make a break
> for it if necessary.
>
> —Michael Connelly

Brian Wilson played a huge part in bringing the American rock 'n' roll
business to Los Angeles. By 1965, it was clear that L.A. was the rock 'n'
roll epicenter. "The sixties called all of the music to the West Coast,"
rock impresario Dick Clark recalled. "L.A. was the place to be. If you
wanted the best [musicians], they were right here in Los Angeles."

A half decade before, the musician magnet was Greenwich Village.
The nation's large-scale infatuation with folk music began at the end
of the fifties, when the well-scrubbed and relentlessly jovial Kingston
Trio arrived. Their first hit, "Tom Dooley," in 1958, might have been
merely a novelty song, but their hits persisted.

The Trio sang cleaned-up, well-enunciated versions of old folk
songs, but unlike the hard-line folk of Woody Guthrie or Pete Seeger,
they generally stayed away from topical songs or political commen-
tary, although their version of Seeger's antiwar "Where Have All the
Flowers Gone?" became a legitimate pop hit in 1961. Meanwhile,
Seeger's unvarnished politics ensured his blacklisting from television
and many concert venues.

The Trio was the gateway drug for young musicians. As soon as
they entered the milieu of folk music, novice performers often cast

aside the Trio in search of more "authentic" folk singers: Seeger, Sonny Terry, Brownie McGhee, and even Guthrie, by then hospitalized and well into his long decline from the degenerative disease Huntington's Chorea. Recording had offered Guthrie a bid for immortality, and the new musicians studied chapter and verse of his songs.

Some singers chose to *remake* themselves as authentic. Elliot Charles Adnopoz was a Guthrie disciple who turned himself into Ramblin' Jack Elliott. Then came Dave Van Ronk, Tom Paxton, Fred Neil, Buffy Sainte-Marie, Eric von Schmidt, Judy Collins . . . why, you couldn't round a corner in Greenwich Village without bumping into a folk singer. Many of them came from semiaffluent middle-class backgrounds but affected the nasal twang and primitive plunking of a Depression-era farmhand.

And the clubs! Greenwich Village had the key venues for folk music and poetry. You might be paid or you might play for free and get whatever change came from baskets passed between tables. The key venues were the Gaslight Cafe, Cafe Wha?, the Bitter End, and Gerde's Folk City. What more could a folkie want?

"Everything I needed was in New York," said Judy Collins, a Colorado transplant. "I lived in the center of the folk music revival. I was a couple of blocks from the Kettle of Fish and a few more from Cafe Fiorello, the Village Gate, Gerde's Folk City on West 4th, and the Gaslight on McDougal."

Folk music made the cover of *Time* magazine in the person of Joan Baez, a nearly academic folk singer with a pure contralto who never shied away from the political involvement inherent in the sinews of folk music.

Into this world ambled young Bob Zimmerman from Hibbing, Minnesota. He arrived in New York in 1961 and invented the persona of Bob Dylan. During his one semester of college at the University of Minnesota, he skipped classes, instead hanging out with a serious folkie contingent of graduate students, who considered him a goofy mascot, somewhat innocent of hygiene. From one unsuspecting friend's house, Dylan absconded with the six-record set of the *Anthology of American Folk Music*, compiled by Harry Smith in 1952. He committed it to memory, becoming a protoplasm jukebox of indigenous music. He also absorbed Woody Guthrie's autobiography, *Bound for Glory*, and took off for New York at age nineteen to meet his idol. He met Guthrie, becoming the dying man's protégé.

Dylan made his mark in Greenwich Village culture. At first, he was like the rest of the singers in the basket clubs and coffeehouses: some kid trying to sound older than he was, droppin' his *G*s, pretendin' to sing country blues laments of the old, weird America. But then Dylan began writing, and some of his songs became enduring additions to the American musical canon: "Blowin' in the Wind," "The Times, They Are a-Changin'," and "With God on Our Side." Instead of singing the same old sea chanteys and doomed-maiden ballads, Dylan wrote songs that revolutionized folk music. Judy Collins, an early fan of Dylan's work, thought his songs subversive. "They ushered in a new musical era," she said.

Greenwich Village was the place to be in the early sixties. After "Blowin' in the Wind" became a Top Ten hit—sung by Peter, Paul and Mary—and his breakthrough *Freewheelin'* album, Dylan was the lodestone. More musicians came to re-create themselves in his image, styling themselves as singer-songwriters: Phil Ochs, David Crosby, Jim McGuinn, John Sebastian, John Hammond Jr., Cass Elliot. With so much talent there, it was hard to be heard above the cacophony.

By 1965, that changed. Greenwich Village looked like Hiroshima after the blast. Everyone was leaving . . . *going west.* Suddenly Los Angeles was the center of the recording industry. Folk music dropped hammer dulcimers, banjos, and reedy voices and plugged in, becoming an amplified version of its former self. Even television's *American Bandstand* moved to L.A., and its creator, Dick Clark, debuted a new show called *Where the Action Is.* Clearly, the action was in L.A., and if you weren't there, you weren't cool.

"The influx of the Greenwich Village folkies in 1964 and 1965 was very important," producer Lou Adler said. "Music changed drastically." Jac Holzman, owner of heavily folk Elektra Records in New York, began scouting West Coast talent. "L.A. was less the promised land than the untilled field," he said. "We'd picked over the East Coast pretty well."

It happened because of the Beach Boys, it happened because of the Beatles, and it happened because the ever-restless Bob Dylan thought it was time to shake the tree. When he plugged in and went electric in 1965, a turning point in American music history arrived.

Jan and Dean sang "(Here They Come) From All Over the World" at the opening of The T.A.M.I. Show in December 1964. It was as if composers Phil Sloan and Steve Barri predicted the future.

Here came a huge influx of young musicians to the West Coast and the birthing of a new rock 'n' roll aristocracy.

––––––––––

The woman who became the Gertrude Stein of this new artistic community was born Ellen Naomi Cohen in Baltimore in September 1941. For seven glorious years, she was an only child. Her father owned several small businesses, including a bakery and a deli. During the deli years, there was a tall young man who became a steady customer. John Phillips had a profound effect on Cohen's life, but at the time, he was just a good-looking guy who liked her father's pastrami on rye. "I remember her as a little, chubby girl, with the stained apron on, behind the counter," Phillips said.

The Cohen family moved to Alexandria, Virginia, then Baltimore again, then Washington, DC. Young Ellen was doted on by her father and had what in retrospect was a normal, happy childhood until she was seven. When sister Leah was born, Ellen had competition for parental attention.

Then she began to eat. "I've been fat since I was seven," she recalled. It was her most marked physical characteristic. People thought of her as the fat girl until they heard her sing. Then they thought of her as the girl with the unforgettable voice. "I'm going to be the most famous fat girl who ever lived," she told friends.

Not an easy path. Though talented, well read, and decidedly witty and charming, Ellen's adolescence was a trial. She was a romantic, and though boys admired her talent and laughed at her jokes, none could get past her weight. She could be quite glamorous, but in the cruel and dictatorial world of youth, not conforming to society's rigid and narrowly defined concept of beauty ensured life as an unwilling wallflower. The world knows no greater cruelty than the disdain of an American teenage girl.

The young women at Baltimore's Forest Park High School were prototypical mean girls, and Ellen was ostracized from the start. The school was structured as a small college, and admission to a sorority was vital for social status. Ellen should have been an automatic admission to the Forest Park chapter of Sigma Pi Sigma, since she had been in that sorority when she attended Georgetown Day School in DC, but the sorority sisters in Baltimore got one look at her and constructed barriers.

Once, Cohen returned to the cafeteria after lunch to find her sorority pin. It had been on her sweater, but while on the way to her next class she discovered it missing. She was back at her table, looking for the pin on hands and knees while a nearby gaggle of sorority girls tittered. Fellow student Ken Waissman deduced what had happened and told the sorority girls to return the pin. They refused. "They were embarrassed to have her seen wearing it," Waissman said. He threatened to expose what the girls had done. "The pin miraculously was later found. It was Ellen's only symbol of status, a kind of acceptance."

(Waissman chronicled the cliquish life of Forest Park High as coauthor of the Broadway musical *Grease*. Another high school classmate and fellow high school outcast, director Barry Levinson, used the same setting as the basis for his film *Diner*.)

Her only girlfriend, Sharon Lisenbee, was everything physically that Ellen Cohen was not. Yet Lisenbee proclaimed herself an outsider because she hated the snobbiness of the mean girls. "I was a cheerleader girl," Lisenbee remembered. "I was everything, probably, that she would like to have been. So each of us probably fed each other something that we really needed—the missing link of our personalities."

Along with Waissman, the girls formed a happy trio of social rebels. Ellen embraced her differences, making controversial fashion choices, including Bermuda shorts with high heels one memorable school day. The mostly rich mean girls wouldn't dream of working, yet Ellen was often late to school because she pulled the dawn shift in her father's food truck. Though extremely intelligent, her school work suffered due to chronic tardiness.

She met rejection with flamboyance, and not just in her clothing. She became high priestess of the smart asses. She stopped holding back and began singing and performing, and she decided music would be her life. She listened to music constantly—at home, in the car, during any free moment. In Lisenbee's basement, the girls pantomimed scenes to the Broadway cast recording of *Gypsy*. They both got parts in a summer community theater production of *The Boyfriend*, which fed Cohen's ambitions.

Unlike classmates, she wasn't drawn to rock 'n' roll. Hefty chanteuse Sophie Tucker became her role model. Tucker performed with a bawdy *Fuck you* attitude that spoke to the soul of any young woman outside the slender norms of fat-shaming society. Ellen *would* have a career in show business; singing kept her going. She dropped out of school before graduation.

As a self-professed performer, Ellen Naomi Cohen decided she needed a better name for the marquee. There are several stories about how she found her stage name, but the one she told most frequently was that she took the *C* from Cohen and the *E* from Ellen and matched them to comic Peggy Cass and poet T. S. Eliot. Hence: *Cass Elliot.*

In 1962, the newly minted Cass moved to New York, where she sponged off an aunt and began auditioning, supporting herself as a cloakroom girl at the Showplace on West Fourth Street in Greenwich Village. This put her in the company of such up-and-coming stars as Liza Minnelli and Woody Allen, who broke in his standup act in the main room. The Showplace manager liked Cass and let her onstage to sing at the end of the night. She auditioned for a number of shows, including the female lead in a new musical called *I Can Get It for You Wholesale,* but lost the part to another novice performer, Barbra Streisand.

The story of her life: great voice, not so great body. Though pretty, her girth turned off Broadway producers. "There wasn't much call for a three-hundred pound ingenue," she said.

She eventually won a role in a touring production of *The Music Man* but left the tour when her father was injured in an automobile accident. She returned home to care for her sister Leah and younger brother. Father lingered a little over a week before dying. In the midst of overwhelming grief, she shared her immense capacity for humor. As her family rode behind the hearse carrying her father, she said, "At least Dad finally got to ride in the frigging Cadillac." The whole family laughed.

Back in the DC area, Elliot made a run at college and was accepted into American University. She liked some classes, loathed others, and treaded water. Uncertain what she wanted to do after her discouraging stint in New York, she figured that if she wanted to sing in public, she'd probably have to embrace folk music, then the rage. The Kingston Trio was at its peak, and campus coffee shops were full of wannabe Belafontes and Baezes.

Cass could sing a medical journal and make it sound swell, but again she discovered she didn't fit the female folk singer image personified by Joan Baez and Mary Travers (of the folk supergroup Peter, Paul and Mary). They were leggy and lithesome, with long, flowing straight hair, everything Cass was not.

Eventually a young singer named Tim Rose crossed her path. "I was *fascinated* with her," he said. "She was the *wittiest* woman I had ever met." They realized they shared a love of music, but their tastes didn't intersect. Cass couldn't believe that Tim didn't have the complete works of Rodgers and Hammerstein committed to memory. He countered by playing "See That My Grave Is Kept Clean" by Blind Lemon Jefferson. *How could she not* know *that?*

Rose convinced Elliot that if she wanted to sing in public—at coffeehouses at least—she needed to get with the program and drop the "Some Enchanted Evening" stuff. Elliot liked Rose and thought he might be her ticket to a real career in music, so she embraced the folkie thing.

Rose's first suggestion? *Let's go to Chicago.* Outside Greenwich Village and Cambridge, that was the folkie hotbed. Rose had a friend there looking to form a trio, à la Peter, Paul and Mary.

"It was the greatest con job of my life," Rose recalled. Cass had a semireliable Volkswagen Beetle and a bit of cash saved from living at home. All Tim brought to the party was the idea.

It was December 1962, and winter was blowing in. The DC-to-Chicago drive was seven hundred miles, all in a car without a heater. The two became friends on the trip and sang most of the way, as Tim taught Cass American folk classics.

In Chicago, they hooked up with Rose's friend John Brown and began blending voices. Everything worked, and they decided to call themselves the Triumvirate. Didn't exactly roll off the tongue, but it was a different kind of name in those days of Peg and Polly, Bob and Biff, and Lucy and Lil.

The Triumvirate got a few bookings in town, then finally scored a coveted gig at Old Town North. During that stand, a dressing room visitor complimented them on their set, then pulled out a guitar and began singing. "I thought, *fucking awful,*" Tim said. "The guy can't sing! Who the fuck is this? Cass said I was wrong. I said, 'No, the guy'll never make it.'" The visitor, whom Rose soon shooed away, was young Bob Dylan.

They began to get bookings around the Midwest, and that's when the Triumvirate began crumbling. Brown had a family in Chicago, and though he claimed he didn't like to be away from his wife, he had no problem burying the weasel with any stranger on the road. It disgusted Elliot and Rose, and when the Triumvirate played Omaha, things fell apart. Brown was asked to leave, and Elliot and Rose talked local singer-songwriter James Hendricks into joining them. Hendricks gave the group an appeal it did not have before. Rose resembled the Pillsbury Doughboy, but Hendricks was square-jawed and movie-star handsome. (Cass later married Hendricks, in 1964, to help him avoid the draft, but theirs was a brother-sister relationship.) The band regrouped back in DC, did a weeklong engagement in Florida, then decided to hit Greenwich Village. By this time they were the Big 3, and though they had not rehearsed a huge set list, their act drew a lot of attention, not always for the quality of the music. They were "the group with the fat chick." If that's what it took to bring in an audience, that was OK. That chick's voice and the chemistry between the performers quickly won over the crowds.

There were three dozen clubs crammed into those few square Village blocks, and so performers all watched each other, traded songs, and stole arrangements. Despite the competition, they developed into a community of outcasts. The performers in the Village were the freaks, the former beatniks on their way to becoming hippies. They were the punch lines in Johnny Carson's late-night monologues and the *New Yorker*'s cartoon captions. The ridicule and scrutiny from outside brought the community together and created lifelong friendships. It was there in the Village, in early 1963, that Cass Elliot met David Crosby.

David Van Cortlandt Crosby had all the arrogance that went with his stuffy name. The Van Cortlandt family was full of political heavy-weights dating from the time of the American Revolution. The Crosby side, of more modest genealogy, brought the scion artistic credibility. David's father, Floyd Crosby, was a respected cinematographer who worked with such revered directors as Robert Flaherty, the father of the documentary, and German master F. W. Murnau, who'd given the world the first movie version of the Dracula tale *Nosferatu*. Floyd Crosby won an Oscar for his pioneering work shooting Murnau's last film, *Tabu*, on location in Bora Bora in 1931.

Despite that accolade, Floyd was firmly on the outside of the Hollywood mainstream and pushed to get into the industry. He took government work during President Franklin Roosevelt's alphabet soup administration and continued government work during the Second World War. He seemed finally on the verge of mainstream success when he shot the classic *High Noon* in 1951. That film, directed by Fred Zinnemann, was a master class in black-and-white cinematography, but also one of Crosby's last high-profile jobs. Blacklisted for liberal political views, Crosby was unable to get work. Zinnemann instructed Columbia Pictures to hire Crosby for *From Here to Eternity*, but the studio refused. For the rest of his career, Crosby was forced to work on lesser films, including sixties schlock for low-budget maestro Roger Corman and American International Pictures, producers of direct-to-drive-in fare such as *How to Stuff a Wild Bikini*, *Bikini Beach*, and *The Raven*, which starred the barely postpubescent Jack Nicholson.

David Crosby and older brother Ethan grew up in a home steeped in arts and liberal politics, giving young David a grounding that followed through his life. "Most of the values I learned I picked up from books like *The Catcher in the Rye*," he said. Though Floyd worked beneath his talent, he was nonetheless able to provide a generous living for his family, and his sons had the best, including a prep school education. But David, suffused with the pompousness and invincibility of an inflated sense of self-worth, treated most everything and everyone with disdain. He was cast out of schools and put into others, where he was soon the festering boil on the new school's rump.

When he reached driving age, David became a hellion. He discovered cars around the time he discovered girls and launched his long and active career in fucking. "I followed my unit the way a caboose chases a train," he said.

Though he assumed he would succeed his father in the film business—on the other side of the camera, as an actor—he found himself drawn to music, mostly because girls were hot and bothered by a boy with a guitar. If he wanted a lifetime full of getting laid, the best way to achieve that goal was to perform in front of an audience, he thought, not on a film set, in front of fellow employees.

As he hit his twenties, the folk music boom began. Armed with the necessary three chords, he fashioned himself as a guitarist and singer, playing coffeehouses around L.A. and Santa Barbara. His parents' liberal politics meant that the Crosby record collection was stocked with the works of Pete Seeger and Woody Guthrie, so David built a repertoire of their topical songs from the forties and fifties, as well as touchstones of classic folk music. He began playing in Arizona and up the California coast, including hip San Francisco clubs, where he schmoozed folk music heavyweights such as Bob Gibson. When

David sought advice from older folkies, the message was clear: *Go east, young man.*

Once in Greenwich Village, David was just a face in the crowd. He'd go to the coffeehouses and check out the competition, and his fierce ambition and arrogance surfaced. He saw Bob Dylan performing his new song, "Blowin' in the Wind," at Gerde's Folk City in early 1963, and the song affected him strongly, though the singer did not. "I didn't like him or his vocal quality because everybody loved him," David said. "I wasn't as big as him and I was jealous as hell." Dylan tried to roughen his voice, to make it sound scarred and authentic, but Crosby was blessed with a pretty voice, a lustrous tenor that turned even the most solemn dirge into something beautiful. It pissed him off that audiences preferred the kid with the faux frog in his throat.

His attitude turned off audiences and would-be friends, but none could deny his talent. "When I got to the Village, I was barely out of prep school," David said. After a somewhat privileged young life, it was a shock to the system to begin his adulthood couch-surfing the Village. He still thought he should be waited upon and those who had been kind enough to put him up didn't like being treated like a servant. David used friends the way others used toilet paper. "David was a bit of a brat," said Billy James, who considered himself a pal.

His manner made him an outcast, which is what drew him to Cass Elliot, outcast of another sort. "I don't think Cass was ever happy," David recalled. "Inside, she was very beautiful, but our society is built on surface and not substance. She wanted to be loved. I think that was probably the single greatest driving force in her character."

Desperate to make a living out of music, David joined a pop music version of a folk group called Les Baxter's Balladeers, a group similar to other pop-oriented acts like the New Christy Minstrels, the Rooftop Singers, and the Serendipity Singers. The idea was to present a jovial Disneyland version of folk music to the masses. The Big 3, Cass's group, had moderate success, including an appearance on *The Tonight Show*. Jack Linkletter, host of television's weekly *Hootenanny* show, decided to put together a package tour of folk performers, along the lines of the rock 'n' roll caravans run by his ABC-TV colleague Dick Clark. *Hootenanny* was exhibit A of the folk music boom, since it was high profile. Yet it lacked credibility with real folkies, especially since Pete Seeger was banned from the show. If it wasn't political in 1963, it wasn't folk music.

Young entertainers like Cass Elliot and David Crosby seized whatever opportunities they could, so they joined the *Hootenanny* bus tour of America.

"Boy, what a *horrible* tour," David remembered. The bus was a standard Trailways model with seats and only one place to lie down—the bench in the back, a place of honor ceded to Cass. "One time, she hurt herself when the driver hit a big bump and it was so bad that it bounced her right off the rear seat and onto the floor." The trip was so awful that after several gigs, David called his father and asked for a credit card so he could fly between stops.

Nevertheless, Cass Elliot and David Crosby cemented their friendship during that rotten bus tour. She discovered that in Greenwich Village, people were more likely to judge you for who you were and not what you looked like.

Barry McGuire, gravel-voiced lead singer of the New Christy Minstrels, scored a hit for his group with his song "Green, Green." During his Village days, he recalled meeting Cass Elliot while she was performing with the Big 3. "Sometimes, you meet people that you have an instant affinity with," he said. "We just looked at each other and went, 'boing!'" The whole Village "was just a fun, exciting time with music floating in every direction," he added.

McGuire was on tour with the Christies when, after a Kansas City one-nighter, another group member suggested he come to a club and listen to a young performer. Barry heard the eighteen-year-old and immediately offered him a job, since another member of the tour was quitting.

At the time, Harold Eugene Clark was barely out of high school and living a semirural life with his parents and twelve brothers and sisters outside Bonner Springs, Kansas. Blessed with classic good looks and a deep, searching voice, Gene Clark was already a fairly seasoned performer. First, he led a group called the Rum Runners, but when Barry McGuire saw him onstage in Kansas City, he was front man for the Surf Riders, which, despite its name, was a folk group, not a surf band.

After listening to McGuire's pitch, Clark had no trouble agreeing to join the Christies. "I wasn't going to turn down something like that," he said. "It was right out of the movies: 'Kid, do you want to go to Hollywood and be a star?' So I said, 'Sure, I'd love to.' So I hopped on a plane and was gone."

The Svengali of the Christy Minstrels, Randy Sparks, created various traveling incarnations of the group so he could maximize bookings. Although he owned a house outside L.A. that was sort of a dormitory for the Christies when they weren't on the road, it was rare that all three versions of the group were not off performing in Keokuk or Kankakee. So much for Gene Clark's Hollywood dreams. He woke up in a Holiday Inn in Effingham, Illinois. Such was showbiz.

Gene lasted only a few months with the group. Sparks expected happy-face razzmatazz, but Gene Clark was a serious and stationary performer. He was on the verge of being fired in early 1964 when he heard the Beatles on a jukebox during a Norfolk, Virginia, stop. "I quit the Christies the next day and went back to L.A. to find a way to start a group like that because I thought *that* was it."

While Cass Elliot and David Crosby froze on the *Hootenanny* tour bus and Gene Clark was hamming onstage with the New Christy Minstrels, Jim McGuinn sat in a Brill Building cubicle, listening to Top Forty radio and trying to write songs like those he heard belching from the transistor. His heart was two and a half miles south, in Greenwich Village, but he was a worker bee in a song factory.

McGuinn was twenty-two but already a show business lifer. Born in Chicago, his life changed one day in high school when a teacher brought singer Bob Gibson to class. McGuinn was captivated by Gibson, who taught songwriting at the Old Town School of Folk Music. Gibson convinced McGuinn to enroll.

Within a year, McGuinn was a skilled player of both six- and twelve-string guitar and five-string banjo. He also began haunting Chicago's prodigious folk clubs, showing up at the Gate of Horn one night with his banjo to hear the Limeliters, a trio led by dazzling tenor Glenn Yarbrough. After their set, McGuinn asked to play for the group. Yarbrough said sure, and he nodded in admiration as the kid played. The next day, the group asked Jim to become their accompanist.

When asked when he could start, Jim let them know he graduated from high school in June.

The group was floored; the kid really was a *kid*, but worth waiting for. That summer, not yet eighteen, Jimmy McGuinn went on the road with the Limeliters as a professional musician. The first gig led him to Southern California, where he met young David Crosby during a Limeliters residency in Santa Barbara. Figuring he might want to hang out with someone his own age, David asked Jim to crash at the family home. Jim recognized David's talent but also saw that he could be an imperial asshole.

After nearly a year on the road with the Limeliters, Jim was hired to accompany the Chad Mitchell Trio, another Disneyfied folk group. That ended badly when Jim challenged their musical integrity and Mitchell punched him in the nose.

Jim had a great reputation as a player and a young man of preternatural maturity, so he did not go long without a job. Singer and movie star Bobby Darin hired him for the folk music segment of his Vegas nightclub act. Darin wasn't simply following a trend; he loved all kinds of music. After several early rock 'n' roll hits, including "Splish Splash," Darin scored a monster success with his full-on pop version of "Mack the Knife." But his love for folk music was sincere, even if he looked a little odd singing Leadbelly's "Rock Island Line" in a tuxedo.

Singer-songwriter Judy Collins had achieved modest success and recorded two albums for Elektra when she went to see Darin in concert after hearing good things about his young accompanist. She assumed Darin was pure showbiz, but was startled by his versatility. "I was unprepared for Darin's sophistication, his down-to-earth humor, and his wonderful voice," she said. "He came onstage, dark-haired, slender, almost like a boy, and showered us with gentle banter between songs and a light touch in his manner." Meanwhile, "Jim McGuinn . . . sat prominently near the front of the band, dressed in clean-lined black pants, shirt, bare-headed, his banjoes and guitars at the ready." Though a sideman performing folk songs, Collins said McGuinn already had the rock-star thing going. "McGuinn was a dreamy guy with a lean and hungry look, almost gaunt," she said. "He wore his dark hair long. He was dressed in a sharp suit and had thick lashes and bedroom eyes. He sang occasional harmony with Darin in a sweet, twangy voice, half country and half crooner."

The strain of singing raw country blues and folk music sidelined Darin, and he took a break from the stage. He wanted McGuinn on retainer, so while he was shooting the film *Captain Newman, M.D.* with Gregory Peck and Tony Curtis, he sent his accompanist to New

York, setting him up in that Brill Building cubicle, paying his protégé just enough to keep him in cheeseburgers.

Jim McGuinn was a junior member of the song factory that included Goffin and King, Mann and Weil, and Barry and Greenwich, the great pop-rock songwriters of that era. The kid had a high standard but accepted the challenge gamely. To cash in on the Beach Boys' success, Jim wrote and produced a single ("Beach Ball" backed with "Sun Tan Baby") under the name the City Surfers. That one single became the relative high point of his tenure at 1619 Broadway.

He continued nocturnal haunts of the Village clubs, which led to the next change of direction. McGuinn was free from Darin commitments, so Judy Collins made him an offer. "I liked Jim's friendly, easy manner on and off the stage," she recalled. "I hired McGuinn to be part of my new album." As accompanist and arranger for *Judy Collins #3*, McGuinn adapted two Pete Seeger songs, "The Bells of Rhymney" and "Turn Turn Turn" to Collins's lovely voice and accessible folk style.

But he kept his day job at the song factory. Jim wasn't nearly as productive as the other Brill Building tenants and was easily distracted. He wanted to be a performer, not a sideman, so he took the subway south to the Village after work and hit the basket clubs, developing a nodding acquaintance with Bob Dylan, already spoken of in elevated tones. Jim joined the crowd that included Barry McGuire, David Crosby, Cass Elliot, John Sebastian, and long, tall John Phillips and his beautiful young wife, Michelle. Collins recalled meeting John Phillips around this time, calling him as "lanky and smooth-moving as a cheetah."

John Phillips was a half-decade older than the others. He'd grown up around Alexandria, Virginia, where he frequented Cass Elliot's deli counter, and earned an appointment to the US Naval Academy. He dropped out after one year, then was in line for a basketball scholarship at George Washington University when he screwed up his knee playing a pickup game. Basketball was the only reason he had to go to college, so he began his long itinerant career in sales. "He sold funeral plots, cars, and Singer sewing machines," his wife, Michelle Phillips, said. "He could actually sell anything and indeed had enormous charm."

He also loved music and led a couple jazz groups, including the Smoothies and the Abstracts. But all roads eventually led to folk, and he assembled a trio called the Journeymen with Dick Weissman and Scott McKenzie. They released three albums and toured the country in the early sixties. During a swing through Southern California, John Phillips met the staggeringly beautiful Michelle Gilliam. Despite being married with two children, John fell into tongue-dragging lust with Michelle. As soon as he could arrange a divorce, he married the beautiful teenager on the last day of 1962, in order to claim the marriage benefit on his taxes.

Though a novice singer, Michelle was folded into John's remade group, the New Journeymen, with Marshall Brickman as the third member. John knew any man with eyeballs craved his wife, so having her in the group—even with her limited singing abilities—was his way to monitor her behavior. They performed in California, primarily at San Francisco's hungry i nightclub, but soon the Greenwich Village allure was too much to resist.

Back in New York, John and Michelle Phillips reconnected with an old friend from days on the road, a Canadian singer named Denny Doherty, who had been part of the Halifax Three when he'd toured with John and his first group of Journeymen. He'd joined a group with the improbable name Mugwumps. That group was on hard times, so when Phillips put out word he needed a tenor for the New Journeymen (Brickman left to become a writer, later sharing an Oscar with Woody Allen for *Annie Hall*), Denny Doherty answered the call.

In early 1964, not long after John and Michelle arrived in the city, they sat with Denny on the floor of their squalid Village apartment, while Denny raved about the friend he had invited over, the chick singer from the Mugwumps. *Meet the Beatles* was playing on their Sears record player. *Meet the Beatles* was playing everywhere.

John and Michelle introduced Denny to LSD, which was all the rage back in California. It was legal then, and they looked forward to tripping. Denny had never done acid.

Then came a knock. "At the very moment the acid began to take effect," Michelle recalled, "Cass appeared in the doorway. I saw her standing there in a pleated skirt and a pink Angora sweater with great big eyelashes on and her hair in a flip, and I just remember thinking, 'This is *quite* a drug!'"

The four clicked immediately. Cass pulled Michelle into a corner conference to profess her gut-twisting love for Denny. To Denny,

Cass was a talented pal. To Cass, Denny was all a man should be, and she urgently wanted to fuck him.

Though Denny continued performing with the Mugwumps even while in the New Journeymen, Cass was eager for success in music, and the Mugwumps, like the Big 3, had been a real struggle. Despite all the talent—and the group also included Zal Yanovsky, one of the most respected guitarists in the Village—nothing clicked. As John pulled out his guitar and began to sing with Denny and then with Michelle, Cass added her voice. A song or two later, she realized she had finally found her musical home. Broadway could wait. This group was what she wanted.

But the group—or, at least, John Phillips—didn't want her. Sure, she was funny and talented, but she was also fat. John was a tall drink of water. Denny's face promised future chubbiness, but he was handsome for now. Michelle was beautiful, in first place on every man's must-fuck list. John reasoned that people wouldn't be able to enjoy the music with the fat chick onstage.

Cass found a gig as a cabaret singer back in the DC area, and John, Michelle, and Denny took a booking in the Virgin Islands. When that ended, with nothing else on the calendar, they made a brief trip back to the mainland and invited Cass and some other friends to come visit them in the islands.

Doherty and the Phillipses were living blissful, stoned, umbrella-drink beach life when Michelle looked up one day and saw Cass's considerable bulk advancing through the sand, steadily approaching the trio's alcohol-soaked base camp. She couldn't stay away, she told them, and the four of them decided they'd hang out until they maxed out the Phillips' American Express card.

Cass and Michelle worked scut jobs on the islands, and John wrote new songs on the beach, trying them out with Denny's soaring voice. Though Cass added to the mix when they sang around their oceanside campfires at night, John made it clear that whatever was happening, Cass was *not* part of this group.

Hearing the Beatles for the first time had the same effect on Jim McGuinn that it had had on Gene Clark. Tuning in to *The Jack Paar Show* on January 3, 1964—well over a month before the British group appeared on *The Ed Sullivan Show*—Jim saw BBC news film of the group and the screaming reaction of the audience. Girls going nuts was intriguing, but Jim responded to the music, not the long hair or the lunacy.

"I might have been one of the first people to dig what the Beatles were into musically," Jim said. "In their chord changes, I could see a degree of complexity that folk music had gotten to by that time, and it struck me as being a groovy thing." He got hold of any Beatles record he could find—the few that were coming out on Capitol, the releases north of the border on Canadian Capitol, and the Vee-Jay collection from mid-1963—and committed the songs to memory. "I started singing their songs in coffeehouses."

He played folk songs as if they were Beatles songs and Beatles songs as if they were folk songs. "They were mixing elements of folk and rock because they'd been a skiffle band," Jim said. "They were doing it kind of subconsciously. They were shooting for a fifties rock style, but they were blending a lot of things together, sort of under the hood. I don't think they really knew what they were doing." With a couple of friends, Jim sat in coffeehouses, analyzing and breaking down the Beatles' songs. "So that's the origins of folk rock, really. It began in Greenwich Village."

This did not go over in the *more authentic than thou* atmosphere of the Village folk community. Jim McGuinn sang Beatles songs before America at large was sure what the Beatles were.

At the end of that winter in 1964, Jim got a call from a friend who had arranged a booking for him opening for singers Hoyt Axton and Roger Miller at the Troubadour in Los Angeles. *Maybe the Troub audience will understand what I'm doing*, Jim thought.

The country was still in its first flush of Beatlemania. Despite that, McGuinn's act didn't go over any better on the West Coast. "I was really getting a terrible audience reaction," he recalled. "The folk purists absolutely hated what I was doing. It was blasphemy."

Not so to Gene Clark. He walked into the Troubadour one night and found Jim McGuinn in the Folk Den, a small performing area outside the Troubadour's main room. *This guy gets it*, Gene thought. He walked up to Jim and introduced himself. "Look," he said. "Do you mind if I play with you?"

"No," Jim said affably. "Have a seat."

For three weeks, they were an informal duo—Gene and Jim—modeling themselves after English performers Peter and Gordon, who were part of the Beatles' inner circle. Soon they began writing songs together that fit the hybrid rock-folk-Beatles style. On occasion, they affected British accents.

One evening as they sat in the Folk Den working on a song, David Crosby walked in and, without an invitation, began adding high harmony. Gene was entranced by the richness David brought to their voices and suggested to Jim that they form a trio. McGuinn, who knew Crosby from his time as a houseguest of the spoiled brat a few years before, was more wary. But he had to admit they sounded good together. Fellow folk singer turned rocker Jerry Yester said the trio sat in the Troubadour lobby every night, heads bent in concentration. "They'd sit there with a twelve-string, just writing songs," Yester said.

Turned out David had a connection in the Los Angeles music world. He'd made some demos for a guy named Jim Dickson, a hyphenated producer-manager-publisher–everything else. The demos were unimpressive, but because of Dickson's work at World Pacific Studios, where the Beach Boys had recorded some pre-Capitol sides, he could use the studio whenever it wasn't booked, no charge. When Crosby told the other two about the studio time, Clark and McGuinn thought a trio might be a good idea after all.

————————

The arrival of the Beatles was like a Vesuvius let loose on American music. Clear lines of demarcation were erased. As producer Lou Adler said, "The Beatles validated rock 'n' roll." In his song "My Back Pages," Bob Dylan pointed out that things were not so simple anymore:

Lies that life is black and white spoke from my skull I dreamed

Case in point: Jackie DeShannon. She was a model for generations of young women seeking acceptance in the often condescending boys club of the music business. As both a songwriter and performer, she had a profound impact on the role of women in rock 'n' roll.

She was in Greenwich Village in 1964 as an agent provocateur. Solidly in the rock 'n' roll camp, she came from California, nearly getting trampled by the mass exodus of folkies heading west to California and a future in the hybrid world of folk rock. A farm girl born on the Kentucky-Tennessee state line outside the village of Hazel, DeShannon began life as Sharon Lee Myers. By age six, she was yodeling on country music radio and within five years hosted her own show. By the time she was a teenager, she was an old pro, asked to appear on a Chicago-based television show hosted by Pee Wee King, composer of the classics "You Belong to Me" and "Tennessee Waltz." She got a record deal as a rockabilly singer in the late fifties and appeared on several package tours, all before she was twenty. Rock 'n' roll dynamo Eddie Cochran heard her work and invited her to California to write songs with his girlfriend, Sharon Sheeley. The two Sharons soon had a hit song, "Dum Dum," for Brenda Lee.

With a new performing name, Jackie DeShannon signed a contract with Liberty Records and began lobbing hits such as "Lonely Girl" onto the charts. She performed Buddy Holly's "Oh Boy!" as part of her set, and during a visit to New York, she planned a sneering visit to Greenwich Village. But then she saw Bob Dylan. "This kid came out in Levis and boots and he did a thing called 'Don't Think Twice,'" she recalled. "I just flipped."

The effect was immediate. DeShannon melded her rock sensibilities with the chord changes and twang of folk, scoring a hit with the folkish "Needles and Pins," written by Phil Spector acolytes Sonny Bono and Jack Nitzsche, and her own composition, "When You Walk in the Room." She recorded that early blend of folk and rock 'n' roll in 1963, and a year later, a British band called the Searchers sent its hit version back across the Atlantic.

Jackie achieved such status that she opened for the Beatles on their 1964 summer American tour. She and the Beatles established an easy rapport and realized they shared a fascination with Bob Dylan. Even though they were squarely in their moptop, *yeah, yeah, yeah* era, the Beatles were already adapting folk sensibilities to songs they had recorded just before starting the tour, such as "I'm a Loser" and "No Reply."

Dylan finally met the Beatles during the New York stop on the tour and introduced them to marijuana, another sign of his influence.

By the end of 1964, Phil Spector was increasingly paranoid, believing the music business was out to get him. He figured everyone was jealous of his success and wanted him to fail. How else to explain the failure of the new Ronettes single, "Walking in the Rain"? Spector considered it another masterwork with the female trio in a string that included "Be My Baby" and "Baby, I Love You." But the new record was a relative stiff by Phil's standards. He heard grumbles that his style, so innovative just two years before, had grown stale. Schadenfreude. People took pleasure watching his fall.

Phil Spector also had a mean streak. He was warned about the relative failure of "Walking in the Rain" by his loyal assistant, Sonny Bono, and decided (figuratively, in this case) to kill the messenger.

Bono had started out at Specialty in the late fifties before moving on to Spector in 1962. He saw Spector as master and himself as apprentice and was deeply, unwaveringly loyal to his idiosyncratic boss. Whether in the studio or marketing product at radio stations, Bono had Spector's back.

Bono was also ambitious and still harbored hope of being a performer. He'd written a song called "Baby, Don't Go," a duet with his girlfriend, Cherilyn Sarkisian. He played it for Spector, hoping the producer would give it the wall of sound treatment. Spector not only declined but also berated Bono for daring to have ambitions not benefiting his boss. Sonny had a few outside productions for Reprise Records—off the clock, on his own time—and Phil let it be known he considered this treachery.

Sonny was flogging "Walking in the Rain" to radio stations in the fall of 1964 when he heard disc jockeys criticize the record as being dated, indicating the Spector sound was tired. One even cringed when Sonny played the record in his office.

Honesty was Sonny Bono's crime. He called Spector and told him perhaps the girl group with the wall of sound was passé. Phil listened, murmured goodbye, then hung up. He immediately called another employee and told him to call Bono and fire him.

The more successful he became, the meaner Phil Spector got. His artists understood how he worked. He'd find a singer, become infatuated, make a couple of terrific records, then cast that singer aside. He loved the Crystals until he heard the Ronettes, and he loved the Ronettes until he heard the Righteous Brothers.

He'd seen the act from backstage when the Ronettes shared a bill with the Righteous Brothers in San Francisco. They were a moderately successful duo comprised of baritone Bill Medley and tenor Bobby Hatfield. They were white boys singing the blues, and they gigged around Southern California clubs and had modest success (principally "Little Latin Lupe Lu") on the regional Moonglow label.

They cut their Moonglow singles at Gold Star, and Stan Ross, the studio's co-owner, told Spector he needed to give the guys a good listen, thinking they might help Spector find a new direction. Bono was gone, and Spector's chief musical arranger, Jack Nitzsche, was doing a lot of outside work, particularly with the Rolling Stones. Irritated by what he considered Nitzsche's disloyalty, Spector began using other arrangers. His Wrecking Crew regulars weren't always available, and the new guys weren't willing to work overtime without pay.

"The enthusiasm was gone," Nitzsche recalled. "It just wasn't the same spirit anymore."

So Spector checked out the Righteous Brothers and found new inspiration. They were the most soulful white singers he'd ever heard, but what he needed was a song worthy of them.

He sent copies of the Brothers' Moonglow releases to Barry Mann and Cynthia Weil at the Brill Building, urging them to listen. *Come out to L.A. I've got some ideas.*

Though Phil Spector was goofy in love with Veronica Bennett of the Ronettes, he still harbored deep love for his not-quite-ex-wife Annette Merar. He waxed and waned in his feelings for her, and when Mann and Weil arrived at the airport, he said he wanted the song to be about reclaiming lost love.

Spector scheduled a Gold Star session and sat at the piano to play "You've Lost That Lovin' Feelin'" for Medley and Hatfield. He described his arrangement, and Medley started backing away from the song, which Spector had designed as nearly a solo for Medley.

"This is not right," Medley told Spector. "We're an act. We sing everything together, but Bobby sings almost nothing in this. It's all me." The song wasn't bad, Medley said. Hell, it was perfect for the Everly Brothers, but not these two purveyors of blue-eyed soul.

Spector persisted. He'd paid off the Moonglow contract, so Medley and Hatfield worked for his Philles label; they had to do as he said. Phil recorded the instrumental track first, with Earl Palmer on drums, Don Randi on piano, Tommy Tedesco and Barney Kessel on guitars, and Ray Pohlman and Carol Kaye on bass. Medley and Hatfield performed with the prerecorded track.

Medley's ball-rumbling baritone began the song:

You never close your eyes anymore when I kiss your lips . . .

Medley sang solo against a slow, magisterial track. After a short bass-and-vibes break in the middle, Hatfield joined him for a gospel-infused call-and-response in the song's last minute.

With recording finished, Phil sat in the control booth, full of doubt. "I don't know," he said to engineer Larry Levine, "it's the only song I've ever done without a backbeat." Levine told Spector he'd just made a great record, but Spector wasn't convinced; he needed an outside opinion. "There was an A&R guy doing something else at Gold Star," Levine said. "Phil brought him into the control room. He was the first person to hear it, and so I played it back and this guy said, 'Play it again.' So I did and he said, 'Play it again. This is the greatest thing I've ever heard.'"

Problem was the record was too long for radio play. It ran three minutes and forty-five seconds, and most radio stations rarely played anything longer than two minutes fifty. But Spector had a plan: he would lie. He listed the running time on the label as three minutes and five seconds.

Disc jockeys across the country were confused when they ran out of time at the end of their carefully planned shifts. Phil's lie fucked up the playlists, and he was caught in his lie, but by then, "You've Lost That Lovin' Feelin'" was the number-one record in the country.

Jim Dickson, the man with the key to World Pacific Studios, opened doors for the McGuinn-Clark-Crosby trio but wasn't interested in another gaggle of retread folkies. He wanted a *band*, something new, something cutting edge. McGuinn, a technofreak, likened the sound he wanted to the sound of a jet. Folk music was a prop plane. Rock 'n' roll was a jet.

They became the Jet Set, working beggar's hours at World Pacific, with a Wrecking Crew rhythm section of Ray Pohlman on bass and Earl Palmer on drums. But nothing seemed to jell, though the voices were pretty and Clark's songs, weepy *She don't love me* ballads, showed a confidence in melody and a facility with words.

But that'll only get you so far, Dickson thought. He put the Jet Set through nightly paces in World Pacific, trying to grow a distinctive sound. After a while, as they collaborated, they helped each other write songs.

"We learned faster than any other garage band you ever saw," David Crosby said. "[Dickson] would sit down and make us listen to the tapes, and boy was that cruelty—aversion therapy. We would look at each other and go, 'Aw, shit! We'll never do this!' But we'd come back and try some more and eventually we got pretty good at it, and it happened a lot faster than it normally would because of that."

Dickson wanted them to start thinking *band*, as in two guitars, a bass, and drums. For now, all they had were three guitarists. McGuinn was a skilled player, but Clark and Crosby were only a few steps above passable. Crosby was assigned to learn bass, but all he learned was that he was a terrible bass player. "Playing bass and singing at the same time is like being able to dial two telephones at once with both hands," he said.

Eventually Dickson persuaded a gifted mandolin player named Chris Hillman to play bass in the group. He was in a successful bluegrass group named after him—such was his level of skill—called the Hillmen. He had earlier served an impressive apprenticeship with the Scottsville Squirrel Barkers. Though only twenty, Hillman had an impressive bluegrass résumé. He wasn't sure he wanted to cast that aside to be part of this sort-of-rock, sort-of-folk group. But he respected Jim Dickson, who told him he didn't have to really leave the Hillmen until he was comfortable with the Jet Set. Hillman grudgingly agreed to learn bass. In his heart, he was horrified and embarrassed. As his friend and fellow musician David Jackson recalled, "Chris told me he'd joined this rock 'n' roll band. He said it with a real sheepish look on his face, like he was betraying the cause."

Most of the stories about finding the Byrds drummer end with the punch line "because he looked like a drummer." Even younger than Hillman—only eighteen—Mike Dick had played bongos, but that was about it. But he had the coolest, most Rolling Stones–like hair in North America. McGuinn and Clark were sharing a fleabag apartment and invited Dick to move in (semi-affluent David Crosby had separate arrangements), but despite shared rent, the group struggled on the brink of poverty, supporting themselves by shoplifting. They certainly couldn't afford a drum kit, so Mike Dick taught himself percussion by using cast-off boxes from a nearby appliance store. And he changed his name to Michael Clarke.

Eventually Dickson told the group that they had produced two songs he would allow to be heard outside the studio. He secured a deal with Jac Holzman's folk label, Elektra Records—home of Judy Collins—to release a single. McGuinn's work for Collins on Elektra was also a selling point. Plus, the country was in the thrall of Beatlemania in fall 1964, and Elektra wanted to branch out.

"Jac was open to all kinds of music, relying on his impeccable taste and an ear for unique, gifted artists," Collins said. "He was a one-man think tank about talent and how to find it. Many times he was simply in the right place at the right time, as he had been with me."

The Jet Set was old hat by now. To reach the Anglophile teen audience, the group decided it needed a British name, and Holzman came up with the Beefeaters. The final tracks—"Don't Be Long" and "Please Let Me Love You"—were recorded by Holzman's number one-producer, Paul Rothchild. Despite the exceptional talent (Rothchild went on to produce the Doors, the Butterfield Blues Band, and Janis Joplin, among many others), the record bombed.

After months of rehearsals and trying to find some way to meld these two styles, the group decided to take a break. An August trip to a movie theater gave the struggling musicians their raison d'être.

A Hard Day's Night, directed by Richard Lester, purported to show forty-eight hours in the life of the Beatles. Filmed after their trip to America in February 1964, the movie was rushed to screens in Great Britain by early July and to the United States a month later. It was presumed to be a quickie exploitation film to cash in on the group's doubtlessly fleeting fame. But owing to a clever script, the unceasing charm of the Beatles, and Lester's skilled, fast-on-the-eye direction, it was not only a surprise hit but a critical success as well. "This is going to surprise you," wrote *New York Times* film critic Bosley Crowther. "It may knock you right out of your chair—but the new film with those incredible chaps, the Beatles, is a whale of a comedy. I wouldn't believe it either, if I hadn't seen it with my own astonished eyes." Nearly a half century later, *Time* magazine proclaimed it one of the hundred greatest films of all time.

Jim McGuinn and the boys left the theater exhilarated. "I can remember coming out of that movie so jazzed that I was swinging around stop sign poles at arm's length," David Crosby said. "I knew then what my life was going to be."

But it wasn't just the witty repartee that got to Jim, David, and company. They studied the music of the film—the captivating chord that opens the proceedings, the band's onstage rapport, and even the equipment the Beatles used. Jim McGuinn fell in love with the sound George Harrison got with his brand-new electric Rickenbacker twelve-string. David Crosby wanted a Gretsch like John Lennon, and Michael Clarke couldn't help but notice the prominent "Ludwig" logo on Ringo Starr's drum kit.

Jim Dickson's partner, Eddie Tickner, came up with a novel scheme to help the group get its equipment up to snuff. He went to an art collector named Naomi Hirshhorn and suggested she invest in the band the way she invested in paintings. Buy the instruments, Tickner told Hirshhorn, and we'll pay you back with interest. It was an unusual proposal, but she went for it and the boys got their instruments of choice.

They wanted to be rock 'n' roll stars, but they couldn't decide what would make the band distinctive. The McGuinn-Clark-Crosby vocal blend sounded like the Wilson brothers, but they didn't sing about life on the ocean. It sounded like surf music without the surf.

Dickson was connected. As part of the music hipster network, he got an acetate pressing of new recordings by Bob Dylan. On June 9, Dylan had gone into the Columbia Recording studios with his guitar and a bottle of wine. That night, he recorded the whole album, to be called *Another Side of Bob Dylan*. Near the end of the night, with the wine supply low, Dylan was joined in the studio by Ramblin' Jack Elliott to take a couple of stabs at another new composition, "Mr. Tambourine Man." Written earlier in the year during a cross-country road trip, "Mr. Tambourine Man" became one of Dylan's most enduring songs, a plea from an artist to his muse. The recordings with Elliott that night were good, but not good enough. The song was left off *Another Side*, but Dickson had the acetate, which he played for his wannabe band. Crosby, still resentful of Dylan, argued against recording the song, but he was outvoted by Dickson, Tickner, and his bandmates. To be associated with Bob Dylan, particularly with a song he had not yet released, was hip cachet.

They recorded the song, along with several originals, such as "Here with You" and "She Has a Way," both brooding love songs. "Mr. Tambourine Man" stood out, managing to overcome its odd arrangement: martial drums, and voices and guitar lines that tripped over each other. It was a sloppy recording, but there was no denying the magic, droning effect of McGuinn's Rickenbacker twelve-string as he picked out the opening notes of the song.

For much of 1964, McGuinn, Clark, and Crosby had been at it—first in the folk den of the Troubadour, then at World Pacific. Now joined by Hillman and Clarke, they finally had a decent demo tape for Dickson to shop around to the record labels. They also knew it was time for a name change. The Jet Set was terrible, and besides, there was already an English group that had recorded under that name. The Beefeaters' one single on Elektra had sunk, so that name was already on the shit list.

They needed to start over. The group and Dickson gathered at Eddie Tickner's house for Thanksgiving, and after the requisite gorge-fest and annual televised loss by the Detroit Lions to the Chicago Bears (27–24), the assembled musicians began discussing their name.

"How about 'Birds'?" Eddie Tickner suggested. The idea was to have a name that suggested their high-flying harmonies.

Jim McGuinn thought it was a good idea. But *birds* was English slang for young women. "We don't want them to think that we're a bunch of fags, right?"

"What if we change the spelling to B-U-R-D-S?" Tickner asked.

McGuinn nearly puked. Who'd want a band whose name was one letter away from *turds*?

Soon, "Byrds" was suggested—a little bit of Old English spelling, with a visual *Y* that might bring subliminal comparisons to Dylan, arbiter of all that was hip and cool.

And so they became the Byrds. Dickson and Tickner continued to bust their asses, shopping the band around to record labels. They were shooting a little higher than Elektra this time.

Somehow the Byrds' demo tape fell into the hands of jazz trum-peter Miles Davis's manager, Benny Shapiro. He played it on his home stereo, and the sound wafted upstairs, to his teenage daughter. Michelle Shapiro raced downstairs, thinking her pop had somehow scored some new music by the Beatles. The next day, Shapiro had breakfast with his moody genius client and talked about his daughter's reaction to the music. Whatever his idiosyncrasies as an artist—and they were legion—at heart Miles Davis was something of a company man. He called the West Coast A&R director for his label, Columbia Records, and urged them to give the band a listen.

Less than a month into 1965, the Byrds were in Columbia's recording studio. Jim Dickson, who'd worked with the band for a year, was not allowed to produce the group he'd nurtured. Instead, twenty-four-year-old Terry Melcher pulled the assignment. He'd given Columbia some success in the surf and hot rod genres, with his studio groups Bruce and Terry (Bruce was Bruce Johnston, Jan and Dean's old friend) and the Rip Chords. His stature at the company was also helped by the fact that his ma, Doris Day, had made a shit-ton of money for Columbia.

Terry Melcher apprenticed at the William Morris Endeavor agency but was unhappy and cut a demo of a song called "That's All I Want." He took an acetate home to play for his multiplatinum mother. She was not amused.

"Oh no, you haven't really made a record have you?"

Terry was crestfallen and sullen through dinner. After dinner, he got his father to listen. He liked it and suggested Terry talk to his mother again.

He led his mother into the den and played the acetate. "She sat there, quite tense, while we put on the record and started it," Terry recalled. "A look of surprise came over her face and she began to relax. When it was over, she turned to me and there was a broad smile on her face. 'Terry was that really you?' she asked. 'I can't believe it. It's good.'"

Talk about a backhanded compliment. "My mother and dad didn't take my singing seriously until they heard my demo record. They were stunned. Neither of them knew I could sing a note. I knew what I wanted—show business."

James Harbert of Columbia recalled how Young Goodman Melcher became a producer for the label. "The whole business was changing in those days," Harbert said, "and he hung out with those groups. I finally made some money for Columbia with the New Christy Minstrels, which I'd developed. But he was into the rock scene, going to all those clubs. I said 'That's great, but you've still got to learn how the business works: Who does the promotions. . . . Who does the distribution. . . . How to handle a session and not waste money while the clock's running.'"

Terry moved to New York to enter Columbia's trainee program. By the time the Byrds came along, he had begun his climb up the ladder.

A prototype for the *beach boy* species, Terry Melcher was good-looking, confident, and cocky. "He was tall, blond, blue-eyed and freckled, with a great infectious grin," said Candice Bergen, whom he dated for several years. "I liked him at once. He was someone special, someone whose luck would never run out. There was a touch of Tom Sawyer about him in spirit as well as looks."

His mother's success was a good boost for her son as he started his career. "Terry had pull because his mother owned a lot of stock," Dickson recalled. "Hell, she practically owned the company. Whatever

Terry wanted to do at Columbia Records he got to do. Luckily, he wanted to do the Byrds."

Terry's mission with Columbia was to help the sleepy old label capture some of that elusive youth market. The major labels had been slow to move into rock 'n' roll, but Columbia wasn't just slow; it was glacial. Its success was based on middle-of-the-road music by Johnny Mathis, Barbra Streisand, the Ray Conniff Singers, and bandleader Percy Faith. The label had its bonafides in folk, with Pete Seeger and Bob Dylan, but its efforts to crack the younger market had been limited to Melcher's surfing music.

The original deal with Columbia was for only two singles, so Terry knew he had to make an impression fast if he wanted to move Columbia firmly into rock 'n' roll.

Covering his bets, Terry contracted with key Wrecking Crew players: Hal Blaine on drums, Leon Russell on electric piano, Larry Knechtel on bass, and Bill Pitman and Jerry Cole on guitars. The only Byrd he allowed to play in the studio was Jim McGuinn. "We've got to have McGuinn because otherwise there's no flavor of what they're going to sound like," Dickson told the producer.

"I'd been a studio musician in New York, so they let me play on it," McGuinn said. "So my feeling was, 'Great, I get to play with this great band, the Wrecking Crew.'"

Chris Hillman and Michael Clarke were doubly pissed. They didn't sing with the band, and only Jim McGuinn, David Crosby, and Gene Clark had actually signed the Columbia contract, because they were singers. Now Chris and Michael wouldn't even be playing on the record. David was likewise furious that he wouldn't get to play on the instrumental track.

Dylan's original version had four verses of startling wordplay and imagery, each separated by the chorus begging the muse to speak to the artist. Few records played on the radio went beyond two and a half minutes, and if the Byrds recorded all of Dylan's lyrics, the song probably would have run five or six minutes and never make the playlists.

So they cut it to chorus, second verse, chorus, and out. Blaine, on drums, helped flesh out the arrangement by basing it in part on the Beach Boys' "Don't Worry Baby." Larry Knechtel, known mostly as a keyboard player (that's him playing gospel-rock piano on Simon and Garfunkel's "Bridge over Troubled Water") played bass on the track, opening and closing the recording with a distinctive, dragging line.

Leon Russell's piano was eventually mixed so low in the recording as to be barely audible. The guitars of Bill Pitman and Jerry Cole were also toned down, to give breathing space to Jim McGuinn's majestic twelve-string. The first notes from the Rickenbacker are among the most distinctive openings in rock 'n' roll, and Jim's voice—folk reedy mixed with a fatigued high—make the song, along with Gene and David's harmonies. It faded out with a lustrous tag as Jim's twelve-string struck an eternal, wandering figure.

The song was recorded on January 20, 1965, and even after mixing, there was something about it that was flat. Terry Melcher realized it needed more postproduction work. His union engineer kept pointing at his watch, telling the kid to wrap it up. Terry wanted to open the echo chambers, a series of concrete block rooms under the studio floor, but the engineer balked.

"You need a written request for that," the engineer said, "and another engineer as well."

"Who's going to care?" Terry argued. "Nobody's around."

"I'm around."

"Look, I think I've got an idea to make this record work."

"No."

It was time to play the mom card. "You know who I am, right?" Terry asked the engineer.

"Yeah, I know who you are," the engineer said, "and it doesn't mean anything to me."

"So you feel OK about pissing my mother off?"

"I don't care who your mother is."

"You think Doris Day doesn't mean anything at Columbia?"

"What are you talking about?"

"You didn't know that Doris Day was my mother?" Terry said. "I didn't want to have to get into that, but I need access into the fucking echo chambers."

"Let me go talk to somebody," the engineer said grudgingly. When he left the studio, Terry barricaded the door with a stack of amplifiers. Working quickly, he broke into the echo chambers and ran reverb on top of reverb until he brought out the sound and felt the music deep in his gut, changing it from a flat, nearly lifeless recording into a record that made the hair stand up on the back of his neck. Once he heard how the chiming twelve-string and deranged choirboy harmonies sounded run through the echo chambers, he knew he had a hit.

"It's alive!" Terry screamed, full of Franksteinian fury.

Pounding on the studio door. "Open this door, Melcher!"

The engineer had company. "This is security. Open the door."

Terry unlocked the door, calm, as if nothing had happened.

The finished and heavily echoed Byrds recording of "Mr. Tambourine Man" clocked in at two minutes, twenty-four seconds. Terry Melcher, the singing Byrds, and the Wrecking Crew had distilled the essence of Dylan into a hit single. Columbia hesitated to release the record and dawdled for months. Finally, Melcher played the mom card again, and Columbia released the song in April, "a fateful moment in the burgeoning history of folk-rock," in the words of record industry mogul Clive Davis.

By June, it was the number-one song in the country.

John and Michelle Phillips heard "Mr. Tambourine Man" emanating from every radio in the Virgin Islands. Cass Elliot recognized the high harmony of her old pal David Crosby in the chorus.

Cass and Denny's old running buddy from the Mugwumps, Zal Yanovsky, had joined forces with another old pal, John Sebastian, and they were lighting up the radio as the Lovin' Spoonful.

Around the bonfire with his friends, John Phillips had an idea. *Hey, that could be us. We're that good.* "Mr. Tambourine Man" was a song that launched a thousand bands.

"The Byrds created a sense of possibility," writer Anthony DeCurtis said.

Barry McGuire, that other Village friend, had decided that he needed to go the route of the Byrds. That meant thumbing a ride to California.

Phil Sloan stopped writing surfing songs and began to write protest songs in the Bob Dylan mode.

And at the beginning of 1965, it seemed that everyone with a guitar converged on Los Angeles.

10

THE DOOR FLIES OPEN

The thing I wonder about is where does Brian's creative spark come from? Not his subjects or anything, but his spark. What makes it so great for me is that I really don't know. There's a mystery behind Brian, even to me.

—Dennis Wilson

As 1965 dawned, Brian Wilson felt liberated. He no longer had to worry about touring and stage clothes and set lists and motel beds and travel itineraries. He was free to stay in his own bed with his young wife at their new home on Laurel Way in the Hollywood Hills. When he felt like it, he wrote songs and went to the studio—Western Recorders, usually—and recorded his ever-more-lush and complicated backing tracks. He called them "pocket symphonies."

The group was on the road by the second day of the new year, all the way across the continent, in Virginia, then North Carolina, then Delaware and Illinois. For a few days, Brian worked at peace in his mad scientist lair with his Wrecking Crew coconspirators. He was halfway through the next Beach Boys album, planning to include some of the singles the group had released in the late summer and fall of 1964, such as "Dance, Dance, Dance," which had made it to number eight, and "When I Grow Up (to Be a Man)," which rose as high as number nine. Also in the can were "Don't Hurt My Little Sister," a guitar-driven piece drawn from his conflicted feelings for the three Rovell sisters, and "She Knows Me Too Well," another in an increasing number of Beach Boys songs in which Brian, now more confident with his high, aching voice, took the lead vocal rather than assigning it to Mike Love.

Brian pushed himself hard that first week of the year, to make sure that when the group returned from the road, he'd have finished tracks that merely required their vocals to become full-fledged Beach Boys records. He called back Glen Campbell from the tour for the tracking sessions, leaving the group to soldier on as a quartet, with Alan Jardine switching to bass for the dates that Campbell missed.

Back at Western, Brian put the Wrecking Crew through twenty-five takes of a new ballad called "Please Let Me Wonder." He'd taken a turn toward the ethereal before, with "Don't Worry Baby," but "Please Let Me Wonder" was a mature step, firmly planted in the realm of the adult experience of love. No more of this teen love at the drag race stuff. He was writing and singing of the love and doubt of marriage. Nothing about the recording or performance of the song rooted it in 1965. It was, and would remain, a contemporary-sounding record.

By the end of the week, he had another track in the can. He put the Wrecking Crew through thirty-one takes of "Help Me Ronda" before pronouncing himself satisfied. In addition to Campbell on guitar for both sessions, the sound was filled out by the usual suspects—Hal Blaine, Carol Kaye, Leon Russell, Don Randi, Bill Pitman, and, from an earlier era of session greats, Barney Kessel on guitar. A surprise guest: former Sun Records recording artist Billy Lee Riley, known mostly for his rockabilly hit "Flyin' Saucers Rock 'n' Roll." Riley was part of Sun's house band and had backed up Jerry Lee Lewis, Warren Smith, and Charlie Rich. He played the distinctive harmonica lick on "Help Me Ronda."

The group came back from the road and immediately went to the studio to see what Brian had done in their absence. He started working on the vocal for "Please Let Me Wonder." Brian had imagined the song with him singing lead, doubled at points by Mike. So clear was his vision that he lost his temper early in the session, accusing Mike of backing away from the microphone to sabotage the song.

"Mike! God!" Brian finally yelled in frustration. "The whole thing is that you just don't realize how important it is to stay in the same spot for the whole fucking time."

After finishing the dual lead, Brian needed nine takes to get the backing vocals finished. He then overdubbed a bass part and pronounced the song finished. Still smarting from Wilson's rebuke, Love stormed from the studio.

Two days later, Brian was behind the board in a different studio: Gold Star, where Phil Spector had made so many of his great records.

Seemingly in Spector's honor, Wilson and the Wrecking Crew cut a dense, smothering track for a cover version of Bobby Freeman's 1958 hit "Do You Wanna Dance?". As with "Ronda" the week before, Brian toyed with volume and modulation. After an intense but subdued opening, the music exploded with the first chorus and never let up. His guitar trinity—Bill Pitman, Billy Strange, and Tommy Tedesco—took their solos to reverb heaven in the Gold Star echo chamber.

The rest of the group watched Brian as he taught the musicians their parts and got a finished take on the third try. Brian tapped Dennis to sing lead, thinking his husky and less-than-perfect voice might be able to match the urgency in the instrumental track. The group then added a thundering wall of voices that climbed toward the song's conclusion. It was the best Phil Spector record that Spector never produced. Apprentice bested master.

He used "Do You Wanna Dance?" as the album's lead-off song and chose Dennis again for the closing song, "In the Back of My Mind." The group was back at Western Recorders on the thirteenth to record this song about the confusion of love, with incomplete thoughts and unresolved questions, highlighted by a string arrangement that wandered in near the end, then seemed to start playing a different song during the tag. Not until the Beatles explored similar dissonant mental territory in "Strawberry Fields Forever" (1967) and "Hey Jude" (1968) would there be songs to so adequately convey such heartbreaking bewilderment.

The studio musicians packed and left, but Brian asked the group to stick around. They pulled chairs into a circle, and Brian delivered his rehearsed speech. This was the way it was going to be: he'd create the pocket symphonies in the studio, and the group would come off the road and add their vocals. He had desperately wanted to show the group that his new system could work, and, after finishing the new album—which he titled *The Beach Boys Today!*—he thought he had done that.

And this is when Brian told them about the beautiful future he foresaw. He asked them to take a leap of faith, and, seeing as they had no choice, they did.

Brian finished the new Beach Boys album by the end of February 1965, and the album was released on March 8. *Today!* followed the classic rock 'n' roll album formula—a rocking side with up-tempo songs such as "Do You Wanna Dance?," "Good to My Baby," and "Help Me Ronda," and a dreamy ballad side with "Please Let Me Wonder," "Kiss Me Baby," and "In the Back of My Mind." But for the inclusion of another spoken track—a tiresome skit with aging hipster/publicist Earl Leaf called "Bull Session with the Big Daddy"—it was a nearly perfect album. Luckily, the "Bull Session" was the last track, so it was easy to lift the needle after the strings from "In the Back of My Mind" wandered off to another room. It was a gutsy, meandering way to end *Today!* and also served as a harbinger of differences to come.

The Beach Boys went back on the road with Glen Campbell, but in addition to his studio work, Campbell was a member, along with Leon Russell and Delaney Bramlett, of the Shindogs, the house band for ABC television's rock 'n' roll show *Shindig!* He had to honor that contract and would miss a few Beach Boys dates. Brian returned to the stage for a week until Glen was again available, but before February ended, Brian was back in the studio. As if to prove the advantage of his new work ethic, as soon as the Beach Boys went back out on the road in February, Brian began polishing his pocket symphonies. He couldn't write—or obviously record—during a concert tour, but as long as someone took his place onstage, he could double the productivity of the Beach Boys.

Getting a steady replacement was critical. Campbell was great at his job, but he was losing money as Wilson's stage replacement and wanted to return to lucrative full-time session work and begin concentrating on his career, developing as a singer.

Mike Love decided to give Bruce Johnston a call. Johnston had been part of the Jan and Dean gang at University High and, at age sixteen, had recorded with Phil Spector. From a moneyed family, he had the right kind of Hollywood connections and was able to work his way into a recording career at an early age. He played on Sandy Nelson's "Teen Beat," and before he reached drinking age, he was staff producer at Del-Fi Records. A few years later, he was one of the few youth acts on Columbia Records and produced an instrumental album, *Surfin' 'Round the World* in 1963, credited to the Bruce Johnston Surfing Band.

That year he hooked up with Terry Melcher, another privileged son of Bel-Air. When crusty old Columbia decided to go for younger listeners, Melcher partnered with Johnston, writing and producing several hits under the names Bruce and Terry and the Rip Chords. As the Rip

Chords, they had a million-selling single with "Hey Little Cobra," written by Bruce's high school classmate and former member of the Teddy Bears Annette Kleinbard, now using her stage name, Carol Connors.

As Bruce and Terry, the duo ranged over the twin genres of surfing and hot rod music. Almost as soon as Phil Sloan and Steve Barri copyrighted and recorded their songs as the Fantastic Baggys or the Super Stocks, Bruce and Terry covered them and scored greater sales than the Sloan-Barri originals. Bruce and Terry's biggest success came with Sloan and Barri's "Summer Means Fun," which, in turn, borrowed the lyric conceit of "Surf City":

> *Summer means fun*
> *The girls are two-to-one*

Sloan and Barri worked for a label just one step up the food chain from a camper truck. Bruce and Terry reaped the benefits of the big time, thanks to being on a major label like Columbia.

So Bruce Johnston knew the territory. Mike Love asked if Bruce could find them a fill-in for Brian on short notice. Bruce made some calls, but no one could make their lives fit the Beach Boys' timetable.

"They wanted someone yesterday," Bruce recalled. "So I said, 'Look, Mike, I can't find anyone, so I'll come. I don't play bass, I play piano, but I suppose I could sing all the high parts if you show me what to do.'"

Bruce joined a touring group already well known for its contentiousness and offstage battles. Rivals Dennis and Mike both saw themselves as the focal point of the group now that Brian was in self-exile. Because of his good looks, Dennis drew most of the attention, especially from the young women wailing in the audience. "In the beginning he was easily the most popular guy in the group," Al Jardine recalled. "Onstage, all he had to do was stand up to stretch and the crowd would go nuts. Mike would be trying to sing, and he'd have to turn around to find out what was going on. Oh, that used to piss Mr. Love off so much." This wasn't calculated on Dennis's part, Al said. "He was a star without evening trying."

Meanwhile, Terry Melcher was rumored to be cutting a much more up-tempo cover of "Help Me Ronda."

Brian knew the song was a hit, and he wanted it to be *his* hit. He rushed into the studio to cut a faster, stripped-down version of the song, now spelled "Help Me Rhonda." The first version included timbales, claves, three saxes, and Billy Lee Riley's harmonica. The remake, recorded as the Beach Boys were finishing *Today!*, featured Blaine on drums, Kaye on bass, Carl Wilson and Glen Campbell on guitars, and Brian on piano. The band was back from its tour, so Brian pulled them into Western Recorders to do the vocal track the same day. As he had on the *Today!* version, Alan Jardine took the lead vocal.

Brian invited his parents to the session. As he tried to get the vocals recorded, Murry Wilson began barking orders on the talkback mic in the control booth.

"Brian, you've got a wonderful tune here," Murry said. "Al, loosen up a little and say sexy 'Rhonda' more. Mike, come in closer on the mic. Carl, 'ooh' better, and Brian, you're awfully shrill tonight, so soften it a little and we've got it. Dennis, don't flat any more."

Murry was rambling and hitting the sauce hard. Brian swallowed his anger and returned to recording vocals. Still, the slurred, condescending voice cut in from the control booth. Mr. Know-It-All wanted to produce the session despite the fact that his son, the hottest producer in rock 'n' roll, was on the other side of the glass.

Finally, Brian urged Murry to sing the song.

Murry harrumphed. "Do you want me to leave, Brian?"

"No," Brian said tentatively, "I just want you to let him sing it."

"Your mother and I can leave now, if you want." Murry addressed the group and the studio musicians: "Brian said, 'Come down and relax,' so I did."

The group took a break from singing and gathered in a corner of the studio to vent about Murry, now neck deep in his cups in the booth. Mike and Brian argued. Alan and Carl counseled *This too shall pass* patience.

When the recording started again, so did Murry. "Fellows, I have three thousand words to say. Quit screaming and sing from your hearts," he advised. "You're big stars. Let's fight for success. Let's go. OK. Let's go. Loosen up. Be happy. OK, fellows? If you've got any guts, let's hear it."

Brian waited a beat. "That's only 82 words."

"Come on, Brian, let's knock it off," Murry said. "If you guys think you're good, let's go. As a team, we're unbeatable."

"Shit!" Brian screamed. "He's driving me nuts!"

Mike tried to calm him. "Don't worry about it."

"God damn it!" Brian screamed.

"I'll leave, Brian, if you're going to give me a bad time," Murry said.

"I have one ear left," Brian said, "and your big bad voice is killing it."

"Loosen up, Al," Murry said, trying to start another take. "Let's roll. Loosen it up, fellows."

Brian turned to Mike. "I can't take it," he said.

Murry offered to leave the session, but when Brian called his bluff, Murry decided to stay. After another take broke down, Brian and Murry went at it again.

"When the guys get too much money, you start thinking that you're going to make everything a hit," Murry said. Then, putting on a show of contrition, he offered to back away. "I'll never help you guys mix another session."

"Why?" Brian asked.

"Because you don't appreciate the good help that Chuck [engineer Chuck Britz] and I have given you. Listen, let me tell you something. When you guys get so big that you can't sing from your heart, you're going downhill."

"Downhill?" Brian asked.

Murry screamed his response into the talkback microphone: *"Downhill!"*

Murry stood up, took Audree by the elbow, and began to leave but offered a parting shot at his eldest son. "I've protected you for 22 years," he said. "But I can't go on if you're not going to listen to an intelligent man."

"Are you going now?" Brian asked urgently. "Are you going or staying? I want to know."

After a few more exchanges, Murry turned to his wife but spoke so that the whole studio could hear. "The kid got a big success and he thinks he owns the business." He put his hand on Audree's shoulder. "I'm sorry. I'm so sorry, dear."

Again, father took a parting shot at son. "Chuck and I used to make one hit after another in 30 minutes," he said. "You guys take five hours to do it."

"Times are changing," Brian said.

"You know why? Because you guys think you have an image."

"Times are changing."

"Don't ever forget," Murry said. "Honesty is the best policy. Right, Mike? You know what I'm talking about, Mike? Forget about your image. You can live for 200 years if you grow. OK, let's forget it. Let's go."

Finally, Murry and Audree Wilson left the session. Brian finished recording the vocals. Within two months, "Help Me Rhonda" was the number-one record in the country.

Murry Wilson never recovered from being fired by his sons, and his relationship with Brian was fractured for the rest of his life. Once, in resignation, he wrote his eldest son a letter: "I cannot believe that such a beautiful young boy, who was kind, loving, received good grades in school and had so many versatile talents, could become so obsessed to prove that he was better than his father."

––––––––––––––

The summer of 1965 was a high-water mark for rock 'n' roll. Tuning the radio dial, it was easy to find the essential elements of "classic rock." The Beatles had "Ticket to Ride," the Rolling Stones hit their stride with "Satisfaction," and Dylan went electric, unleashing six minutes of anger and bile called "Like a Rolling Stone" that forever changed the definition of the popular song. Who would have known that rage and resentment could make a hit?

In some ways, 1965 was a continental divide in rock music. Standing on the crest of that year, it was easy to look back and see the black vocal groups in their tuxes and the Beach Boys in their striped shirts and the Beatles in collarless Pierre Cardin. Turn the other direction, and the Stones and the Byrds set a new style not only of clothing but also of subject matter. And Bob Dylan sat above them all as the arbiter of cool. It stopped being *rock 'n' roll* and became *rock*.

There was a lot of soul on the radio, from Barbara Mason's "Yes I'm Ready" to the breakthrough song from the hardest-working man in show business—"Papa's Got a Brand New Bag" by James Brown.

The new mutant gene known as folk rock was in evidence with the Byrds ("Mr. Tambourine Man" was still on the charts as the summer began), Dylan, and the Dylan covers: Cher's "All I Really Want to Do" and the Turtles' "It Ain't Me Babe." Dylan's use of *babe* inspired Cher's partner Sonny Bono—the former Specialty A&R guy who became Spector's gofer—to try it out with "I Got You, Babe."

Motown was at a peak with "I Can't Help Myself" by the Four Tops and "Back in My Arms Again" by the Supremes. The year had kicked off auspiciously with the Temptations classic "My Girl."

Even bad songs were good on the radio in 1965. Radio belched the jive of "Wooly Bully" by Sam the Sham and the Pharaohs. The most coy of British Invasion bands, Herman's Hermits, covered Sam Cooke's "Wonderful World." Billy Joe Royal addressed the American class system in Joe South's "Down in the Boondocks."

The Beatles and all things British still dominated the charts, but Brian managed to garner the top spot on the charts with "I Get Around" in 1964 and "Help Me Rhonda" a year later.

At home and left to his own devices, Brian began to explore and make other friends outside the tight family circle. He also tried to navigate his rise to maturity while taking tentative steps into the mysterious new world of marriage. Marilyn was young and both protected and baffled by her talented and unpredictable husband. When she learned that Brian and agent Loren Schwartz, one of his new best friends, had smoked marijuana, she was hurt, scared, then angry.

No longer surrounded by his brothers and cousin, Brian began seeking other friends like Schwartz, wringing everything he could from the friendship, and then moving on. He had a new best friend every other week or so, and some of these relationships went far beyond marijuana. By the summer of 1965, Brian had tried LSD and found that he liked it. He said he saw God.

Marilyn Wilson, then still a teenager, carried the responsibility of trying to protect her erratic husband from these people she called the "drainers" in his life. "I could kill the guy that gave him acid," she said. "That was the worst experience for Brian to go through. Jesus, do you realize how sick that is for people to give people acid?"

Mike Love was never one to turn down a good time, but he got a little worried about Brian's marijuana use, then went into all-out panic mode with the LSD. When Murry learned about the acid, he lectured his eldest son as if Brian were nine. Murry and Brian were in the car, on their way to a recording session. "I read in the *Times* that you experimented with LSD," Murry said. "Is that a put-on to the newspapers, or did you do it?"

"Yes, Dad, I did."

"Well, tell me Brian, do you think you're strong enough in your brain that you can experiment with a chemical that might drive you crazy later or maybe you might kill somebody or jump out of a window if it ricochets on you?"

"No, Dad," Brian said. "It made me understand a lot of things."

"Who're you trying to kid, Brian?" Murry asked. "What did you understand, except seeing like a nightmare in your brain, colors and things like that maybe? You know, Brian, one thing that God gave you was a brain. If you play with it and destroy it, you're dead, you're a vegetable. And we haven't heard the end of this. There are going to be people killed and people in sanitariums and insane asylums because they played with God."

But it was too late to stop now.

———————————

The drugs and the enlarging circle of admiration made Brian want to reach higher and go for more. He thought of what he could do with music and came to the conclusion that he could create a musical sunrise. He would record a track that would be the *sound* of the sun rising. Mike Love was dubious. *Great. That ought to sell well.* Eyebrows arched. Eyes rolled.

But Brian did it. And the result was the piece of music he always said was his favorite thing he wrote: the instrumental introduction to "California Girls," released in the summer of 1965. "The song was a big record for us," Brian said, "but I never really liked anything but the intro." The irony was that disc jockeys talked over the introduction, shutting up only when the carnival-style organ kicked in and Mike Love, in full swagger mode, began singing:

> *Well, East Coast girls are hip*
> *I really dig the styles they wear*

But the sunrise was beautiful. With the pinpoint of a guitar, the sunlight pierced the darkness. Then came other shafts of light played on strings, and the sky grew lighter with the sigh of brass until, by the end, day had arrived.

"California Girls" was credited solely to Brian Wilson, primarily because the music publishing company for the Beach Boys, Sea of Tunes, was run by Murry Wilson. Murry's practice begat decades of resentment. "I wrote every last syllable of the words to 'California Girls,'" Mike said, "and when the record came out, it said 'Brian Wilson'—there was no 'Mike Love.'"

With *Today!* and "Help Me Rhonda" riding high, Brian began assembling the parts of what would become the next group album, *Summer Days (and Summer Nights!!)*. "The door starts to fly open on that album," Carl Wilson said. "Musically speaking—the recording process and, you know, that whole total sound."

The door had already been opened with *Today!*, but Brian did include some backing-track experiments on the album, including a fairly grandiose setting for his aching ballad "Let Him Run Wild." Remarkably, he was expanding the boundaries of popular music within the narrow confines of the dictates of the music industry: what record companies would release, what radio stations would play. In doing so, he subversively began to expand those boundaries.

An important commandment fell away in 1965, though Brian had no hand in the change. Radio program directors, as standard operating procedure, would not authorize the play of any record longer than three minutes. Most artists had learned to work within this structure and had produced several small masterpieces. Phil Spector was especially adept at squeezing so much drama and teenage angst into his songs, and they were all shorter than two minutes. Brian's greatest asphalt drama, "Shut Down," was a complex and jargon-filled tale of a drag race on an L.A. street, and it clocked in at one minute and forty-nine seconds. Another car paean, "Little Deuce Coupe," had been a mere minute thirty-eight.

Two rock 'n' roll artists broke the three-minute barrier. The first assault was Phil Spector's 1964 recording of the Righteous Brothers' "You've Lost That Lovin' Feelin'."

The barrier finally fell in the summer of 1965 when Bob Dylan released "Like a Rolling Stone." Columbia Records executives had been surprised when a New York discotheque had success playing the record in its six minutes of furious glory without the dance floor screeching to a halt. People were actually dancing to Bob Dylan. The company briefly thought of cutting the record in half, the way rhythm and blues artist James Brown dealt with his long songs: divide them, with "Part 1" on the A-side and "Part 2" on the B. But "Like a Rolling Stone" became a hit without any edits for length. And so the three-minute barrier fell.

Brian was working within the confines of the three-minute radio-friendly song. Nearly every track on *Summer Days* had some new touch he'd cook up, then execute with his ace studio band. The Beach Boys were on the road, breaking in new guy Bruce Johnston, on a tour when the group had such support acts as Sam the Sham and the Pharaohs and Bobby Goldsboro. Brian was mostly cloistered in the studio but appeared with the group on ABC Television's *Shindig!* Despite the fact that Glen Campbell and Leon Russell were part of the show's house band, Campbell did not play, and neither did Johnston. Brian donned the striped shirt and joined the group in lip synching "Do You Wanna Dance?"

Summer Days threatened to become the first non–Beach Boy Beach Boys album. As Brian labored in the spring and early summer, he found himself employing the Crew almost exclusively, and but for a couple of songs (most notably "Girl, Don't Tell Me" and the Spector tribute "Then I Kissed Her"), the band members played hardly a note on the album. Brian was expanding his roster of musicians as well, working with string sections on some of his ballads. When the album was released, "Summer Means New Love," a dreamy instrumental that showed off Tommy Tedesco's guitar playing, featured not a single Beach Boy.

Brian pushed the musicians hard. It took forty-four punishing takes before he was satisfied with the track for "California Girls." He had a full infield of guitar players to simulate the sunrise, and if one of them missed or flubbed a note, he *heard* it.

OK, let's go again.

Adding the voices made it a Beach Boys album. Brian also ticked off the vocal contributions on the back cover's track listing. His piano blues, the confessional "I'm Bugged at My Ol' Man," was credited to "Too embarrassed," but there was no hiding Brian's voice. For only the second time (not since "Pom Pom Play Girl" on *Shut Down, Volume 2*), Carl Wilson took a lead vocal. "Girl, Don't Tell Me" shared a similar twelve-string and drum sound as the Beatles' hit of that summer, "Ticket to Ride." It was also the first Beach Boys song with no backing vocal. It became a showpiece for Carl, who began assuming more lead vocals at Brian's urging.

Released to coincide with the Fourth of July, *Summer Days* was the quintessence of the early Beach Boys, right down to the cover. They were tanned and windblown on a sailboat (Al Jardine wasn't pictured, home with the flu), and "California Girls" became a key part of that summer's soundtrack.

The opening was beautiful, but Brian also knew how to end a song, how to get the right fade-out. "I love the way Brian has faded out some of his records," Dennis said. Carl agreed that Brian had a special talent for knowing how to end a song. "We call fadeouts 'tags,'" he said. "We're big tag fans. 'Surfer Girl,' 'Surfin' U.S.A.'—I think that's when Brian got the knack."

In a way, *Summer Days* was a regression for its creator. Brian had spelunked deep into his soul for those longing ballads on the second side of *Today!* But for the shrill "Let Him Run Wild," there was nothing comparable on *Summer Days*. Brian was willing to share his heart, if he could figure out how to do it.

————————

Making hit records was like being a gerbil on a treadmill. Both the industry and the audience had a *What have you done lately?* attitude toward musicians. A hit record in 1964 didn't mean much a year later.

In 1964, Barry McGuire was the cob-rough lead singer of the New Christy Minstrels' hit "Green, Green," which he coauthored with Christies mastermind Randy Sparks. He'd quit the Christies at that peak and gone out on his own, without much luck.

In 1965, he was doing much better with marijuana than singing. He became known among friends as a great source of killer weed. Everybody knew McGuire. Jim McGuinn was a pal from the Village, and so when the Byrds became the house band at Ciro's, the venerable Sunset Strip nightclub, McGuire showed up to support the band with his dance-floor flailing that seemed to help loosen the room.

McGuire wasn't alone on the dance floor. The Byrds were still somewhat inept as musicians. Only McGuinn and Hillman approached professional levels, but Hillman wasn't playing the instrument he'd mastered and was still adapting to bass guitar. But in those months before "Mr. Tambourine Man" hit number one, the Byrds turned Ciro's into the place to be, with the help of the action on the dance floor.

As Jim Dickson watched his clients onstage help create a *scene—the* scene—he noted the action unfurling before him: "We had them all. We had Jack Nicholson dancing, we had Peter Fonda dancing with Odetta, we had Vito and his Freakers . . ."

"Vito" was Vito Paulekas, who—with his band of mirthful dancers—drew much of the crowd to Ciro's. "We made lines in front of Ciro's that hadn't been seen since Peggy Lee played there," Dickson recalled.

Some might claim Vito as the first hippie. Four hundred miles north, you'd get an argument on that point from Ken Kesey and his

Merry Pranksters, who had driven their psychedelic bus cross-country the summer before, freaking out straights across America, a journey chronicled in journalist Tom Wolfe's *The Electric Kool-Aid Acid Test*.

Vito Paulekas presided over a commune that may have predated Kesey's Pranksters. (Only your sociologist knows for sure.) The Byrds had hooked up with Vito and his "freaks"—a term the dancers embraced and encouraged.

During the months of rehearsal that Dickson demanded, the group had often practiced in Vito's loft, as did another band, called Love, led by an enigmatic and supremely talented Arthur Lee.

In the "first hippie" argument, Lee cast his vote with Vito over Kesey. Vito and the Freakers "started the whole thing," Lee said.

It was obvious to the Ciro's managers that the dancers had a drawing power at least equal to the band, so Vito and his pals not only got in for free, they were comped drinks and treated like valued employees. "A band didn't have to be good as long as the dancers were there," said producer-musician Kim Fowley.

Barry McGuire wasn't a card-carrying member of Vito and the Freakers, but he certainly could pass the audition. He flailed in that arrhythmic twist-a-frug-jerk that became ubiquitous in the hippie years (and still on view wherever decedents of the Grateful Dead gather). Of course, McGuire's dope also helped loosen the mood at Ciro's.

Taking a break from dancing to suck down a beer, McGuire ran into Lou Adler. Adler had split his partnership with Herb Alpert, who had begun to have success with his Wrecking Crew studio band, under the name Herb Alpert and the Tijuana Brass. His records on his own label, A&M, were so successful that by 1965, he'd recruited musicians to take on the road to meet an overwhelming demand for concert appearances.

Adler had also started his own label, Dunhill Records, and was searching for talent. When he saw McGuire doing his spastic dance at Ciro's, he thought lightning might strike twice. If America had lapped up McGuire's gruff growl on "Green, Green," maybe they'd like to hear that voice again. Adler made McGuire an offer, and the singer seemed game for another ride on the pony.

A few days later, at the Dunhill office, Adler realized McGuire was a good writer but not prolific. He did not have enough songs to carry an album, so Adler played him a stack of demos, none of which McGuire liked. He was ready to leave for another night on the Ciro's dance floor when Adler suggested he go see the kid.

"Phil Sloan is down the hall," Adler told McGuire. "He's got some songs that I don't get but maybe you'd like to hear them."

Sloan, until recently one of the recognized Shakespeares of surf music, played McGuire several of his new, more mature tunes. Sloan *was* still a kid, living at home with his parents. The ascendance of Bob Dylan had had a profound effect on him, and he cast aside the surf-and-turf songs. In what he called a moment of divine inspiration that spring, he'd written four songs in one night. One of them was a status update of a world in chaos called "Eve of Destruction." Dark and brooding and finger-pointing, it was the yin to the yang of "Summer Means Fun." Sloan had played his new songs for Lou Adler, who immediately said he hated them. Sloan still believed in his songs, but he set them aside and awaited further orders from Adler.

So when Barry McGuire stuck his head in the closet-sized office Phil Sloan shared with Steve Barri, the kid played "The Sins of a Family."

"I like it, Phil, but it's not what I'm looking for," Barry said.

Phil kept spinning off songs, always getting the same polite turndown, until he played "What's Exactly the Matter with Me?". Lou resisted the idea of recording the song. But Barry was insistent.

Adler scheduled a session in Western Studio 3, with Hal Blaine and Larry Knechtel, with Sloan on guitar and harmonica. They recorded a couple takes of "The Sins of a Family," then took a break and had some fried chicken delivered. Adler wanted to knock out a B-side for the single, so they cut another "mature" Sloan song, "Ain't No Way I'm Gonna Change My Mind." They nailed that one and still had twenty minutes left on the session clock. Like all independent record men, Adler never wanted any paid-for time to go to waste, especially when he had paid for the talents of Blaine and Knechtel.

McGuire decided to do "Eve of Destruction." *Really?* Adler despised the song, which to him was merely a litany of ills plaguing the country—the war in Vietnam, the bloody struggle for civil rights, the looming threat of nuclear annihilation. But McGuire was again insistent.

Unfortunately, someone had set their paper plate of greasy fried chicken on top of the lyrics Sloan had copied on notebook paper. McGuire rolled with it, assuming he was laying down a rough guide vocal, to be erased when something more polished could be recorded. At one point, unable to read through grease stains, he groaned with frustration but kept singing. (Years later, singer Jackson Browne described the record as akin to Yosemite Sam singing Bob Dylan.) There was no time to recopy the lyrics, so McGuire gruffly sang into the mic, *hmmm*ing and *mmmm*ing as he struggled to read the words.

When all parties gathered in the booth to listen to the playback, Blaine and Knechtel were most enthusiastic, quoting their favorite lines, saying they'd never heard such a song before. Engineer Bones Howe also spoke up. "You've got a hit track here, Lou," he said.

"The track is great, guys," Adler told them, "but this song? I don't think so."

That was the consensus. McGuire grunted his way through the song like a man in the middle of a particularly difficult shit.

After hearing the playback, McGuire was as dubious as Adler, but Sloan thought the song had resonance. He'd offered it to the Byrds, who'd turned it down. The Turtles recorded it but buried it as a filler track on their "It Ain't Me Babe" album, reasoning that if they put out such a controversial song as a single, they'd be blackballed. Sloan thought McGuire might be his last chance with the song, which had great meaning for him.

The kindly McGuire acknowledged Sloan's enthusiasm by picking "Eve of Destruction" as the B-side of "The Sins of a Family." The record fell promptly out of sight, dead on arrival until a small-market disc jockey in Wisconsin decided to play the flip. Calls came in. *Play that again. And again.* Pretty soon bigger markets picked it up, and word of broadcast mouth began spreading. The song was banned in Boston, then New York, then Chicago. Tasting forbidden fruit, teenagers snapped up the record and grooved to the sound of racism and social injustice, as growled out by a big, hairy teddy bear of a man.

Once again, and against almost everyone's better judgment, Barry McGuire had a hit.

John Phillips still resisted the idea of having Cass Elliot in his group. As far as he was concerned, he and Michelle and Denny were the latest iteration of his trio, the *Newer* Journeymen. He worried that the addition of a "fat chick" might limit the group's appeal or make them into something of a joke. Still, he could not deny the pure beauty of Cass's singing.

Elliot decided to leave the Virgin Islands and go see Jim Hendricks in California. It was understood that the other three also would leave island life soon. They were impatient to get rich and famous, now that some of their friends were doing so well.

John heard the Byrds, and he heard Barry McGuire on the radio. These were people he knew—they all knew—from their days in the Village. Hell, if *they* could do it, then there's no reason he and his rag-tag group couldn't do it. Plus, maybe McGuinn and McGuire could open some doors.

Turns out it was Cass Elliot who opened the doors. Upon arriving in California, Elliot hooked up with Hendricks and his new girlfriend, Vanessa. Jim and Vanessa were pitching themselves as the next Sonny and Cher and had signed a song publishing deal with music impresario Kim Fowley. Cass sponged off Jim for about a month before John, Michelle, and Denny arrived in L.A. The gang slept on Jim and Vanessa's living room floor.

Fowley's fingerprints were everywhere on Los Angeles rock 'n' roll. A former Uni High classmate of Jan and Dean, as well as Bruce Johnston and Nancy Sinatra, he had also gravitated toward show business. His father was a steadily employed character actor named Douglas V. Fowley, who showed up in such film credits as Second Drunk or Indian Chief. Son thought he might follow father into acting, but Fowley's prematurely craggy looks made him better behind-the-scenes fodder, though he was occasionally the talent on a record. With Gary Paxton, he recorded the hit "Alley Oop," which they credited to the nonexistent Hollywood Argyles. But mostly, Fowley stayed in the business arena, scouting talent, making deals, stoking the star-making machinery.

So her estranged draft-dodger husband's deal with Fowley was at least an opening for Elliot. She called Fowley, bullshit her way through a quick interview, then held up the telephone receiver while John, Michelle, and Denny sang. Fowley liked what he heard. Cass got the usual *I'll call you* brush off, but then he did call.

Fowley phoned his old pal Nick Venet, the man who'd brought the Beach Boys to Capitol Records. Venet was trying to assemble talent for a new label called Mira and so eagerly arranged an audition. Elliot went along as driver, and at first Venet thought she was part of the group. John Phillips told him no, with an emphatic eye roll. But Venet saw how the four of them acted together, and then he asked Elliot to sing with the others. Finally, he said he needed to arrange a second audition with the label boss, Randy Wood, but was pretty sure he'd be offering them a Mira contract. One stipulation: Cass Elliot had to be part of the group.

After John finished gulping, the four of them returned to the Hendricks apartment. They were dizzy with excitement, so Cass decided they needed to chill, or their nerves would bungle the audition. She also knew Barry McGuire from her Village days, and now that he had a big hit with "Eve of Destruction," she figured he'd be happy to *give* them some of his famous weed.

Barry came over almost before he hung up the phone. He sat on the floor and rolled joints as the four scraggly wannabes began singing. "Man, this is awesome," he said when they finished a song. He was in the middle of recording his second Dunhill album. (The "Eve of Destruction" single rose to number one and the follow-up album rose to number three.) He wanted to introduce Cass and the others to Lou Adler and maybe get them on Dunhill.

The burly singer insisted on bringing the four of them along to the studio. His reason, he told Adler, was to use them as backing singers, even though what he really wanted for them was a full audition. Adler insisted on hearing them anyway, so he found one of Western's empty studios and told them to do their stuff. John allowed Cass to sing along, thinking her strong voice might lift Michelle's thinner warble. They ran through several John Phillips originals.

Adler always played his cards close to his vest. He turned to Bones Howe, his engineer. "What do you think?"

"If you don't take them, I *will*," Howe said.

They were so odd looking, but Adler began to see that as a plus: here was long, tall John; stunningly beautiful Michelle; handsome, dimple-chinned Denny; and earth mother Cass. They were "a visual that was unbelievable," Adler recalled.

Adler still wanted to play it cool. He went ahead with the business at hand—Barry McGuire's recording session—and employed the disheveled foursome for their intended purpose: singing background. They decided to cut one of the songs John Phillips had just played in the vacant studio down the hall. It was a love song to California on a cold winter's day in New York. Though credited to both John and Michelle Phillips, they argued over its authorship for years. John Phillips always claimed he wrote it in the middle of the night, back in the Village days, and woke up Michelle merely to type his dictated lyrics. To convince her to get out of bed, he promised her composer credit. Michelle Phillips denied that story. *She* was the California girl, after all, and she knew what it was like to miss home and had provided the central image of being alone in a church.

Adler decided to record the track "California Dreamin'," with his Wrecking Crew stalwarts and Phil Sloan, who played the acoustic guitar introduction. McGuire growled through the song, and the four back-up singers did their job. Later, Phillips pulled McGuire aside in a studio corridor and asked him if they could record the song as their debut single for Dunhill. Of course they could, McGuire assured them. *It's your song.*

The new foursome used the same Wrecking Crew backing track, replacing McGuire's vocal with their own.

Though impressed with their talent, Adler played it cool when it came to discussing business, but John Phillips knew a contract was in the offing. "I'll give you whatever you want," Adler finally said. "Just don't go see anybody else." Phillips chose not to mention Venet. "What we want," Phillips said, "is a steady stream of money from your office to our house."

When the contracts were laid before them, there were four copies—for John, Michelle, Denny . . . and Cass. She was part of the group, which was now known as the Mamas and the Papas.

It was an exhausting year for Brian Wilson. As soon as it was clear that *Summer Days* was another resounding success, Capitol Records began howling for a new album, but Wilson wasn't ready. The pressure to write all the songs for yet another album was daunting.

He recorded some things he liked but wasn't sure what to do with them. Al Jardine had long suggested the Beach Boys should do the traditional folk song "The Wreck of the Sloop John B." The Kingston Trio had some success with it, and it was a favorite of Jardine's, going back to his community college days with the Islanders. He mentioned it one day, and the next time he saw Brian in the studio, Wilson played the Wrecking Crew's effervescent backing track for the song. Jardine was stunned. All the song needed were the voices. But Brian set it aside, unsure what to do with it.

He threw all of his energies into another groundbreaking single, "The Little Girl I Once Knew." The song's subject was the usual boy-girl stuff, but the production was elaborate, dominated by an organ played with unusual gusto and other symphonic touches.

The vocals were superb and Brian resurrected the "bow-bow-bow-bow" backing vocals from "Help Me, Rhonda." It was a stunning single, but Brian's production worried disc jockeys. "They were confused by changes in tempo and several breaks in the music that caused dead air," Wilson said. The single made *Billboard*'s Top Twenty—a hit for almost any other artist but a relative failure for Brian Wilson.

Still, Capitol hounded him for more. To appease the record company, Mike Love suggested another live album—only it wouldn't be live. It would be a bunch of cover songs and remakes, recorded to *sound* as if it was taped during a party. It was one of Mike's more brilliant ideas.

Put together quickly in the fall of 1965, *Beach Boys' Party!* gave listeners the illusion of being a fly on the wall in the Wilson living room during a guitar and hand-clap sing-along. In fact, the boys were at Western Recorders, recording as usual. But this time noise-making tracks—such as crunching potato chips and bottle tops popping—were added to the recordings to create a party atmosphere. Brian led the group through nearly one hundred songs in the studio, though only twelve were used on the album. Left in the vaults were Beach Boys covers of "Hang on Sloopy," "Ticket to Ride," and Dylan's "She Belongs to Me."

Party! carried modest expectations yet became a huge bestseller. It rose to number six on the American charts and was number three in Great Britain. The package was elaborate for its time: an all-color gatefold album with sixteen cut-out wallet-sized photos of the boys. It also was a brilliant time-buying move, since it required no new songs and allowed the group to cash in on the Beatles' success (recording a couple Lennon-McCartney tunes) and to engage in self-parody. Mike sang a new version of "I Get Around" in a haughty Brit vocal. Most of the songs were goofy ("Alley Oop" and "Papa-Oom-Mow-Mow"), but there were a few semiserious recordings, primarily Brian and Mike's cover of the Everly Brothers' ballad "Devoted to You."

Al Jardine did Bob Dylan's "The Times They Are a-Changin'," and Dennis soloed on John Lennon's "You've Got to Hide Your Love Away." Brian was still looking for more songs to cover, when Dean Torrence wandered in. He and Jan were down the hall in a smaller studio at Western, trying to finish a track called "You Really Know How to Hurt a Guy." Jan was relentless, and Dean wanted to put the song to bed. Jan couldn't deal with his partner's growing impatience and told him to leave.

Dean ambled down the hall to Studio 3 and found his friends the Beach Boys, drunk as monkeys, chugging away on acoustic guitars and singing songs by other people.

Hey, Dean, you want to sing a song?

Hell yes he did. The Regents had recorded Fred Fassert's "Barbara Ann" in 1961, and the next year Jan and Dean included their version on their *Golden Hits* album, though it had not been a hit for them, golden or otherwise.

So when Brian asked the question, the first thing out of Dean's mouth was "Barbara Ann." Within fifteen minutes, the song was in the can, with Dean Torrence as lead vocalist. Two months later, it was the number-two record on the *Billboard* Hot 100 chart. "I was alone among the group in not celebrating the triumph," Brian wrote in a memoir. "It might not have been out of step with the times—not yet anyway—but it was definitely out of synch with what I wanted to do."

By the end of the year, the Beatles had proven to be more than a short-term phenomenon. In 1964, they had arrived in America as lovable, loony moptops with simplistic songs. But time revealed them to be more.

As 1966 began, the Beatles were approaching the second anniversary of conquering America. They were nearly four years into their British fame, and the nucleus of the group had been together for eight years. They had advanced from their days of tossing around songs full of personal pronouns and were now writing about things a bit more complex than simple teenage lust.

Rubber Soul, loosed on the public on December 3, 1965, was a revelation. The Beatles had produced a stunning album without a weak track among its dozen tunes. The American version deviated from the British album because Capitol Records knew the public would accept only ten to twelve songs on albums, while the British, as a rule, generously offered fourteen songs. The American company also put all of the Beatles' hit singles on albums, which was not the practice in Great Britain. This allowed Capitol to manufacture albums such as *Something New*, *Beatles '65*, and *Yesterday and Today*—collections that did not exist in England.

So the American *Rubber Soul* that Brian Wilson heard was not the same as the one the Beatles released in England. But both versions of the album had the scent of marijuana. It was an album made stoned, to be heard stoned.

Since the Beach Boys shared the American record label with the Beatles, Brian could have scored an early copy of the album. But even when it was released, he did not race to listen to it. He heard some of the songs on the radio but never heard *Rubber Soul* straight through until it had been out for a month. Then he felt the hammer come down.

He was astonished. He'd never before heard such an exquisite recording by a rock 'n' roll band. Hell, the group's *name* wasn't even on the cover, as if to say they were above the normal requirements of fame. The album cover was different in other ways, with its wicked, distorted faces of the group. *Moptops no longer!* The songs were strong, Brian thought. *No filler at all!* No "Bullshit with the Big Daddy," no big-twang, space-filling instrumentals. Every song was a winner. It was all *good stuff.*

And Brian could smell dope in the record grooves.

It was simultaneously exhilarating and depressing. The album was so good, but what did *he* have to offer in response? A few weeks after *Rubber Soul* came out, the Beach Boys released "Barbara Ann" as a single from the *Party!* album. Its semimoronic sing-along would reach number two on the US charts and give listeners the impression that the Beach Boys were nowhere near as cool as the Beatles.

No doubt, *Rubber Soul* was a game changer. The album was both catalyst and challenge for Brian. A half century later, the album was still held in the highest esteem. When *Rolling Stone*, in one of its massive best-of issues, rated the greatest albums of all time, *Rubber Soul* clocked in at number five.

"They put only great stuff on that album," Brian told pot-smoking buddy Loren Schwartz. "That's what I want to do."

Later, he shared his excitement with his young bride. "I just finished listening to *Rubber Soul*," he exclaimed. "It's unbelievable. It inspired me."

"That's great," Marilyn said.

"I mean it," he told her. "I'm going to make the greatest album—the greatest rock album ever made!"

11

THE LONERS

Our language has wisely sensed the two sides of being
alone. It has created the word loneliness to express
the pain of being alone. And it has created the word
solitude to express the glory of being alone.

—Paul Tillich

The surf was never up in Winnipeg. The namesake lake, one of the
largest freshwater lakes in the world, was thirty miles north of town,
too shallow and placid for even the most skilled of surfers. Still, Winnipeg teenager Neil Percival Young became infatuated with surf music.

The Young family—Mom, Pop, Bob, and baby boy Neil—lived in
the Northern Ontario village of Omemee for several years. There was
enough breathing space for the boys. "The open and wild countryside
was only about three miles away," Young wrote in a memoir. He saw
Elvis first in the Omemee home, wriggling on television. That black-
and-white moment when Neil was ten changed the boy's life. He first
got a ukulele, the instrument of choice for sleepy-eyed television host
Arthur Godfrey. That made its purchase more palatable for his parents.

By the time he was fifteen, his parents had separated, and the
boy, his older brother, and his mother ("Rassy") moved to Winnipeg,
where Neil was given a Harmony acoustic guitar as solace for the
broken family. The boy found a new path.

"There really wasn't anything more important in my life than playing music," Young said. "There was nothing else that interested me."

Neil's father, Scott, lived in Toronto, where he was one of Canada's most respected journalists, proprietor of a section-front column
in Toronto's *Globe and Mail*. Neil shuttled back and forth between

parents, trading life in Winnipeg for occasional stays in Toronto. Omemee grew in his mind as a symbol of an ideal past, and he would return to the village all of his life.

Young had formed and disbanded several rock 'n' roll groups by the time he started the Squires over the Christmas school holiday in 1962. He was a *my way or the highway* kind of leader and kicked out lots of friends from the band over the years until he had what he thought was the right mix. He'd worried his mother by writing notes and pinning them to his walls—mostly notes of the *Who cares?* variety. Rassy fretted that her son was depressed and figured he needed to express himself, so for his birthday in 1962, she bought him a Gibson Les Paul Junior, the youngster version of the guitars he saw his favorite players sporting on their album covers. He practiced until his fingers ached. Rassy also helped her son buy an Ampeg Echo Twin amplifier.

———————

Surf music was not just about surfing. It was a style of guitar playing—generally instrumental (the Beach Boys being a major exception), with lots of twang and heavy reverb. There were several such nonsurf surf songs during the boom years of the early sixties.

One of the most masterful examples of the genre was by Dick Dale, the king of the surf guitar. "Misirlou" was a Greek song first recorded in 1919, which Dale turned into a dark tour de force.

Likewise, "Walk, Don't Run," by the Seattle-based Ventures, was another instrumental whose title bore no direct connection to surfing, but twang and reverb made it part of the milieu.

The style was a worldwide phenomenon. In England, the launch of the Telstar satellite inspired the beat group the Tornados to create their swelling six-string celebration called "Telstar." The Shadows, backing band for England's Elvis, Cliff Richard, had a hit with "Apache," showcasing the mighty twang of guitarist Hank Marvin.

So it wasn't beyond the realm of possibility for a band in Winnipeg, Manitoba, to play surf music. Neil Young's first professional recording was "The Sultan," a 45 RPM by the Squires, which he also wrote. It was released in the summer of 1963, just as the Beach Boys were beginning to crest with a national audience. The Squires' record was on V Records, which to that point had exclusively been a polka label. A reputable addition to the surf-guitar canon, "The Sultan" featured a gong at its conclusion, hence the exotic title.

For the eighteen-year-old rock star–in-waiting, having the seven-inch piece of vinyl was a defining moment. "We were recording artists," Young recalled. "I will never forget the thrill of hearing it on the radio for the first time."

Young went from the Squires to a number of famous collaborations, but the band he formed as a high school student had a longer life than his high-profile bands.

Then and throughout his career, Young's eclecticism was his strong suit. Though the Squires began as an instrumental combo, Young's restless spirit led him elsewhere, even into the realm of folk music. This was in 1964, as folk was fading before the onslaught of the Beatles and other soldiers of the British Invasion. But Young valiantly took up folk music, fusing the old songs with an electrified approach a year before the success of the Byrds, Bob Dylan, and others with the genre the industry labeled "folk rock."

Of course, this meant someone had to sing, and that job fell to the leader.

"My voice is a little strange," Young said. "People told me I couldn't sing, but I just kept at it." Despite catcalls from the crowd—"stick to instrumentals!"—Young had his mother's steadfast encouragement and continued to sing, despite his quavering and unorthodox voice. Young recalled, "Some people would yell out, 'Stick to guitar playing' and stuff like that, kind of like heckling at a hockey game."

The Squires became one of the most successful bands in Winnipeg. "We had the most original material of all the bands," Young recalled. As he steered the band to more folk music and vocals, the band did rock arrangements of "Oh Susannah," "Tom Dooley," and "Oh My Darling Clementine," influenced by Jan and Dean's sped-up surf version of the folk ballad.

Young knew that amped-up folk songs and covers were not enough to launch and then sustain a career in music. "I was writing a lot because I was always thinking about music," he said. "First it was instrumentals, then it was songs with words that I had to start singing. Original music was the key to moving up."

The Squires became Winnipeg favorites, playing high school hops and church dances. "We started at five dollars for our first night, and

moved up to twenty or thirty-five bucks a night as we got better,"
Young recalled. "We actually started to get a little following."

The Squires' reputation spread so fast that soon the band and its
eighteen-year-old leader began performing out of town. One of their
first road gigs was in Fort William (now Thunder Bay), Ontario, the
point of origin for Highway 61, which ran south along the Mississippi
River, connecting Canada to the music of the Delta and New Orleans.
The Fort William performance turned out to be a key moment as
Young defined his style. While the Squires were wrapping up "Farmer
John," Neil responded to an unexpected cymbal crash from his drummer and a roaring thunder from his bass player. It affected Neil in
an unusual way.

> Somehow I started on the wrong notes, lower than
> the ones I was trying to hit, but it didn't sound bad.
> I slipped up to the higher notes and something hap-
> pened. I lost track of time. My fingers were flying all
> over the neck! I reached down and turned my amp
> up all the way, then I just took off. Hyperventilating,
> I felt a cold breeze behind my eyes. Time stood still
> as we slashed and bashed at those three chords with
> power that seemed to come from somewhere else. . . .
> After the set ended, the crowd was going crazy,
> screaming and clapping as we left the stage. I felt
> amazing!

To get players and equipment to the shows, Neil needed a vehicle,
and mother Rassy's squat Ensign sedan was no longer adequate. The
Squires could shoehorn their equipment into the car but had to use
rope to keep the trunk closed.

Young found a 1948 Buick Roadmaster hearse for sale. "I thought
a hearse would be the ideal band vehicle," he said, figuring that the
rails on wheels that helped roll caskets in and out of the back would
work just as well with amplifiers, drums, and guitars. With help from
Rassy, he bought the car, naming it Mortimer Hearseberg, or "Mort"
for short.

"I loved the hearse," Young recalled. "Six people could be getting high in the front and back, and nobody could be able to see in
because of the curtains. And the tray . . . the tray was dynamite. You
open the side door and the tray whips right out onto the sidewalk.

What could be cooler than that? What a way to make your entrance. Pull up to a gig and just wheel all of your stuff out onto the tray."

The more he played, the better he got. Neil kept rotating other players into the band until he had a tight, professional-sounding unit, and the music lovers of Winnipeg took notice. After a gig at the Fourth Dimension in March 1965, he was high from the enthusiasm of the crowd. "The crowd really went nuts," he said. "To be accepted like that and have people actually clapping and yelling after we played. We were buzzing heavily as we loaded our equipment back into Mort's cavernous form."

Around this time, Neil was diagnosed with epilepsy. He decided to keep his condition secret, so as not to scare off promoters. In the course of his long career, rarely did his condition interfere with his performance. But the uncertainly and unsteadiness, matched with his tentative, sometimes gasping singing style, helped him project an image of fragility that contrasted with his fiery and manic approach to electric guitar.

Young's frailty came naturally. At age six, he had suffered a bout with polio and was confined to the Toronto Hospital for Sick Children for a week. When he returned home, his first words to his family were "I didn't die, did I?"

He recovered, but the polio defined him. His mother always said her famous son was so stubborn because he'd battled polio at such a young age.

Since the Squires were from the foreign and mysterious big city of Winnipeg, the band held the denizens of Fort William's Flamingo Club in thrall. "Neil was different," said Tom Horricks, a Fort William musician. "He was from out of town so everyone thought he knew something they didn't know." The Squires became a frequent Flamingo attraction, and the crowd no longer catcalled when Young sang.

He celebrated his nineteenth birthday with a gig at the Flamingo and spent that night in the Victoria Hotel, writing "Sugar Mountain," his melancholy look back on childhood from the perch of a newly minted adult. He'd quit school after failing to pass tenth grade for the second time, so at a tender age, he was a professional musician, out on his own. But he always had his mother, and Winnipeg, as home.

It was at the Flamingo where Young's path first crossed that of Stephen Stills, a member of the touring American folk group called the Company. Beatlemania had sucked the life out of folk music in the United States, and club gigs had largely dried up, so the Company was working its way across Canada, where traditional music still had some teeth in the marketplace.

Stephen had grown up a nomad, part of a military family, a life of frequent moves and short friendships. He spent some of his teenage years in the same high school in Gainesville, Florida, as fellow future Rock and Roll Hall of Famer Tom Petty and was in a local band with Don Felder, later a member of the Eagles.

In 1964, Stills arrived in Greenwich Village just as most of the action in the music world was packing up and heading west. The Beatles had changed things, and the performers at the clubs in the Village were those who predated—and outlasted—any so-called folk music boom. Something of a musical dilettante at this point, the best Stills could do was find a job as part of a faux folk group called the Au Go-Go Singers. He recorded an album with the aggregation, but the record, like the band, reeked of blandness. The group had been struck as prefab folkies in the model of the Serendipity Singers or the New Christy Minstrels. Stills was smart enough to figure it all out but went along with the forced-smile performances. A paycheck for playing music was the important thing.

Stills moved on to the Company, another folkish group—this one with a pinch more integrity than the Au Go-Go Singers—and was on the Flamingo's stage in Fort William when Neil Young saw him for the first time. "There was a guy singing in that band who was really great," Young said. "He played guitar and sang, and it sounded like he was a soul singer. You had to look at him to be sure he was white."

The Squires and the Company were both spending off time at the Sea Vue, a squat park-at-your-door motel with kitchenettes and a view of Lake Superior. Stills and Young soon became friends, realizing they shared the same compulsion: the pathological need to make music. "We got on quite well right away," Young said. "We didn't talk about forming a band together then, but we knew we wanted to get together later. I knew he was going back to the States and I wanted to go to the States and now I knew a musician in the States."

They exchanged addresses and Stephen and his band headed off to complete their Canadian tour in Winnipeg and points west. Neil and the Squires were headed east, to the clubs in Yorkville, Toronto's version of Greenwich Village. Young had been encouraged to try out some of his music with a more sophisticated urban audience. Young wanted to keep the Squires going but also wanted to pursue a solo career. This *I'm in a band/I'm a solo artist* dichotomy would continue through his performing life.

The Yorkville audiences were tough, though, particularly on the fragile kid with the quavering voice. A review in a local newspaper accused Young of trafficking in clichés and shopworn ideas. It was brutal, but he forged on, even when the other Squires drifted west, toward home.

It was easier to cross the border then, so Young moved on to New England. His shows there were also not well received, but he remained undaunted, and by November 1965, he had arrived in Greenwich Village, where remnants of the folk music boom were on life support.

Stills had invited Young to crash at his place in the Village if he ever got there. Young eagerly showed up at Stills's apartment on Thompson Street. He knocked, and a fresh-faced kid from Yellow Springs, Ohio, opened the door. Stephen was gone, the kid said, seeking fame and fortune in California.

The kid was Richie Furay, and he was taking a few days off from his factory job at Pratt and Whitney in Hartford, Connecticut, to audition for singing and acting roles. Stills had offered his apartment.

Furay had met Stills when he first came east, trying to get a folk singer gig in the Village. When things didn't immediately work out, Furay latched onto the Pratt and Whitney security, but still longed for success in show business. He came down on weekends to see what sort of work he could rustle up. He and Stills would hit the clubs together and became infatuated with the good-time music of the Lovin' Spoonful.

Led by John Sebastian, one of the Village basket-house regulars, the group was one of the early bands to blend folk and rock. They named themselves after male ejaculate—from a line in an old blues song, "I love you 'bout a lovin' spoonful." Sebastian teamed with drummer Joe Butler, bassist Steve Boone, and guitarist and goofball Zal Yanovsky, who'd been part of the Mugwumps with Cass Elliot and Denny Doherty.

The Spoonful was out-of-the-box successful in 1965, with "Do You Believe in Magic" and "You Didn't Have to Be So Nice," which used the aggressively folk instrument the autoharp. That these guys suddenly went from playing gigs for beer to chart-topping success made them the envy of their social scene in the

Village, so much so that Stills daydreamed about joining them, if only they would ask.

Stephen and Richie mused over beers about starting a band, but that didn't go anywhere. At that point, Pratt and Whitney financial stability outweighed rock 'n' roll dreams. Stephen went back on the road, with the goal of landing in California, where everything seemed to be happening.

When Neil showed up at the door and introduced himself, Richie beamed. He'd already heard all about Neil Young from the stories Stephen brought back from Canada. Neil and Richie exchanged songs, and Richie was awed by Neil's "Nowadays Clancy Can't Even Sing," which he began to play at his auditions. "Neil really struck me, right from that moment as someone who was completely different," Furay said.

Young scammed an audition at Elektra Records while he was in New York. Label president Jac Holzman was eager to move his eminent folk label into the new folk-rock genre but considered Young too eccentric at this early stage in Elektra's new history. Frustrated, Young decided to head back to the frozen tundra. He and Furay had become good friends, and he admired the boy's all-American looks and pure, soulful voice. But he didn't seem committed to music, since he held on to the factory job. If his heart was pure, he'd be on the road, headin' for another joint.

Neil told Richie to tell Stephen he said hello.

On the way back home, Young cadged a folk club gig in Detroit, then went back to Toronto and took another stab at Yorkville, where he met Bruce Palmer.

"I met Neil walking down the street, carrying his guitar," Palmer said. "We were looking for a guitar player at that time in the Mynah Birds, and he was there. He was looking for people to play with, so I asked him to join."

Palmer had been in the Mynah Birds for almost a year when he recruited Young. Though he was a year younger, Palmer was already a veteran bass player, serving in a variety of Toronto bands, which eventually begat Steppenwolf (lead singer John Kay and organist Goldie McJohn) and songwriter Mars Bonfire ("Born to Be Wild"). Palmer was attracted to the Mynah Birds by the band's charismatic lead singer, Ricky James Matthews. The Birds were a proto–Rolling Stones band, but Matthews, who was black, infused his singing and stage presence with a level of soul generally not found north of the border.

Desperate for a gig—but also admiring Matthews and Palmer—Young joined the band. In his mind, he was merely putting his dreams of solo success on hold. "I had to eat," he said. "I needed a job and it seemed like a good thing to do."

Things quickly picked up. The Mynah Birds became so popular in Toronto that Motown Records heard the buzz and signed the group to a contract. Working with producer-performer Smokey Robinson, the group began recording an album in Detroit, but Matthews's arrest put an end to the proceedings. Turns out he was absent without leave from the US Navy. (It would be merely a rock 'n' roll dream deferred for Matthews, who—as Rick James—became a successful recording star in the eighties.)

Young and Palmer had become close and, with the Mynah Birds at a dead end while Matthews served his one-year prison sentence, they decided to load their equipment in the back of Young's hearse. This wasn't Mort, which had died a sad death near the Trans-Canada Highway. Young parked it at a roadside motel and walked away. This second addition to the Neil Young hearse collection was a 1953 Pontiac, which Young and Palmer used to head off to the promised land of California. Neil estimated the hearse got a maximum of ten miles per gallon, but gas was cheap then, and he didn't have anything remotely resembling a normal car. "I had to go down to California because I knew that the music I was interested in was coming from there," he said.

Two months later, nothing much had happened for Young and Palmer. They were the new guys in town, and one of them, the one that sang, sounded a little like a dying cat onstage. It was kind of hard to get gigs or pull together a band. Still, they were in California, the land of the golden dream. "We had made it to the Pacific Ocean and California, home of the West Coast Sound," Young recalled. "This is where the Beach Boys had come from, the Byrds, the Mamas and the Papas, and so many others. We had made it."

All the while, Young was looking for Stephen Stills. He felt that he was destined to work with Stills. He scouted the bars for him, planning to suggest they start a band.

In the meantime, Stills had made it to L.A. and found it rough going. He'd made a few friends, such as Dickie Davis, stage manager of the Troubadour. Davis not only gave Stills a slot on the Monday open mic night at the celebrated club but also put him up and kept him in SpaghettiOs. He also introduced him to Barry Friedman, who saw Stills as the starter kit for a rock 'n' roll band he could manage.

> Madness!! Auditions. Folk & Roll Musicians-Singers
> for acting roles in new TV series. Running Parts for
> 4 insane boys, age 17–21. Want spirited Ben Frank's
> types. Have courage to work. Must come down for
> interview.
>
> —*Daily Variety*, September 8, 1965

Stills saw the advertisement in *Daily Variety* and lined up with every young musician in L.A. for the audition. The producers wanted a television series about a rock 'n' roll band. The audition ad offered a few clues: they wanted "Ben Frank's types," and Stills thought he fit the description. Ben Frank's was a Sunset Strip diner frequented by musicians, a triangulated site for several recording studios.

Stephen, part of that culture, figured, *What the hell?* He was turned down, in part, because of his crooked teeth. He did pass news of the audition to his friend Peter Torkelson, a fellow Greenwich Village basket-house renegade. Peter ended up getting one of the four coveted parts in the television show, shortening his name to Peter Tork.

The producers, Bob Rafelson and Bert Schneider, pitched the show to television executives in the afterglow of the Beatles and their innovative film *A Hard Day's Night*. At first, they thought they'd use an existing band, the Lovin' Spoonful. But John Sebastian, the Spoonful leader and a prolific songwriter, learned that the television deal would require him to turn over his publishing to Colgems, the big money behind the production. The group declined.

Rafelson and Schneider didn't really care about musical ability. The program they were creating was *about* a rock 'n' roll band. The actors didn't have to *be* a rock 'n' roll band. Yet Tork was a musician. The producers already had a front man—a young English performer named Davy Jones, who'd won a Tony nomination for his role as the Artful Dodger in the original Broadway production of *Oliver!*

The cattle-call audition drew every starving musician in Southern California. Paul Williams, the diminutive composer of songs for the Carpenters and Three Dog Night, was turned down. So was future Three Dog Night lead singer—and Brian Wilson drug-gobbling pal—Danny Hutton. Brian Wilson's future lyricist Van Dyke Parks was also dismissed. The producers wanted eccentric, but the effete and intellectual Parks was deemed more than Middle America could stand on its television set. The producers said no to singer Harry Nilsson and countless others. For many years, a rumor persisted that future mass murderer Charles Manson had also auditioned, but that was an urban legend. Manson was in prison in the fall of 1965, not yet part of the California music scene.

The make-believe group was dubbed the Monkees, and the four members—Jones, Tork, Michael Nesmith, and Micky Dolenz—initially balked at the arrangement made by the producers and musical director Don Kirshner. Kirshner wanted his Brill Building composers to supply the material and the Wrecking Crew to play all the instruments. Three of the Monkees had decent musical chops. The exception was Micky Dolenz, who had been a child actor with his own television series, *Circus Boy*. He was selected to play the drummer and quickly went about learning the instrument.

The problem was, the Monkees wanted to actually be a band, not just play one on television. It took a couple of years, but the band eventually found its independence and became a self-sustaining musical entity. *The Monkees* was one of the most popular programs during the two years (1966–68) it ran on NBC, and the group sold more records in that era than the Beatles and the Rolling Stones combined.

Stills watched Tork, his friend and former roommate, be swallowed up in the star-making machine. Nearly overnight, Peter became rich and famous, but Stills didn't fret too much about his lost opportunity. He wanted to be in a real rock 'n' roll band, not a television facsimile.

———————————

Back east, tired of factory life drudgery, Richie Furay decided to give music one last chance and called Stephen Stills in California. Stills lied, saying everything was great. *I'm starting a band, and all I need is you.*

So there they were, months later, on Sunset. Furay was feeling that Stills had sold him a bill of goods. When he got to L.A., no one met him at the airport. Stills had a *Take it or leave it* thing going on, not caring that Furay had uprooted his life and changed coasts with the promise of *something*.

Meanwhile, Neil Young and Bruce Palmer had been driving around. "We couldn't find Stills anywhere," Young said. "Eventually, we gave up on L.A. and decided to head north to San Francisco, where Flower Power was in full bloom, with Jefferson Airplane and Big Brother and the Holding Company. Human Be-Ins were happening in Golden Gate Park. Hippies were everywhere. We were on our way to Mecca."

Barry Friedman was driving a white van, and Stills was riding shotgun, with Richie between them, leaning over from the backseat. They were waiting at a light on Sunset Boulevard when Furay noticed a hearse stopped on the opposite side of the intersection, going the other way. Squinting, he saw that the front license tag was from Ontario. He nudged Stills and pointed across the intersection.

"Bruce and I were just leaving to go to San Francisco," Young recalled. "Then Stephen and Richie saw us in traffic."

"I know that guy," Stills shouted. "It's Neil."

Friedman executed a U-turn to catch up to the hearse once it started moving. "We pulled off Sunset Boulevard around the corner a block away," Friedman said.

Young remembered the moment: "I looked around out the driver's window of the hearse. It was Stills! We got out and hugged right there on Sunset Boulevard in the middle of traffic. Horns were honking! To us, it seemed like everybody was celebrating. Something was happening, but we didn't know what it was." They headed off to Friedman's house to smoke some dope and talk.

"Everything just fell into place," Bruce Palmer recalled. All they needed was a drummer, which Friedman quickly obtained through his friendship with Byrds manager Jim Dickson. Dewey Martin had grown up in country music, touring with Patsy Cline, among others. He was offended that Stills and Young insisted that he audition, since he hadn't had to when the Everly Brothers and Roy Orbison hired him. But, grudgingly, he did as they asked and joined the group.

By mid-1966, surf music was passé, so Neil Young figured he'd have to put his stinging guitar to some other use. Bob Dylan and the Byrds had come up with something that *Billboard* magazine was calling folk rock, and that seemed to make sense for three Greenwich Village washouts. Stills, Young, and Furay all wrote songs, and two and a half of them could be a lead singer. (At first, the group decided Neil should not sing, for fear of scaring away the customers.)

All the group needed was a name. A road crew was resurfacing Fountain Avenue in front of Friedman's house, where Stills and Furay had been staying. The crew parked a steamroller right in front of the house, and Stills liked the sign on the back of the machine that listed the manufacturer. He ripped off the sign when the crew broke for lunch and hung it on the wall of Friedman's living room.

BUFFALO SPRINGFIELD, it read.

Life was hard out there on the Western Plains of Canada. Their home was so remote that they got their soap from vendors traveling by wagons. Soap was a luxury, so rare that when it arrived, the family lined up to bathe, to wash clothes, to give the dishes a good cleaning.

Thus was life in Alberta and Saskatchewan in the late forties. Roberta Joan Anderson was an only (and somewhat lonely) child growing up in outposts previously the sphere of only wild animals and the Royal Canadian Mounted Police. Her mother, Myrtle McKee, had grown up in the remote wilderness and vowed to do better than her own mother had done with marriage. She met and married—within two weeks—Bill Anderson of the Royal Canadian Air Force while he was home on leave during the Second World War. Their daughter was born November 7, 1943, in Fort Macleod, Alberta. She was rarely called by her first name. From the start, she was Joan, then Joni.

After the war, Bill Anderson found work as a butcher and began his rise through the ranks of the grocery business. As Joni grew up, she fed herself on stories of her ancestors, particularly her grandmothers. Both had lived unfulfilling lives in service of husband and family. They accepted that meager lot in life. Her grandmother Anderson had dreams of being a pianist, but the reality of marriage to a belligerent alcoholic and regularly birthing children extinguished her dreams.

"She raised eleven children and lived a horrible life," Joni Mitchell said of her grandmother. "Giving, giving, giving—a self-sacrificing animal to her many children."

Her grandmother McKee endured a similar fate—a life lived enslaved to men and children—but unlike her counterpart, she didn't cloak her sorrow. She lashed back, expressing her bitterness regularly and with vigor. She passed on to her daughter Myrtle, Joni's mother, a desperation to get away from a life of traps—emotional and sexual, as well as geographic.

The agonizing frustrations of her grandmothers made young Joni determined not to suffer their soul-crushing fates, but to live her life for them and to speak for them. It laid out a path that, from an early age, Anderson could see leading her to art. Her mother encouraged her, energized by the desperation in her genes.

Her mother started her on a course of piano lessons when she was seven, but within a couple of years, Joni fell victim to the Canadian polio epidemic of the early fifties. When Joni did not wake one morning, her mother tried to pull her from bed, but the girl fell to the floor. She was flown to the provincial capital of Saskatoon, becoming the envy of her social set for being one of the first to fly in an airplane. She was hospitalized for over a month, then returned home, where her mother schooled her as she recovered.

During her convalescence, she listened to music daily and decided that she wanted to compose. Her obsessions were Rachmaninov's "Rhapsody on a Theme of Paganini" and the songs of Edith Piaf. She spent hours in a local furniture store that had listening booths and a tolerant attitude toward teenagers obsessed with music. She saved her money from part-time jobs in high school and bought a ukulele and a collection of Pete Seeger sheet music. It was 1961, and she was following the Joan Baez model. That's what you did if you were a young woman who wanted to play music.

The final move of Anderson's childhood was to Saskatoon, a metropolis compared to the towns of her early life. It was there where she began an all-on assault on the arts: through music (piano, ukulele, guitar), then painting. As happened with so many aspiring artists, a teacher played a key role in her life. As she hung one of her paintings in the school hall, teacher Arthur Kratzmann stopped to admire it. "If you can paint with a brush, you can paint with words," he said. When she began taking classes from him in high school, he pushed her to do better work and to be original. Deep into a Nietzsche phase, Kratzmann channeled the philosopher when he told his pupil, "You must write in your own blood."

She liked seeing her work in print. She loved to wear fine clothing and began writing a fashion column for the school paper at Aden Bowman Collegiate. She'd done some modeling and also waited tables at a coffeehouse where local musicians played folk songs. She ditched her grown-up clothes and embraced the late-blooming black beatnik wardrobe. She worked at the hippest coffeehouse Saskatoon had to offer. Named after a Canadian revolutionary and the founder of Manitoba, the Louis Riel was the northernmost stop on the folk music/coffeehouse circuit that included Greenwich Village, the Yorkville area of Toronto, the Gate of Horn in Chicago, and the Flick in Coral Gables. On Halloween 1962, a scant few days after the resolution of the Cuban Missile Crisis, Joni Anderson gave her first paid public performance at the Louis Riel. She became known as the coffeehouse's premier singing waitress.

She sang the standard repertoire of the time, ancient ballads, with a few examples of the pop folk of the Kingston Trio mixed in. She became the go-to performer. A year into her singing career, she quit and moved one province over to attend the Southern Alberta Institute of Technology. Despite its name, the school offered a strong arts program, and Joni embraced the nurturing atmosphere, keeping her musical skills intact by playing Calgary's high-profile coffeehouses. "I discovered I was a ham," she said.

She'd fallen in and out of love a few times by then, and in the summer of 1964, while Canada joined its southerly neighbor in reeling in Beatlemania, Joni discovered she was pregnant. She and her boyfriend traveled to Toronto to stay out of sight while she bore the child. Toronto had a network of maternity homes for unwed mothers.

She bargained with her soul. Keeping the baby seemed out of the question. She was young, not yet fully educated, and knew her boyfriend was not the sort of man with whom she wanted to spend her life. Anderson remembered her grandmothers and their sacrifices. She thought about the sacrifices that women always made. They have talent and dreams yet are forced to put all that aside for two decades while raising a child. As she sat on her bed in the maternity home, she worked on the new songs she'd written. If she had to give up her daughter, she thought, she'd make that sacrifice *worth it.*

In her mind, she was leaving the baby until she was ready to care for her. She met a folk singer and actor named Chuck Mitchell. "Thirty-six hours after I met Chuck, he asked me to marry him," Joni said. "But we waited two months." Chuck was older, more experienced, and expected his new wife to defer to him.

The Mitchells continued to tour folk clubs of Canada, turning two single acts into a duo. "We are both strong-minded people," Chuck said, "and we both had our own ways of doing a number. There were some hectic times until we blended our styles."

The two had enough success to attract a *Detroit News* reporter, who profiled them in the newspaper. They were a beautiful couple and conveyed a sense of marital and musical bliss. The article concluded with this scene of domesticity: "Chuck said, 'Joni and I have developed our solo act. We are not just folk singers now. We do comedy, sing some ragtime and do folk-rock. We're ready for the big clubs now.' Joni nodded her approval, as any dutiful wife would do."

Joni's grandmothers were always present on her shoulder, and they began whispering of traps and dead ends and lost dreams. Before long, Chuck Mitchell would lose his dutiful wife.

One night in Winnipeg, Joni met Neil Young, then still touring with the Squires. Young found himself stunned silent by her voice and stage presence. He *aw-shucks*ed and hands pocketed through a conversation afterward and they decided to stay in touch, to try to help each other in this new and frightening world of performing. Two years older (an eternity at that age—she a worldy twenty, he still a teenage boy) and married, Joni Mitchell was an experienced and wise counselor who would prove invaluable in Young's life and career.

When Young played her "Sugar Mountain," his song of lost innocence, Mitchell was moved and responded by writing "The Circle Game." The gates opened, and she began writing songs constantly. Husband Chuck was content to sing the songs of others, and their drift had begun. He had promised her that once they were on solid ground financially, they would go rescue her daughter from foster care. But then *when* became *if* as their commitment faded.

Giving up her child had imbued Joni Mitchell with a passion for work and led her to leave the Canadian provinces and her husband and head south, to America.

Brian Wilson was surrounded by friends and hangers-on and syco-phants, but he never felt more alone. The only place where he felt welcomed was in the recording studio, with those superb musicians who helped him get the music out of his head and on to tape.

As he set about to make the next album, and to make it the greatest rock album ever made, he briefly considered whether he should do it alone. He had the Wrecking Crew. He could overdub his voice and do all the singing; he didn't really need the other Beach Boys. But fear or loyalty or the realization of how many people were dependent on him would not permit him to step into a solo career. The group was his family, after all.

He wasn't getting any help from the hangers-on. They liked Brian's money because Brian's money could buy drugs. They spoke the standard gibberish heard at the beginning of the American Stoned Age that was just beginning: *Yeah, man* . . . *Groovy* . . . *Out of sight* . . . *Far-out* . . .

Brian was skilled musically but was not particularly articulate. He'd written with Gary Usher and Roger Christian because they knew the world of cars and girls and surf that he matched with his music. To pathologically shy Wilson, it was as if Usher and Christian were writing science fiction.

Mike Love had proven to be a compatible and clever lyricist. His work would never be mistaken for the wit of Cole Porter or Lorenz Hart, but he was fine in the surf-and-turf milieu. And that's why Brian did not want to collaborate with his cousin on the new project. If he was ready for his music to evolve, the words had to be better than "I been all around this great big world and I've seen all kinds of girls."

Tony Asher was a twenty-six-year-old copywriter at Carson /Roberts, the largest agency in Los Angeles. Terry Gilliam was one of Asher's Carson/Roberts colleagues before he joined Monty Python's Flying Circus and began directing films.

Because Tony had a background in music and was comfortable speaking with musicians, he drew assignments to create radio jingles for the agency's clients, including Mattel, Baskin-Robbins, Learjet, and Gallo.

Asher liked recording at Western and generally knocked out his jingles in the mornings. Rock 'n' roll stars were nocturnal creatures, and Western was usually booked in the evenings and all night. So Asher was surprised to run into Brian Wilson at the studio's hallway water fountain. Tony recognized Brian immediately, and they began talking about their work and music. Brian showed Tony a couple figures on the piano he was using in one of the smaller studios. They had a good time, and that was it.

Until one day in January 1966, when Asher came back to his cubicle to find a message that Wilson had called. He thought it was a joke until he called the number on the pink message slip.

Characteristically, Wilson did not beat around the bush. "Listen, I have to finish this album," he said. "The boys are in Japan touring and I don't have anybody to write with and besides, I don't want to write with anybody I've written with before anyway. I want to do something totally new."

He'd figured that maybe a guy who wrote ads might be able to excavate the emotions from his head and turn them into lyrics. Asher was startled that Wilson didn't suggest doing one song and seeing how that went. He wanted Asher for the whole enchilada.

"Do you want to write this album with me?"

"I thought you wrote with Mike," Asher said.

"I don't think he's capable of what I have in mind," Wilson said. "I need someone sensitive."

Tony agreed immediately and negotiated a three-week leave from Carson/Roberts. But the first day he showed up at Brian's house, he began to have second thoughts. Tony reported at 9 AM and cooled his heels in the living room until the rock star awoke around 11. Then Brian delayed work even further because he demanded that Marilyn make him a huge breakfast.

Brian was struggling. "The most difficult part of songwriting has always been the first ten minutes," he said. "It's a time of utter anxiety. Will anything come? Am I dried up? Am I the loser my dad said? The same with every day. After opening my eyes, the first few hours were filled with fear."

Asher was frustrated. He had only a three-week window to complete this project and Wilson was perfecting his impersonation of a sloth. When they did actually meet face to face, the frustration did not ease. Brian was easily distracted by his friends, his dope deliveries, his dogs, his flights of sexual fantasy. But Tony was a pro, and so he put on blinders and focused on what Brian wanted to say with these new songs. Because he was also a musician, Tony could speak Brian's language—a good thing, since Brian was not excessively verbal.

He had difficulty expressing himself to Tony, but he had lofty goals for his work in progress: "I just wanted to make the music sound whole, to convey the timeless, emotional content inherent in great works of art—paintings, poetry, symphonies. What I've always described as the presence of God."

Wilson made it clear that he wanted Asher to forget he'd ever heard any of those songs about surfing or cars. "I want people to hear it and say, 'Wow, that can't be the Beach Boys.'" He had already produced a track called "In My Childhood," complete with bells and bicycle horns. He recorded a guide vocal with his lyrical sketches but became dissatisfied and erased his voice. He handed a tape of the track to Asher, telling him he wanted the lyrics to be about devotion. "Why don't you take it home and give it a shot?" Asher came back with "You Still Believe in Me."

He played it for Wilson, and the reaction was immediate. "Oh this is great, man, I love it!" Asher had passed the audition.

They were only a few years apart, but Asher felt he was dealing with an overgrown child. Wilson needed help with so many daily tasks and was so easily swayed by his friends and their revolving enthusiasms. Even the decorating of the house was off-kilter to Asher, a man of mature tastes. Wilson was basically a kid, and his bride was still a teenager.

"The only times I actually enjoyed myself or even got comfortable with Brian were when I was standing by the piano working with him," Asher recalled. "Otherwise, it was hideous."

Blinders. "For the most part, all I ever heard was Brian playing in a very simple way, tunes on a piano," he said. "I knew that he heard a lot of things in his head that I had no idea of, and when I heard what he'd come up with, I was just blown away."

Beyond the tacky decor and strange tastes that Brian showed, Tony was most appalled when Brian opened up to him about his feelings for his sister-in-law Diane. He was still in the newlywed stage with Marilyn and yet telling his collaborator, this guy he hardly knew, how much he wanted to fuck his wife's sister.

"He was a genius musician but an amateur human being," Asher said.

Brian had no filter when it came to expressing his sexual desires— whether for Diane or for an actress who showed up on the television or for a girl who walked into the coffee shop where they met to discuss their songs. Brian had melodies and, in some cases, completed tracks for the album. Usually he also had a song title and a lyrical idea, maybe a phrase or two. He knew he wanted the songs to have cohesion and to explore feelings of love, longing, and loss.

"Did you see how beautiful she looked yesterday?" Wilson asked Asher.

"Who?"

"I was watching Diane, and God, she's so beautiful."

"Brian, you're married," Asher said.

"I know," he said. "But wouldn't it be nice if I could lie down beside her and nestle myself in her long hair?"

"Come on, man," Asher admonished. "Do you hear what you're saying?"

"I'm in love with the idea of falling in love."

Somehow, Tony found in Brian's constant talk about Diane the inspiration he needed for "Wouldn't It Be Nice," destined to become the theme song for thousands of young couples wishing they could be older so they could love the way that they wanted.

> *Oh, we could be married*
> *And then we'd be happy*

Asher was unimpressed with the hangers-on—there to feed off of Brian, smoke his dope, and bask in his creative weirdness. Schwartz was the most irritating Brian friend, mostly because he was like a puppy, with new enthusiasms every day—new books to read, new drugs to try, new religions. Brian latched onto these enthusiasms and turned into a puppy. Asher did not like working with a puppy.

"I found Brian's lifestyle to be damn repugnant," Asher said. "For every four hours we'd spend writing songs, there'd be about 48 hours of the dopey conversations about some dumb book he'd just read."

Somehow, they managed to finish the lyrics for the album during Asher's leave. They quickly found the right words to go with the song Wilson planned for the album's conclusion, a meditation on lost love called "Caroline, No."

"The general tenor of the lyrics was always his," Asher recalled, "and the actual *choice* of words was usually mine. I was really just his interpreter." When they worked on the album's centerpiece, Wilson was worried that the song would doom the album because it contained references to God. Asher talked him off the ledge, and together they wrote "God Only Knows."

"With 'God Only Knows," Asher said, "I always felt like we barely got started. I felt like saying, 'Wait a second, can't we put another section in this song?' because there was not very much to it."

There were other songs that found new life. An old melody was reused for Asher's lyrics on "I'm Waiting for the Day." Brian wrote a dreamy instrumental called "Let's Go Away for Awhile," with a track featuring swaying Hawaiian guitars—great dope-smoking music. He didn't think it needed words. Another track began life as Brian's

daydream of writing the theme for a James Bond film. He called it
"Run, James, Run," but when the Bond producers turned it down, he
decided to use it on the album as well. There were a couple more self-
reflective songs, including a strong Wilson-Asher confessional called
"I Just Wasn't Made for These Times." Prior to Tony's arrival, Brian
had collaborated with road manager Terry Sachen on a song about
his experiences with LSD called "Hang on to Your Ego." Brian also
decided to resurrect the track he'd recorded the previous July, the
folk song now called "Sloop John B," for inclusion on the album.

The tracks were beautiful. Brian had gone deep into the Wrecking Crew bullpen and brought in strings, harpsichords, oboes, far-
ting tubas, glockenspiel, vibes . . . a whole orchestra. The tracks
were unlike anything heard before on a rock album. As he began to
sequence songs on the album, he put "Caroline, No" as the closer,
augmented by the sound of his dogs—Louie the Weimaraner and
Banana the beagle—barking after a disappearing train. He'd recorded
guide vocals to help the group but decided his would be the only
voice on "Caroline, No."

The touring Beach Boys spent most of January 1966 in Japan,
with a stopover for a show in Hawaii on the way home. After a short
break, they showed up at Western Recorders on February 9 to hear
Brian's new tracks.

Brian held his breath. He was proud of the music, but it was
markedly different and might worry the group. They'd just returned
from a tour in which they played "Fun, Fun, Fun," "Surfer Girl,"
and "Surfin' USA" every night. How would the audience respond to
a song called "Hang On to Your Ego"?

"Hey, Brian," Al Jardine said during the vocal tracking. "This is
a little tricky."

Mike, for his part, openly mocked the lyrics, singing them as
imitations of big-schnozzed comedian Jimmy Durante and movie
tough-guy James Cagney.

Mike and Al were supposed to be singing together, but Mike kept
belching into the microphone to distract Al. Brian barked over the
speaker from the control room: "Hey you guys. Don't fuck around.
Please, we've got to do it. Come on."

Mike Love was emphatic: he didn't like anything about the
work in progress, especially the Wilson-Asher partnership and the
strange instrumentation on the tracks. "Love's main concerns were
success, money, and pussy in no particular order," Asher said. "Art

and self-expression did not appear to his set of values in any way whatsoever."

Mike was disrupting the session as his way of protesting Brian's drug use and the effect it was having on the music. "I was aware that Brian was beginning to experiment with LSD and other psychedelics," Love said. "The prevailing drug jargon at the time had it that doses of LSD would shatter your ego, as if that were a positive thing. I wasn't interested in taking acid or getting rid of my ego."

The group began to split like musical amoeba. Brian was off on his own, and now Mike was spinning the other direction. Carl and Dennis followed their adored big brother, and Al Jardine was caught in the middle, a rarely heeded voice of reason.

"It was a whole new horizon for us," Jardine recalled. "We were a surfing group when we left the country at the start of 1966 and we came back to this new music. It took some getting used to. The vocals were arduous, tedious, and long."

To avoid a fight, Brian ditched Terry Sachen's lyrics to "Hang on to Your Ego," and, with Mike, rewrote the song as "I Know There's an Answer." But Brian wasn't willing to compromise any more. He assigned Mike certain lines to sing, and when his cousin refused, Brian took the parts himself. He ended up singing most of the lead vocals on the album, with the help of his brothers, Al Jardine, and Bruce Johnston.

Wilson wasn't sure what to call this new work. "We were standing in the hallway in one of the recording studios, either Western or Columbia, and we didn't have a title," Love recalled. "From the speakers we heard the sound of a train passing into the distance. That's how the album ended—the train passing, the clanging of a bell at a railroad crossing, and two dogs barking. . . . With the sound of the dogs echoing in my ears, I said, 'What about Pet Sounds?'" Another story ends with the title coming from Mike's sneering remarks that these were the pet sounds of his obsessive-compulsive cousin. Wilson retitled his failed James Bond theme "Pet Sounds," using the instrumental as the album's penultimate track.

The group finished the vocal tracking, then got ready to go back on the road. Mike Love was terrified of what might happen next. He warned Brian, "Don't fuck with the formula."

(Irked by the oft-repeated *Don't fuck with the formula* quote, Mike attempted to set the record straight in his memoir. He claimed the quote was an invention attributed to him in a 1971 *Rolling Stone* article on the band. It wasn't just a case of a quote being taken out of context. "Actually, the quote had no context, because it was never spoken," Mike wrote. "When Brian, whose memoir invoked the same line, was asked under oath in 1998 if I ever said, 'Don't fuck with the formula,' Brian responded, 'No. No. Absolutely not.'")

Brian supervised the mastering of the album at Capitol's studios, insisting that all lights be off, in keeping with the record's intimate mood. The technicians worked by the lights on their control panels. His friend, concert promoter Fred Vail, attended the session at Wilson's insistence. "Throughout the whole thing, Brian gave instructions to the mastering guy," Vail said. "He'd say, 'Fade it here' and 'Turn up the highs a little bit.' Straight through to 'Caroline, No' and the trains and his dogs at the end of the album. It faded out and I was just mesmerized." Another masterful tag.

"Well, what do you think?" Wilson asked Vail.

"It's great, Brian. I love it. It's fabulous!"

Wilson told Vail he worried about the other Beach Boys and how they'd feel about the finished record.

Vail reassured him: "Whatever they think, it doesn't really matter. It's your best effort yet."

Brian brought an acetate home and walked into the house carrying it like a holy relic. He summoned his young wife; it was time to share with her. "We went into the bedroom," Marilyn recalled. "He said, 'OK, are you ready?' He was serious. This was his soul in there. We just laid there all night, alone on the bed, listened and cried. It was really, really heavy. He was so proud of it."

In early May, the Beach Boys were on the road—in Providence, Knoxville, and the Bronx. They wore their striped shirts and played the surfing songs as the crowd sang along.

Back home in California, Brian Wilson was ready to release *Pet Sounds* to the world. The group was gone, but his world was filled with the Wrecking Crew, his wife and her family, and the entourage of hangers-on that came by his house to get high and listen to music. Despite the crowd, and in a way he'd never quite felt before, Brian was completely alone.

12

THE TEENAGE SYMPHONY TO GOD

People fear death even more than pain. It's strange that
they fear death. Life hurts a lot more than death. At the
point of death, the pain is over.

—Jim Morrison

Phil Spector made it up to Bobby Hatfield. As tenor for the Righteous
Brothers, Hatfield had been relegated to a supporting role to partner
Bill Medley for Spector's great production of "You've Lost That
Lovin' Feelin.'" In 1965, Spector produced "Unchained Melody," and
Hatfield sang solo. It became a Top Five hit, and the same recording
made number one in 1990.

By the end of 1965 and after several successes with the Righteous
Brothers, the parties moved on. Medley and Hatfield had been modestly successful before Spector, and now they wanted their careers
back. The duo self-produced their number-one single "Soul and Inspiration" in 1966, which sounded like great imitation Phil Spector.

Spector fell in love with another voice: Tina Turner's. Born
Anna Mae Bullock in Nutbush, Tennessee, she had hooked up with
bandleader Ike Turner and his Kings of Rhythm in 1958, when they
both lived in St. Louis. Bullock was a fan of the band and dated the
saxophone player, singing with the group now and then. Ike Turner
took her away from his saxophonist and decided to groom her and
add her to the act, changing her name and calling the new attraction
the Ike and Tina Turner Revue.

Their shows on the chitlin circuit kept food on the table, and
when she wasn't performing, Tina raised Ike's children and ran his
household. They had several hits on the rhythm and blues charts—"A

228

Fool in Love," "I Idolize You," and "It's Gonna Work Out Fine"—but barely registered on *Billboard*'s Hot 100.

Spector loved the Revue. "The show was just mesmerizing," he said. "I said, God, if I could make a number-one record with her she could go on *Ed Sullivan*, she could go to Las Vegas, she could break the color barrier. I was just devastated by her."

The problem was Ike. Phil wanted Tina's voice with the Wrecking Crew. No Ike. He described his terms to Ike, who had no issue as long as his name was on the record and he got paid.

Phil needed a special song, so he flew back to New York to create something with Jeff Barry and Ellie Greenwich. Their marriage had just ended, but their songwriting partnership continued. Together with Spector, they knocked out three likely songs in a week.

Back in Los Angeles, Phil began working with Tina on "River Deep–Mountain High," Barry and Greenwich's song of hopeless and impossible devotion. The sessions were brutal for Tina, a natural, improvisational singer. Phil didn't want improvisation. He wanted everything his way. At times, she was shoehorned into Gold Star with forty other musicians and backing singers. Spector invited Brian Wilson to the sessions, but only to observe, not participate.

Later, after he had finally gotten the vocal he wanted from Turner (she said she thought she'd sung it five hundred thousand times), Spector overdubbed strings. After mixing the record, he listened to it in the control booth with his guests. When it ended, he embraced his longtime arranger, Jack Nitzsche. Later, Nitzsche said that he and Spector agreed that "River Deep–Mountain High" was as good as it would ever get.

It was an overwhelming record that twice built to epic peaks, only to stop, drop, and start again. Individual instruments blended into one breathtaking whole. In the middle of this beautiful chaos, Tina Turner sang as if she would combust.

Released in May 1966, "River Deep–Mountain High" was a colossal flop, barely making it onto *Billboard*'s Hot 100. Heartbroken by the failure of the greatest record he'd ever made, Phil Spector retired at age twenty-six.

"Caroline, No," the somber finale to *Pet Sounds*, was released as a single on March 7, 1966, credited to Brian Wilson. It *was* a solo recording—just Brian and the Wrecking Crew, including four flutists. The flip side was Tommy Tedesco's guitar-driven instrumental from *Summer Days*, "Summer Means New Love." "Caroline, No" reached number thirty-two on the *Billboard* charts.

There was some speculation that this would be the start of Brian's solo career, but two weeks later, the Beach Boys released a single.

As Brian readied *Pet Sounds* in the early spring, he decided to include "Sloop John B," recorded the year before. It was the only nonoriginal song on the album and was credited as a Brian Wilson arrangement of a Bahamian folk tune. When released, the single became a worldwide hit and reached number three on *Billboard*'s Hot 100.

Pet Sounds was released on May 16. Though it eventually reached *Billboard*'s Top Ten, Capitol saw it as a disappointment. It was so different.

There were no American rock critics then—none to speak of, at least—and no serious reporting on the music industry. The mainstream press looked on rock 'n' roll records with bemused disdain, if it looked on such records at all. *Billboard* commented on the recording quality of *Pet Sounds* and its potential to deliver hit singles. That was all.

"When it wasn't received by the public in the way that he thought it would be received, it really hurt him," Marilyn Wilson said of Brian. "It made him hold back. He couldn't understand it. He said, 'Why aren't people willing to expand and accept more and grow?'"

In England, critics lavished the album with glowing prose. Music publications praised the album, and musicians spoke admiringly of it in interviews. Andrew Loog Oldham, manager and producer of the Rolling Stones, called *Pet Sounds* "the Scheherazade of pop music." The reception in Great Britain drove *Pet Sounds* to number two on the English charts.

Two months after the album's release, Capitol issued a single of "Wouldn't It Be Nice" and "God Only Knows." The American single was promoted with "Wouldn't It Be Nice" as the A-side, and it rose to number eight. The flip side just squeaked into the Top Forty at number thirty-nine.

In foreign markets, "God Only Knows" was promoted as the A-side and rose to number two in Great Britain. It was a Top Ten hit in most other countries around the world that cared about rock music.

In hindsight, the album is seen as a masterpiece, but at the time—despite its Top Ten showing—Capitol Records judged it a qualified failure. It sold, but it didn't sell *as well* as earlier Beach Boys albums.

Six weeks after *Pet Sounds* was released, Capitol issued *Best of the Beach Boys*, an anthology that drew heavily from the surf-and-turf years and didn't feature any of Brian's elaborate recent productions.

The anthology was a huge success, giving Mike Love a chance to *I told you so* cousin Brian. It outperformed *Pet Sounds*, and its success depressed Brian. He had moved beyond all of that surfing stuff, and now *that's* what was selling, not his from-the-heart magnum opus, the album into which he had poured his soul. "Artistic freedom in those days was a concept that ran contrary to the way the record industry functioned," Brian said.

But Brian was already off in another direction. He'd started on a major production during the *Pet Sounds* session, and when its recording grew beyond his expectations, he set it aside. Now he wanted to get back to it.

He'd also met someone he thought might be an even better match than Tony Asher as lyricist. Instead of mourning the tepid response to *Pet Sounds* and Capitol's *Best of the Beach Boys* low blow, he got back on the pony and decided to produce the best rock 'n' roll single ever made.

He had big plans. "My real intention was to redraw the entire map of pop music."

Ray and Jim lived at the beach, but they didn't sing about surfing. They'd met at UCLA's film school, and in the summer of 1965, they decided to form a band. Emulating the music of the Beach Boys was the furthest thing from their minds.

Ray Manzarek was a little older than the typical rock 'n' roller, already married and with a master's in film from UCLA. No film studios had yet asked him to become the next John Ford, or even the next Roger Corman. He and his wife, Dorothy, were living in a garage apartment on Venice Beach. He was a California boy by way of Chicago and comfortable in the oceanside life. Until Hollywood called, he planned to hang out at the beach by day and play organ by night in Rick and the Ravens, a band fronted by two of his younger brothers. One day on the beach, he ran into that charmingly obnoxious underclassman he'd known at UCLA.

Jim Morrison always had trouble answering the question "Where you from?" Like all children in military families, he grew up a nomad. Dad was a naval officer, so Jim was regularly uprooted during childhood. As a teenager, he attended George Washington High School in Alexandria, Virginia, where he was a classmate of Ellen Cohen, still a couple of years away from becoming Cass Elliot.

Jim was the weird kid in school—whichever school he attended. Pudgy, angry, and insulting, he was a trial for teachers and parents. His father was on his way up the ranks, but Jim continued to embarrass him at required military family gatherings, so he and his wife sent Jim to live with his grandparents in Clearwater, Florida.

Once in the Tampa Bay area, he began dating Mary Werbelow, a beautiful first runner-up for Miss Clearwater in 1963. Statuesque, with a considerable Jackie Kennedy bouffant, she was enamored of Jim's new persona as a literary madman. Her support and encouragement made him feel secure about pursuing an artist's path. He carried notebooks wherever he went and frequently pulled them from his ass pocket to scrawl new insights or revelations. When Jim was driving, Mary took custody of his notebook. "Write this!" he'd yell, then dictate a Great Thought or two, which she obediently wrote down.

Music was not part of Jim's developing art. He showed no more than routine interest in song and was rhythmically impaired, hopelessly Caucasian, and incapable of dance. "He didn't sit around and sing," Mary said. "Jim, no, he was a poet. He wrote poetry."

What he was doing was . . . *different*. He didn't fit the candy-striped Beach Boys model of an American male in 1964. When the Beatles came along, Jim grew his hair, but to prove his severe love for Mary, he bucked fashion and got a crewcut at her request.

"He was a genius," Mary recalled. "He was incredible." As she recalled, the writers he most admired—and imitated in his early days—were William Burroughs, William Blake, Norman Mailer, Friedrich Nietzsche, Karl Marx, Arthur Rimbaud, and Jack Kerouac.

He attended nearby St. Petersburg Junior College, then transferred to Florida State University. Mary accompanied him to Tallahassee, over the objection of her parents. Things did not go well. He was arrested for being drunk and disorderly at a Seminoles football game.

Beyond the crime of underage inebriation, he committed Tallahassee's greatest sin: in the South, where football is religion, he yelled insults at godlike players.

Morrison transferred to UCLA later in 1964. Again, Werbelow defied her parents and announced she would go with him. Their chaste relationship became sexual. They arrived in Los Angeles as another beautiful, sunny young couple in the world's entertainment capital. Both of them had aspirations in the arts. For his part, Jim embraced Hollywood life, began studying film, and expected to make his mark onscreen. Mary watched as he transformed, changing colors like a chameleon.

And then Jim met Ray. Ray Manzarek was four years older and already in graduate school. Ray knew Jim as a chubby junior varsity blowhard, so full of shit it poured from his ears. But the more time they spent together, the more Ray became fascinated with the kid. Jim mocked nearly everyone he saw, without having accomplished anything himself. He was arrogant without portfolio.

Manzarek invited Morrison to see Rick and the Ravens and coaxed him on stage—not hard, considering how drunk Jim was—to belt out the frat-rock anthem "Louie Louie." He was terrible, but he had fun and a presence.

Ray and Jim circled each other as casual acquaintances, and in early summer 1965, when Ray finished his master's, they went different directions. But somehow, those directions led them to a meeting on Venice Beach later that summer.

As soon as he arrived in California, Jim began gobbling acid like M&M's, and his personality went from aloof to extrovert. He was always stoned or tripping, and Mary began to think the Jim she knew was gone. A couple months after their arrival, she found him with another woman and knew it was over. He helped her move into a new apartment, and she told him they needed to take a break. "He clammed up after that," she recalled. "I really hurt him. It hurts me to say that. I really hurt him."

Ray Manzarek thought Jim's breakup with Mary Werbelow was a turning point. "She was a great girl, and she really seemed to be in love with him," he said. "But that was also the summer Jim went through some kind of transformation—physical, mental, emotional, on every level—and I don't think any relationship he'd had could have survived that." Everyone who knew Mary loved her, he recalled. "She was Jim's first love. She held a deep place in his soul."

Determined to finish college, Jim buried himself in school. As artist and writer Eve Babitz recalled in a memoir, "My friend Judy Raphael, who went to film school, too, remembers Jim as this pudgy guy with a marine haircut who worked in the library at UCLA and who was supposed to help her with her documentary term paper one night but ended up talking drunkenly and endlessly about Oedipus, which meant she had to take the course over that summer."

Jim graduated, but in order to prove he was not another sheep, he skipped his commencement ceremony.

When Jim and Ray ran into each other on the beach, they played catch-up and soon realized they were both busy doing nothing. Jim was cut off from the UCLA meal plan—he used to gorge on the student trough—and so he'd lost more than twenty pounds. Ray said he was unemployed. *God bless Dorothy for having a job.* He told Jim he was just woodshedding with his brothers' band, trying to get something going there. He said they might record a demo, but they needed original material and it wasn't happening.

"I've been writing some songs," Jim said, squinting into the sun.

Really? Ray asked Jim to sing, but he demurred. After a few minutes of hemming and hawing, Jim closed his eyes and began reciting, not singing, his words.

Let's swim to the moon, let's climb through the tide

"This is incredible," Ray said. "Do you have anything else?"

In his delicate, high voice, Morrison began softly singing his pseudo–beat poetry. Wheels spun in Manzarek's head. Rock music was changing. This was the summer of the Byrds, whose "Mr. Tambourine Man" winked openly about LSD: "Take me for a trip on your magic swirlin' ship." Gone were striped shirts and matching suits and simple boy-girl songs. Ray conceived of a band that would push boundaries and combine theater and cinema with rock 'n' roll. Jim's words certainly pushed those limits. No "da do ron ron" here.

Ray saw Jim as his ticket. Since his parents had cut him off, Jim needed a place to stay, so Ray told Dorothy they had a roommate. Jim boosted steaks from the local market to earn his keep. Ray brought him to Rick and the Ravens gigs, pushing him up front to sing. Ray's younger brothers weren't sure about Jim, but deferred to big brother. The Ravens were unhappy with their drummer, and Ray suggested a jazz player he'd met named John Densmore, a much better drummer than the Ravens deserved. Eventually the younger Manzarek brothers realized they were in danger of losing their group and suggested to Ray that he take his friends and start his own band.

Morrison named the new band the Doors, from his infatuation with William Blake and Aldous Huxley (*The Doors of Perception*). One fan theory claimed the name was because the band members were swingers and had big knobs.

The name beat the hell out of Rick and the Ravens, Ray thought. They'd found Robby Krieger, a skilled slide guitar player with a dazed, perpetually stoned look. Robby figured this was just another band, but as his first rehearsal ended, a dope dealer showed up and suddenly Jim Morrison went wild—he went *off*, with a fierce anger that stunned Robby. "Jim just went nuts," he said. "I thought, 'Jesus Christ, this guy's not normal.'" Rather than being scared off, Robby saw the band as a way to maintain his equilibrium, thanks to Ray Manzarek's maturity and steadiness behind the keys. "Jim was just so out there," Robby said. Ray could bring things back to earth. His methodical personality "created a good balance."

The band decided to go without a bass player until the right one came along, but Ray covered the low parts on the organ, which they figured was OK for stage performances. Their demo tape was rejected by every label. One record executive gave the tape minimal attention, then blithely said he couldn't use it. Jim bellowed, "We don't want to be *used* anyway!"

The Doors hoped for word of mouth, so they played any gig they could get. Morrison grew confident and even charismatic in performance, allowing his inherent weirdness to come forward, crafting with the band songs unlike anything on the radio. Happiness was absent. The songs were bitter and scornful. Even Jim's attempt at a love song, "Hello, I Love You," was snide.

The band's darkness and its sneering songs set it apart from other groups. Crowds came to their gigs, which got better and better. Jim, Ray, Robby, and John began playing around town, still without a bass player.

By early 1966, the Doors were the house band at the London Fog on the Sunset Strip. It was a wretched dive that stunk of rotting beer and had a floor sticky with spilled drinks, gum, and, no doubt, bodily fluids. The stage was ten feet above the dance floor, and the band had to climb a ladder to play. But they had a steady gig (forty bucks a night), and word spread.

This is where Jim became *Jim Morrison*. Four nights a week, five sets a night, they played everything from dumb frat rock to original tunes. Jim performed his somber ballad "The End," about his breakup with Mary. Onstage, Jim improvised, made space for bandmates to solo, and called down from the gods spontaneous bursts of rhyme, turning the short, simple dirge into an epic prose poem. Robby contributed a song with a South American rhythm called "Light My Fire." Again, onstage, Jim toyed with it, improvising lyrics and pushing the band and the song in another direction. The London Fog audience became lab rats for musical experimentation.

The rats loved the band: John Densmore, enigmatic behind the drums; Ray Manzarek, mad professor at the keys; Robby Krieger, frizzy-haired, slack-jawed stoner on guitar; and Jim Morrison, leather pants, no shirt, all sex. "Like everyone back then, Jim hated his parents, hated home, hated it all," Eve Babitz wrote. "If he could have gotten away with it, Jim would have been an orphan."

The live act came together, and Jim was a *presence*. He'd been on the LSD diet, eating acid instead of cheeseburgers, and the new, slimmed-down Jim Morrison drew arched eyebrows from Babitz. "He had the freshness and humility of someone who had been fat all his life and now suddenly a morning glory. I met Jim and propositioned him in three minutes even before he so much as opened his mouth to sing."

He had allure. Ronnie Haran, a young woman who booked bands for the Whisky a Go Go—premiere venue on the Strip—secured an audition for the Doors and then marshaled friends to deluge the owner, Elmer Valentine, with requests to book the band with "that sexy motherfucker with the black pants." Indeed, Jim spent his offstage hours roasting his broomstick all over Hollywood.

The Whisky was a cosmic leap from the London Fog, and the band—so unlike any other rock band until that time—drew the amorous, the furious, and the curious.

The Doors soon had a large, loyal following, and as the members continued to work through their original repertoire onstage, the songs continued to evolve. "The End" radically matured from a simple breakup song to balls-out Oedipal drama. One night at the Whisky, Jim improvised a segment that ended with the cry "Mother, I want to fuck you!" That was it for Elmer Valentine, who suddenly decided he needed a new house band.

The Oedipus incident watered and manured the Doors' growing reputation as the most *out-there* band in Los Angeles.

Billy James, a young and hip Columbia Records executive stationed in L.A., liked the look of the band, if not the music. He thought they had potential just because they were so different. "They appealed to the snob in me," James admitted. "They were UCLA graduates and I thought, 'Great, here are some intellectual types getting involved with rock 'n' roll.'" James signed the group to make two singles for Columbia, but none of the staff producers, including red-hot Terry Melcher, wanted to work with them.

In retrospect, it's hard to imagine the Doors on stuffy, corporate Columbia. Esoteric Elektra Records was a better home, and in 1966, the company was trying to get a foothold in the rock 'n' roll world. Founder and president Jac Holzman was used to dignified folk acts such as Judy Collins and Tom Paxton. The Byrds would've made sense on Elektra, but their first Elektra single bombed and they moved on to Columbia.

Holzman wasn't a big rock 'n' roll fan but wanted his label to move in that direction. He signed Love, the band led by the shaman singer Arthur Lee and guitarist Bobby Beausoleil. Critics loved Love, but the group never clicked commercially. What was the point of going into rock 'n' roll, Holzman reasoned, if not to make money? Like Billy James, Holzman was drawn to the seriousness of Ray Manzarek's playing and his classical flourishes. He did not think much of Jim Morrison at first.

Holzman signed the band to Elektra in the summer of 1966 and was ready to produce the debut album, but then got to know Jim Morrison well. That's when he handed off the job to one of the few producers on his tiny staff, Paul Rothchild. Paul was in his early thirties, had done some time for marijuana possession, and had a good career producing small but important folk records for the label. Rothchild was insulted to be asked to produce this bar band, but Holzman had been steadfast during Rothchild's imprisonment, promising his job would be waiting when he got out of the pokey. Rothchild owed Holzman.

By the end of August, Rothchild and the band he so loathed were ensconced at low-rent Sunset Sound Recorders, a studio with no rock 'n' roll track record, known mostly for Walt Disney movie soundtracks.

As Rothchild circled the band, getting to know them, he began to see why Holzman arranged the shotgun wedding. "You're talking about a band where the guys were all very smart and frequently about different things," Holzman said. "Ray and Jim were super-smart, and you needed a guy who was as well read as they were, and Paul was that. So I thought he was the ideal person. I thought he could really whip them into shape."

Rothchild brought in Larry Knechtel from the Wrecking Crew to solve the bass problem, and they began working out arrangements for the group's original songs at Sunset Sound. The band decided to credit all of the songs to the Doors, even though "Light My Fire," for example, was ninety percent the work of one member, Robby Krieger. The group credits were a sixties peace, love, flowers thing— the community-of-man spirit. As they began working with Rothchild, the band members began to appreciate that he wasn't a button pusher or an executive. He shared their artistic sensibilities, and when he pushed the band in one direction or another, he was doing so for artistic reasons, not commercial reasons.

Engineer Bruce Botnick ran the board. He was a much-in-demand engineer freelancing around town. He'd seen it all, and then he saw the Doors.

"They were totally different than anything else I was recording," Botnick said. "I was recording the Beach Boys, the Turtles, the Ventures, and a lot of pop music as well—and they were totally different. It was the beginning of that era of American sixties music."

While calling the Doors a well-oiled machine might insult well-oiled machines, their five sets a night helped the band find the heart of its original songs and develop a style unlike any other rock 'n' roll group. Jim Morrison had, in the space of one year, gone from a pudgy, smart-ass do-nothing into a sex symbol poet poured into leather pants with a provocative and confrontational stage presence.

Throughout the fall, the Doors played bars and small clubs. The album was in the can, but the record manufacturing process took *forever*. Though some copies of the album—simply called *The Doors*— were released in December 1966, the album was not in most stores until its official release date in the first week of January 1967.

Fitting: a new year, a new sound, something unlike anything anyone else had done.

Brian Wilson met Van Dyke Parks when he was nipple-deep in *Pet Sounds*. Though soon absorbed into Brian's floating entourage of stoners, hangers-on, and ass kissers, Parks was not really part of that group. Van Dyke Parks was an original, not part of any group.

Because of geography and precociousness, it's tempting to compare Parks to Truman Capote, the great American writer who became the model for the character Dill in his friend Harper Lee's *To Kill a Mockingbird*. Capote and Lee grew up in Alabama. Parks was from the next state over, born and raised in Hattiesburg, Mississippi, a couple decades after Capote. His childhood home had two grand pianos. Papa was a physician, and Mama was a Middle East scholar.

Parks began music lessons when he was four, first playing the clarinet. "I always sat first chair," he said. "My brothers played trumpet, French horn, and double-barrel euphonium. Each Advent season, we hit the neighborhood with Noels."

The gifted child was sent to Columbus Boychoir School in Princeton, New Jersey. At one school event, he sang in German while Princeton professor Albert Einstein accompanied him on violin. He sang at the Metropolitan Opera when he was ten, had a continuing role on the Jackie Gleason television comedy *The Honeymooners*, and got a coveted role in Grace Kelly's final film, *The Swan*, in 1956. He began as a music major at the Carnegie Institute, studying composition under Aaron Copland. At twenty, he dropped out and moved to Los Angeles to see what he could do in the music business.

He had a number of jobs in the music industry. With one of his older brothers, he played in a series of folk groups. At twenty-one, he was hired by Disney Studios to arrange "The Bare Necessities," the showstopper in the animated film of *The Jungle Book*.

Soon, Van Dyke Parks's path led him to David Crosby of the Byrds, and they became pals. One day in summer 1965, Crosby asked Parks to join him on a visit to Brian Wilson's home, where the head Beach Boy played an early dub of "Sloop John B." Wilson had a love-hate relationship with the song. It was done, but he didn't know what to do with it. Parks loved surfing and didn't like the Beach Boys and what he considered their faux surf music, so despite the fact that the acetate Wilson played was engaging, he did not change his opinion.

Parks stayed in Crosby's orbit, and one of his early arranging/performing gigs was on the Byrds' third album, *Fifth Dimension*. He played organ on Jim McGuinn's title song, a tune banned by overly cautious radio station programmers who assumed it referred to drugs.

Oh, how is it I can come out to her and be still floating
And never hit bottom and keep falling through

Terry Melcher no longer produced the Byrds but was still one of the most connected movers and shakers in the city's musical universe. At one of Melcher's glorious house parties, Brian again met Van Dyke Parks. It was February 1966. Parks was working with the Byrds, but Melcher took no offense to Parks consorting with his latest enemies. He was producing Paul Revere and the Raiders, a band with more teenybopper appeal than the Byrds, making money ass over fist.

"I had lots of music-business gatherings," Melcher said. "I had huge music speakers all over the house, all over the grounds, and these people would arrive from the studios in L.A., New York, London and they would bring their acetates of unreleased material."

Melcher's home was the place to be in those heady days.

Brian, meet Van Dyke; Van Dyke, meet Brian. "Brian needs a lyricist," Terry said. He was a great fan of Brian's, but always wished he'd work with a lyricist as sophisticated with words as he was with music. "He writes fantastic melodies," Melcher said. "He's like a classical composer. Brian can do a Bach thing. Give him 90 pieces and he'll give you a Bach thing; then give it to an expert and he'd have a hell of a time finding the difference. But he isn't a lyricist, so he's been put down a lot for being an asshole. But the people who put him down, if they were really musicians, they'd forget the words and get into the structure of the thing."

Brian and Van Dyke decided to get together at Brian's house on Laurel Way. Wilson played sections of his new music—he called them "feels"—and asked Parks what he thought. Parks admitted that he did not like the Beach Boys until he heard *Pet Sounds*. The surf songs and car songs did nothing for him, but *Pet Sounds* did.

"Brian was the most powerful creative force in the business in terms of teenage records sold," Parks said. "He did it all—he didn't have [Beatles producer] George Martin. He was a magnetic field."

Brian first asked Parks to help with a song he'd worked on with Tony Asher in the middle of the *Pet Sounds* sessions. He was excited about it musically but thought Asher's lyrics misfired. The idea came from something his mother said to him when he was a child. He wanted to know why dogs growled at some people and not at others.

They could feel vibrations, his mother told him. *Bad vibrations and good vibrations.*

He had the basic structure and had spent several sessions in the studio on the song. "That started with one little riff," Brian said, "and we waited a month and started another section. We started recording individual sections and then at the very end we spliced all these sections together."

The song's instrumental track was evolving with an unusual dynamic—interplay between three lead instruments: drums, cellos (a Van Dyke Parks suggestion), and a theremin, an electronic instrument mostly associated with the alien sounds in science fiction films (*oooeeeooo*).

Asher's lyrics did not fit Brian's ambitious musical terrain. Parks turned down Wilson's offer, saying he didn't want to take on anyone else's problems. He'd rather start from scratch. "I told Brian that I wouldn't touch it with a 10-foot pole and that nobody'd be listening to the lyrics anyway once they heard that music."

Instead, Mike Love came up with the words for "Good Vibrations." In one of their greatest collaborations, Brian's avant-garde music was perfectly matched with Mike's *You come here often?* guy-girl lyrics. Hurt by the lyrical freeze-out of *Pet Sounds*, Mike was happy to see another Wilson-Love credit (and the eventual royalty checks). But he didn't care too much for the recording sessions.

They went on. And on. And furthermore, *they went on.* Eight months on one song. The whole summer of 1966. Brian would record at Gold Star, then move his operation to Western because of the studio's special sonic quality. And then move to Sunset Sound for its unique acoustics.

He began on February 7, 1966, during a session booked for *Pet Sounds* at Gold Star. Though he did a few full takes of the song, he began a new approach to making records: he'd record bits and pieces, then bring everything together. It was an expensive production, paying the Wrecking Crew to come to the studio du jour and lay down the same bit over and over and over. Van Dyke Parks participated in one session on his hands and knees, playing the same bit on organ pedals over and over.

Brian tinkered with the recording for months, shifting between studios, eventually doing some recording and tweaking at Columbia Studios. He knew it was good. Finally, Mike got the words right. But was it too weird, too far out for the audience? Brian debated whether to release it at all. "It's still sticking pretty close to that same boy-girl thing, you know, but with a difference," Brian told writer Tom Nolan. "It's a start, it's definitely a start." A start to what, he did not say.

Wilson finally let go, and Capitol released "Good Vibrations" on October 10. It sold nearly a quarter million copies in its first week and by December was the number-one record in the country. The single's success was repeated around the world.

Mike's lyrics kept the song grounded in the Beach Boys milieu, though a "blossom world" and "the wind that lifts her perfume through the air" were nods to the *peace, love, flowers* mantra voiced by the era's hippies. Brian balked a little at Mike's line about the worshipped girl in the song "giving me the excitations." He thought people would think they were singing about erections.

If the lyrics broke little new ground, the music was something else. It stayed within the basic structures of Beach Boys music but at the same time was revolutionary. Who had ever used cellos before on a rock 'n' roll record? And had anyone ever used them in *this* way?

Mike Love saw *Pet Sounds* as a misstep but figured it was something Brian needed to do to get that desire for experimentation out of his system. "Good Vibrations" vindicated them both. Mike was right, but Brian was right too. But despite Mike's urging, Brian did not want to be exclusive with his cousin as lyricist. He wanted to try something new and radically different with Van Dyke Parks.

———————————

The Whisky a Go Go was more or less in the middle of the mile-and-a-half-long section of Sunset Boulevard known as the Sunset Strip. The Strip ran through West Hollywood, cheek by jowl with L.A. but not *in* L.A. That meant the rowdiness in the Strip's restaurants and clubs could not be curbed by the Los Angeles Police Department. The Strip fell under the jurisdiction of the more laid back sheriff's department.

This was where Hollywood royalty of old—Clark Gable, Bette Davis, Gary Cooper—had hung out in the thirties and forties. Ciro's was the go-to nightclub of the Hollywood clerisy. This was where Humphrey Bogart dined, smoked his cigarettes, and eyeballed the action.

But those were the bygone days. By the sixties, Ciro's and a lot of other clubs on the Strip had degenerated into sleazy dives. No one in his right mind would go into them without a hazmat suit.

And then Elmer Valentine opened the Whisky a Go Go in January 1964, taking the name of a celebrated French discotheque. To draw people to the Strip, Valentine wanted to have live entertainment, and so he booked Johnny Rivers.

Though born in New York as John Ramistella, Rivers (disc jockey Alan Freed gave him the stage name) grew up in Baton Rouge, Louisiana, steeped in swamp rock and the varied and delightful music of nearby New Orleans. He began performing and recording in the late fifties, but lack of success led him to Nashville, where he hoped a music publisher would sign him as a staff songwriter. One of his songs got to television rock 'n' roller Ricky Nelson out in Hollywood. Nelson recorded it, so Rivers headed to Los Angeles as the sixties dawned.

He was still a staff songwriter and had pretty much given up on performing when he was asked to play at a club on the lower Strip, Gazzari's. He generated some buzz, which is why Elmer Valentine came calling.

Rivers knew he needed familiar material to keep a good-time rock 'n' roll show going. Though a proficient songwriter, he chose to fill set lists with reinterpretations of rock classics such as Chuck Berry's "Maybellene" and "Memphis." Almost immediately, Valentine had an audience and Rivers had a performing career.

Lou Adler was in the audience for an early show, and he approached Rivers and asked to record him live at the club. *Johnny Rivers at the Whisky a Go Go* came out at the end of February. It happened that fast.

Rivers signed a year's contract with the Whisky and ended up recording five live albums there, though the nature of their "live" status came into question. Music historians still debate whether they were truly live or whether the Rivers albums were recorded in the studio with the Wrecking Crew, with audience overdubs and tinkling glasses added, à la the Beach Boys' *Party!* album.

Whatever the case, Johnny Rivers became a popular recording artist, regularly scoring hits for the Imperial label. When a British television series called *Danger Man* was licensed for broadcast in America, producers sought a new theme song. The request landed on Lou Adler's desk, and he gave the assignment to Phil Sloan and Steve Barri. They came up with "Secret Agent Man." Rivers recorded it, and the result hit number three on the *Billboard* charts.

The success with Johnny Rivers gave Lou Adler the capital he needed to establish Dunhill Records.

Rivers put the Whisky on the map. Ciro's begat the Byrds, but that group moved west down Sunset for a Whisky residence. Love played the Whisky, as did Buffalo Springfield and the Doors.

The Whisky drew crowds and the once-dead Strip became Rock 'n' Roll Avenue. Among the clubs were the Trip, the Melody Room, the Galaxy, the hip eatery Ben Frank's, Ciro's, It's Boss, the coffeehouse Fred C. Dobbs, and Pandora's Box, the purple-and-gold palace where Brian Wilson met Marilyn and Diane Rovell during an early Beach Boys gig.

Pandora's was a tiny place on a plot little bigger than a traffic island, where Sunset met Crescent Heights. By 1966, all the way from Pandora's west to Gazzari's, the Strip was a teenage wonderland but hell for the local gentry in their fine restaurants. They stayed away from the Strip rather than share airspace with increasing unhygienic and hirsute young folk. Kids ambled down the Strip, clubs along the way taking a few bites out of the crowd or spitting out a few, who rejoined the crowd, moving on. The kids were pissing off grown-ups. "It's not a pleasant thing to see them walking around," said Bruno Petroletti, owner of the fancy pants La Rue restaurant. His place had some quality customers. Frank Sinatra was frequently at La Rue that summer, romancing starlet Mia Farrow. *Mr. Frank Sinatra wants peace and quiet!*

Petroletti and other owners of "mature businesses" complained to the sheriff's department about the scraggly, smelly longhairs walking the circuit, and, as often happened with law enforcement officials in the sixties, they overreacted, using a Howitzer to swat a gnat.

Deputies announced a strictly enforced ten o'clock curfew. *Enough with the walking! Enough with the hair! Enough with the music!* The deputies began rounding up kids and carting them to jail for the crime of walking while young. Still the kids came, doing the whole Strip walk, being loud, being hairy. It was too much for the older folk.

Some of the young folk organized a protest and passed out flyers on the Strip, urging people to gather across from Pandora's on Saturday night, November 12, 1966. It was time to stop the oppression.

There was a *kumbaya* vibe to the gathering when it started, as the demonstrators held hands and sang. Several staged a street sit-in, blocking traffic. A two-car accident with a sedan full of marines led to street fights and boiling tempers. Deputies with billy clubs moved in, ordering everyone young to leave. Protestors numbering around a thousand coiled with anger. The crowd let loose on anything that symbolized the older folks, "the establishment," the people wanting to tuck them in by 10 PM, just when fun awakened.

The protestors began rocking a city bus, dragging out passengers and the driver. They broke bus windows with rocks, let air from the tires, and tried to set the thing on fire.

In the face of chanting protestors, the establishment stood firm. "We're going to be tough," county supervisor Ernest Debs vowed. "We're not going to surrender that area or any other area to beatniks or wild-eyed kids."

The riots continued for a few nights. Stephen Stills of Buffalo Springfield witnessed the scene. "Riot is a ridiculous name," Stills said. "It was a funeral for Pandora's Box. But it looked like a revolution."

A revolution with an audience. Celebrities dropped by to see what was going on. Actors Peter Fonda (recording it with his home movie camera) and Jack Nicholson were there, though Jack Nicholson wasn't *Jack Nicholson* yet. Sonny and Cher stopped for a look. Just being on the Strip that night meant guilt by association and cost the married singing duo an important gig. They were supposed to ride on a New Year's Day float in the Tournament of Roses parade, but the float's sponsor did not want to be associated with "their type." Sonny and Cher had not taken part in the riot but merely observed and offered counsel to kids. "I told them to be peaceful," Sonny Bono said.

Stills rushed home after the riot. "I had to skedaddle and headed back to Topanga," he said. "I wrote my song in about fifteen minutes."

> *There's something happening here*
> *What it is ain't exactly clear*

Stills never mentioned the Sunset Strip or curfew or Pandora's Box in his song. He was vague, but sometimes vague is good (as with the First Amendment). But he described menace, fear, resentment, and anger—the dominant feelings of the young people of that era. They could be drafted to fight in a war on the other side of the world, but they could not vote. They could not legally drink alcohol.

The song was about teenagers pissed off about early closing times, but it became something else to those who heard it on the radio. Unfortunately, Buffalo Springfield had just finished its first album, due to be released at the beginning of December, so it was too late to add this new song.

Stills, Neil Young, Richie Furay, and Dewey Martin had bonded quickly the previous summer and for a time became the house band at the Whisky and opened frequently on Beach Boys tours. They signed to New York–based ATCO, the subsidiary of Atlantic, the great rhythm and blues label, and recorded their debut album *Buffalo Springfield* at Gold Star in July and August. There were twelve songs on the album, five written by Neil Young, but he sang only two vocals, because his voice was deemed so unconventional.

Stills believed in what he had with his Sunset Strip song, but recording a second album wasn't guaranteed. ATCO had to see how this first one did. Nevertheless, he gathered the group at Columbia Studios on December 5, 1966, to record. When he presented the tape to label owner Ahmet Ertegun, he said, "I have this song here, for what it's worth, if you want it."

"For What It's Worth" became the title, though the phrase appeared nowhere in the song.

Pandora's Box was closed in the aftermath of the riot but was opened for Christmas Day. Buffalo Springfield played at Pandora's that night, debuting "For What It's Worth." Early in the New Year, the county bought Pandora's and demolished it over the summer.

The Beach Boys might've helped create the rock 'n' roll world of Los Angeles in the sixties, but by middecade, the Byrds rivaled them for influence on other bands.

Buffalo Springfield would not have happened without the Byrds. The Turtles followed the Byrds in covering Bob Dylan songs ("It Ain't Me, Babe"), and the folkish tunes turned out by Phil Sloan and Steve Barri also reflected their influence. Sonny Bono and his teenage bride, Cher Sarkisian, took a brief stab at being Caesar and Cleo but scored a success as Sonny and Cher, following the folk-rock trail and dressing in flamboyant garb that often worked animal fur into their ensembles.

Sonny was a little older than the typical folk rocker—after all, he'd started as A&R man with Specialty Records in the fifties, then served as Phil Spector's gofer—so he relished his new role as a hairy folk-rock rebel. Cher and he made a beauty-and-beast couple, and their mere appearance inspired outrage.

Cher's cover of Dylan's "All I Really Want to Do" sold more than the Byrds' version—her single hit number fifteen, and the Byrds only got to number forty. The Byrds had created a formula by then, and producer Terry Melcher, a good friend of Mike Love's, did not like messing with the formula.

Still, the group's *Mr. Tambourine Man* album was riding high (it reached number six on *Billboard*'s album chart), and the group soared on its success rather than focusing much energy on creating singles. The teenybopper press called them America's Beatles, and in the fall of 1965, the Byrds toured Britain, showing that the Beatles had nothing to fear. Aside from Jim McGuinn, the group was still not fluent on its instruments.

That summer was the apogee of folk rock, when the high priest of American folk music and rebellion started playing rock 'n' roll. Bob Dylan appeared onstage with the Byrds at Ciro's, giving the group his blessing. Until 1965, Dylan's albums had been all acoustic, but that March, he released *Bringing It All Back Home*, on which half of the songs had electric accompaniment. That summer he recorded his monumental "Like a Rolling Stone," a six-minute rant that not only helped bring down radio's three-minute barrier but also pushed away most confines for popular songs. If he could sing *this* and *this* could become a hit, nothing was off limits. Dylan irritated his folk-protest disciples in July at the Newport Folk Festival when he blasted rock 'n' roll from the stage. He followed that by recording a scorching all-electric *Highway 61 Revisited* in September 1965 and released the mammoth and magnificent two-record set *Blonde on Blonde* in May 1966.

The Byrds returned to Dylan's well, but few efforts were successful. Gene Clark was the only prolific Byrds songwriter. He wrote or cowrote five of *Mr. Tambourine Man*'s twelve songs. Four songs were by Dylan, and Jackie DeShannon and Pete Seeger each contributed a tune.

The *What have you done for me lately?* attitude in the music industry pressured the Byrds to quickly follow their first success. After the miserable live performances in Europe, they returned to Columbia Studios in Hollywood to see if they had a second act. The first session fell during the Beatles' American tour, and the British group set up housekeeping in L.A. for a five-day break. George Harrison and Paul McCartney attended the session, a de facto Beatles seal of approval to their so-called American rivals.

One of the first things the Byrds tried in the studio was Dylan's "The Times They Are a-Changin'." Confident this was a sure-fire success, Columbia announced it as the group's next single before it had been recorded. When the band finished the song, it clearly wasn't anything special. Melcher soldiered on, pushing the band to get something down on tape. Columbia expected *product*.

Then Jim McGuinn reached into his past and brought in "Turn! Turn! Turn!" If the band couldn't connect with Dylan, maybe they could connect with God. "Turn! Turn! Turn!" drew its words from the Book of Ecclesiastes and was arranged by Pete Seeger into a brilliant folk song. Before Seeger could record it, the Limeliters released a cover version of it (as "To Everything There Is a Season") in 1962. The group's accompanist, Jim McGuinn, just out of high school, played the song nightly onstage. When he went to work for Judy Collins, he reworked the arrangement for her third album, *#3*. Now, with his electric twelve-string Rickenbacker, he found it was a natural for folk rock.

In 1965, America escalated its war in Vietnam. The war had gone from a distant murmur to the number-one issue for young Americans. The song's chilling closing message resonated with the antiwar movement:

> *A time for love, a time for hate*
> *A time for peace—I swear it's not too late*

The Byrds were back—with a number-one single and soon with a Top Twenty album. *Turn! Turn! Turn!* was released in December. Once again, Gene Clark was the dominant Byrds songwriter, and when the royalties started coming in, he bought a Ferrari. The other band members began to resent his conspicuous wealth.

By the end of January 1966, McGuinn, Clark, and Crosby had collaborated on "Eight Miles High," which became the group's most innovative single. Beginning with a pumping bass line from Chris Hillman, musical chaos ensued as McGuinn's twelve-string boiled and gurgled, pointing toward the vocal—all three composers singing together—as mysterious as anything in popular music. Hypersensitive program directors, seeing the word *high*, assumed it was another drug song and banned it from some airwaves, though it still hit number fourteen on *Billboard*'s Hot 100 chart. It was clearly a pop song but showed the influence of jazz saxophonist John Coltrane.

During his days traveling with Les Baxter's Balladeers, Crosby happened upon a Chicago club gig and saw Coltrane play. He was astonished by his virtuosity and creativity. Crosby leaned against the puke-green tiles in the club's bathroom, draining his main vein, when Coltrane kicked the door open and came in to hear how his sax sounded in the bathroom. Sounded great, as Crosby recalled.

"It really affected me," Crosby said. "I realized that there were levels that I could never get to but, suddenly, I could see what direction I wanted to go in. There were things that jazz musicians could do that I could never hope to do. I knew that somehow I wanted to reach for more."

The Byrds were not America's Beatles, certainly not in terms of sales. But one quality the group shared with the Brits was fearlessness about change. They were the progenitors of folk rock but soon moved into the realm of jazz and electronic music and played a major role in the emergence of country rock at the end of the sixties.

So "Eight Miles High" was a major step, but by the time it was released in March 1966, its primary composer, Gene Clark, was out of the band. To answer to those who wondered what the song was *really* about, Clark said he left the group because he feared flying.

McGuinn was last on the plane for a trip with the band to New York on February 22, and as he walked to his seat, he noticed Clark blocking the aisle. "I walked up to him and felt this fear for five feet around him," McGuinn said.

"I gotta get off this plane," Clark said, terror in his eyes.

"Hey man, it's cool," McGuinn counseled.

"I can't make it now," Clark said.

"If you can't fly, you're gonna blow it, man."

Gene got the flight attendant to open the cabin door and let him leave. Then Jim began to worry.

"Cold sweat came over me," he said. "Maybe he's psychic and knows something I don't know."

The pilot, knowing several passengers were unnerved by Clark's scene, delayed the flight by requesting another check of the plane's engines.

"They found the engines were messed up and they fixed them," McGuinn said. "He probably saved us all by getting off that plane."

The Byrd who would not fly. That was not Clark's official exit from the group. His bandmates were determined to maintain a five-piece unit, but McGuinn thought there might be other factors affecting

Clark's decision. "Maybe the guilt factor was there, because [Gene] was in Ferraris and things and we were still starving. He was making thousands and we weren't making anything yet."

Clark was soon gone, and the Byrds became a quartet. Within eighteen months, the group was a trio.

———————

There was a new aristocracy in the Los Angeles music world. Sinatra's era as grand exalted mystic ruler was passing. Brian Wilson could have assumed the role of leader/shaman/spokesman for the new musical elite, but for the fact that he was socially awkward and not especially verbal. When Terry Melcher introduced Brian to his beautiful girlfriend, actress Candice Bergen, Brian was so shy he put a fishbowl over his head so he'd have an excuse not to talk.

No, the leaders of the new rock aristocracy were the Mamas and the Papas—specifically Papa John Phillips and Mama Cass Elliot, the woman whose membership Phillips worried would doom the group. Instead, Cass became the group's star. Denny Doherty sang most of the lead vocals, but Cass gave the group its identity.

She also built ties within the music community. Her house was a salon for serious discussion, as well as serious dope smoking and LSD eating. When a musician from Great Britain—Eric Clapton, say—visited L.A., Elliot invited him to her house and asked over friends. Thus were long-term relationships born and much great music conceived.

Though John Phillips was social, he was more interested in the business side of the new rock community.

The Mamas and the Papas scored two huge hits right off the bat: "California Dreamin'" and "Monday, Monday." The title of their first album reflected Lou Adler's response to seeing them for the first time when they showed up at Barry McGuire's session: *If You Can Believe Your Eyes and Ears.* Dunhill released the album in March 1966, but its cover upset some retailers and was withdrawn. The cover photo showed the group squeezed into a bathtub, and it happened by accident. Guy Webster, the photo Boswell for Los Angeles musicians, was assigned the cover shoot. While Webster readied his equipment at the group's communal house, his subjects went elsewhere in the house to hide.

"You could hear him all over the house—'Come on you guys, we gotta get some pictures,'" Denny Doherty said. "We were hiding from him, fuckin' with him. We were all loaded out of our minds, and we'd been up all night." They decided on the bathroom and closed the door. "We were all giggling, and then he opens the door, and says, 'Oh, great!' and started shooting." Webster's image had John, Cass, and Denny in the tub, with Michelle sprawled over them. The look on Michelle's face was both coy and aggressive and became part of many American boys' sexual highlight reels.

Unfortunately, the cover photograph included a toilet. Shopkeepers outraged by this indecency refused to stock the album, so Dunhill—a growing company but still new—took back those covers and reissued the album with a sticker ticking off song titles over the toilet.

Indecent or not, the album was hotter than lightbulbs, and thanks to generous airplay and key television appearances, the Mamas and the Papas were America's new favorite hippie band by the summer of 1966. Adler was right: they were a great visual. They were soon rock 'n' roll royalty, and John and Michelle bought a splendid house in Bel-Air. Cass lived in Laurel Canyon, where she established her salon.

Sessions fell apart as the group began to record songs for a second album. The dynamic would have made an excellent afternoon soap opera: *As the Mamas and the Papas Turn.* John and Michelle's marriage was held together with tissue. Cass wanted to fuck Denny. Denny wanted to fuck Michelle. Michelle wanted to fuck Denny. John just wanted to gobble as many drugs as he could.

John's songs for the second album were weak and paled next to the classics on the first record, and he was worried that he'd shot his wad.

"John was a really good songwriter who really hit his peak with one album," said Mark Volman of the Turtles, a group traveling in the same social and creative circles as Phillips. "If you listen to that first album, *If You Can Believe Your Eyes and Ears,* it was John's *one* contribution. If you go to the next album, those songs were not as great. There were sporadic moments of good songwriting, but John Phillips's contribution to the landscape of music history was on that one album, those twelve songs."

Somehow in this creatively troubled and whacked-out environment, they went into Western Recorders with Hal Blaine, Joe Osborn, Larry Knechtel, and the kid Phil Sloan and tried to repeat the past. But there was too much tumult for the album to be recorded without drama. "I knew something was up when Michelle punched Denny at a session," Lou Adler recalled.

Almost as soon as John and Michelle moved into their new house, John moved out, after learning that Denny and Michelle had done the deed. John berated his young wife for breaking his one rule about her role in the group: *Don't fuck my tenor.* Michelle was also getting grief from Cass. Standing next to gorgeous Michelle onstage, Cass felt like the *before* picture, and although she joked about her weight, she was hurt, and hurt often, and she took it out on Michelle. And when Cass learned that Michelle had made the beast with two backs with dreamboat Denny, she was outright hostile.

When John moved out, *of course* he moved in with Denny. Who would spy on Denny otherwise? He wanted to make sure he wasn't lusting and thrusting with his wife. In what Michelle considered an act of pure sadism, John insisted that Denny help him write a song, "I Saw Her Again," about the affair.

They plugged away recording and still did concert dates, playing nice together onstage until they did a show at Melodyland, a theater-in-the-round in Anaheim. That's when the group's condition went from delicate to critical.

Michelle was by then having an affair with Gene Clark, who'd recently left the Byrds. When she walked out on the stage with the group, she saw him immediately. *How could she not?* He'd wrapped his tall, handsome body—*in a bright-red sport coat*—into a front-row seat. To shield Gene from John, Michelle took an odd placement onstage, blocking John's view. Despite her resentment of Michelle, Cass quickly intuited the situation and also stood in the way.

The concert was uneventful until John shifted position onstage and saw Gene grinning up at the woman who was still, on paper at least, John's wife. The audience heard an explosive *fuck!* from John's microphone. The word was not yet a common part of performance, so it startled. John recovered, and the group finished the show.

They were barely offstage when John lit into Michelle, telling her she was fired, and within a day he had a letter drafted and insisted that Cass and Denny sign it.

> This letter is to advise you that the undersigned no longer desire to record or perform with you in the future. Moreover, the undersigned desire to terminate any business relationship that may have heretofore existed.

John was a musician but also a businessman. He knew that the Mama and Two Papas probably wasn't going to work. He needed to find a new mama, and he immediately thought of Jill Gibson.

"I found out Michelle was fired from the group at the same time I was asked to be in the group," Gibson said. "I was excited at the opportunity to sing the songs John had written because I thought they were great songs and I loved the harmony."

Although the second album was still being recorded, the cover had already been shot: the group looking out an adobe window, with Michelle sitting on the sill. A photographer posed Gibson in the same windowsill and pasted her picture over Michelle's. Doing the same with the music would not be so easy.

Jill Gibson was best known in the Los Angeles music world as a backing singer, songwriter, and photographer. She was also Lou Adler's girlfriend. She'd recently started dating Adler after her long relationship with Jan Barry came to an end early that year.

Jan Berry, the mastermind of Jan and Dean, was in a coma.

At the end of 1964, Jan and Dean hosted the mega rock 'n' roll concert The T.A.M.I. Show (the Teenage Awards Music Internationl, or Teen Age Music International, depending on who you asked). Filmed at Santa Monica Civic Auditorium on October 28 and 29, director Steve Binder edited the best of both concerts into a film shown on December 29 in something called Electronovision, a euphemism for *We were careful to make sure everything was in focus.*

The duo introduced the show with a filmed skateboard tour of Los Angeles while they sang "(Here They Come) From All Over the World," written by Phil Sloan and Steve Barri. Considering the acts on the show, Jan and Dean's selection to host was a sign of affection and respect.

The T.A.M.I. Show was the musical equivalent of a NATO summit. The Beatles did not appear, and Bob Dylan was not yet a rock 'n' roll artist. But most everyone else was there: Chuck Berry, a founding father; from Motown, Marvin Gaye, the Supremes, and Smokey Robinson and the Miracles; from all over the rest of the nation, Lesley Gore, the Barbarians, James Brown, and the Beach Boys; and from England, Gerry and the Pacemakers, Billy J. Kramer and the Dakotas, and the Rolling Stones.

The house band was essentially a union meeting of the Wrecking Crew. Hal Blaine, Leon Russell, Glen Campbell, Plas Johnson, Tommy Tedesco, and Lyle Ritz formed the heart of the band, and Phil Spector's right-hand man, Jack Nitzsche, was music director. As Bill Wyman of the Rolling Stones recalled, "The film was fairly incidental to the importance of the occasion. What was important was that we met a whole string of artists and other people here who would figure into our career. Jack Nitzsche, Phil Spector's arranger on his records, was conducting the big band that accompanied all the other acts."

During rehearsals, James Brown approached the director. "Of course I'm the last act on the bill, right?"

"No," Steve Binder said. "Actually you're going to be followed by the Rolling Stones."

Brown smiled and told the director, "Nobody follows James Brown."

For the young white kids who watched this superconcert unfold onscreen, Brown's appearance was a relevation and, perhaps, life-changing. He was not widely known to white audiences, so to the Caucasian kids in the crowd (and watching in their movie theaters at home), his act was stunning. He did what he had been doing every night for a decade on the chitlin circuit.

For years onstage at those all-black clubs, he'd been vamping a routine as he sang his first hit, "Please, Please, Please." At T.A.M.I., Brown begged, pleaded, and fell to his knees as he beseeched his woman not to leave him. Appearing so bereft he could no longer walk, he implored his woman to stay while his backing singers shrouded him in a cape and consoled him as they led him offstage. At stage right, he threw off the cape, ran to the microphone, sinking to his knees to beg his woman some more. He did it again, but when that song ended, he still had the energy to dance in a way that defied gravity. James Brown moonwalked before Neil Armstrong.

Backstage, in the green room, the Rolling Stones watched. "During an incredible set from James Brown and the Famous Flames, all the acts [in the green room] went as crazy as the audience out front," Bill Wyman said. "We now knew what James Brown meant and were petrified at the prospect of following him."

Brown's performance at The T.A.M.I. Show is one of the high points of rock 'n' roll history, and the Rolling Stones had to follow it. Keith Richards said the Stones' agreement to follow Brown was the biggest mistake of the band's career.

The T.A.M.I. Show was a peak for rock 'n' roll, and it was also the peak of Jan and Dean's career. As 1965 began, the downhill slide began.

That year's arrival of the Byrds signaled rock music more mature than drag race and hang-ten juvenilia. The Beatles moved on to more sophisticated themes, and the Rolling Stones finally hit their stride with the fallen satire of "Satisfaction." Bob Dylan's coronation as a rock 'n' roll star hammered the nail in the coffin of surf and car songs.

The Beach Boys moved past those genres and focused their lyrics on the generics of summer and young love, with their *Today!* and *Summer Days* albums. *Party!* was a fitting farewell to the era. *Pet Sounds* was the final warning for those who hadn't been paying attention: *the Beach Boys had evolved.*

The other surf and car groups gradually disappeared. Phil Sloan and Steve Barri no longer aped surf and hot rod groups. Sloan followed Dylan's star and wrote more meaningful songs such as "The Sins of a Family" and "Eve of Destruction."

Jan and Dean did not make an easy transition. An attempt to have the Bel-Aire Pops Orchestra play Jan and Dean songs—*Jan and Dean's Pop Symphony No. 1 (in 12 Hit Movements)*—did not chart. A second *Golden Hits* package, which this time *did* include some golden hits, could not crack the Top One Hundred.

Thanks to Frank Sinatra, they had been dropped from the film *Ride the Wild Surf* the previous year but had signed for a new movie, *Easy Come, Easy Go.* The first week of filming, Jan and the director were seriously injured when a train ran into the camera's flatcar. The track was supposed to be closed, which led to speculation that someone out there was still trying to derail Jan and Dean's career and make them pay for their sins. Jan was in a cast from ass to toes, and the film was canceled.

The cast slowed Jan but did not keep him from medical school and recording-career commitments. He just began using the studio at odd times and was often at war with Liberty Records over expenses. He received an invoice with a note scrawled on it.

"This work was not scheduled in advance," it said. "Engineer had to put be held on overtime—Abnormal scheduling."

Jan and Dean split over efforts to inaugurate a new style. Torrence objected to Berry's conservative "Universal Coward" and insistence on recording much of the album without him. *Folk 'n' Roll* crawled to 145 on the charts.

The next year got off to a similarly bad start. *Jan and Dean Meet Batman* did not chart, and despite its cleverness, it looked like just another effort to cash in on a craze, ABC's new tongue-in-cheek television show *Batman*.

After moving into a new home together off Mulholland Drive and (finally) talking seriously about marriage, Jill Gibson and Jan Berry called it quits.

On April 12, 1966, Jan was on his way to work when his Stingray rounded a corner and slammed into a parked truck on Whittier Drive. His injuries were severe. For two months, he lay in a coma at UCLA Medical Center. When he awoke in June, he discovered a disconnect between his thoughts and his ability to speak. He was paralyzed on his right side.

He refused to believe his career was over, and his partner and friend, Dean Torrence, promised to keep his seat warm. In the summer of 1966, Dean recorded *Save for a Rainy Day*, a concept album collecting songs about rain. He did all of the vocal parts and asked Ken Berry, one of Jan's younger brothers, to stand in at the cover photo session. A combination of a tinted, grainy shot and a semipsychedelic design made it look as if all was well with Jan and Dean.

It was not. Jan and Dean switched to Columbia Records, and the mighty label released one single, "Yellow Balloon," from the sessions. Columbia scheduled the album release but scuttled it at the last minute. Though Dean intended the album as a labor of love for his partner, Jan—still bedridden at UCLA Medical Center—was outraged. Dean pressed a few copies for friends (J&D Records he called the label), and that was the last heard of *Save for a Rainy Day* for thirty years.

It was going to be a long road back for Jan Berry.

Cass Elliot, always insecure about her appearance, flowered with stardom. Much like Gertrude Stein in 1920s Paris, Cass Elliot in 1960s L.A. had a knack for getting the right people together. She was a natural and gracious host and seemed to reach inside her friends to develop a profound understanding of them, all the while pondering which of her other friends this friend might want to meet. Assembling bouquets of chums was one of her greatest talents.

Michelle was back in the group. She and John achieved a rapprochement and decided to give martial fidelity another spin. They coexisted in their massive house in Bel-Air. Jill Gibson graciously backed out, took to caring for Jan Berry, and concentrated on her photography.

It didn't matter to Cass whether it was Jill or Michelle; she had always feared being onstage next to a slim, beautiful woman. She despaired of being the laughingstock. But a funny thing happened on her way to self-loathing: Cass became the breakout star of the Mamas and the Papas. Soon her house was the epicenter of the scene in Laurel Canyon, the somewhat seedy colony that with a little paint and baling wire was getting gussied up as the neighborhood of the stars.

When the English group the Hollies toured America, they fell in love with it. "We soaked up American culture like sponges," said guitarist Graham Nash. Visiting the West Coast for the first time changed Graham's life. "LA was uptempo, vivace: the Beach Boys, the Ventures, Jan and Dean, the Mamas and the Papas. Hollywood! Blondes! I was in love with it before I ever set foot there. Flying over the city, I was already sold. There were turquoise-blue pools spread across the landscape, the ocean licking across the western shore, sunshine as bright as klieg lights."

In Los Angeles, their L.A.-based label, Imperial Records, celebrated Graham and the other Hollies with a party. An eager teenager named Rodney Bingenheimer hung around the band all evening, asking what they wanted to do when the party was over. Other members of the group thought he might be hitting on them, but Nash finally asked the Bingenheimer kid what he had in mind. He said he wanted to take him to Western Recorders, where the Mamas and the Papas were recording their second album. Nash loved their records, especially the blend of voices on "California Dreamin'" and "Monday, Monday." But he eagerly went to the session because of lust. "I had seen the album cover and wanted to fuck Michelle," Nash said.

The group, with producer Lou Adler and engineer Bones Howe, was working on a new John Phillips song called "Dancing Bear." Still nursing his double-standard heart after Michelle's alliance with Denny, John immediately gave Nash, the good-looking Englishman, the stink eye. He figured every healthy man with a John Thomas wanted to sleep with Michelle. Graham picked up John's hostility immediately, and so he observed a perimeter with Michelle and fell in with Cass.

Elliot was a hopeless anglophile and between takes quizzed Nash relentlessly about the Beatles and her fantasy man, John Lennon. She was dying to meet him, and Nash had been friends with him for five years by then. When the session ended in the wee hours, Elliot told Nash she would swing by his hotel at noon the next day to pick him up.

When she arrived in her Porsche convertible the next afternoon, he asked where they were going. "Oh, it's a surprise," Cass said.

She whisked Graham off to Laurel Canyon and brought him into the living room of David Crosby. Nash knew of Crosby and admired him. "Crosby intimidated the hell out of me," he recalled. "He gave off this don't-fuck-with-me vibe and seemed unapproachable." David had no idea who Graham was. He was occupied with rolling joints, so he didn't stand up to greet his visitors. Graham already admired David's high, pretty voice from the Byrds' records. Now, he discovered David's other great talent.

"Without much effort and without much concentration," Nash recalled, Crosby was "rolling some of the finest joints I'd ever seen. They were almost packageable by Camel, those joints." They were also the first ones Nash had smoked.

A deep friendship eventually formed between the two men, thanks to Elliot. Nash soon left L.A. with the Hollies, but he would be back. Years later, he thought of everything he would have missed if he hadn't gone along with that kid. "That small decision that I made in going with Rodney Bingenheimer changed my life in a drastic way."

In the fall of 1966, all eyes were on Brian Wilson. He was attracting unprecedented attention. The great maestro Leonard Bernstein had since 1958 educated adolescents with his celebrated Young People's Concerts on CBS television. CBS producer David Oppenheim began assembling material for a show with a reverse approach: Bernstein planned to showcase rock 'n' roll musicians and learn from them.

Oppenheim's camera crew focused on Brian Wilson. Writer Jules Siegel specialized in rock artist profiles for the *Saturday Evening Post*. His piece on Bob Dylan appeared in the issue dated July 29, the day Dylan suffered the motorcycle accident that sidelined him for nearly two years. Siegel also joined the Brian Wilson entourage, observing every movement.

The Beach Boys hired publicist Derek Taylor, the English gentleman who helped build the Beatles' career. After surveying the scene at Wilson's home and in the studio, he began asking those hip and in the know what they thought of Brian. The consensus was *genius*. "I thought, 'If that is so, why doesn't anyone outside think so?'" Taylor said. "Then I started putting it around, making almost a campaign out of it. But I believed it. Brian Wilson is a genius. It was something that I felt could be established."

Brian was recording a new Beach Boys album, initially titled *Dumb Angel*, then changed to *Smile*. He called it his "teenage symphony to God."

Van Dyke Parks formed a close partnership with Brian Wilson. The rest of the group was on the road, playing the songs that filled the *Best of the Beach Boys* album, along with "Good Vibrations" and a couple of token tunes from *Pet Sounds*.

Meanwhile, Brian was at home with a flock following him around, calling him a genius. "I'm not a genius," he said in response to the hype. "I'm just a hard-working guy."

Things were odd at the Wilson home. There was always a congregation, strangers to Marilyn, often mere casual acquaintances to Brian. They chanted the *genius* mantra while smoking dope and dropping acid with Brian.

Oppenheim had just finished a documentary on Igor Stravinsky when he got the CBS assignment to follow Wilson. Oppenheim blended in with the entourage, got high with Wilson, and witnessed his subject's need for instant gratification. Oppenheim recalled the time in the middle of the night when Wilson insisted on getting a telescope.

"Brian, there's no place open at three in the morning to sell telescopes."

This came as a surprise to Brian and pissed him off. "Well, let's buy a telescope place, man, we'll have it open 24 hours a day."

"Brian, who's gonna want a telescope other than you at three o'clock in the morning?" "Somebody does, and if somebody does, they should have it."

The next night it was something else.

"Wouldn't it be great to play ping-pong? Let's get a ping-pong table."

"Brian, it's four in the morning."

"Get those Yellow Pages. Somebody must know—you must know somebody who knows how to get a ping-pong table."

Brian turned his dining room into a sandbox and put his grand piano there so he could wiggle his toes on the beach while he composed. The Bedouin tent went up in the living room. Meetings were held in the swimming pool. At dinner parties, he insisted that guests play their plates and silverware as musical instruments, then entertained them by playing unlabeled acetates he recognized from groove patterns. These were his *feels* for the teenage symphony to God.

Beyond the at-home weirdness, the music he recorded at the studio was unlike anything he'd done before, unlike anything most anyone had done before. He did fifteen or twenty takes of a song, different instruments each time, then married the disparate sounds in a master. The musicians were stunned by his prescience. *He heard all that in his head?* The assembly was fascinating to most but frightening to the other Beach Boys. The band had acceptably reproduced "Good Vibrations" onstage without cellos (and Mike learned how to play theremin). But the stuff Brian was doing for *Smile*—that was just too weird.

Jules Siegel described the sessions for Brian's fire music, an intense piece he called "Mrs. O'Leary's Cow":

> "All right, let's go," said Brian. Then, using a variety of techniques ranging from vocal demonstration to actually playing the instruments, he taught each musician his part. A gigantic fire howled out of the massive studio speakers in a pounding crash of pictorial music that summoned up visions of roaring, windstorm flames, falling timbers, mournful sirens, and sweating firemen, building into a peak and crackling off into fading embers as a single drum turned into a collapsing wall and the fire-engine cellos dissolved and disappeared. . . .
>
> For the next three hours, Brian Wilson recorded and re-recorded, take after take, changing the sound balance, adding echo, experimenting with a sound effects track of a real fire.
>
> "Let me hear that again." "Drums, I think you're a little slow in that last part. Let's get right on it."

"That was really good. Now, one more time, the whole thing." "All right, let me hear the cellos alone." "Great. Really great. Now let's do it!"

With 23 takes on tape and the entire operation responding to his touch like the black knobs on the control board, sweat glistening down his long, reddish hair onto his freckled face, the control room a litter of dead cigarette butts, Chicken Delight boxes, crumpled napkins, Coke bottles and all the accumulated trash of the physical end of the creative process, Brian stood at the board as the four speakers blasted the music into the room.

For the 24th time, the drum crashed and the sound effects crackle faded and stopped.

"Thank you," said Brian into the control room mic. "Let me hear that back." Feet shifting, his body still, eyes closed, head moving seal-like to his music, he stood under the speakers and listened. "Let me hear that one more time." Again the fire roared. "Everybody come out and listen to this," Brian said to the musicians. They came into the room and listened to what they had made.

"What do you think?" Brian asked.

"It's incredible, incredible," whispered one of the musicians, a man in his fifties wearing a Hawaiian shirt and iridescent trousers and pointed black Italian shoes. "Absolutely incredible."

"Yeah," said Brian on the way home, an acetate trial copy or "dub" of the tape in his hands, the red plastic fire helmet still on his head. "Yeah, I'm going to call this 'Mrs. O'Leary's Fire' [sic] and I think it might just scare a whole lot of people."

As strange as the music was, the lyrics matched the melodies in joy and experimentation. When Mike Love heard "dove-nested towers," "blind-class aristocracy," and "columnated ruins domino," he was incensed. *He* should be writing the lyrics, not that effete little dilettante bastard Van Dyke Parks.

"'Surf's Up' was the first song that Brian and I wrote," Parks said. "I was in a position of defending my lyrics. They went from 'ding woodie pearl, hang ten'—I mean, I didn't know that language—to 'columnated ruins domino.'"

Mike Love was bewildered. "Who the fuck knows what you're talking about?" he asked Parks.

Van Dyke, the word sprite, ran into a brick wall when Mike heard some of the lyrics he was supposed to sing. "Mike Love made my life hell because he was jealous," Parks said. "Sibling rivalry. Highly adolescent. But I don't want to talk about Mike Love anymore than I want to talk about your urologist. Because it's not fun."

Years later, Parks still seethed with frustration: "Mike Love said to me one day, 'Explain to me what this means—"over and over, the crow cries uncover the cornfield."' It was an American Gothic trip that Brian and I were working on. I said, 'I don't know what these lyrics are about. They're unimportant. Throw them away.' And so they did."

Van Dyke left in late spring 1967, entrusting his lyrics to Brian with an order to take them or leave them. "It just got too much for me. It was an expensive decision for me not to continue my association with the most powerful artist in the music business at the time, but I made the only decision I could. I walked away from that funhouse."

The *Smile* sessions stretched from fall 1966 through summer 1967. Brian had bits and pieces, his *feels*, and kept tinkering with them, adding flourishes. Each day brought new and more insane ideas. *Let's make it a comedy album! Let's make it a health food album!* Mike tried to bring Brian back to earth: *What does that even* mean?

Capitol announced a Christmas 1966 release, and that deadline passed. "Good Vibrations" was not going to be on the album, and then it was. Capitol had a list of tracks but no tracks. The company designed a record jacket (Frank Holmes painted a shop selling smiles) and listed song titles on the back cover, with a note to "see label for sequence." Translation: *We don't know what the fuck Brian Wilson is doing.*

The gatefold illustration was Brian—enigmatic and inscrutable, sitting behind his piano: the genius, looking like one. The Beach Boys (now with Bruce Johnston) were pictured separately, in checkerboard-shirt glory, on the back cover, looking like the good *old* Beach Boys.

Him . . . *and them.*

"We're his fucking messengers," Dennis Wilson said.

Yes, Dennis, but what was the message?

By the summer of 1967, it wouldn't matter anymore.

13

CAPTIVE ON A CAROUSEL

I like to think of my behavior in the sixties as a learning experience. Then again, I like to think of anything stupid I've done as a learning experience. It makes me feel less stupid.

—P. J. O'Rourke

In Jim McGuinn's view, David Crosby had always been an arrogant prick. As they say, you are born an asshole, you die an asshole.

The Byrds were born from dysfunction, built on a shaky foundation of mediocre musicianship, resentments, and jealousy over songwriting royalties. Gene Clark left the band in 1966, in part because he was a white-knuckle airline passenger, in part because his prolific songwriting elevated his income and stature over the rest of his bandmates.

McGuinn had the signature sound, the twelve-string Rickenbacker, and the voice—the reedy one generally heard on the hits. But Crosby battled for a greater role and challenged McGuinn's leadership. Chris Hillman, the great mandolin player converted to bass player, was past his discomfort with the new instrument and by the summer of 1966 was a virtuoso, playing bass the way John Coltrane played his sax—with revel and abandon. He was ready to step up now that Clark was gone, and began writing songs for the next album.

The Byrds were a talented band, but their greatest talent was squabbling. Luckily, the Columbia producer hired to squeeze the next album out of the band was experienced with bickering over music.

Brian Wilson's old collaborator Gary Usher was prolific during the surf and hot rod years. In addition to writing for the Beach Boys, he produced and performed on records credited to bands that did not exist outside the studio: the Tri-Five (including Carl and Dennis Wilson), the Four Speeds, the Sunsets, the Competitors, the Roadsters, the Super Stocks, the Roadrunners, and Mr. Gasser and the Weirdos.

"The height of the hot-rod fad climaxed during a one-month period when Roger [Christian] and I actually wrote, and I recorded, over 50 car songs," Usher said. "By that time, I had purchased a new 426 Plymouth Hemi Superstock. It's interesting that I never did own a 409 Chevy; by the time I had 'saved my dimes' the 426 was considerably faster. I should add that I won many events at the San Fernando drag strip with my 426 and a young, exuberant Dennis Wilson by my side."

Usher's greatest success came with a group he managed and produced called the Hondells, which scored with a hit version of the Wilson and Love composition "Little Honda." Usher's version made it to number nine on the charts, while the Beach Boys' version languished.

All of that car-crazy stuff was old news by 1966, but Usher had proven successful enough to get a staff producer's job with Columbia and get assigned to the Byrds. As far as the group was concerned, Usher was a huge step up from Terry Melcher and Allen Stanton. Stanton was an executive, but Usher was a hyphenate—writer-musician-singer-producer. He spoke music.

Usher and the four Byrds gathered in the studio in late October to see what they had for the next album. Hillman's songs, his first, were particularly impressive: "Have You Seen Her Face," "Time Between," "Thoughts and Words," and "The Girl with No Name," which showcased his country influence.

With help on the bridge from McGuinn, Hillman also wrote a music business satire called "So You Want to Be a Rock 'n' Roll Star" that Usher lavished with sound effects (screaming girls) and skidding runs from South African trumpeter Hugh Masekela. The world-weary song was believed to be autographical. "That song was just a slight jab at the Monkees," Hillman said. "Not at the people but at the process of taking a contrived thing and making it a watered-down version of *A Hard Day's Night* on a weekly sitcom."

McGuinn added a science fiction song ("C.T.A.-102"), complete with alien voices, and composed a couple tunes with Crosby. The band went to the Dylan well again and recorded "My Back Pages," perhaps the most beautiful recording the Byrds ever made.

Crosby stepped up with two solo compositions. The first, "Everybody's Been Burned," was an exquisite jazz-influenced song that showcased Hillman's newfound mastery of the bass. To call Crosby's second solo contribution a piece of shit was an insult to pieces of shit. "Mind Gardens" was atonal gibberish that his fellow Byrds begged him to leave off the album. Crosby refused, and the song became a carbuncle on an otherwise beautiful record titled *Younger than Yesterday*. "Mind Gardens" was strike one for David Crosby.

Bobby Fuller was a big fish in the small musical pond of El Paso when he heard the *Go west, young man* siren call that drew so many rock 'n' roll hopefuls to Los Angeles in the sixties.

Fuller's family followed his father's jobs around the New Mexico and Texas gas fields, and by the time Bobby was a teenager, the Fullers lived in the westernmost city in the Lone Star State, separated only by the Rio Grande from Mexico.

The boy was musical from birth and played drums and trumpet in the school band, while little brother Randy played trombone. They were close, didn't constantly fight like a lot of brothers, and in love with music. They started a rock 'n' roll band in high school. Bobby decided he was the front man and told Randy if he wanted to be in the band, he had to play bass.

It didn't take Bobby long to become proficient. "Once Bobby got a guitar," his drummer Dalton Powell said, "it only took him a year to get good—I mean really good."

Bobby was formidable onstage. "He had incredible presence," said local disc jockey Steve Crosno. "Once he came on, you couldn't take your eyes off him." The women in particular liked the classic handsomeness of the Fuller brothers. As the singer, Bobby got the most attention. "Bobby was a real show off," said his bandmate Rod Crosby. "He was pretty egocentric and sometimes went overboard with it. But you sometimes have to be that way to be a successful entertainer."

By nineteen, Bobby Fuller was releasing singles on a small Alamogordo, New Mexico, label called Yucca, and his modest success led him to cut out the middleman and create his own label to release his product. He turned the family home into a recording studio and built an echo chamber in his backyard. He recorded songs by his idols Eddie Cochran ("Nervous Breakdown") and Buddy Holly ("Not Fade Away").

The group was the shit in El Paso, drawing six thousand fans to a shopping center parking lot in the searing sun. It was the surf music era, so Bobby and Randy took a pleasure trip to Southern California to check out surf bands up close, taking in a Dick Dale show at the Rendezvous Ballroom. Bobby's band had a twangy sort-of surf sound, and after the California sojourn, Bobby decided to accentuate that element in his playing.

He made assloads of money—relative to rock 'n' rollers in El Paso—so on his return, he opened a club called Bobby Fuller's Teen Rendezvous, which officially served nothing stronger than Coke, though mucho Lone Star was smuggled in. When Bobby and his band weren't playing, he booked local acts or touring rockers. The biggest outsider he got was Bobby Vee, who packed the joint on June 27, 1964.

Bobby and Randy Fuller also founded two record labels to distribute their work and that of other artists. By the time he hit 21, Bobby was a music impresario.

"It was a sight to behold," Randy Fuller recalled, "playing surf music at our teen club." There were elements of Dick Dale guitar in their music, but geography was responsible for much of the band's style. "It's a border sound," Bobby said. "We take sounds from Mexico with maracas. One time we used a bottle. And little finger cymbals." His idol was Buddy Holly, from Lubbock, up in the Panhandle. Since Holly's death in the February 3, 1959, plane crash, many artists tried to fill Holly's Thom McAns: Buddy Knox, Tommy Roe, and Jimmy Gilmer—but Fuller had the voice, the guitar, and the sound *down*. He could've passed as Buddy Holly's kid brother. Bobby made a pilgrimage to Lubbock, and then to Clovis, New Mexico, to record at the studio where Holly worked with producer Norman Petty.

Bobby Fuller billed himself as the rock 'n' roll king of the Southwest, but as he kept playing around Texas and New Mexico, the title lost luster. After the Beatles hit, a lot of American rock 'n' roll seemed passé. But Bobby Fuller's channeling of Buddy Holly seemed somehow contemporary. The Beatles were Holly fans, after all. Their name was inspired by Holly's backing band, the Crickets, changing *beetles* to *Beatles* to accentuate the beat of their music. Fuller recognized the revolutionary effect of the Beatles when he first heard them on the radio, though when he heard them do Holly's "Words of Love," he scoffed, saying the British band would "never be able to do Buddy Holly like Buddy Holly because they're not from Texas."

Eventually the Teen Rendezvous closed. "The club became too popular," said Bobby's high school friend Ty Grimes. "Things got out of hand. Too much fighting, too much beer, too much fun. Everyone was sorry to see it shut down."

The *El Paso Herald-Post* boosted its hometown son—ENGLAND HAS BEATLES BUT EL PASO HAS BOBBY cheered a headline—but Bobby wanted to be part of the larger music world, and so he and the band, now called the Bobby Fuller Four, moved to Los Angeles in November 1964. Bobby researched and tracked down Bob Keane, owner of Del-Fi Records. Since Keane had released a lot of surf music, Fuller figured he would like the big twang of his Texas guitar.

He was right. Keane's open-door audition policy paid off, and he snapped up the group and created the Mustang label just for Bobby's product. He also helped the transplanted Texans find their way around Los Angeles, securing club residences that included the fairly high-profile P. J.'s, on Santa Monica Boulevard. The club was known for smooth jazz, showcasing exquisite guitar played by Wrecking Crew veteran Barney Kessel. In 1965, P. J.'s opened its back room to rock 'n' roll hordes and bands such as the Standells ("Dirty Water") and the Bobby Fuller Four. They also were the opening attraction at the soon-to-be-cool club called It's Boss.

Keane had unconventional ways to break talent. Exhibit A: he created a band tie-in with radio station KRLA. The first Bobby Fuller Four album in 1965 had radio call letters in the title. Despite its dumb-ass name, *KRLA King of the Wheels* was a good introduction to the band. Side two was laden with now old-fashioned car songs, but side one showcased Fuller's Hollyesque rock 'n' roll. Defiantly out of step, the retro band quickly became hot locally. "Let Her Dance," his first big hit, was perfect for clubs.

Bobby took a deep dive into L.A. He dated Nancy Sinatra and hung out with actors Ryan O'Neal and Sally Field. He was on all the key television shows: *Shindig!*, *Hullabaloo*, *Where the Action Is*, *American Bandstand*, and *Shebang*. On *The Dating Game*, bachelorettes twice rejected handsome Bobby, but he didn't seem to mind. The group even made a big-screen appearance with Boris Karloff in *The Ghost in the Invisible Bikini*, a *Citizen Kane* for the beach-blanket set.

Bobby was young, handsome, talented, and in the center of the rock 'n' roll world. Bob Keane managed the group, outfitting them in matching red suits. Keane had Fuller groomed by Jay Sebring, hairstylist to the stars. The flamboyant Sebring, a rock star of follicles, nurtured Brian Wilson's mop and supervised Frank Sinatra's sixty-plus toupees. Sebring gave Bobby a modernized Elvis upsweep style. In the wake of the Beatles, everyone combed forward, but Sebring took Bobby's thick hair *up*.

In late 1965, at Randy's suggestion, Bobby rerecorded a song he'd done a couple of years earlier. Bobby's new version of Sonny Curtis's "I Fought the Law" charged into the maelstrom of the British Invasion and a legion of folk rockers with throwback rock 'n' roll. The song made *Billboard*'s Top Ten.

Bobby Fuller was hot. He followed "I Fought the Law" with Holly's "Love's Made a Fool of You," which went Top Thirty. Though a prolific songwriter, Keane kept pushing Bobby to record songs by other writers, including "The Magic Touch" by Ted Daryll. Bobby planned to make over the R&B song in his West Texas style. But when Bobby was on tour, Keane overdubbed horns, and the result, in Bobby's opinion, was a shambles. Out on the road, Bobby stewed, often fighting with his brother. Keane upset other members of the band by pushing Bobby to go solo.

Fuller reached a wider audience—Mustang now had reliable nationwide distribution with Roulette Records—but the group was on its way to falling apart.

Bobby spent much of Sunday, July 17, 1966, at home relaxing and drinking beer with his buddies. The band was just in from the road, with a little down time before hitting the recording studio. Several Texas pals were visiting, along with Bobby's parents.

In the early hours of Monday, Bobby was still up drinking beer in his apartment when the phone rang. He spoke briefly, hung up, and then asked his mother if he could borrow her car. He took her keys and left quickly, still wearing slippers.

Bobby missed a meeting he'd set that morning at the Del-Fi studios. The next day, shortly after noon, Bobby was still not home. Worried, his mother began calling Bobby's friends to ask if anyone had seen him. Early in the afternoon, Loraine Fuller looked outside and saw her car was back, but Bobby still had not come home.

She went outside and opened the door of her blue Oldsmobile, and was overcome by the noxious stench of gasoline. Bobby's body was splayed over the front seat, his face shoved into the console. He'd been beaten, and his dead hand gripped a short length of hose leading to a gas can.

Loraine screamed. One of her first calls was to Randy, at the nearby art studio of a former high school classmate and transplanted El Paso friend, Boyd Elder. The phone rang, and when Elder answered, all he heard was "I've got to talk to Randy."

"Hello?" Randy asked.

"Bobby's dead," his mother said, and hung up without another word.

Randy and Boyd rushed to the apartment, hoping for a mistake, that Loraine had been wrong. She was not. A police officer on the scene threw the gasoline can in a Dumpster and removed the hose from Bobby's hand. Police allowed gawkers a good view of Fuller's mutilated body. His slippers were covered in dirt, indicating he'd been dragged somewhere and not killed in the car. His nearly detached right arm was draped across his back.

The coroner's report said Bobby "was found lying face down in front seat of car—a gas can, ⅓ full, cover open—windows were all rolled up & doors shut, not locked—keys not in ignition." When an ambulance arrived, attendants pulled Bobby's body out by his head.

"I was in a fog," Randy said. "I watched them take Bobby's body away."

It was ruled a suicide—comical in a macabre way. Judging from the body's condition, that would mean Bobby killed himself, then, while drenched in gasoline, drove back to the apartment. Rigor mortis indicated he'd been dead several hours before being found, but the car containing his corpse appeared at the apartment moments before his mother's discovery.

Suicide sounded like bullshit. "He was not self-destructive at all," said Boyd Elder. "He seldom even drank. He was polite and gentlemanly, and the girls loved him. He was on his way to stardom. Whatever happened, it wasn't suicide."

The ridiculous coroner's ruling saw "no evidence of foul play," but the family pressed further. An uncle went to the police department and was told to keep his mouth shut if he knew what was good for him.

In October, the coroner changed the ruling to accidental death by means of asphyxiation. The murder was never solved. The most likely theory states that Bobby Fuller was a victim of organized crime connections, an affiliation dating Mustang's distribution deal with

Roulette Records. One of the more lunatic theories advanced in the years since the singer's death was that Fuller had been murdered by the associates—or the "family"—of a criminal named Charles Manson. Impossible, of course, because the month before Fuller's mysterious death, Manson had been sentenced to Terminal Island for his second stretch in that particular prison and had not yet begun gathering the waifs who became his murderous family.

Roulette was an open secret in the music business. The mafia essentially ran the label, using it as a front to hide and launder money. Roulette was operated out of New York by Morris Levy, one of its four cofounders. The trade publication *Variety* called Levy the Octopus because he had a hand in nearly every part of the music business, from talent acquisition through sales and distribution. He was a man used to getting his way. Whatever Mo wanted, Mo got. If he wanted a songwriter's publishing royalties, he took them. If he got resistance, he strong-armed composers.

Tommy James was a journeyman in a midwestern bar band when he had a from-out-of-nowhere hit in 1966 with "Hanky Panky," a song recorded two years before. James was signed to Roulette and made a lot of money for himself—and much more for Morris Levy—as Tommy James and the Shondells. The hits included "I Think We're Alone Now," "Mony, Mony," "Crystal Blue Persuasion," and "Crimson and Clover," among many others. He sold over one hundred million records.

James had one of rock 'n' roll's great rags-to-riches stories. Just out of high school in 1963, he formed the Tornados and played bars straddling the Michigan-Indiana line, heady days for a teenage rock 'n' roller. "Motown and surf music were hot that year and we did them to death," he said. "[We played] practically everything by the Beach Boys. On a Friday night at Ronnie's Pavilion, we'd start at eight, and by midnight we usually had more than a thousand kids on a dance floor built to hold only a few hundred."

The onstage euphoria didn't last, though, and within a year, James was married, with a colicky baby and a job selling Preparation H at a South Bend dime store. He decided to give music one last chance and scored a regional hit with "Hanky Panky," a throwaway by Phil Spector collaborators Jeff Barry and Ellie Greenwich. It became a

1964 hit on Snap Records, earning steady and consistent regional airplay. Disc jockeys loved it, and, although it took two years and the words of many mouths, by 1966, Tommy James heard from suitors wanting national distribution rights: Atlantic, RCA, and Columbia. The industry heavyweights were fighting over Tommy James and his bar band hit.

Then suddenly they weren't. The label reps called, bowing out. As James wrote in a memoir, "One of them, Jerry Wexler from Atlantic Records, admitted that he had received a call from Morris Levy, the president of Roulette, who informed him, 'This is my fucking record! Leave it alone.' We had heard rumors about Morris Levy and Roulette—how the company was 'connected' and how Morris was known as the Godfather of the music business."

Stories about Levy went trans-Atlantic. In 1965, Graham Nash was in the Hollies, a British Invasion band, when he and his partners had dinner with Levy to discuss a music publishing deal. "We'd heard stories," Nash wrote, "how he put his name as writer on all the records Roulette released, how at one point he owned the phrase 'rock 'n' roll' and held the mortgage on Alan Freed's house. But we heard other things that scared the shit out of us. (He'd have cut off my dick and put it on a keychain had he discovered I was sleeping with his secretary, Karen.)"

James signed to Roulette and spent his million-selling years looking the other way, though he recalled Levy interrupting convivial office chats to confer with "associates" in the hallway about whose legs they'd just broken on Levy's instruction. Once, Morris introduced the singer to these "associates." Tommy wasn't sure what to say. "*Wonderful,* I thought as we all shook hands. *What am I supposed to say now? How did your beating go? Was this a business beating?*"

James kept his head down and didn't dispute Levy's controversial business practices. "In some ways, having a guy like Morris in control was a great safety net," he said. "It was wonderful because nobody messed with you. You didn't make much money, but nobody messed with you."

In the end, Tommy James was one of the lucky ones. Frankie Lymon ("Why Do Fools Fall in Love?") planned to sue Levy over copyright and was found dead. Jimmie Rodgers ("Honeycomb," "Kisses Sweeter than Wine") disputed Levy's accounting and was found on the side of the San Diego Freeway with a fractured skull. In his memoir, Tommy James said he'd heard that Levy orchestrated the beating. When Hank Ballard ("The Twist," "Sexy Ways") told Levy he wanted the copyrights on his songs returned, Levy said, "No, no, no—keep it up and you're going to go the route of the rest of these guys."

And Bobby Fuller was found in his mother's Oldsmobile, soaked in gasoline and severely beaten, dead at twenty-three.

Since she made the decision—or rather, since it had *been* made—Joni Mitchell worked like a woman possessed. As she turned twenty-one, she had made the most difficult choice of her life, putting her career first. Sometimes she said the idea to leave her child in foster care was hers. Other times she shifted the responsibility to husband Chuck Mitchell. He was thirty, nearly a decade older, and to him it was obvious what his young wife wanted. Music and writing and art—that was her life, not a child.

But Chuck Mitchell couldn't see the turbulence inside her. She was often an enigma to him. The happy young folk music couple played Moose Jaw and Saskatoon, splitting their sets, with Chuck—the obvious headliner—doing some solo songs, then Joni, then some duets. They traveled to Toronto, but America was the main attraction. Chuck was from Detroit, and Joni was eager to start a career across the border.

When they set up their folktastic hippie pad in Detroit, it became a regular stop for touring singers. Whenever one of them—Eric Andersen or Ramblin' Jack Elliott or Tom Rush—came to play the Chess Mate, they crashed on the Mitchell couch.

Chuck wasn't a writer, but Joni was. The price for free crash and food was listening to her small but growing repertoire of original songs. Rush began his recording career in 1962, so to Mitchell he was something of a grand master. A fine but not prolific songwriter, Rush was a conduit for young writers. Though he covered Buddy Holly's "Love's Made a Fool of You" as well as other rock 'n' roll standards ("Money Honey," "Too Much Monkey Business"), his heart was with folk. He'd grown up in New Hampshire and begun playing the coffee shops of Cambridge while attending Harvard. He was a human folk jukebox, with an uncanny ability to find songs before anyone else. He was one of the first to record songs by James Taylor, Jackson Browne, and Joni Mitchell.

Joni played Tom "Urge for Going" in the living room while he was staying over. Chuck was there, and if he'd listened carefully to the lyrics, he would have understood his young wife's inner torment. Tom loved the song, learned it, and said he planned to record it.

Back home in Cambridge, Tom got in touch with Joni and asked if she had more songs. She'd met Neil Young on the Canadian circuit, and he'd played his *farewell to childhood* song, "Sugar Mountain." It was simple, at turns comical and deeply sad. It gestated in Mitchell, and she began writing what she dismissively called an answer song. When Rush called, she decided to finish her song of lost innocence. She sent Rush a tape of several compositions but saved "The Circle Game" for last. Before she began playing, she offered Rush an aside: "It sucks and you're going to hate it. I don't know why I'm putting it on."

She sang, in that precise and ethereal voice, of a childhood gone too soon:

> And the seasons, they go 'round and 'round
> And the painted ponies go up and down
> We're captive on the carousel of time

Rush called back, sputtering praise, and said he wasn't just recording "The Circle Game"; he was making it the title song of his next album on Elektra. Rush included a third Joni Mitchell song on the album, "Tin Angel."

The Mitchell marriage was foundering, and their careers spiraled in opposite directions. Chuck was happy to be the folkie du jour onstage singing ancient ballads each night. Joni was increasingly filling her sets with the homegrown repertoire she'd assembled with the encouragement of her pad crashers. The decision to tour separately put the marriage on life support, and when Chuck confessed his insecurities to his wife, she responded angrily. He pulled her across his legs and spanked her. Fate was sealed.

In early 1967, she moved out of the Detroit apartment and headed for Greenwich Village. For his part, Chuck claimed she'd used him to get a green card, but they had fashioned separate careers and separate lives. In New York, she found herself picking through the remains of the early sixties folk music world and developed deep friendships with the artists she'd hosted in Detroit. Eric Andersen helped her find early gigs, and she expanded her circle to include Steve Katz, Roy Blumenfeld, and Al Kooper of the Blues Project.

Kooper was a rock 'n' roll Zelig. His talented hands were everywhere, from recording "Short Shorts" by the Royal Teens to writing "This Diamond Ring" for Gary Lewis and the Playboys to supplying the signature bleating organ sound for Bob Dylan's foray into rock 'n' roll with "Like a Rolling Stone." His term in the Blues Project was about to end, and he planned to soon unveil his new brass-infused rock band, Blood, Sweat and Tears. As she had with so many others, Mitchell played her songs for Kooper one night in July 1967.

"One song especially killed me, 'Michael from Mountains,'" Kooper wrote in a memoir. "I thought it would be great for Judy Collins."

It was 5:30 in the morning, but Kooper was so excited he called Collins and told her he had a new song for her album in progress. She was not happy. "I have to get up soon and drive all the way to the Newport Folk Festival," she said. "I wanted to get some sleep for a change." She told Kooper the song could wait.

Kooper had a *eureka* moment. "Judy," he said, "why don't you, room permitting, take this girl with you to the festival? She could play the song and others for you on the way up and make your trip that much more pleasant. Then, being that you're on the board of directors, you could see if maybe they could fit her into the schedule somewhere to play, huh?"

No response. Had she fallen back asleep?

"Judy?"

"Kooper, you bastard," she said. "Yeah, I'll do it."

Except she didn't. Mitchell packed a bag and sat around waiting for a call. Finally, she realized she'd been stood up. Collins called the next day, bulging with apology, to report that someone had sung one of Joni's songs at the festival. The performance sucked, but the song was brilliant. Collins told Mitchell she'd send a car. Getting Mitchell onstage was a bit of a battle because her reputation for talent and beauty preceded her and "Big Joan" Baez—mother of Joan and Mimi Farina—thought the Canadian newcomer would detract from her daughters. Judy Collins would not budge, and so Mitchell was added to the festival's closing day, Sunday, July 17, in a workshop session with another Canadian songwriter Collins had boosted, Leonard Cohen. Joni, filled with stage fright in front of the Newport crowd, asked Judy to stand by her side as she sang. "As her blond hair hung over the guitar as she sang, I wept once more, as I would when I heard many of her songs," Collins wrote. "She was a muse to me in many ways: her great beauty, the light in her eyes, the sadness I felt in her soul."

Wildflowers, released by Elektra that fall, featured the first three self-penned songs to appear on a Judy Collins album. It also included two Cohen songs ("Sisters of Mercy" and "Hey, That's No Way to Say Goodbye") and "Michael from Mountains" and "Both Sides, Now." The album was a Top Ten hit for Collins, and word soon spread about the preternaturally talented singer-songwriter Joni Mitchell.

From July to December 1966, Brian Wilson logged forty-three recording sessions at Gold Star, Western, and Columbia, all for *Smile*. Breaking from conventional rock 'n' roll wisdom, he taped a series of increasingly less commercial songs, decidedly out of step with popular music. He wrote a love song for vegetables, a tune about health called "I'm in Great Shape," and a ditty called "Teeter Totter Love" for photographer Jasper Dailey to sing. He and Hal Blaine recorded a mock argument to be used as comic filler on the album.

At one session, after the group smoked a particularly potent shipment of hashish, they lay on the studio floor and had microphones lowered to their mouths to record the fatigued-high celebration of "Wind Chimes." There was that song about fire, so there was a song about water, a chant called "I Love to Say Da Da." Another wordless, spiritual piece called "Our Prayer" praised the powers and principalities of air. *Small moments of life . . . praise of the immediate . . . a teenage symphony to God.*

"It was a crazy time," Mike Love recalled. "People fucked up out of their minds on stuff. You do a lot of pot, LSD, cocaine, you name it, paranoia runs rampant." This was why, Mike figured, Brian responded so dramatically to his criticism of the work. Capitol printed 466,000 copies of the *Smile* album jacket and the twelve-page booklet of artwork by Frank Holmes and photos of the group.

Wilson shifted gears and began concentrating on getting a single on the market, the hotly anticipated follow-up to "Good Vibrations." He announced that it was called "Heroes and Villains."

As winter gave way to spring in 1967, Brian's eccentric behavior went beyond cute and became troublesome for Capitol executives.

When he refused to come to the Tower for meetings, executives were instructed to meet him in his pool. He wanted a level, if liquid, playing field. "If you take a bunch of businessmen and put them in a swimming pool, with their heads bobbing out of the water, then they really get down to fundamentals because nobody can bullshit while they're in the water," Wilson reasoned.

It wasn't a matter of just mastering a single. "Heroes and Villains," like *Smile*, was a collection of ideas. There were so many possible permutations of the song—one of them operalike and a half hour long. The sessions on the single and the album continued through the spring. At this inopportune juncture, the Beach Boys sued Capitol for alleged unpaid royalties.

Seventy sessions and counting for *Smile*! "Do You Like Worms?" . . . "He Gives Speeches" . . . "Cabin Essence" . . .

That last one had lyrics that made Mike Love puke:

Over and over the crow cries, "Uncover the cornfield!"

But then Brian stopped recording. He scheduled session after session, kept musicians waiting, then often canceled after two hours of deliberation because "the vibrations" weren't right. Thousands of dollars spent without a note being recorded.

The world still watched Brian Wilson, the genius. He was atop L.A.'s musical pyramid and needed a new home befitting such a king, so he moved with Marilyn into a Bel-Air mansion once owned by Edgar Rice Burroughs, creator of Tarzan. He immediately outraged neighbors by painting the house purple. *Damn crazy rock 'n' roll star.*

On April 10, Wilson had a visitor during the seventy-seventh *Smile* recording session. Paul McCartney was on a Los Angeles turnaround, having nearly finished the latest Beatles album, due for release in June. Brian was doing a vocal session on his song "Vegetables," and he put McCartney to work crunching celery for a track to be played under the vocal.

At the Wilson home later, McCartney sat at the piano and played a new, heartbreaking tune about a girl running away from home. Marilyn cried, it was so beautiful. After dinner that night, the Wilsons and their guest grabbed a bottle of wine and walked over to the home of John and Michelle Phillips. They sang and drank until dawn, when McCartney boarded his private plane to London, where he put the final touches on the new Beatles album.

On April 25, CBS aired the Leonard Bernstein music program called *Inside Pop*. The centerpiece was Brian at the piano playing "Surf's Up," one of the songs with lyrics by Van Dyke Parks.

> *The glass was raised, the fired rose*
> *The fullness of the wine, the dim last toasting*
> *While at port adieu or die*

David Oppenheim, the CBS producer who assembled the special, introduced the song by warning the audience it was too complex to understand at first but demanded further listening.

The Los Angeles music world had been hearing the *Brian is a genius* drumbeat for a year. Now it was confirmed, thanks to CBS and Leonard Bernstein.

John Phillips and Lou Adler decided to put on a festival that brought together the great bands of Los Angeles and San Francisco. The motive, in part, was to co-opt the San Francisco bands. Groups in that city were exciting and revolutionary, operating outside the mainstream. They'd brought an evolution of music and lifestyle, and Phillips and Adler sought to package the San Francisco bands with the L.A. bands and run the festival, presenting it as L.A.'s music czars offering a warm howdy-do to the scruffy San Francisco bands. They even decided to hold it closer to San Francisco turf, in Monterey.

When Adler and Phillips formed a board of governors for their festival, they invited Brian Wilson to serve. Other L.A. representatives included Johnny Rivers, Terry Melcher, and Jim McGuinn. The board was heavy with British artists—Donovan, Mick Jagger, Paul McCartney, and Rolling Stones producer Andrew Loog Oldham. Despite Phillips's and Adler's pandering, neither Jagger nor McCartney got their bands to play. Bob Dylan was also approached but was still in seclusion after his July 1966 motorcycle accident. No San Francisco artists were on the board, though Phillips wrote a beautiful song called "San Francisco" that issued the dress code for the festival: "Be sure to wear some flowers in your hair." He recorded the song not with the Mamas and the Papas but with his old friend from the Journeymen, Scott McKenzie.

May 1967: More canceled Brian Wilson recording sessions. The vibes were all wrong. *Smile* sessions eighty-three, eighty-four, eighty-five . . . *Smile* scheduled and delayed and scheduled and delayed. The new single, "Heroes and Villains," still not ready for release.

And then on June 1, 1967, the Beatles released *Sgt. Pepper's Lonely Hearts Club Band* in England. It came out a day later in the States.

There had been nothing like it before. The Beatles presented an astonishing collection of songs, from operatic rock to music hall tunes to Indian sitar music to something with the weight and power of epic poetry. The effects were perfect and stunning, including a note that was pitched too high for human ears but made dogs prick up. Everything about the album, including its packaging, was without precedent. This was the bar set high.

Suddenly no one cared about *Smile* or Brian Wilson. The entourage left, and Brian was alone at his palace in Bel-Air with his sandbox, his Bedouin tent, and thousands of hours of recordings for an album that would never be released.

———

Lou Adler was present at the creation of the Los Angeles rock 'n' roll world, and John Phillips had quickly become his protégé. They were the Holmes and Watson of L.A. The success of the Mamas and the Papas made Adler and Phillips rich men. They staged the Monterey International Pop Festival June 16–18, 1967, in part, to announce their presence with authority. Yet the Brits, the San Francisco groups, and far-flung out-of-towners stole the show.

Brian Wilson could see it coming. "Brian was afraid that the hippies from San Francisco would think the Beach Boys were square and would boo them," John Phillips said. Brian thought when the Bay Area hipsters got a load of the boys in their candy stripes, it would be all over. The Beach Boys were scheduled to headline the last night of the festival, but Brian pulled the plug at the last minute. There was a convenient excuse: after receiving his induction notice for military service, Carl Wilson had filed for conscientious objector status. He was arrested for draft avoidance and missed a few shows earlier that summer. So the cancellation announcement was tagged to the furor over that, but Brian wasn't sure the hippies bought it.

The last-minute cancellation no doubt stunted the group's career, but Brian's greatest fear was appearing unhip. Still, their friends were on the bill—they'd headlined shows with the Byrds and Buffalo Springfield, and they were held in high esteem—but the San Francisco bands were another proposition entirely.

The Grateful Dead, Big Brother and the Holding Company (with lead singer Janis Joplin), Jefferson Airplane, Quicksilver Messenger Service, and several other Bay Area bands performed.

Booker T. and the MG's, perhaps the most skilled group of musicians to play rock 'n' roll in the sixties, came from Stax Records in Memphis, playing an instrumental set on Saturday night, then backing Otis Redding, the king of soul music, for a moving performance that introduced Redding to a wide (and white) audience.

The Animals and the Who were the primary British representatives. The Animals had been part of the 1964 post-Beatles invasion. The Who had also been around, but Monterey was the group's coming-out party. Pete Townshend spun guitar windmills, and drummer Keith Moon kicked over his kit and set off smoke bombs while singer Roger Daltrey lassoed his microphone over the first rows. The audience was astonished by the anarchistic performance, but even the Who could be topped.

Jimi Hendrix was from Seattle and had paid his dues on the chitlin circuit backing Wilson Pickett, Little Richard, and Curtis Knight, hiding in plain sight in his home country. But after moving to England in 1966, he was discovered by Chas Chandler, the bass player for the Animals, who wanted to get into management and producing. He signed Hendrix, who electrified British audiences. At Monterey, the energy of Hendrix's set and his Martian approach to guitar shocked the crowd, as did his antics at the end of his performance, when he set his instrument on fire.

The Mamas and the Papas had to close the show after Hendrix and were lame by comparison. Most of the Los Angeles groups would have gone home early if Monterey had been a battle of the bands. Buffalo Springfield and the Byrds were two bands in turmoil, and it showed onstage.

Neil Young was in an *off* cycle of his on-and-off relationship with Stephen Stills in the Springfield. Right before Monterey, Young announced he would not play, so Stills got David Crosby of the Byrds to sit in. This did not sit well with Jim McGuinn, who was already upset with his fellow Byrd. He didn't know Crosby would join the Springfield onstage until he saw him step into the spotlight next to Stills.

The night before Crosby defected to the Springfield, he performed a seven-song set with the Byrds, focusing mostly on newer material from *Younger than Yesterday*, which had been released four months before. Thankfully, "Mind Gardens" was not on the set list. Before doing the traditional "He Was a Friend of Mine," which McGuinn had rewritten as a remembrance of President Kennedy, Crosby—wearing a Cossack hat to cover his eroding hairline—addressed the crowd.

"They're shooting this for television," he said. "I'm sure they're going to edit this out. I want to say it anyway, even though they will edit it out. When President Kennedy was killed, he was not killed by one man. He was shot from a number of different directions, by different guns. The story has been suppressed, witnesses have been killed, and this is your country, ladies and gentlemen."

McGuinn was furious. *Not the time or place, Croz.* But they leaned in and sang into the same microphone, and the song rarely sounded better. Anger brought out harmony.

But Crosby wasn't through. When the song ended, he told the crowd: "As I say, they will censor it I'm sure. They can't afford to have things like that on the air. It'd blow their image."

Crosby also encouraged the crowd to give LSD a try, if they hadn't already, and handled most of the "host" duties for the band. McGuinn was not amused. Crosby was right about one thing: because of his rants (and a relatively lackluster performance), the Byrds were not featured in televised coverage of the festival or the marvelous D. A. Pennebaker documentary *Monterey Pop*.

Monterey was strike two for David Crosby.

Joni Mitchell was a solo act, fully emancipated from Chuck Mitchell, though not from his name. After her Newport appearance, she was the word-of-mouth new performer to hear on the folk club circuit. She made a haunting impression and several connections at the Monterey festival, one of which (with producer Joe Boyd) led to her first European performances, in London.

She also had decided her career was at the stage where it required a manager. Elliot Roberts was one step above a gofer at the agency run by Robert Chartoff and Irwin Winkler (the duo whose second act would be in film, as producers of *Rocky*, *Raging Bull*, and *The Right Stuff*). Roberts told her he would manage her and wouldn't take no for an answer. He even went on the road with her—at his expense—until she finally relented.

Roberts pledged his life to Mitchell. He counseled her to not accept the first recording contract offered but to instead wait until the stars were aligned. He shopped a tape of her original compositions around to New York record labels, but the A&R guys there saw her as a manufactured relic of an archaic era. *Who gives a shit about folk music anymore?*

Roberts got Joni steady bookings in more and more impressive venues. As winter 1967 loomed, he was ever thoughtful, booking her into the Gaslight South in Miami Beach and the Flick in Coral Gables.

The Byrds were back in the studio, struggling to complete their fifth album. The sessions were all-out war between Crosby and his bandmates.

The summer 1967 single from the group was "Lady Friend," a Crosby composition featuring vigorous vocal and brass harmonics. The group's voices had not been good enough for Crosby, however, so he had Gary Usher erase the other Byrds from the track and multitrack his voice. The result was a beautiful piece of music that inspired disinterest among consumers. It staggered to number eighty-two on *Billboard*'s chart. (The single's flip side for the British market was "Don't Make Waves," a McGuinn-Hillman composition for a film of the same title, starring Sharon Tate and Tony Curtis. At the end of the song, Crosby offered a sarcastic comment on-mic: "Another masterpiece." It was cut before release.)

From the start of the sessions for a new album that fall, Crosby was at Michael Clarke's throat. He'd never been satisfied with Clarke's drumming, considering him a belt notch above an amateur. Crosby argued over everything. He was most opposed to recording songs from outside composers. The Byrds chose to do "Goin' Back," a beautiful song of childhood recalled, from Brill Building veterans Gerry Goffin and Carole King. Feeling that inclusion of a Tin Pan Alley tune might keep one of his songs off the album, Crosby vowed he would boycott the track. He refused to sing on it. McGuinn recorded the song, among the Byrds' most beautiful performances.

It was 1967, and, as Jim McGuinn said, musicians "were all trying to out-weird each other." The Beatles set the standard with the studio whiz-bang effects of *Sgt. Pepper* and even groups that should have known better—the Rolling Stones being the primary example with *Their Satanic Majesties Request*—jumped into the spacey, flower power studio trickery. No one pulled it off as well as the Beatles.

But the album the Byrds were fighting over would be one of the finest of the 1967 weirdness competition. When not insulting each other, Crosby, McGuinn, and Hillman wrote terrific songs and sang exquisitely.

Then David brought in a new song to record called "Triad," an enthusiastic endorsement of group sex. The group recorded it, McGuinn and Hillman pulling a Crosby and not singing on the track. It just wasn't right for the band, Jim and Chris argued. But David was adamant.

The Notorious Byrd Brothers came from this tumult. A masterpiece of its era, the album's birthing was a long and arduous process, overseen by Gary Usher, who played the Brian Wilson/George Martin role as the in-booth collaborator with the musicians on the floor. Usher contributed a lot of the album's special effects and oversaw the wide range of material and instrumentation—everything from acoustic and steel guitars to Moog synthesizers.

Out of the group dysfunction came the antiwar "Draft Morning" (complete with battlefield sound effects); "Dolphins Smile," one of Crosby's jazziest and most lyrical songs; and a McGuinn science fiction epic called "Space Odyssey."

As the four Byrds worked on "Dolphins Smile" at Columbia on August 14, Crosby's frustration with Clarke's clumsy playing boiled over, though the fight started meekly enough. "Michael? Uh, can you," Crosby began, then backed up and started over. "Maybe I'm not right. . . . If you really wanted to, you could really do it."

"You mean the first time I ever play it?"

"Ah, sure man," Crosby said. "I've heard you do stuff first time really good." Clarke mumbled disgust, and Crosby offered some ideas how to play. "Instead of that fast, choppy stuff, see, it's supposed to be a long, smooth slow-floating thing, like a boat." Clarke mumbled more discontent, but Crosby cheered him on: "Come on, let's try it."

After a couple bars, the next take broke down and Usher spoke over the talkback, encouraging Clarke to glide over his drums instead of doing a choppy style. "Come on, fellas," Usher said.

David continued to push Michael, miming the drum sound he wanted: *chicka chicka boom boom chicka chicka boom boom . . .*

Michael, grumbly and sullen, sat behind the drum kit. This was not the first time David had told him how to play his instrument.

"Try something gentle," Crosby implored. "Try something *pretty*. That's what it's supposed to be. It's not beyond you, Michael. You don't like anything, man, until you get it down right, and then you like it a lot."

Usher chimed in again, trying to encourage the pissed-off drummer. "Let's try it a few times, we got plenty of time," he said.

Crosby still insisted that Clarke didn't *have it*, and then the argument turned into a shouting match.

"Try playing right!" Crosby finally yelled at Clarke.

No longer mumbling, Clarke exploded. "What do you mean, 'Try playing right'? What do you know what the fuck's right or what's wrong? You're not a musician."

"I know you're just fucking up when you're playing," Crosby said. "Dig it."

McGuinn tried to intervene, but it was too late. Crosby would not back down. "You're just fucking up," Crosby yelled at Clarke. "You're doing your number."

Despite the tension, the group attempted a couple more takes, which soon dissolved into chaos.

David threw up his hands. "Can't you play the drums? Shall I learn you how to play?"

"If you don't like me," Michael shot back, "send me away."

"We love you man," Crosby said, sincere as a used-car salesman. "We want you to play the drums right!"

"Send me away. I don't even like the song."

"What are you in the group for?" Crosby asked. "The money?"

Clarke stormed from the studio. It was time to call the Wrecking Crew, and drummer Jim Gordon played on the rest of the album.

Halfway through recording the album, McGuinn and Hillman realized they could not continue working under such stress. In mid-September, they got in their Porsches and went to see David Crosby.

Crosby was sitting in his living room when he heard McGuinn's and Hillman's Porsches roaring into his driveway.

They ran through their arguments: *Not working. Too many disagreements. You're difficult. Your songs don't fit. You're impossible to work with . . .*

"They tossed me out," Crosby wrote in his autobiography. He recalled the last thing they said: "We think we'll do better without you."

The Notorious Byrds Brothers was David Crosby's third strike. "Triad" did not make the album.

———————

David Crosby's buyout from the Byrds netted him about $10,000 cash. He decided to use that and another twenty grand borrowed from his rich pal Peter Tork, of the Monkees, to finally buy the boat of his dreams, a schooner named the *Mayan*. David had long wanted to sail around the world, and now—footloose, fancy-free, and fired—seemed like the best time. His father had done it during the years he was blacklisted by the big studios. David understood now that need to escape.

He first sailed through the Caribbean with his pals Stephen Stills and Paul Kantner of Jefferson Airplane. When the cruise was over, Stills and Kantner returned to their day jobs and David Crosby hung around South Florida. A young singer he was eyeing as a fuck buddy suggested he listen to the other performer on the Gaslight South bill—Joni Mitchell.

He was dismissive at first, but the more he listened, the more he fell in love, both with the songs and the woman. "I thought I'd been hit by a hand grenade," Crosby said. "Her voice, those words . . . she nailed me to the back wall with two-inch spikes."

Joni Mitchell's first thought when she laid eyes on David Crosby was of cartoon character Yosemite Sam. Out of the Byrds, he'd let his hair grow to his shoulders, and his mustache mutated into something huge and droopy. He still carried a layer of baby fat, and even though he had been in the Byrds (his story was that *he* had left the group), Mitchell was not impressed by his looks or his celebrity. But Crosby was nothing if not persistent, and within a week, she had moved on board the *Mayan*.

David was a puppy dog around Joni. The assholery from his days with the Byrds receded as he licked his ego's wounds, and he walked around Miami Beach declaring his love for Joni wherever he went. His career was over, he told a friend. The debut issue of *Rolling Stone* hit newsstands that October with the news of his firing. He was at a low point. But now he had a new mission: produce Joni Mitchell and make her a star.

"David was wonderful company and a great appreciator," Mitchell said. "When it comes to expressing infectious enthusiasm, he is probably the most capable person I know."

He made some calls that opened doors in Los Angeles for Elliot Roberts, and the young manager took Joni's tapes to Warner Bros., where she was given a contract with Sinatra's label, Reprise. David was signed to produce.

So much for sailing around the world. At the end of 1967, Crosby set aside his mariner dreams and headed back to Los Angeles with Mitchell, his ticket back into the big-time music business.

———————

The Notorious Byrd Brothers was released on January 15, 1968. With David Crosby gone, Michael Clarke came back and Gene Clark rejoined for three weeks of recording, but then quit again.

There were only three Byrds when court photographer Guy Webster got the album cover assignment. He took the trio to Topanga Canyon, where he photographed them on horseback. Then he found an abandoned stable and decided he wanted a shot of the group looking out the barn's four windows. One of the horses was eating nearby, so Webster posed the nag in the fourth window, looking out. That was the image Columbia chose for the cover.

"It wasn't to replace Crosby," Webster insisted. "It wasn't to insult anyone. It was just to balance the composition."

Crosby was incensed when he saw the cover. He howled about it, but Webster and the other Byrds pleaded innocence. *No offense intended. It was an accident, Croz, really.*

"An accident? An accident!" Crosby fumed. "Do you believe that? It's bullshit. You *know* it is. *You* know why *he* did it."

The *he*, of course, was Jim McGuinn, who said there was no attempt to use the horse to represent Crosby. "If we had intended to do that, we would have turned the horse around," McGuinn said.

14

PEACE, LOVE, AND FLOWERS

> The world would have been a very different place
> without the ideals that generation stood for. Slogans
> like "peace and love" may be clichés now, but back
> then we meant it. With all our hearts.
>
> —Jo Nesbo

The word *hippie* derived from San Francisco beatnik culture in the fifties. Those finger-snapping, beret-clad nonconformists were alternately known as hipsters, from whence came *hippies* a decade later, used to describe the next step in the evolution of coolness. Though the lifestyle celebrated nonconformity, hippies did have a uniform of sorts: lots of hair, sandals, torn jeans, tie-dyed shirts, maybe some face painting if the occasion warranted, an "occasion" being Tuesday.

And flowers. As John Phillips wrote in his theme song for the Monterey International Pop Festival:

> *If you're going to San Francisco*
> *Be sure to wear some flowers in your hair*

Phillips promised there were "some gentle people" there. The music culture of San Francisco helped begat the new counterculture, and soon Los Angeles musicians cloaked themselves in raiment of peace, love, and flowers.

The hair, the flowers, the fermenting *mellowness* of it all—these were required for entrée to the counterculture. Many of those barefoot hippies walking around town were from affluent backgrounds. Their parents found and exploited the American Dream, and now their grubby-by-choice kids rejected it. The kids had affluence but shrugged it off. Others wanted affluence but couldn't attain it. The unacknowledged American class system imploded along the hippie divide.

Being barefoot in frayed and disintegrating jeans and threadbare T-shirts—this wasn't a fashion choice for many of the hirsute multitudes strolling San Francisco's Haight-Ashbury district. This was all they had. "A *hippie* was sort of the unwashed, unkempt kid," groupie Pamela Des Barres wrote. "A *freak* was someone who put a lot of care and intention into their appearance."

San Francisco was the new magnet for teenagers. Gray Line added hippie neighborhoods to its San Francisco bus tours, and the folks from Ohio and Iowa looked out to see the world of the freaks. San Francisco's new world order became fodder for Johnny Carson's monologues and the punch lines of stand-up comics. The pop world regarded the hippie world with fascination and occasional revulsion. Figuring there was money in them-there hippies, the pop world sought to embrace and co-opt the milieu. In summer 1967, the Cowsills, a clean-cut mom and her kids (models for television's soon-to-be Partridge family), released a song steeped in the watered-down world of free love. "The Rain, the Park and Other Things" was written by Artie Kornfeld, former car song collaborator of Jan Berry and Brian Wilson, and seemed to hit all the high points of the time. The infectious chorus of "I love the flower girl" brought a diluted G-rated sense of San Francisco into the homes of teenagers across the country.

No doubt: San Francisco was the hippie Mecca.

Uncharacteristically, L.A. eyes looked north, taking cues from the chilly city on the bay. New rock 'n' roll Bel-Air millionaires began going barefoot in artfully shredded jeans and designer T-shirts, getting Jay Sebring to style their hair in the new shaggy, carefully unkempt look.

It was hard to tell friend from foe when all wore garments of love. In was into this world of peace and flowers—specifically into Haight-Ashbury—that a career convict named Charles Manson strode.

Manson had spent most of his teen and adult years in one prison or another. When paroled from California's Terminal Island on March 21, 1967, at age thirty-two, it was against his will. Uncertain he could navigate the outside world, Manson asked to stay behind bars. Prison was comfortable, the only life he'd ever known.

Manson's mother was a sixteen-year-old alcoholic and prostitute uninterested in her son, unsure of his parentage. The boy's life was as unstable as a house of cards, and his mother—with *thief* also on her résumé—sent him to reform school. He ran away, developed a specialty in grand theft auto, and was regularly sent to the slammer throughout adolescence and early adulthood.

Manson married during a short prison sabbatical but was ill prepared for life or love. After spawning a son, he was divorced while in the pokey. He betrayed no geographic loyalty, and though a product of the Great American Midwest, he relocated to the West Coast to advance his criminal career. Charming and quick-witted, he was somewhat inept as a crook, always getting caught.

In prison, he read voraciously about religion and also raped a fellow prisoner at knifepoint, which enhanced his rep in the big house as a dangerous man. Eventually he expediently adopted the traits of a so-called model prisoner and learned guitar under the guidance of celebrity inmate Alvin "Creepy" Karpis, the only FBI-proclaimed public enemy number one ever taken alive. The Depression-era con was pushing sixty when he met Manson and was happy to tutor the young man.

Manson also met Phil Kaufman in the joint. "Charlie was in the yard singing," Kaufman said. "He was rather like a young Frankie Laine—he had that kind of loop in his voice. I thought his voice was good and I thought he would fit in." On the outside, Kaufman worked as a road manager ("road mangler" he called it) in the music business, and he vowed to help Manson when he got out of the pen.

Release was terrifying. "I don't want to leave," Manson told the guard supervising discharge. "I don't have a home out there. Why don't you just take me back inside?"

The guard laughed. "I'm serious, man," Manson said. "I don't want to leave." The guard laughed again, ignoring the request.

The world he reentered shocked Manson. When he was locked up in 1960, men wore neckties and hats and women dressed in June Cleaver dresses. In 1967, he saw a hairier world, people wearing the kind of stuff he wore, and it wasn't hard to get laid. In the joint, he'd heard that there was a world of peace, love, and flowers in San Francisco, and his L.A. parole officer granted him permission to move there.

"My guitar, my voice, my songwriting, and my homeless state put me right at home," Manson recalled. "I was just one of thousands who called wherever they were at the moment home. My hair grew a little longer. I lugged the guitar every place I went."

He quickly began making enough money to get by singing on street corners, but getting laid took a little longer. His hair needed to grow, and he hadn't yet mastered the mellow hippie vibe. Charlie was a lot of things, but mellow was not on the list. That was learned behavior. Eventually the tightly wound ex-con learned to fake it and, with his killer smile, attracted some of the nubiles. "I was on the street many days before I got my nuts out of hock," he said.

During a torrential rainstorm, Manson took shelter in a front stoop alcove and was soon joined by a young girl carrying a guitar, soaked to the skin. He urged her to take off her clothes and curl up in his sleeping bag to get warm. He wrung out her clothes and hung them up in the alcove to dry. Then she invited him to share the sleeping bag. "The little broad was an acid freak and not all that pretty, but she completed my welcome to Haight-Ashbury. It wasn't love and I don't even remember her name."

It was the perfect con for a con man of Manson's abilities. Bruce Davis, who would become part of Manson's gang serving life in prison for murder, thought unleashing Manson on the gullible and innocent was opening the henhouse door to a wolf.

"Peace and love . . . the sixties . . . flower children . . . dah dah dah . . . that's the kind of thing that would give him an entrée into the most vulnerable market," Davis said. "If he could have thought he could control some other group, he would have got their nomenclature down. But this was the most vulnerable. It was morally deficient, it was young and inexperienced, a great vacuum of what to do and where to go—a very good opportunity. So he learns to say, 'Peace and love.' It was the right bait for the fish."

To infiltrate this vulnerable community, Manson had to be a good actor. "I'm not a child of the sixties," he scoffed. "I'm not a hippie."

Yet the hippie culture was awfully appealing to a career prisoner. Music writer Greg Shaw lived in the Haight-Ashbury neighborhood when Manson arrived. "When Manson came here, it was probably the kind of scene he would enjoy very much: a lot of available women, a lot of drug traffic, a lot of psychic energy. Everybody was using drugs every day and walking down the street stoned out of their heads or having bad trips, and it was an environment I think he might've enjoyed. It was kind of hellish, something like Hieronymus

Bosch might enjoyed painting if he were alive in those times. There were so many freaks and so many extremes, but the good people, the original people, had left. They were gone. So all you had here was these biker gangs, speed freaks, and these innocent young people who came looking for the promise of peace and love and got exploited by these kinds of characters."

Shaw spoke of "the good people, the original people," most of whom took great offense at having Manson lumped in with the hippies just because he looked the part. "Manson was not a hippie," said Paul Krassner, the counterculture lion who edited the *Realist* magazine. "He was the Frankenstein product of the American prison system who brought all those values of racism and violence out of the prison with him into society."

Manson's pal from the joint, Phil Kaufman, was amused when he discovered that Charlie was passing himself off as a hippie. "Charlie didn't like the hippies or the hippie movement," he said. "Charlie used the hippie movement for his own benefit. I don't think he had that real love that people were trying to put out."

As Manson's hair grew, he gulped down acid and worked on his hippie-dippy smile. The outside world wasn't so bad after all. Finally, he could blend in.

Even Carl Wilson, most fervent disciple of brother Brian, thought it time to pull him from the precipice. *Smile* was over. Gone. History. All right, so the Beatles *had* won. So what? No one would ever top *Sgt. Pepper*—that was a given, Carl figured. What the Beach Boys needed to do in the fall of 1967 was make some music that would allow Brian to cool out.

After the whole *Smile* mess, Brian was in serious need of cooling out. By midsummer, he'd been tinkering with the "Heroes and Villains" single for a half year, and it was nearly eight months overdue when Brian finally thought the vibes were right to release it.

In July, just before the Monterey festival, Brian's astrologer said the time had come. Brian called the other Beach Boys, solemnly announcing he was ready to release the record. *Mount your chargers!* The Beach Boys' Rolls-Royces formed a procession (the funeral analogy would come later) down to KHJ, the radio station judged hip enough to receive this *gift* from Brian Wilson.

He delicately carried the "Heroes and Villains" acetate as if it was the Holy Grail. Even the record company was unaware the new single was finished. The caravan arrived at the station, and after a little *ahem*ing (they had no appointment, after all), security guards let the cars through the gate. Brian and the others found their way to the studio, and suddenly the head Beach Boy was face to face with the on-air disc jockey.

"Hi, I'm Brian Wilson," he said. "Here's the new Beach Boys single. I'd like to give you and KHJ an exclusive on it."

"Can't play anything that's not on the playlist," the disc jockey said.

Terry Melcher was in the entourage and said Brian nearly fainted. "It was all over," Melcher said. "He'd been holding the record, waiting for the right time. He'd had astrologers figuring out the correct moment. It really killed him. Finally they played it, after a few calls to the program director or someone, who screamed, 'Put it on, you idiot.' But the damage to Brian had already been done."

After waiting so long for a follow-up to the number-one brilliance of "Good Vibrations," the new single was a qualified disappointment. Capitol undercut interest in the record by releasing another surf-turf compilation, *Best of the Beach Boys, Vol. 2*, the same day as the single. Unlike the first best-of, this album didn't crack the Top Forty.

"Heroes and Villains" only made it to *Billboard*'s number twelve. But there were new creatures in the land: rock critics. The first significant of these, Paul Williams, was rhapsodic. Williams (not to be confused with the songwriter with the same name) was founder and editor of *Crawdaddy*, the rock 'n' roll journal that predated *Rolling Stone* by a year. In a later testament to the greatest records in rock 'n' roll history, Williams hinted "Heroes and Villains" may have been ranked number one. Alas, he presented his hundred best in chronological order.

Williams understood the agony, frustration, and joy that Wilson spent on the three minutes and thirty-six seconds that ended up on vinyl. "We are most human, most mortal, when we are reaching for something," Williams wrote. "And though we will never obtain what we reach for, our vulnerability at these moments of hyperextension is a gateway through which the most wondrous possessions can and do arrive. In 'Heroes and Villains' . . . something comes to life that I have never heard on any other recording."

Yet . . . *failure*. Brian retreated to bed. After neighbors blew their high-end gaskets over the Wilsons' purple house, he and Marilyn repainted it a southwestern mellow-gold color, and then—as long as they were remodeling their new house—they turned the living room into a recording studio, mostly at the behest of the other Beach Boys.

Few artists had this extravagance, but Carl thought an in-house studio would lure Brian from bed to make music without the usual pressures. A couple houses down, John and Michelle Phillips put in a studio, doing it off book to get around Beverly Hills code enforcement officers.

The home studio was the new status symbol, but Brian wasn't sure it was the best thing for him in his fragile mental state. The home studio wasn't Western or Gold Star, but it was there.

Hal Blaine thought it was a terrible idea. "I think the main period of hit-making for the Beach Boys ended when they put that studio in his home," he said, "because the other guys were around 'making decisions' and getting in the way, whereas before Brian was in control. In a regular studio, it was a more professional environment."

To the cost-conscious Beach Boys, there were economic advantages. No more need to book (and cancel) sessions. The studio was always open. The group could come and go at will, keeping Brian on a short leash. Marilyn Wilson recalled this as the time when her husband began staying in bed for two- or three-day stretches, finding reasons not to come downstairs.

The first iteration of the studio was not soundproofed. Instruments and microphones were in the living room, and the control booth was down the hall, in what had been the home office, where the previous owner churned out his Tarzan novels. Walking down the hall was dangerous because of cables snaking between rooms.

Mike Love announced the group was scaling back on Brian's musical experiments from *Smile* to fashion a quieter record called *Smiley Smile*, sort of a son of *Smile*. Officially released on Brother Records, with its Frederic Remington end-of-the-trail Indian logo, Capitol still manufactured and distributed the album.

"Most of *Smiley Smile* was done at Brian's house," Carl said, "with his own equipment and in his studio which he had built in a couple of days. We did part of it in his gym, part in his back yard, and even in his swimming pool."

When *Smiley Smile* was released on September 18, the credit read, "Produced by THE BEACH BOYS." Despite the inclusion of "Good

Vibrations" and "Heroes and Villains," two masterful Brian Wilson productions, and even though Carl did most other in-booth work, the album was credited to the whole group. The album oozed a weary marijuana high, best exemplified by the drowsy, dopey, and beautiful "Wind Chimes," the silliness of "She's Goin' Bald," and the laughing sing-along of "Little Pad." Much was adapted from *Smile*'s fragments and musical ideas. Full of touching, splendid moments, it's still accurate to call the album "slight." It clocked in at less than a half hour.

Smiley Smile went Top Ten in England but coasted to number forty-one in the States. But the fact that the Beach Boys had finally released *something*—some *product*—was a great relief to Capitol Records. Mike Love wanted to make sure the group made up for its year in the recording wilderness by getting its meal ticket back to his old self.

Mike sought to buy time for Brian, so he suggested another live album. The group scheduled its annual summer spectacular in Honolulu (with support acts Bobbie Gentry; Paul Revere and the Raiders; and Dino, Desi and Billy), recording back-to-back shows for an album they planned to call *Lei'd in Hawaii*. The concerts were made special by Brian's presence onstage. The shows were deemed great successes.

But back in California, the group discovered the Hawaii recordings were subpar, almost entirely unreleasable. After making a few attempts to rerecord the songs in the studio to create a fake live album, the project was abandoned. Mike Love convened the group at Brian's home to record something else—quickly. The Beach Boys *had* to get back in the marketplace. Mike brought a raft of lyrics to marry to old melodies by Brian.

No Wrecking Crew. The self-contained band worked through new tracks in Brian's studio, with or without Brian. Sometimes he'd listen upstairs, music leaking through the floorboards. Not yet twenty-one, Carl took the lead on production.

Meanwhile, Brian was two-timing the Beach Boys. When they toured, he worked with a trio he'd dubbed Redwood, whom he wanted to sign to Brother Records. One of his dope-smoking pals, Danny Hutton, brought together fellow singers Cory Wells and Chuck Negron, and Brian enjoyed working absent the tension and baggage of the family band. At Wally Heider Studios, Brian cut tracks with Redwood for two new songs he'd written, "Time to Get Alone" and "Darlin'."

It didn't take long for the other Beach Boys to discover Brian's infidelity. One afternoon, Mike, Carl, and Al appeared uninvited at Wally Heider and confronted Brian during a Redwood session. "They maneuvered Brian into the control booth and reduced him to tears," Chuck Negron recalled in a memoir. "Danny, Cory, and I were in the studio and could see it all happening through the control-booth window." The conversation was intense, Brian listening as Mike ranted. When Brian tried to leave the booth, Mike blocked his exit.

Eventually Brian returned to the studio floor, crying. "His head was lowered and his shoulders sagged," Negron wrote. "It was the body language of a child who had just been scolded and punished."

Wilson told the singers, "We can't do this. I have to give the songs to them. They're family, and I have to take care of my family. They want the songs."

No matter who produced the group, Mike Love adamantly opposed signing Redwood to Brother Records. Within a year of the incident at Wally Heider, Redwood landed a deal with Lou Adler's old Dunhill label (now owned by ABC) and, as Three Dog Night, launched a career that included twenty-one Top Forty hits, three of them number ones, and sales of forty million albums.

Brian returned to help finish the new Beach Boys album, *Wild Honey*, released in December 1967, just two months after *Smiley Smile* and on Capitol, not Brother. It was another piss-poor chart performer, dismissed by *Rolling Stone* with the most damning criticism of that post–*Sgt. Pepper* era: it didn't *matter* . . . it was *inconsequential*. It came out during a great trans-Atlantic weirdness competition between British and American bands, and the Beach Boys record sounded simplistic and decidedly homemade.

Nearly alone among critics, Paul Williams praised it, writing in *Crawdaddy* that *Wild Honey* was "a lovely record full of exuberant singing" that was "new and fresh and raw and beautiful."

"I celebrate *Wild Honey* as a work of joy," he wrote, "and one more gift of music from probably the most creative musician alive."

By the close of 1967, the homemade style heard in *Wild Honey* was the new fashion. The same month of its release, Bob Dylan returned from hiding with his muted masterpiece *John Wesley Harding*, using only a guitar, bass, and drums (and steel guitar on two tracks).

(Dylan's old backing band, the Hawks, continued the trend. They woodshedded with Dylan during 1967 and recorded some of their debut album in their home in the Catskills. *Music from Big Pink* was eventually released in July 1968, becoming a defining and deeply influential album of the times. For their second album, the group rented an L.A. home from Sammy Davis Jr. and recorded in the pool house out back. The result was another classic back-to-basics album, *The Band*.)

As the 1967 weirdness competition wound down, there was a late entry from an unlikely source: Jan Berry.

After his automobile accident, Berry was in a coma and his prognosis was grim. But after two months, he awoke. He had suffered significant brain damage and was partly paralyzed. He had to learn to walk and talk again and endured extensive and exhausting physical therapy. Miraculously, he was back in a recording studio the year after his accident.

It took him longer to process his ideas, but he still felt melodies in his body. For six months, he labored on an adventurous work, which was nearly a solo project.

Dean Torrence had recorded *Save for a Rainy Day* solo during Berry's hospitalization but credited it to Jan and Dean. Jan planned to make his new album, *Carnival of Sound*, a Jan and Dean project. The duo signed a contract with the hippest label in town, Warner Bros., and released three singles, but *Carnival of Sound* was considered too dense and challenging to see release and was shelved by Warner for thirty years.

Not everyone was temperamentally suited to go back to basics. Word of mouth about the lyrics of *Smile* created buzz around young Van Dyke Parks, and Warner Bros. signed him as a solo artist in 1967. By the end of the year, he had prepared *Song Cycle*—innovative and dense with melody and lyrics that would have made James Joyce proud.

Parks's intelligent and beautiful album was historic in its noncommerciality. The heavily orchestrated pieces blended together, punctuated with plunking pianos and Parks's sly, conspiratorial voice. Label president Joe Smith did not writhe with enthusiasm when he first heard it. "If it's called *Song Cycle*," he said. "Where's the song?"

Others recognized Van Dyke's achievement. Parks recalled, "Warners would have killed the whole thing right there if Jac Holzman hadn't said to Mo Ostin, 'Look, if you don't wanna put this out, I do; how much do you want for it?'"

Song Cycle's producer was Parks's greatest champion. Lenny Waronker was a second-generation record man. His father, Simon, ran Liberty Records, which he rescued from bankruptcy by signing a novelty act called the Chipmunks. Simon also signed Eddie Cochran, Billy Ward and His Dominoes, and Jan and Dean to the label. Liberty was a player, but Waronker's health problems brought on an early retirement before son Lenny could work in the family business.

Instead, Lenny Waronker joined Warner Bros. Records, where he set to work transforming the label's corporate identity. Jack Warner started the label in 1958 to keep lucrative soundtracks from Warner Bros. Pictures in house. Among the first releases on the label was *Music for People with $3.98 (Plus Tax, If Any)* by Ira Ironstrings—who, it turned out, was swing band leader Alvino Rey in mufti because he was signed to another label.

Warner Bros. had a few novelty hits but then began to turn things around when the Everly Brothers signed in 1960. The Brothers Everly supplied the brothers Warner with "Cathy's Clown," its first million seller. The following year, the label lucked into Peter, Paul and Mary, the folk supergroup that made a mint for the label. Then Frank Sinatra tired of running his boutique label, Reprise, and merged with Warner (huge financial windfall for the Chairman). From Reprise, the company got its president, Mo Ostin. Warner brought in former Boston disc jockey Joe Smith. Together, Ostin, Smith, and then Waronker built Warner-Reprise as an artist-friendly label.

Parks the artist did not transform the label, but Parks the producer and executive did. With one of Waronker's boyhood friends, Randy Newman, another child of a showbiz family (his uncles Alfred and Lionel wrote film scores; Liberty's first release in 1954 was an instrumental by Uncle Lionel), Parks attracted to the label a number of bold and idiosyncratic artists who would certainly be cut adrift by RCA or Columbia. Columbia had signed guitar prodigy Ry Cooder, then seventeen, as part of a band called the Rising Sons, led by singer Taj Mahal. The album Terry Melcher produced for the band went unreleased, and when the group folded, Mahal stayed with Columbia, where he became a celebrated roots 'n' blues singer. Cooder joined Warner-Reprise, where Parks, Newman, and he collaborated on several albums.

Waronker enlisted both Parks and Newman for a new Warner act that came from its acquisition of San Francisco–based Autumn Records. The Tikis became Harpers Bizarre, and with the advice and counsel of the Parks-Newman brain trust, their version of Simon and Garfunkel's "The 59th Street Bridge Song (Feelin' Groovy)" was so successful it more than covered the Autumn purchase price.

Ever the company man, Parks helped revive the career of Warner-Reprise labelmate Frank Sinatra. The Chairman of the Board was so depressed over the rise of rock 'n' roll that, at age fifty, he pondered retirement. Impish Van Dyke Parks helped Sinatra climb from his self-pitying abyss. Parks suggested bringing Ol' Blue Eyes out of his emotional tailspin by having him record one of his brother's songs. "Somethin' Stupid," by C. Carson Parks, was released as a duet with daughter Nancy and became the elder Sinatra's first million-selling single.

Despite helping create an artist-friendly sanctuary, Parks was frustrated by the massive commercial failure of *Song Cycle*. Critics loved the record, and some even named it album of the year. But crowds did not line up asshole-to-bellybutton to buy the thing. This disconnect inspired one of Warner-Reprise's most notorious ads.

Advertising was a major factor in the label's image. Joe Smith credited advertising with not only raising the corporate profile but also attracting artists. The main man behind it all was Stan Cornyn, who supervised advertising and was the Charles Dickens of liner notes. Seizing on the Parks/poor sales dichotomy, he headlined an ad, How WE LOST $35,509.50 ON "THE ALBUM OF THE YEAR" (DAMMIT).

The ad infuriated Parks. "It was such a painful experience to be a joke at Warner Bros.," he said. "They didn't even lose money! Not a cent!"

Cornyn meant no harm with his ad copy or his promotional material. He articulated a smart-ass personality for Warners and worked hard to draw attention to Parks, Cooder, Newman, and other idiosyncratic artists, with two-record sets (for only two dollars!) that showcased nearly every artist on the roster. Cornyn won two Grammy Awards for his notes on Sinatra albums and was nominated three other times. His writing conveyed attitude, whether it was the Pigpen Lookalike Contest (Pigpen was the Grateful Dead's keyboardist), the Win-a-Date-with-a-Fug Contest (the Fugs being a group of gratuitously hairy poets), or the weekly promotional rag called *Circular*.

For new artist Joni Mitchell, Cornyn would concoct one of his most notorious ads—JONI MITCHELL IS 90 PERCENT VIRGIN.

Back in Los Angeles, David Crosby told Joni Mitchell to scrub off her makeup and confront the world with her resolute and natural face, beauty without need of enhancement. Crosby supervised Mitchell's coming out to L.A. music society. He took pride in his musical debutante, introducing her to Stephen Stills, Cass Elliot, John Phillips, and the rest. At parties of music royalty, she pulled out her guitar and enraptured audiences in a slew of Laurel Canyon homes.

"When Joni would sing over that guitar, men were riveted," recalled Cass Elliot's sister, Leah Kunkel. "They stopped doing what they were doing, they were absolutely enamored. Before that, it was always women riveted by the male guitarist. This was the first time it changed. Joni got introduced to the cream of the pop rock world, and she was accepted right away."

Crosby was smart enough to know that the best way to produce Joni Mitchell was to *not* produce Joni Mitchell. His role as producer was written into her Reprise contract, mostly because the last thing he wanted was to have someone *produce* her by adding drums and bass and electric guitar. "David did me a solid favor," Mitchell recalled. "The way David put it, he'd produce me minimally." Crosby saw his job as aiming microphones and pushing the record button.

David booked Sunset Sound in late 1967, and almost as soon as Joni and manager Elliot Roberts got to L.A., she was in the studio working on *Song to a Seagull.* "At the time I made the first album," Mitchell said, "[I] was still very concerned with childhood. It was full of the remnants of fairy tales and fantasia." She guest-roomed a bit, stayed with David a bit, then got herself a nice little cottage in Laurel Canyon, neighborhood of the stars.

Crosby had finally figured out who Graham Nash was. He was preoccupied with joint rolling when Cass Elliot introduced them, but by the time he was working with Mitchell, he'd long since made the connection that the British guy was in that nice pop group the Hollies. He was impressed because, as an addict of great singing, he'd admired their blend on the radio. Through Crosby, Nash met Mitchell again. They'd had a one-night stand in Winnipeg when their touring paths crossed a couple years earlier.

"There was a party at David's house and Joni was there," Nash said. "I was already totally intrigued and in love with this woman and she invited me home. I went with her and didn't leave for a couple of years. It was a cute little house. That was an incredible time for me, probably the most intensely creative, free, and special time I've ever experienced."

David didn't lose sleep over Joni and soon rekindled a romance with an earlier girlfriend, Christine Hinman. If Joni left him for someone else, might as well be a friend rather than some jerk. "I subscribed to the hippie ethic of non ownership," Crosby said. "I didn't feel that anybody owned anybody and I tried my level best not to be jealous or territorial about that kind of thing because I didn't want it done to me. I used to tell girls, 'Look, you don't own me. I'm going to make love to whomever I feel like. This is just how it is. I love you and I'll give you all the love I can, but I'm not going to be possessed. It's not happening and if that doesn't suit you, leave now.' Christine, because she was really in love with me, was willing to live with that."

Laurel Canyon had changed from a run-down enclave of fading homes into the epicenter of the rock world in Los Angeles. The Byrds were the first band to set up housekeeping. Graham Nash and Joni Mitchell shared a cottage on Lookout Mountain Avenue. Frank Zappa lived in the big log cabin up the road. David Crosby roared through the streets on his motorcycle, cape flowing behind him like some gone-to-seed Superman.

The place was a magnet. Songwriter-impresario Kim Fowley recalled willowy hippie girls suddenly showing up. "All these chicks would hitchhike up to the Canyon Store from the Strip, girls from Kansas who'd heard about Laurel Canyon: 'Hi! Folk-rock musicians! I'll clean your house and fuck you and I'm a vegetarian and I can make you macrobiotic stuff as you're shooting heroin.'"

Everybody who was anybody lived in Laurel Canyon, with the exception of Bel-Air dwellers named Wilson and Phillips and a few other outsiders, such as Dennis Wilson, who lived in a log cabin estate off Sunset Boulevard.

The center of Laurel Canyon society was Cass Elliot's house. Cass was a guaranteed entry to rock 'n' roll society, and as soon as Joni hit town, Cass introduced her to a social circle she could not enter otherwise. When English guitar god Eric Clapton from Cream came to L.A., he didn't know anyone and was too shy to thrust himself into parties. Elliot invited him over and called Crosby, who brought along Mitchell. "Whenever things weren't going right," Nash recalled, "we'd go over to Cass's house. She was a magnificent creature. She knew how crazy and fragile artists were."

Elliot had issues with her fellow Mamas and Papas. Recording the third album, *Deliver*, was a trial. A gulf yawned between them, and the group saw each other only in the studio or onstage. Far from holding back John's ambitions, Cass's coattails carried the group. Her role as salon diva also upset John, mostly because he could not control her.

There was another reason recording *Deliver* was strained. "No one knew Cass was pregnant," Denny Doherty said. "She was already six or seven months pregnant before anyone knew." Cass would not (and never did) identify the father of her daughter, Owen Elliot. And still there were other tensions in the studio. "Jill had come and gone," Denny said. "Michelle had come and gone and now she was back in the group, and John and Michelle are back together and they moved into Bel-Air. Supposedly, 'business as usual.' Ha-ha . . . *right*. . . . The thing with her and I was over, and the group was supposedly continuing on. But she was running around seeing other people and that was driving John crazy, and it became an untenable situation." One of Michelle's paramours was a hot new filmmaker from Poland named Roman Polanski.

Rather than hang out with her bandmates—each of whom she had license to loathe—Cass connected dots, bringing people together under her roof, introducing them and constructing new friendships. Jackson Browne was a young, handsome singer-songwriter taken under her wing. "She was very important not only as an individual artist and a great singer," Browne said, "but also for knowing who would be good with who, who should be working with or singing with who. She had a great instinct for that."

Crosby was so often at Elliot's house he was morally obligated to pay rent. "I always got a lot of delicatessen food in because I know David is going to come over for a swim and things are going to happen," Elliot said. Parties spilled from living room to yard, and rock 'n' roll stars rolled in the grass with baby Owen. It was a welcome refuge, a retreat for rock stars and their fragile egos.

"Music happens in my house," Elliot said, "and that pleases me."

The Byrds, those elder statesmen of Laurel Canyon, were reduced to a duo. Gene Clark left, returned, then left again. David Crosby was dismissed, and Michael Clarke, happy to return once his nemesis was fired, left again. Roger McGuinn (he changed it from Jim after converting to Subud) and Chris Hillman surveyed the wreckage of their band and decided to soldier on. After the failure of the Rising Sons—the band with Ry Cooder and Taj Mahal—the Byrds recruited its drummer, Kevin Kelley, who was Hillman's cousin. McGuinn mapped out an ambitious plan for the next Byrds album and he needed another member to carry it off—maybe a full-time pianist, which they'd never had.

Gram Parsons was born Ingram Cecil Connor III in Winter Haven, smack dab in fertile Polk County, Florida's breeding ground for musicians. After his father, known as Coon Dog, offed himself with a shotgun, the boy took the surname of his stepfather, Bob Parsons. Raised in wealth and pampered, Gram Parsons formed a series of Central Florida bands (the Legends, the Shilohs), before heading off to Harvard, a good college to drop out of. He arrived in Cambridge, Massachusetts, as a folk-rock musician, but by the time he left college after one semester, he considered himself a country-and-western singer. Hearing Merle Haggard changed his life, but he didn't want to completely submerge himself in the genre. With a couple of other folk-rock renegades, he formed a loosely tethered group called the International Submarine Band that played the Boston club circuit.

His mother was from wealth, and when she died of cirrhosis, Parsons inherited enough money for a *go to hell* fund. He used it to go to California and recruit new musicians with whom he used the Submarine Band name. Far from Porter Wagoner–type country, he began expounding on his blend, which he called cosmic American music, blending country with rock, gospel, and rhythm and blues. He garnered enough attention to draw sniffing interest from Lee Hazlewood. Hazlewood was the producer, songwriter, and sometimes singing partner of Nancy Sinatra ("These Boots Are Made for Walkin'"). He had helped Dean Martin top the charts again with his song "Houston." Hazlewood formed a label, LHI Records, and Parsons and his Submarine Band were among the first artists signed.

Unfortunately for Hazlewood, McGuinn and Hillman heard about the Sub Band's shows at the Palomino Club, so they checked out the band and liked what they saw: Gram Parsons. He joined the Byrds in February and by March was recording with the group. By the time the Submarine Band's album (*Safe at Home*) was released, Parsons had moved on.

McGuinn intended to follow the adventurous *The Notorious Byrd Brothers* with a music history lesson. "My original idea," he told *Rolling Stone*, "was to do a double album, a chronological album starting out with old-timey music—which I'm into too—not bluegrass but pre-bluegrass, dulcimers and 'In Nottamun Town . . .', nasal Appalachian stuff, and then get into like the thirties advanced version of it, move it up to modern country, the forties and fifties with steel guitar and pedal steel guitar—kind of do an album on the evolution of that type of music. Then cut it there and kind of bring it up into electronic music and a kind of space music and going into futuristic music. That was my original idea, but it didn't come off because I didn't have any support. It was a nice idea, but harder to pull off than to think of."

When it came to the country music, Parsons fit neatly into McGuinn's plan. But then he nearly hijacked the group, and his contract with Hazlewood created complications McGuinn did not need for the Byrds. With the zeal of a recent convert, Parsons turned himself into a country music jukebox and used the Byrds to recognize his dream of recording in Nashville and appearing on *The Grand Ole Opry*, the Saturday barn dance show on clear channel WSM. They were mocked as the first rock band to play there (and they mocked back with "Drug-Store Truck-Drivin' Man," a song McGuinn and Parsons wrote about the Opry's condescending emcee, Ralph Emery), but they got a week's worth of recording done in Nashville, then finished up in Los Angeles.

Sweetheart of the Rodeo was much less than the album Roger McGuinn intended yet was still one of the most influential records in rock history. McGuinn managed to get demos of unrecorded songs from Bob Dylan, still in semiseclusion after his 1966 motorcycle accident. With two songs by Dylan and two songs by Parsons, the album was filled out with straight-faced versions of the Louvin Brothers' "The Christian Life" and Merle Haggard's "Life in Prison." Gun-shy about a Lee Hazlewood lawsuit, Columbia insisted that several of Parsons's lead vocals be erased and McGuinn's voice substituted. Parsons remained on his wistful back-home ballad "Hickory Wind."

Hello, I must be going. Groucho Marx could have been speaking for Gram Parsons when he coined that signature line. Parsons was gone before *Sweetheart of the Rodeo* was released that summer. By then, he had met Keith Richards of the Rolling Stones during a brief tour of England. Parsons and Richards became music and drug buddies, and when Richards heard that the Byrds planned to tour apartheid South Africa that summer, he urged Parsons to back out. *South Africa ain't cool, mate.*

As the plane was preparing to leave London for Johannesburg, McGuinn realized Parsons wasn't coming. Chris Hillman, Kevin Kelley, and he fulfilled their Byrds obligations as a trio. "I was curious," McGuinn said, "I was hip to it, knew it was a fascist country and Miriam Makeba—I'd worked with her with the Mitchell Trio and the whole Belafonte Enterprises trip—she told me the whole thing, how the Nazi stormtroopers work down there, shooting people in the head in the middle of the street and just leaving them there." Still, he thought the experience was valuable.

For his part, Chris Hillman said he felt stupid up onstage with only McGuinn and Kelley. When they returned to America, Hillman and Kelley quit, and McGuinn, the last Byrd, was starting over from scratch.

From the moment Buffalo Springfield came together, the band was coming apart. Stephen Stills and Neil Young were immensely talented and strong-willed, and if a rock 'n' roll band wanted to survive, it could support only one specimen of that personality type.

"For What It's Worth" got the group on the radio, but constant power feuds between Stills and Young crippled the group. Richie Furay was a peacemaker but was well over his head in epic squabbles. Bruce Palmer's drug use put him on a treadmill of busts and deportation. (Other bass players were drafted to fill his spot onstage—Ken Koblun, Jim Fielder, and finally Jim Messina.) Drummer Dewey Martin, the old pro, just looked the other way, often in disgust.

The first album suffered from poor production by managers Charles Greene and Brian Stone, who were rank amateurs in the studio. On the second album, *Buffalo Springfield Again*, each song bore a different production credit, Stills working with label president Ahmet Ertegun, Young with Spector's former arranger Jack Nitzsche.

During long retreats from the band, Young hid out in his cabin, writing songs that with Nitzsche he turned into the elaborate productions "Expecting to Fly" and "Broken Arrow." Furay mediated the Stills-Young wars, writing and singing "A Child's Claim to Fame" and "Sad Memory" and even writing a quasi-soul tune for Dewey Martin, "Good Time Boy."

Recording was torture. Members were rarely in the studio together, so most tracks were cut with the Wrecking Crew. Despite the dissonance, the album became a great artifact of L.A. rock in that era.

Young was in and out of the group, depending on mood. When his ethereal "Expecting to Fly" couldn't even infiltrate *Billboard*'s Hot 100, he again questioned whether this was the band for him, and boycotted several performances. Messina joined Richie Furay in trying to find peace in the band. He was both a bassist and a recording engineer. "I didn't contribute as to what their musical ideas would be," Messina said, "but I was their technical adviser, at their request, as to how a particular thing should be done."

The album had several virtuoso moments, and to listeners at home, there was no evidence that the group was all but in name broken up. Perpetually moody, Young came and went, talked openly about a solo career, then joined the group in concert and sparred on guitar with Stills, turning "Bluebird" into a thirty-minute epic. Such peaks made valleys endurable. The group vowed not to let the album sound cheap and crappy, as its first album did. They worked at Sunset Sound, taking breaks to play basketball in the half-court out the studio's back door. "These old studios are so wonderful," Young said. "Imagine a building constructed so that music would sound good in it."

Through Cass Elliot's house parties, Stills met David Crosby. Over the years, their friendship deepened and they began collaborating. They wrote "Rock and Roll Woman" for the new Springfield album, though Crosby kept his name off the publishing to avoid legal complications. He'd pissed off his fellow Byrds by committing public adultery at the Monterey festival with the Springfield. Now fired, and with Neil Young increasingly erratic, it might make sense to switch teams.

"David wanted to be in the Springfield so bad when he was having problems with the Byrds," Chris Hillman said. "He would have joined them in a minute if he had been asked." Out of the Byrds, Crosby might've joined the group, but by then there wasn't much of a group left, and, besides, he'd found Joni Mitchell.

Buffalo Springfield Again hit the market in October 1967, and the band pulled together long enough to appear, with Strawberry Alarm Clock, in support of the Beach Boys on a short pre-Thanksgiving tour. Touring with the Beach Boys was a master class in dysfunction. When Brian stopped touring, the Beach Boys morphed into a group dominated by a bully (Mike), quietly led by a compromising peacemaker (Carl), and ready to implode at any moment because of onstage impetuousness (Dennis). The Mike-Dennis battles were incendiary.

Those battles could be tamped down because of shared DNA. Stills and Young didn't have blood ties, and their resentments burned unchecked. As they began recording a third album, Stills boycotted Young sessions and Young skipped Stills sessions. Young soon withdrew from all group activity but did show up with a solo recording of "I Am a Child," which he handed to Messina for the next album.

In a rare moment of same-place, same-time harmony, they all took part in recording the new Neil Young tune, "On the Way Home," with a vocal Neil passed off to Richie Furay. But soon, the Springfield began erupting.

Charles Manson's first follower was Mary Brunner, a library assistant recently transplanted to Berkeley from Wisconsin. Manson busked streets around the Bay Area and was doing a set near the Berkeley campus, hoping to pick up spare change from rich college kids. Brunner was somewhat plain and charmed by Manson's constant praise of her beauty, so she invited him to sleep at her apartment, though she did not promise sex. Soon, they were sleeping together. Manson had sonar for detecting the lonely.

"I admit wanting to make it with anything that wore skirts," he wrote. "I had a heart crying for love. And there isn't much doubt about my craving some attention and wanting to be accepted. These are all the things I had in common with the kids I met."

Charlie began gathering followers while living with Mary. He seduced the lonely and unlovely with proclamations of peace and love and a philosophy stitched together from various religions he'd learned about in prison libraries, including Scientology.

He quickly found another lost soul and brought her home. His Mary experience gave him the blueprint, and eventually there were eighteen girls living with him in Mary's apartment. It was like plucking blueberries from a bush. They were all enraptured by Charlie Manson and thought he might be the new Christ. They regarded his every belch, wheeze, and fart as some sort of Holy Writ, and when he gathered them to travel the country in a modified old school bus, they did. They stole for gas money. Manson pimped them out, telling them that fucking others was a way to show their love for him. They went to Washington State, then back through Oregon, down to California, then all the way down to Los Angeles and its beach environs.

Once, spare changing on a street corner, Manson saw a young, red-haired girl sitting nearby. He planted himself a few feet away and watched her. He sensed deep sadness, one of the qualities he liked in young women. Girls were more vulnerable when hurting.

"You look like you have problems," he said softly. "Is there anything I can do to help?"

The girl looked at him, a spray of freckles decorating her pixieish nose. "It isn't anything I can't handle," she said.

"OK, if you're sure I can't help," Manson said, setting the hook. "I just thought you might need a friend."

He stood up and began walking away. He turned, and she was right behind him. "Where are you going?" she asked. "Can I come along?"

That was how he found Lynette Fromme, the damaged young woman he renamed Squeaky. He renamed them all: Squeaky, Gypsy, Yellerstone, Sadie, Ouisch, Dopey, Sleepy, and Grumpy. Instead of seven dwarves, Manson soon had dozens of drones. "He changed everybody's name and stressed that nobody could be the leader," said David Smith of the Haight-Ashbury Free Clinics. "But by ridding everybody of power, he became the all-powerful leader."

They were lost souls, these girls he gathered. "We were alienated from our culture," said Sandra Good, one of Manson's followers. "When I met Charlie, what impressed me most—that I did not see in my own culture growing up—was the strong sense of brotherhood, loyalty, honor. And that immediately struck a chord in me."

Los Angeles County prosecutor Vincent Bugliosi became the world's expert on Charles Manson and understood his modus operandi. "He gathers around him a bunch of kids from average American families," Bugliosi said. "You don't expect them to be mass murderers. He convinces them that he is the second coming of Christ and the devil, ultimately gets them to kill total strangers at his command."

Once Manson began assembling his harem, he began taking them on trips to visit his freed pals from the joint. "I had a lot of pride in those girls," Manson said. "Some of the traveling we did was not to see a new place or search for an experience, but to show off my good fortune, and maybe make some of my old partners envious of me."

Manson found empty houses for his gaggle. For a while, they squatted in a condemned house in Topanga Canyon, which they named Spiral Staircase, after its dominant feature. Manson and his girls spray-painted graffiti on the walls, proclaiming Manson's gibberish.

Since he was in the entertainment capital of the world, Manson called on one of the Hollywood contacts Phil Kaufman had given him in prison. This guy wanted to make a movie about Jesus in the modern world, and Manson—bearded, with now shoulder-length hair—looked the part. Alas, those talks went nowhere, though the producer found Manson fascinating in a repellant way.

Manson set up housekeeping with the gang at Spiral Staircase, but eventually they were routed out and found a home at Spahn Movie Ranch, a half-hour drive up State Route 27 from Topanga. George Spahn owned the place, and fast-talking Charlie Manson told him his gang would live rent-free in exchange for taking care of the ranch and helping with his trail-riding business. He also offered Spahn whichever girl he wanted. Despite being eighty and blind, Spahn still responded with tumescence to naked flesh.

"Spahn Ranch was very peaceful," said Catherine Share, the girl Manson named Gypsy. "Everyone was loving to each other. Everyone was trying to get away from the cities and society." The ranch dated from the thirties and was used for movies—including *Duel in the Sun*, David O. Selznick's western follow-up to *Gone with the Wind*—and boomed with the nearly all-western-all-the-time format of network television in the late fifties. By the time Manson arrived in 1968, the ranch was little used, save for the occasional birthday party trail ride, which the girls handled ably, their smiles too happy.

Manson knew how to keep Spahn happy. As writer Gay Talese reported:

> Manson would visit his shack on quiet afternoons and talk for hours about deep philosophical questions, subjects that bewildered the old man, but interested him, relieving the loneliness. Sometimes after Spahn had heard Manson walk out the door, and after he had sat in silence for a while, the old man might mutter something to himself—and Manson would reply. Manson

seemed to breathe soundlessly, to walk with unbelievable silence over creaky floors. Spahn had heard the
wranglers tell of how they would see Charlie Manson
sitting quietly by himself in one part of the ranch, and
then suddenly they would discover him somewhere
else. He seemed to be here, there, everywhere, sitting
under a tree softly strumming his guitar.

Spahn Ranch was just the sort of place Manson needed in order
to live the life he wanted with his girls. "It was an isolated existence
in an isolated setting," said Bugliosi. It also was not exactly hygienic.
Al Springer was a member of the Straight Satans, a generally passive motorcycle gang that rode their hogs on weekends but worked in
cubicles during the week. Springer was appalled when he visited the
ranch with other Satans. "There was flies all over the place," he said,
"and they were just like animals up there. I couldn't believe it, you
know." Springer was not fond of the Spahn Ranch ambiance. "I've
never been to a nudist colony. . . . I've never seen real idiots on the
loose," he said. The sex on demand was attractive to the Straight Satans
at first, but only for a while. "Everybody got sick of catching the clap."

Manson's followers were mostly women, though there were a few
men in his orbit. Bobby Beausoleil was a drop-dead gorgeous rock star
wannabe who'd played guitar in Love for a while before the band was
signed to Elektra. He still hoped to make it in the music business but
was mostly concerned with staying high and screwing all the women
he could. Threatened by such a good-looking man, Manson decided
to co-opt him, bring him into his circle, and use him to recruit more
and better-looking women for the family.

Manson's ever-widening net was intended to help him make ties
in the music business so than he would get a recording contract and
become a bigger star than the Beatles. When two of his minions got
picked up by Dennis Wilson, things seemed to be falling into place.
Dennis wasn't a Beatle, but a Beach Boy might be a good start.

For a decade and more, Dennis Hopper had been Hollywood's favorite self-destructive actor. He came along in the midfifties with James
Dean, playing small but significant roles in *Rebel Without a Cause* (his
first film) and *Giant*. He earned a rep as a hard-headed and pretentious actor and was such a pain in the ass during the filming of *From*

Hell to Texas that director Henry Hathaway vowed to blackball him from the business.

He did for a while, and Hopper dwelled in the ghetto of series television. (*Petticoat Junction* was a highlight.) He developed other talents and became a respected photographer. He'd become friends with Phil Spector, who had him photograph Ike and Tina Turner during their time with Spector.

Phil Spector did not handle retirement well. He was unwilling to admit that popular music had passed him by and yet too proud to try again and, perhaps, fail.

Like a rock 'n' roll Charles Foster Kane, Spector walked through his overlarge, echoing mansion, where he kept his wife a virtual prisoner, and recalled past glories. He lived well off royalties and investments, but at twenty-eight, he was too young to truly retire, with a long life gaping before him.

Sensing Spector's restlessness, Hopper came to him in early 1968 with a proposal: *Why don't you appear in my new movie?*

Hopper was back from the wilderness. Henry Hathaway generously hired him to appear in the John Wayne and Dean Martin western, *The Sons of Katie Elder*, in 1965. Later, he cast Hopper as the most sympathetic of the bad guys in *True Grit*.

Back in the film business, Hopper seized exploitation opportunities offered by low-budget producer Roger Corman and American International Pictures. He had his first lead role in *The Glory Stompers*, a motorcycle epic. Hopper was pals with Peter Fonda of the great acting family. Jane Fonda rose to the top of her profession, but for a long time, Peter Fonda had been unable to break away from exploitation land. He'd done *Tammy and the Doctor*, as well as other crapola, but achieved box office success with *The Wild Angels*, a biker flick costarring Nancy Sinatra. With Dennis Hopper, he appeared in *The Trip*, a Roger Corman film about LSD written by another member of their social set, the young actor Jack Nicholson.

Fonda owed American International another biker movie, and Hopper hatched a plan: let's make a *good* biker movie, something with meaning for the times. Hopper wanted to direct, if Fonda would produce. Fonda wanted to do a story about a cross-country bike trip that would end with the bikers getting murdered.

Hopper and Fonda pitched the idea to Terry Southern. He was part of the *Paris Review* crowd, a postwar expatriate who wrote well-received novels (*Flash and Filigree*, *The Magic Christian*) and underground classics (the satire *Candy*), and discovered his darkly humorous voice worked brilliantly onscreen. He'd coauthored scripts for *Dr. Strangelove*, *The Loved One*, and *The Cincinnati Kid* and did a lot of uncredited script-doctoring work. When Hopper and Fonda approached him, he'd just done everything he could to salvage *Don't Make Waves*, a film that existed primarily to show off the bikinied body of beautiful young actress Sharon Tate.

Arguments raged for decades about who did what on the screenplay for the biker flick. Southern maintained that he wrote it and Hopper and Fonda only took cowriter credit when they realized the film was going to be a huge hit. It was Jack Nicholson's breakthrough; he crossed over from schlockywood to major stardom. It's always been acknowledged that Southern wrote all of the brilliant material for Nicholson in the film.

Hopper wanted Phil Spector in the film, thinking *some* activity might get the great music producer out of his slump. But could he act? Even if he could, was he too strange—jumpy, rough voiced—for the picture? Would he be a distraction?

Hopper finally cast Spector in a small but important role in the film: he played the cocaine buyer who gives Hopper and Fonda (playing Billy and Wyatt) the money they need to subsidize their cross-country trip. The drug-buy scene included surroundings familiar to Spector: a stretch limo. But it was shot under the landing lanes for airlines at Los Angeles International Airport. Every time a plane roared over, Spector withdrew with a terrified flinch that did not require acting ability.

That role, along with a guest appearance on *I Dream of Jeannie*, accounted for all of the experience on Phil Spector's acting résumé.

The Hopper-Fonda biker movie became *Easy Rider*, a title Terry Southern brought to the party. When finally released in the summer of 1969, it became one of the touchstones of American cinema and a landmark in the history of independent film.

Formerly chubby Jim Morrison enjoyed his new life as a sexy rock 'n' roll star and front man for the Doors, which increasingly annoyed his bandmates. Drummer John Densmore thought Jim worked overtime to embrace the tortured artist thing instead of concentrating of carrying his weight in the band. "Self-destruction and creativity don't *have* to come in the same package," he said. "Picasso lived to be ninety. But in Jim, they came together, so I had to accept it. We all had to. That was the card we were dealt as a band."

The Doors and "Light My Fire" had been huge in early 1967. Their next album, *Strange Days*, did not sell as well, nor did it yield a successful single. This didn't matter to Morrison the artist, but it was of major concern to Holzman the label owner. He was learning how to love rock 'n' roll, though still a folkie at heart. As long as he had rock 'n' roll on his label, he wanted hits. Earlier in the year, Love—the band led by Arthur Lee and that for a time featured guitarist Bobby Beausoleil—cut a menacing reimagining of Burt Bacharach's "My Little Red Book," but it peaked at only number fifty-two. Holzman expected more from the Doors. "People Are Strange" got to number twelve, but two subsequent singles, "Love Me Two Times" and "The Unknown Soldier," couldn't crack the Top Twenty.

Holzman made it clear: the Doors must spew singles. Morrison saw Top Forty as a relic. Albums were key; singles were nowhere.

Pressure within the band. Nothing they wrote smelled remotely commercial. Jim's lyrics were increasingly obtuse. He wanted to do poetry recitations with Ray tinkling on keyboards and Robby noodling on guitar.

To satisfy Holzman, they reached into the Rick and the Ravens vault and withdrew "Hello, I Love You," a song long ago dismissed as lame. Filled with contempt, they recorded it, Morrison singing with a cadaver's enthusiasm. It worked; a song that could have been a simple teen chant became a cynical theme song for a stalker. It went to number one.

Morrison intended one side of the new Doors album to feature his epic poem "Celebration of the Lizard." The other Doors balked, and only a four-minute section of it was used. They wrote a song called "Waiting for the Sun," decided it would be the album's title, but the song was left off.

Joan Didion, the diminutive titan of literary journalism, attended a *Waiting for the Sun* session and published her observations in the *Saturday Evening Post*. Few writers better impersonated a fly on the wall than Didion, who sat off to the side, watching the dynamic—or lack thereof—of the Doors.

The group was worthy of interest, Didion wrote, because it stood decidedly apart from the peace, love, flowers crowd. "The Doors seemed unconvinced that love was brotherhood and the Kama Sutra," she wrote. "The Doors' music insisted that love was sex and sex was death and therein lay salvation. The Doors were the Norman Mailers of the Top Forty, missionaries of apocalyptic sex."

She watched Manzarek, Krieger, and Densmore seethe in the studio for more than an hour, waiting for Morrison.

> It was a long while later. Morrison arrived. He had on his black vinyl pants and he sat down on a leather couch in front of the four big black speakers and he closed his eyes. The curious aspect of Morrison's arrival was this: no one acknowledged it. Robby Krieger continued working on a guitar passage. John Densmore tuned his drums. Manzarek sat at the control console and twirled a corkscrew and let a girl rub his shoulders. The girl did not look at Morrison, although he was in her direct line of sight. An hour or so had passed, and still no one had spoken to Morrison.

Morrison's appeal—Didion cited the black vinyl pants with no underwear—was the golden goose for the Doors, so the musicians in the band tolerated, but barely, his antic preening. They were, as Morrison said, "erotic politicians," and he was president of this new sexual nation.

He took his role and his appearance seriously, engaging the services of celebrity hair stylist Jay Sebring—whose pelts included those of Brian Wilson, Steve McQueen, and Frank Sinatra—to style his leonine mane.

"What do you want it to look like?" Sebring asked when Morrison fell into his salon chair.

"Like this," Morrison said, pointing to a photo on a page ripped from a book. "Like Alexander the Great."

Morrison drew interest from mainstream publications because he was different. Most rock stars were college dropouts, but Morrison (and Manzarek) were UCLA grads, and Morrison read actual books, not just comics or teen rags.

He was also changing in another and more destructive way. Around the time of *Waiting for the Sun*, he tapered off his LSD consumption and became a serious boozer. Alcohol soon consumed his life, and he began seeking out dive bars—decades before such places became trendy—becoming a regular, along with a flock of professional all-day drinkers, staring into mugs and muttering epithets at the world.

The Doors could handle the acid that brought out Morrison's pretensions. The belligerence of booze was too much. Morrison became . . . embarrassing. When he was the poet, the Arthur Rimbaud in satyr mode, he was Jim. The drunk was Jimbo, just another bloated rummy.

Smoothie singer John Davidson, he of high cheekbones and inoffensive television demeanor, invited Morrison and other rock gods to his house for a party. Singer Janis Joplin was there, and at first she and Morrison appeared to be great pals. Then Jimbo showed up. Jim pulled Janis close, and for a while, they were a four-legged beast. "Mr. and Mrs. Rock 'n' roll," proclaimed fellow partygoer Paul Rothchild, who produced both of them.

Morrison turned brutal, grabbing Joplin by the hair and shoving her face in his crotch, holding it there while she flayed with her fists. "Finally she broke free," author Jerry Hopkins wrote, "fleeing to the bathroom in tears. Jim was wrestled into a car. Janis came running after him. She reached inside the car and began hitting Jim over the head with a bottle of Southern Comfort. Jim was laughing as they pulled away."

Finally, fully embracing the drunkard life, Morrison moved into the Alta Cienega Motel, within staggering distance of Elektra's new studios with its paisley-covered walls. No longer would he have to drive drunk to sessions. He could show up and spew his boozed-addled poetry, then stagger home, hitting his circuit of bars on the way back to his ten-bucks-a-night flophouse. While peers nested in Bel-Air with their home studios or joined the communal never-ending lovefest singing parties in Laurel Canyon, Morrison pulled away, preferring the company of wheezing drunks.

The enduring appeal of the Doors indicates that darkness and gloom always find an audience. All souls go dark on occasion, and Morrison was willing to perform the soundtrack for malaise and foreboding. Critic Lester Bangs cautioned fans and critics not to underestimate the Doors and the band's role in awakening atavistic fears and impulses. "The Stones were dirty but The Doors were dread," Bangs wrote. "The difference is crucial, because dread is the great fact of the '70s, and the Stones didn't learn it until it was almost too late. For them and us."

There was no final blowout that ended Buffalo Springfield. Things slowed and finally stopped in early 1968. It fell mostly to the new guy, Jim Messina, to assemble recordings to make another Springfield album. In addition to "On the Way Home," a true group effort, he had bits and pieces from each member. Messina was the sole producer and pulled together "I Am a Child" from Young and "Questions" from Stills. He wrote "Carefree Country Day" and sang lead and brought in steel guitarist Rusty Young to accompany Richie Furay on "Kind Woman," the gentle ballad that closed the album.

Unable to be in the same room for the cover photograph, *Last Time Around* featured a pasted-together portrait: band members in Buffalo nickel profile, Neil Young turned the other direction.

As bands splintered and dreams diffused, the wayward musicians always had a warm place to stay and a shoulder to cry on: Cass Elliot's house. Elliot was the rare rock star of that era who could please Mom and Dad. No one could deny the warmth and beauty of her spectacular voice. She was also blessed with the hospitality gene, the ability to make everyone feel at home. She embraced her role as the counterculture's premier hostess.

"My house is a very free house," Elliot said. "If you come over to my house and you see Eric Clapton and David Crosby and Steve Stills playing guitar together and Buddy Miles walks in, it's not because I got out my Local 47 book and called up and said let's get a bunch of musicians together."

Her home on Woodrow Wilson Drive in Laurel Canyon was known for its parties, some of which lasted days. All sorts of characters would show up, sample the food and drink, and perhaps leave with a new friend. It wasn't cool to ask for résumés and references at the door, so even the likes of Charlie Manson and his harem were invited in. Manson was stuck to Dennis Wilson like a barnacle, so wherever his benefactor went, the scruffy little dude also went.

"That was a fascinating house," David Crosby said, "and I spent a *great* deal of time there. She probably had the nicest house of any of us and there was plenty of room and she was a person that liked having people come over because she was lonesome."

Cass was loved, but not *loved*. She had her share of relationships, but they were often with needy or opportunistic men. She had many talents, including attracting sleazebags. Her business partner, Denny Doherty, remained the love of her life. One night, she drove to see him, unannounced, and found him drunk with a gaggle of hangers-on littering his living room floor. There had been some business issues with the Mamas and the Papas—missing royalties, for one thing—and that was her pretense for the visit. She took him aside.

"Dennis, get your head out of your ass," she told him. "You're getting *fucked* and you don't care? You're going to get screwed man. You're gonna lose your house. You'll lose everything."

Doherty, backed up against the wall, was too drunk for a coherent response. As if a cloud crossed the sun, Elliot's mood changed, and she came closer and whispered, "Come on. Let me take care of you. *I* could make you happy. If you marry me, I can make you happy."

Doherty sobered immediately. This was the first time she'd made such a declaration, though he'd been pretty sure she was crazy about him. "I wasn't man enough to deal with that," Doherty said, years later. "I made some stupid joke. She left and something was lost forever."

Doherty regretted hurting her but wrote it off to his insensitivity and stupidity. "She did weigh three-hundred pounds," he said. "But you don't look at the *value* of relationship [when] you're being led around by your dick." Her confession came as no surprise. "I knew she loved me and I loved her too, but not like she wanted me to."

———

Decades later, they still argued over where it happened—whether it was at Joni Mitchell's cottage or Cass Elliot's house. They all agreed on one point however: it happened because of Elliot.

Elliot had a vision that these three people in her life—David Crosby, Graham Nash, and Stephen Stills—would sound great together. All of them had recently gone through ugly musical divorces: Crosby fired from the Byrds, Stills standing helpless while the Springfield disintegrated, and Nash leaving the Hollies because he wanted to record original songs, while the others wanted to sing Bob Dylan songs.

Elliot made things happen. "David and I were messing around," Stills recalled, "and she comes up to me and says, 'Do you think you need a third voice?' And I said, 'Yeah.' She said, 'OK, don't say anything, especially to Crosby. And when I call, *come*.'"

So there they were in L.A., Elliot nudging them together. Nash recalled it as being at Joni Mitchell's house. Others held that it was in Cass's living room. It was in Laurel Canyon somewhere. It was a party, so Stills brought his guitar. He sat center circle with Crosby.

They knew they had great chemistry because they'd sung so beautifully on "Rock and Roll Woman." But what next—hop from one band into another? Crosby wanted to make his bones as a producer, making strides in that direction with Mitchell's debut.

At the party, Crosby and Stills sang a new Stills song called "You Don't Have to Cry." When they were done, Nash stuck his head into the circle, complimenting them. *Would you do it again please?* Eyebrows arch; a nod. But they did.

Again, please, Nash requested. Crosby and Stills exchanged looks, shrugged, then sang the song again. Afterward, he hold them it was beautiful. *Would you mind singing it again?* "Three times, the same song," Nash recalled. "They must have thought I was stoned out of my gourd."

Third time through, Nash leaned in, adding harmony. When they finished, the room shimmered from the blended voices. Crosby's grin spread across his face. "That's the best thing I ever heard," he said.

Nash turned to Joni Mitchell. "Did that sound as incredible to you as it did to me?"

"Yeah, it sounded pretty incredible," she said.

Jim Messina wrapped up the mastering of Buffalo Springfield's *Last Time Around* in April, and by the time the album was released midsummer, the members had gone their separate ways.

One afternoon in July, Neil Young decided to make a house call. Still licking his wounds from the Springfield breakup, he was unsure about the road he was taking. He and producer David Briggs were about to record his first solo album, but with his unconventional voice, he was dubious about success in the fickle rock 'n' roll marketplace. Buffalo Springfield was good, but other than its one big hit, it didn't build a big following.

Young worried he'd have to get on with another group and didn't know if his temperament was right for a group. Bands were bullshit, with warring egos and rock-star trappings. The thought depressed him, so he decided to visit a friend and try out some of his new songs. Well-placed words of encouragement might help with the whole solo thing.

So he drove over to Rustic Canyon to see Dennis Wilson. The Beach Boys: now *there* was a group with warring egos and oceans of bullshit, but Dennis managed to excuse himself from much of the day-to-day rock-star crap. He wasn't pretentious, and he reveled in the small pleasures of life: hanging out, fucking, surfing . . . the usual stuff.

Dennis lived in a log cabin mansion, a party boy with an open-door policy. Word on the marijuana telegraph these days was that Dennis's house was filled with young, naked women and orgies were common.

Sure enough, when Young sauntered through the back door, a batch of mostly topless young women greeted him. There were about eight of them, and word was the girls kept house, served meals, and vigorously fucked any swinging dick. Dennis's house was base camp for L.A.'s hedonistic culture.

Wilson enthusiastically welcomed Young and made one-name-only introductions. Soon, Young was sitting on the couch, good-naturedly strumming his Martin, trying out songs from his upcoming solo album. He had a couple of songs he'd been kicking around for a year or so, "The Old Laughing Lady," "The Loner," and a ten-minute piece of strangeness called "The Last Trip to Tulsa." The girls circled him like grinning dunces, loving whatever it was that came out of Neil's mouth. Dennis walked around the room shirtless, smoking, and taking an occasional swig of beer.

The girls sang along as best they could to Young's idiosyncratic songs, and Wilson's friend—introduced just as "Charlie"—filled the space between songs by talking about his life on the road and his time in and out of jails. Young hadn't met Charles Manson before, though he'd heard of him. Everyone who'd spent time with Dennis knew about the short little dude who went everywhere with him. Charlie's nose was so far up Dennis's ass it stuck out his navel. The Beach Boys had made some noise the year before about starting their own record label, Brother, and Dennis said he was going to produce this Charlie guy's album on Brother Records.

Eventually Manson asked to borrow the guitar and began to play some songs he wrote. Young was immediately impressed by Manson's style, though he said he was more of a "song-spewer" than a songwriter.

Young listened attentively and at one point freestyled on guitar while Manson pulled lyrics from the recesses of his brain. "This guy is unbelievable," Young said. "He makes the songs up as he goes along, and they're all good." Young liked Manson's music, saying he'd put in a good word for him at his record company. "The songs were fascinating," Young recalled. "He was quite good." Manson's eyes lit up.

The session with the adoring topless women gave Young a confidence boost, and he left buoyed by the visit. "I was finally going to create my masterpiece," he said. He booked time at Wally Heider Studios on Selma Avenue in Hollywood and began recording his first solo album in a couple of weeks.

Neil liked Dennis, who was so unlike the other Beach Boys. When Springfield was just weeks old and got a gig opening for the more established Beach Boys, Dennis treated him like an equal, not like some loser in the third band on the bill.

A man of his word, Neil Young soon suggested to Mo Ostin, president of his record company, that he sign Charlie Manson to a recording contract. "He's good," Young told Ostin. "He's just a little out of control."

Ostin passed.

————————

Judy Collins could take some credit for bringing Joni Mitchell to public attention, and she decided to plumb Mitchell's songbook as she began to prepare her next album. *Wildflowers* made it to number five on *Billboard*'s album chart, and the Mitchell-penned "Both Sides, Now" became a Top Ten single. Such success was rare for an acoustic artist barely on the fringe of rock or popular music.

But Collins also did not want to sink into formula. She wrote a song, "My Father," for the new album and dug back into the Leonard Cohen songbook. And to make sure things were different this time around, she worked with a different producer. David Anderle had most recently been in the employ of the Beach Boys, who charged him with setting up Brother Records. But with that vanity label's future in doubt, Anderle moved on. He brought another recent Beach Boy employee to the sessions, Van Dyke Parks. Parks played piano with a studio band that included the Wrecking Crew's latest go-to drummer, Jim Gordon, along with James Burton on guitar and Chris Ethridge on bass. Stephen Stills was also tagged to play guitar on the album, which would have as much of a rock 'n' roll feel as a Judy Collins album would ever have.

Even before the last Springfield album was released in summer 1968, Stills branched out to work with Al Kooper. Kooper helped give Bob Dylan his rock 'n' roll sound in 1965 and wanted to make an album with the fiery guitarist from those Dylan sessions, Mike

Bloomfield. They had a productive day in the studio, but Bloomfield didn't show for day two. Kooper called Stills, unemployed guitar hotshot, and they recorded several tracks. The result, *Super Session*, became a huge bestseller.

By now, Stephen Stills was in the throes of early love with David Crosby and Graham Nash, and they began working on material for a debut album. Recording with Judy Collins was more than a paycheck for Stills. He admired her work and, of course, her eyes. At Anderle's prerecording session party, Collins discovered mutual attraction.

"All during the evening," she recalled, "Stephen and I sang songs, traded verses, swapping harmonies. I remember leaning against the window and sneaking a closer look at this handsome man with his eyes of a blue different from mine. I sensed Stephen was an old soul with a vivid imagination."

That late summer and fall was a grim time in the year when everything came undone: the hopelessly lost Vietnam War, the assassinations of Martin Luther King and Bobby Kennedy, and the police riot at the Democratic National Convention in Chicago, which showed the nation's divisiveness in a bloodbath on the city's streets on prime-time television. In November, gloom settled after Richard Nixon's election. Into this year of dread, Collins released the delicate and beautiful *Who Knows Where the Time Goes*, yet another attempt to bring justice and beauty to a sinful world.

Phil Spector's marriage to Veronica Bennett was troubled from the start. The young retiree was around and in the way. Though Ronnie had one of the great voices in rock 'n' roll, Phil controlled her and would not allow her to record with anyone else. He retreated to his home, with its gates, security dogs, and bodyguards. He dragged her with him into a de facto retirement.

Spector was so jealous of his new wife that he never wanted anyone to see her alone. He had a plastic blow-up doll made of himself— Inflatable Phil—so that when she was out in the car, it would appear that Phil was by her side.

Directors did not line up to hire him after his *Easy Rider* cameo. Being out of the music game was difficult for him, but he so feared failure. He was paralyzed. Money was no problem, but boredom was. His isolation fed his eccentricities and paranoia.

Like Spector, Brian Wilson also was entering Howard Hughes territory. Reclusive, his hygiene was the first thing to go. He wandered around his house and occasionally other people's neighborhoods wearing only a bathrobe. He'd sometimes show up at the end of a friend's driveway, waiting for them to come outside so they could talk. Why he didn't ring the doorbell, only he knew.

Linda Ronstadt was still little known when this wounded bear lumbered to her house. "I discovered him at my back door," she recalled, "studying a little pile of coins he held in his hand, which he said was ten or fifteen cents shy of the price of a bottle of grape juice. He said it was important for him to drink grape juice in order to solve some health problem that was troubling him. He didn't say what it was, nor did I ask."

Brian returned to the Sunset Strip, showing up at clubs in his bathrobe. He might be called up to the stage by starstruck young performers, only to puzzle everyone in the room with his antics. The band would sing one song while Brian sang another.

While Brian was lost and aloof, Mike Love was on the other side of the world in a remote ashram in Rishikesh, India. Through Dennis, of all people, he'd discovered transcendental meditation and its greatest proponent, Maharishi Mahesh Yogi. To investigate further, Mike joined a trip to the maharishi's retreat, along with the Beatles, actress Mia Farrow and her sister Prudence, and Scottish folk singer Donovan. Together they abstained from drugs, ate healthier food, and meditated several hours a day.

They also composed music. The Beatles wrote so many songs in India that when they returned to England, they needed to produce a double album to hold them all. Paul McCartney came to breakfast one morning in Rishikesh with a half-finished song about Russia, a long-delayed answer to Chuck Berry's "Back in the U.S.A." Mike suggested he add a bridge drawn from those old Beach Boys odes to women: "The Ukraine girls really knock me out." McCartney used it in "Back in the U.S.S.R."

Mike was increasingly infatuated with the maharishi and began hatching a plan for a joint tour as Brian and the rest of the group, back home in California, began work on another album. Instead of being treated for mental illness, Brian was instead expected to produce ten or twelve songs for an album to restore the Beach Boys to commercial prominence.

Brian's longtime lust object, Marilyn's sister Diane, assisted Brian by scheduling the sessions, and the home studio was opened to several veterans of earlier recordings, including bassist Lyle Ritz and Jim Gordon, the Crew's hot young drummer. Together with Brian, the musicians cut some tracks that would remain instrumentals, enhancing the disconnect between Brian and his band.

Brian was at the controls, but he wasn't. The confident young man was replaced by this prematurely burned out twenty-six-year-old. "Brian worked really hard for the first seven years and he needed a break," Carl said. "He just took a look and saw how fucked up the world was—he's not a dummy—and he said, 'The world is so fucked up, I can't stand it; it's unspeakable how fucked up everything is.' And I think it really broke his heart."

Martin Luther King was assassinated on April 4 in Memphis, just as the Beach Boys were boarding a plane for Nashville to open a tour. As news of King's murder spread, riots erupted in several cities. The Nashville date and eighteen other shows were canceled, costing the Beach Boys a bundle. After rescheduling as many of the shows as was viable, the group was back on the road by midmonth.

Mike returned from India with a few songs to flesh out with Brian, but most of the group's album was written and recorded in Mike's absence, perhaps why Brian often said the resulting album, *Friends*, was his favorite of the group's career. It was a true collaboration. The composer credit for the title song read, "B. Wilson—C. Wilson—D. Wilson—A. Jardine." The songs of hippie domesticity—odes to awakening, pregnancy, and pencil sharpening—were homespun tunes with the lyric references meaningless beyond the group's circle. In the middle of "Be Here in the Mornin'," the group coyly sang, "No calls from Korthof, Parks or Grillo." Translation: cousin Steve Korthof, Van Dyke Parks, and manager Nick Grillo. Brian's pencil-sharpening song called "Even Steven" during gestation was retitled appropriately as "Busy Doin' Nothin'."

As disastrous as the April tour was, the May tour became notorious in the annals of rock concert history. The planned joint tour with Maharishi Mahesh Yogi was to feature the giggly voiced meditation guru as the opening act, nudging crowds toward cosmic consciousness in their inner and outer lives.

The problem was the crowds—or rather, lack of same. The marriage of a rock concert with a lecture by a tittering little man in white robes was ill-advised at best, spectacularly moronic at worst. The Beach Boys lost thousands and scuttled the tour, canceling a dozen shows.

Yes, it *was* possible to make matters worse: when *Friends* was released in June, it became the group's lowest-charting album. No one was listening.

The group needed income and turned its attention to other artists who might deliver revenue through Brother Records. Dennis thought his roommate might be the answer to their financial problems. He brought Charles Manson, whom he called the Wizard, to Brian's home studio and with Carl produced hours of music and preaching by Manson, occasionally accompanied by his band of young women. The group hired engineer Stephen Desper to oversee recording. He was impressed by Manson's songs and his singing. Mike Love was not moved. "Just chanting, fucking, sucking, and barfing," Mike termed it. "It was a million laughs."

Though Brian had essentially checked out of working with the Beach Boys, he'd still sneak downstairs to the studio when no one was around to record tracks, playing all the instruments himself. He knew when Manson and the girls were in the house, and he was not impressed with the music or the man. "Everything I heard about Manson gave me the creeps," he said. He understood why Dennis was so fascinated by Manson. "He was waited on hand and foot by Manson's nubile, often semi-naked girls and allowed to participate in the orgies Charlie orchestrated." Brian wouldn't leave his room when Manson and the girls were downstairs, but he could hear the music coming through the floorboards. "I never saw them," Brian said. "The bad vibes filled the house and I locked myself in the bedroom."

Desper recalled Manson being totally unprepared for the session, spending more time smoking dope with his girls than actually recording. They recorded several songs, which Desper thought were pretty good. But after hours in the studio, Manson dropped the easygoing facade and became himself. "We were in there two or three nights," Desper recalled, "and then he got pretty weird. He pulled a knife on me, just for no reason, really." That was the end of the sessions at Brian's house.

Manson changed the narrative: he wasn't being kicked out of Brian Wilson's house; rather, he couldn't work with all of those bad vibrations around.

The feeling was mutual for Marilyn Wilson. She was looking for an ultraviolet toilet seat because Manson's girls would use the family bathrooms and she feared their crotches in such proximity to the family throne. She complained to a secretary in the Beach Boys office, "Dennis is bringing those crummy girls up here with Charles Manson and I'm afraid they're going to give us or the children some disease."

The presence and willingness of the Manson girls was not enough for insatiable Dennis, who began an affair with Mike's wife, Suzanne. Once, while Mike was out of town, Dennis and Suzanne went out to dinner and asked Manson family member Susan Atkins to babysit. Mike learned of this a few years later during his divorce procedings. He made Atkins an issue. "She was convicted of participating in eight murders," Love said, "and she was our babysitter." He was awarded custody of his two children from that marriage.

There was so much tension about Manson that manager Nick Grillo investigated his background. When he discovered Manson's voluminous criminal record, he informed the Beach Boys. "The Wizard was a convicted thief on probation," Brian said. "That, combined with the changes in Dennis was enough to frighten me. I became convinced the Wizard was experimenting with evil powers and immediately sent word to Dennis: neither Charlie Manson nor any of his family members were ever to set foot on my property again."

Dennis tried to help his hairy little friend. "Dennis Wilson was fascinated with Charlie's mind and the kind of music he wrote," said Catherine Share, known as Gypsy during her time with Manson. "He tried to record the family at his recording studio, at his brother's house. He saw great potential in Charlie."

Those recordings didn't lead to a recording contract, because the other Beach Boys were dubious about launching Brother Records with the little dude. Dennis didn't give up. "Dennis introduced Charlie to people in Hollywood," Share said. "He was always talking him up. Dennis took Charlie to parties. At one of the parties, he introduced him to Terry Melcher, who was Doris Day's son."

It seemed unlikely that Manson would help the Beach Boys get out of their creative and financial abyss.

Backstage before a concert in New Haven, Jim Morrison was canoodling with a girl in a dressing room. He looked like any other unkempt kid—certainly not a big-time singing star—so he was maced by an overzealous police officer apparently upset at the display of affection. During his performance that night (at the end of 1967), Morrison began talking about the officer from the stage and, in the parlance of the time, called him a pig. The show was stopped, and Morrison arrested.

Early the next year, in Miami, he was charged with public indecency for flashing his joystick for the Dinner Key Auditorium crowd. For decades, the *Did he or didn't he?* debate rang. The upshot was that Morrison was losing his shit. Drunk onstage and off, his belly bloating, the drama and fire of his early lyrics were lost in the spinning world of a habitual drunk.

During summer 1968, the Doors toured Europe, and George Harrison invited Morrison to a session as the Beatles tried to record the scores of songs written during their Indian sojourn. Impressed by the varied instrumentation the group was using, Morrison went along with Paul Rothchild's efforts that fall, back in L.A., to enlarge the Doors' musical palate with strings and horns.

The Beach Boys' great years coincided with Charles Manson's prison residency. He was nevertheless aware of the group's career, and it didn't take any scientific analysis of the *Billboard* charts for him to realize the Beach Boys no longer sold records by the woodie-full. Manson wasn't into the Beach Boys' music. Words were important to him, and words to Beach Boys songs—excepting those by Tony Asher and Van Dyke Parks—either were innocuous or made no sense.

Still, Manson saw Dennis Wilson as his ticket, not because of who he was but because of who he knew, which was just about everybody in L.A.'s rock 'n' roll community. Dennis also was a generous bastard, turning over his house, his cars, and his money to Charlie and his girls. Dennis's friend Gregg Jakobson dubbed Manson and his mostly naked chicks the "family," a name that stuck. "Dennis was just divorced," Mike Love said. "I suppose the lifestyle appealed to him." It did not appeal to Carole Freedman, his former wife. Dennis adored his children, Scott and Jennifer, but Carole took a couple bites out of the Manson crowd and put her foot down: all of Dennis's visitations would take place at her house.

Dennis praised the Wizard's songs and planned to produce him for Brother Records. That's why Dennis brought Gregg into the tent.

He was one of Dennis's collaborators on everything from songwriting to sound engineering. They both enjoyed the Manson ambiance, which included ready-to-fuck girls, as well as Charlie's sharp, distinctive voice. The song lyrics were a little weird, but with some work, Dennis thought they'd be commercial.

Dennis was full of stories about Manson and his family when he spoke to a reporter from England's *Record Mirror*. "I found he had great musical ideas," Dennis said. "We're writing together now. He's dumb, in some ways, but I accept his approach and have learn[ed] from him." Of his many female roommates, he said, "They're space ladies, and they'd make a great group. I'm thinking of launching them as the Family Gems." As Manson recalled Wilson's infatuation with his music: "Dennis himself thought I was some kind of wizard when it came to playing and writing music."

Generous to a fault, Dennis invited Charlie into his social circle, with Jakobson and Terry Melcher. As the "Golden Penetrators," their informal boys club, Wilson, Jakobson, and Melcher hit the night spots, competing to see who landed the most beautiful woman.

Melcher wasn't married, though he might as well have been. As a son of Hollywood royalty, he intended to mate inside his social circle and had been dating Candice Bergen, actress daughter of radio ventriloquist Edgar Bergen, for nearly eight years (since she was fifteen). They lived together in a rented pseudochalet on Cielo Drive in Benedict Canyon, but as an in-demand film actress, she was often away on location. In her long absences, Terry enjoyed playing with Charlie's girls, especially Ruth Ann Moorehouse, the beautiful young woman Manson renamed Ouisch. Manson's decree was that the girls had to have sex at least seven times a day, so Melcher and other rock 'n' roll visitors always found willing partners.

"Dennis was a hell of a guy," Manson recalled. "For all his success and wealth, he still enjoyed the simpler things in life." He'd seen Dennis glory in the rock-star role, but it was just a performance. "Inside, he was a rebel and had long ago tired of catering to the whims of a public who wanted him to be the 'All-American Boy.'"

Manson felt right at home in the log cabin estate. "Dennis opened the doors of his house to us," he said, "and, as much as his business agents would let him, he opened his pockets." Wilson often said he couldn't bear to see people going without, so he gave large amounts of money to strangers, and lavished gifts on mere acquaintances. Being generous to Manson was par for the course.

"They were sleeping all over the house," said Croxey Adams,
one of Dennis's girlfriends in that era. "Charlie always had these
girls providing for him—sewing, cooking, doing anything he wanted."
Adams discovered that Manson had a jones for her, and she fought to
keep him at bay. "It's not very complimentary to know that Charlie
Manson has a crush on you," she said. "I told Dennis, 'You'd better
get these people out of here, because I have a feeling you're going
to get busted.'"

Manson tagged along with Wilson to the Beach Boys' offices,
where Dennis pressured Grillo to help his protégé's career. "Charlie
was a very bright guy," Grillo said, "and his major concern was public
acceptance of his music. Dennis was enamored with Charlie and the
other members of the group were enamored with the fact that he had
twelve or thirteen women. The other guys were looking to get laid."
The office staff referred to Manson as "Pigpen."

If Dennis was an open book, then Terry Melcher was a cipher.
Manson could never tell where he stood with Melcher. They palled
around together, but Manson was always subtly reminded he was on
the outside. He was *in* their world but not *of* their world.

Late that summer, as *Friends* was stinking up the charts, the
Golden Penetrators made an outing to the Whisky a Go Go, with
Dennis bringing Manson along in his Rolls-Royce. The Penetrators
were regulars and big spenders, so they were squired to their usual
ringside table, despite the scruffy little dude in their party. As Wilson,
Melcher, and Jakobson sat at their table, sipping drinks and sharing
chick-bagging strategies, Manson unfurled his unique style on the
dance floor.

In his biography of Manson, writer Jeff Guinn described what
happened next:

> Looking around, [Dennis, Melcher, and Jakobson] saw
> something unique in the history of the Whisky a Go
> Go: Instead of vying to get on, everyone was struggling
> to clear off the hallowed dance floor, where they had
> packed in so tightly that they now had trouble squirm-
> ing apart. Melcher, Jakobson, and Wilson exchanged
> puzzled glances. They stood up to get a better look,
> and that was when they saw that smack in the middle
> of the floor a single figure remained—Charlie Manson,
> gyrating to the music. His dancing grew increasingly

maniacal; he tipped back his head and threw out his arms and they agreed later that it seemed as though electrical sparks flew from Charlie's fingers and hair.

The crowd had surged off the dance floor as if driven from it by some irresistible force field. Now it circled the floor, mesmerized by the sight of the whirling dervish who seemed oblivious to everything but the pulsating beat.

As Jakobson told Guinn several decades later, "That was when we realized that he was something really different, that night at the Whisky."

Manson looked the part of a free-love hippie, doing his spastic dance at Cass Elliot's and hanging out with David Crosby and Frank Zappa. He looked like everyone else, but it gradually became obvious that he was unilaterally *unlike* anyone else.

Among Manson's songs was "Cease to Exist," about losing one's self into the soul of another—*We're all brothers,* that sort of thing. Perfect for the peace, love, and flowers world. Manson said watching the warring members of the Beach Boys inspired him to write the song. Dennis liked it and thought there was a good melody in there somewhere, so he changed it to "Cease to Resist," turning the song into a tract for sexual, not spiritual, submission. That was more like it. Sexual submission . . . that was right up Dennis's alley.

Dennis recorded it at Brian's home studio in September 1968, just four months after meeting Charlie at his back door. Not bad for Manson: from nobody to composer of a Beach Boys single in four months. Carl helped Dennis turn the song into a major production, with sleigh bells and strings part of the dense sound. The new title was "Never Learn Not to Love," and it was the B-side of the "Bluebirds over the Mountain" single. It was going to be part of the next group album, *20/20*, a "very un-Brian album," in the words of his onstage substitute, Bruce Johnston. Carl had learned to mimic Brian's style so well that between Carl's production and a couple of scraps from *Smile* and the Redwood sessions, it still appeared as if Brian was part of the group. He wasn't, really. He was lying in bed. He didn't even appear on the album cover.

When Dennis played Charlie "Never Learn Not to Love," Charlie became infuriated because the words had been changed. He demanded that his name be removed. The episode convinced Manson that Wilson was not to be trusted. By then, Dennis had also tired of the freeloaders who had trashed his house, totaled his Ferrari, caused $20,000 worth of damage to his Rolls, and given away his gold records and clothes. "Dennis ran up the largest gonorrhea bill in history the time the whole family got the clap," Mike Love said. "He took them all to a Beverly Hills doctor—it took something like a thousand dollars in penicillin."

"Manson's blending of psychedelics, sexual servants, rock music, and new-age rhetoric was too much for Dennis to resist," Mike Love wrote in a memoir. "In a few short months, Dennis swerved from Maharishi to Manson, two diminuative but hypnotic figures who promised a better world for their followers."

But the luster wore off for Dennis. He was generous, but even he had a point of intolerance. He moved out of his home and had Nick Grillo evict Manson and his family. Dennis's lease was up, so he moved to Gregg Jakobson's house, figuring he was done with Charles Manson.

Knowing rock stars only went so far. No matter how much Dennis Wilson liked him, nothing would happen in Manson's career until he met someone with the power to offer a contract. Dennis Wilson, Frank Zappa, Neil Young, Cass Elliot—none of them could get him a record deal. But Terry Melcher could.

After months of serenading the producer, Manson came to believe Melcher was merely stringing him along in order to satisfy his need for amorous congress. Melcher listened to Manson's songs on visits to Spahn Ranch but was preoccupied with the nubile Ouisch. Catherine Share—Gypsy—recalled Manson preparing for one of Melcher's visits to the ranch: "I remember that Charlie was very nervous. Terry Melcher was the person who might make him a star. Charlie waited for that call, and he never got that call."

Meanwhile, Manson began basic training with the family's women. He'd clothe them all in black, then send them out on what he called his creepy-crawling missions. He'd tagged along with Wilson and Jakobson to parties, so he'd been to the homes of rock-star royalty, such as Cass Elliot and John Phillips. Manson dug that life; he thought he deserved such a life. He'd gotten used to riding around in Dennis's Rolls-Royce and attending the parties in Bel-Air, where people like Brian Wilson and John and Michelle Phillips had their own state-of-the-art recording studios in their homes.

As Guinn wrote:

[Dennis] Wilson was part of a rock star social set where everyone was in the habit of dropping in on everyone else. No call ahead was deemed necessary. If one celebrity pal wasn't in, you just went on to the home of the next. Hanging around at Wilson's, Charlie constantly met other people who might be able to get him his record deal. He kept his guitar handy and played songs for anyone willing to listen. That wasn't unusual; at any given time, just about all the successful L.A. musicians had protégés hanging around, hoping for their own chance at stardom. Wilson made it clear he was sponsoring Charlie.

Manson and the girls returned to the homes, uninvited, under cover of dark. Michelle Phillips remembered her husband waking her up one night and grabbing his gun from the closet. He ran downstairs and Michelle waited in the bedroom until he returned a few minutes later. "I saw six people," he told her, "all dressed in black, in tights and leotards, men and women, and they were in the Rolls-Royce, out in the garage, and when I went to the door, they all tiptoed away like penguins." Only later did that nighttime visit make sense to Michelle. "John and I had been visited by Charles Manson's people, 'the Creepy Crawlers,' and we had survived."

Creepy-crawling missions were usually fun, a mind fuck. They'd break into occupied houses and rearrange all the furniture—just to fuck with people. They didn't steal anything or hurt anyone.

"I don't deny disappointment at not reaching my goals as a musician," Manson said. He was ready to wash his hands of the whole rock-star bunch.

Manson brought the issue to a head. "I went to see Melcher," he said. "Melcher was friendly enough but beat around the bush about another recording date. 'Goddamn, Terry,' I told him, 'We've been going through this kind of crap for the last year. Is it ever going to happen or not?'"

"Charlie, there's mixed emotions about promoting you," Melcher said. "You're unpredictable. You amaze me at times, and, at other times, disappoint the hell out of me." Melcher told Manson there was a rumor going around that he'd shot some black guy. Manson left, stomach in knots.

"If I had left Melcher's feeling down and sorry for myself, by the time I got back to Spahn's, the pity was well shadowed by hatred and contempt," Manson said.

One story about Dennis and Charlie took on the status of a folk tale in L.A.'s rock community, the events told repeatedly until no one could be certain of its truth. "One day, Charles Manson brought a bullet out and showed it to Dennis, who asked, 'What's this?' And Manson replied, 'It's a bullet. Every time you look at it, I want you to think how nice it is your kids are still safe,'" Van Dyke Parks recalled. "Dennis grabbed Manson by the head and threw him to the ground and began pummeling him. . . . He beat the living shit out of him. 'How dare you!' was Dennis' reaction. Charlie Manson was weeping openly in front of a lot of hip people. I heard about it, but I wasn't there. The point is, though, Dennis Wilson wasn't afraid of anybody! Dennis was a total alpha male."

Infuriated, Manson ranted to the family about Dennis Wilson's and Terry Melcher's betrayals. These betrayals were biblical in nature, much like Judas's betrayal of Jesus, he said. His followers believed him. "At that point, they had little choice," according to Jeff Guinn. "They'd surrendered their lives and wills to Charlie. They moved forward in preparations for Helter Skelter, but as they did, they sensed a permanent change in their leader."

Manson was angry, and he wasn't done with Wilson, or with Melcher. He carried resentments like a holy plague.

15

THE DREAD

On August 9, 1969, I was sitting in the shallow end of
my sister-in-law's swimming pool in Beverly Hills when
she received a telephone call from a friend who had
just heard about the murders at Sharon Tate Polanski's
house on Cielo Drive. The phone rang many times
during the next hour. These early reports were garbled
and contradictory. One caller would say hoods, the next
would say chains. There were twenty dead, no, twelve,
ten, eighteen. Black masses were imagined, and bad trips
blamed. I remembered all of the day's misinformation
very clearly, and I also remember this, and wish I did
not: I remember that no one was surprised.

—Joan Didion

Back then, there were no televised talent contests with a recording
contract as grand prize. And if there had been such a thing, imagine
Charles Manson's outrage if he didn't win and suffered monumental
public humiliation.

Manson felt entitled to fame. Since he rubbed shoulders with rock
stars, that was the life he felt he deserved. When it wasn't forthcoming,
he lost his shit. He'd been in the homes of rock stars, sang for them,
danced for them, jabbered for them, been their trained monkey. He
amused. To those hosts—Dennis Wilson, Terry Melcher, Cass Elliot,
Frank Zappa, John Phillips, Neil Young—Manson was just another
hippie, until he wasn't.

Life at Spahn Ranch for Manson and his family was a festival of
drugs, orgies, and stolen cars. Manson stage-managed the LSD-fueled

orgies, never taking as much acid as the others, so he could maintain control. "Manson became a maestro," Vincent Bugliosi said. "While they were on these trips, he would reach down deep into their psyches and remove long-standing convictions. The subversion of sexuality was one way he broke down the ego. They would do whatever he wanted them to do if they had no ego."

Selling stolen cars provided the family's cash flow. After Melcher rejected him, Manson stewed and fell back into his familiar world. He'd been so close, though, it was hard to let go of his dreams of musical fame.

In March 1969, Manson again went to see Melcher at his house on Cielo Drive and discovered that he'd moved out just before Christmas. The new tenant was a beautiful young woman floating on an air mattress in the pool, being photographed, Manson learned, for a magazine spread. The photographer told him Melcher now lived somewhere in Malibu.

November 22, 1968, was the fifth anniversary of the assassination of President Kennedy. It was also, coincidentally, the fifth anniversary of the release of *With the Beatles* in Great Britain. On that date, the Beatles released a massive two-record set called *The Beatles*, which fans soon renamed the White Album for its austere avant-garde cover. It was a colossal, varied, virtuoso collection, mostly of songs written in India while staying at the maharishi's ashram with Mike Love, Mia Farrow, and other celebrity meditators.

Charles Manson saw the album as confirmation that the Beatles were trying to communicate with him. Each song spoke to him and affected the family's nomenclature.

One of the damaged girls Manson brought into the family was Susan Atkins. Pretty and big busted, she was a runaway, dancing topless when Manson found her and drew her into his life of dependency, renaming her, as he did all members of the family. Susan became Sadie Mae Glutz, and so when John Lennon sang of "Sexy Sadie" on side three of the White Album, Manson knew that he had not just imagined a connection.

George Harrison's song "Piggies" was a not too subtle jab at the establishment (the piggies were "clutching forks and knives to eat their bacon"), recorded, of course, by a millionaire. Paul McCartney's

"Blackbird," with its call to "arise," was an obvious signal for black people to begin a revolution. But the song that affected Manson the most was McCartney's "Helter Skelter," around which he built a philosophy and conceived a plan for a race war. Too bad he didn't realize the song was about an amusement park ride.

Manson played the album nonstop and its world—with Bungalow Bill, with Desmond and Molly, with Honey Pie and Rocky Raccoon and Sexy Sadie—came alive in his daily sermons, and he shared his demented philosophy with the family. The girls lapped up every word out of his yap. "He had this phenomenal ability to gain control over other people and get them to do terrible things," Bugliosi said. "Eventually, he convinced them that he was the second coming of Christ."

The songs were at times demented and subversive: "Why Don't We Do It in the Road?" "Everybody's Got Something to Hide Except Me and My Monkey," "Happiness Is a Warm Gun."

Side four of the White Album, a dark and disturbing set of songs, included an eight-minute sound montage that John Lennon produced with his artist-companion Yoko Ono and fellow Beatle George Harrison. He wanted it to be the sound of a revolution, and it was named "Revolution 9." Manson took note. *Revolution 9, Revelation 9 . . . dig it?*

The chaos of "Revolution 9" paralleled the apocalyptic ninth chapter of the Book of Revelation. Manson, now discarded by his L.A. music business pals, saw imminent death and destruction and seized on the ninth chapter's references to a bottomless pit. He decided said pit was in Death Valley and began telling his family that a race war called "Helter Skelter" was coming. They just had to listen to the song by that title (side three, track six of the White Album); then they'd understand.

"Manson was a racist," Bugliosi said. "He believed that blacks were sub-human, less-evolved than the white man. It was their turn to win the war, but he said, 'Blackie will never be able to handle the reins of power, because blackie only knows what whitey's told them to do.' So he said that the black man would have to turn over the reins of power to those white people that survived, whereupon, he would come out of the bottomless pit and take over leadership of the world. He convinced them that this Armageddon was going to bring about a new and better social order. He used the Bible and the Beatles as foundations and support for what he said."

Manson wanted to take his family to the desert, to the bottom-less pit, and wait until the war ended. Since he said blacks would not be competent enough to govern the new society, he planned to step forward as mankind's savior. He was the new Christ, after all.

"They were anticipating, at that point, a war between blacks and whites, but they were not going to be part of it," Bugliosi said. "He said the bottomless pit was a land of milk and honey."

Manson was entranced by the chaotic and magnificent album. "When the Beatles' White Album came out, Charlie listened to it over and over and over and over again," Gypsy said. "He was quite certain that the Beatles had tapped into his spirit. He thought that the Beatles were talking about what he had been expounding for years. Every single song on the White Album, he thought they were singing about us."

That was the way Manson saw it. He was not inspired by the Beatles; the group was inspired by *him*, and the album proved that they were receiving his thoughts telepathically. *No shit—this is what he told his followers.*

Hanging out with Dennis Wilson and Terry Melcher, Manson had developed a certain lifestyle, and despite now being cut off from that world, he wanted to somehow maintain that level of living. That meant a return to what he did best—crime—hence the stolen cars. But he wanted to find other sources of income.

Time to squeeze his network of associates. Manson knew Gary Hinman, a compassionate and amiable dude who had been nice to various members of the family, letting some of them stay at his home in Topanga Canyon when they needed a place to crash. He was a music teacher and nearly finished with his doctorate in sociology. He was nice to everybody, and that was his downfall.

On Friday, July 25, Manson sent family member Bobby Beauso-leil to shake down Hinman. Beausoleil took along Susan Atkins and Mary Brunner. Things began cordially enough—Hinman was nothing if not a kind host—but when Beausoleil began demanding money, things grew heated. Manson had told Beausoleil Hinman had stocks and bonds he could cash in. Maybe he should be encouraged to also give up the pink slips to his two cars.

Hinman kept telling Beausoleil he had no money, no stocks, and he wasn't giving up his cars. He politely but firmly asked the family members to leave. Instead, Beausoleil called Manson at the ranch. "You'd better get up here, Charlie," he said. "Gary ain't cooperating."

Manson showed up carrying a battle sword and with family member Bruce Davis in tow. Hinman at first thought Manson was there to help him, but soon Manson began badgering him for money. "Come on, Gary," Manson said. "Money ain't worth all this hassle. Tell us where your stash is and we'll get out and leave you alone."

Hinman, the Buddhist pacifist, was now furious. "It's all your doing, you phoney little bastard," he spat at Manson. "Get out of my house and take these maniacs with you."

Manson didn't speak, instead whacking the side of Hinman's head with the sword, slicing his ear so severely that it hung like shredded melon from his jawline as his head spurted blood.

"We ain't going to get nothing out of him," Beausoleil told Manson. "He ain't going to give up nothing. And we can't just leave. He's got his ear hacked off and he'll go to the police."

Manson looked at Beausoleil. "You know what to do," he said, then left with Davis.

Beausoleil stabbed Hinman, sending him to death with the words "You're a pig and society don't need you, so this is the best way for you to go. You should thank me for putting you out of your misery." Atkins and Brunner held a pillow over Hinman's face to muffle his screams. Hinman comforted himself in his last moments with a Buddhist chant.

Part of Manson's plan with his new agenda of murder was to make blacks appear to be the killers. Beausoleil, on Manson's orders, dipped his hand into Hinman's blood and made a paw print on the wall—the symbol of the Black Panthers organization. The girls wrote POLITICAL PIGGY and PIG on the wall. The Panthers had begun using *pig* to refer to members of the white establishment.

Beausoleil hot-wired Hinman's two cars, a Volkswagen bus and a Fiat wagon, and he and the girls drove back to Spahn. Danny DeCarlo, another member of the Straight Satans, said Beausoleil strutted around the ranch that afternoon, reveling in the glow of becoming a murderer. He told Charlie what he'd done, then began to worry that Charlie might be right about something: he *might* be identified because he'd used his palm to make the paw print. His palm might be just as identifiable as his fingertips. After fretting a few days, Beausoleil decided to remove that evidence.

Five days after the murder, he went back to Hinman's house
to scrub off the paw print. No one had found Hinman's body, still
slumped in a chair. Beausoleil said he "could hear the maggots eating
away on Gary." He was unable to remove the paw print.

Hinman's body was discovered the following Thursday, nearly a
week after the murder. Police learned from neighbors that Hinman
had two cars, both now gone. Searching the house, detectives found
paperwork with the license numbers of the cars. They also found a
letter on an end table. It was addressed to Bobby Beausoleil, who'd
left it behind.

On Wednesday, August 6, the police picked up Beausoleil driving
Hinman's Fiat. He told detectives that he and two girls visited Hinman
the week before and found him already beaten up and stabbed, blam-
ing the Black Panthers for attacking him after a political disagreement.
Hinman then offered to lend Beausoleil his car. Or so he said.

Detectives asked the names of the girls who'd accompanied him.
"I'll talk to you," Beausoleil said, "but I want to see an attorney before
I involve anyone else." He was charged with murder and arraigned
on August 8.

Word got back to Manson fast. He knew Beausoleil wouldn't
give him up—at least not right away. Since Beausoleil was locked up,
Manson figured the best thing he could do was to kill some more
people and make it look like the people that killed Hinman were still
on the loose.

More killing would serve another purpose. "They wanted to start
the revolution and blame the murders on blacks," said Steven Kay,
a deputy district attorney in Los Angeles.

Beausoleil was arraigned in the morning. By nightfall, Manson
put together a team. "On that night, August 8, 1969, I was aware of
being totally without conscience," Manson said.

His right-hand man with the family—a group that included few
men—was Charles Watson, called Tex around Spahn. Dennis Wilson
had brought Watson into the family the previous year. Watson was
driving down the Pacific Coast Highway when he stopped to pick
up a hitchhiker, who turned out to be Dennis Wilson. Watson took
him home. "Wilson, always gracious, asked Watson to come in for a
while," Manson remembered. There he met Manson and other family members. "He left, with Dennis's invitation to visit anytime he
wanted." He did, and soon joined the family.

Manson asked Tex Watson to lead the mission and picked Susan Atkins and Patricia Krenwinkel, one of the hitchhikers Dennis picked up that first day he met Manson.

Manson also plucked Linda Kasabian from his harem. She was a new arrival, a refugee with a child from a failing marriage. Gypsy had befriended her and invited her to come live at the commune at Spahn Ranch. "I immediately decided to go with her," Kasabian said. "There was no second thought. I was searching for love and freedom. I was searching for God." After married life, living with the family was an approximation of heaven. "I was comfortable with communal living," she said. Gypsy said, "Linda was very quick and very open to coming to the ranch and being with people that would love her and take care of her and Tanya."

Kasabian slept with Tex Watson her first night at Spahn. "Tex was gruff and greasy," she said, "but he just always had this beautiful smile, and these beautiful eyes. He had me the first night. He made me feel like I'd never felt before."

"Tex had told me she was a hell of a lay," Manson said, "so that night I checked her out myself." Checking her out meant stage-managing a four-way—Charlie with Kasabian, Gypsy, and another family member named Brenda. "She wasn't stingy with her body," Manson said.

Kasabian had only been there a month and was still neck-deep in Manson love. "There was a magnetism about him—charisma, charm, power," she said. "He gave me the feeling that I would be cared for. He took care of everybody. We were like his children. We *were* his children."

Getting picked to go along with veteran family members on this . . . adventure—whatever it was to be—was unusual for one of the new people. "I felt special, excited, chosen."

She thought they were going on another creepy-crawling mission, since Manson insisted on black clothes. She figured Charlie chose her because she had something few members of the family had: a valid driver's license.

"Now is the time for Helter Skelter," Manson said. Even a newbie like Kasabian knew what he meant. "What it meant was the Negroes were going to come down and rip the cities all apart," said another Manson disciple, Paul Watkins. "Before Helter Skelter came along, all Charlie cared about was orgies."

The girls piled into a stolen Ford sedan with Watson. Manson leaned in the window and told them to leave a sign, "something witchy." Manson selected Terry Melcher's house. He knew the place well, and Watson had been there as a guest of Dennis Wilson's. Manson knew that Melcher no longer lived there. He told Watson to kill everyone inside and mused about how much shit would be scared out of Terry Melcher.

Melcher was long gone from the house. His dealings with Manson had freaked him out, and when he told his mother, Doris Day, about the wild man with the knives and the sheeplike followers, she insisted that Terry and Candy Bergen move into her Malibu beach house. "A mother's intuition," Mike Love called it, "and it may have saved his life."

Watson drove straight to the house, which took just a shade over a half hour at that time of night, midnight. The house was at 10500 Cielo Drive, a quiet enclave in Benedict Canyon, with pretty fair space between homes.

"The seclusion of the house was a major consideration," Manson said. Watson parked on the street, jumped the chain-link fence, and scurried up the telephone pole to cut the wires. Then he directed Atkins, Krenwinkel, and Kasabian to jump the fence and follow him up the driveway toward the house, which was on a slight rise.

As they started up the driveway, a car approached from the direction of the house. Watson motioned the women to hide in the bushes off the driveway. He stood his ground, waited for the car to stop, and when it did, went to the passenger-side window and shot the driver four times.

Kasabian recoiled. This was not in the bill of fare. Watson, immediately sensing Kasabian's discomfort, told her to stay by the car while he, Atkins, and Krenwinkel went to the house to do their business. Kasabian moved to the car slowly and in a daze. From outside, she could hear screaming inside the house, but she remained frozen in the yard.

After Terry Melcher and Candice Bergen had moved out of 10500 Cielo Drive in the spring, film director Roman Polanski moved in with his new bride, actress Sharon Tate. Tate was a star-in-waiting with a couple of highly visible roles, in *Valley of the Dolls* and *Don't Make Waves*, the latter of which had a title song by the Byrds. But she had put her career on hold that summer as she prepared for the birth of her baby. She was eight and a half months pregnant on the night of August 8. Polanski, riding high from the success of his first American film, *Rosemary's Baby*, was in London preparing his next film, *The Day of the Dolphin*. To keep Tate company, Polanski asked one of his young Polish countrymen, Wojciech Frykowski, and his girlfriend, coffee heiress Abigail Folger, to move into the house.

That night, Sharon Tate had another houseguest, Jay Sebring. The haircutter to the stars was Tate's former boyfriend, long sentenced to the friend zone since she'd been with Polanski, but that didn't keep him from carrying a massive torch. He was the compassionate listener as Tate talked of her concerns about motherhood and her insecurities about her husband. She'd recently learned that since their marriage, Polanski had an affair with the beautiful Michelle Phillips of the Mamas and the Papas. Though Tate was stunningly beautiful and by all accounts genuine and kind, she was monumentally insecure, in part because of Polanski's compulsive philandering.

As Kasabian stood in the yard and listened to the screams, she had no idea who was being killed. She didn't know Sharon Tate from Ernest Borgnine. She just knew she was standing in the middle of a nightmare. "My body was there, but I wasn't," she recalled. As she waited, a man—Frykowski, as it turned out—staggered out of the house, bleeding profusely from several stab wounds. "He looked right into my eyes and he was dying," she said. "I felt he was dying because of me." A few moments later, Watson emerged from the house and stabbed Frykowski until he no longer fought.

Watson, Atkins, and Krenwinkel delivered over a hundred stab wounds to the four occupants of the house. For trying to protect Sharon Tate (*Can't you see she's pregnant?*), Jay Sebring was shot. In addition to being viciously stabbed, Tate was also hanged—she had rope burns on her neck—and when Watson and the girls left, Tate's and Sebring's bodies were connected by rope wrapped around their necks. Remembering the command to write something witchy, Atkins dipped a towel in Tate's blood and wrote PIG on the front door.

"Manson, on the night of the Tate murders, was trying to ignite Helter Skelter," said prosecutor Bugliosi. "It didn't matter who the victims were. The residence symbolized the show business establishment he was trying to penetrate, and they had rejected him."

A few yards away in the guest house, William Garretson, a caretaker hired by the 10500 Cielo Drive owner, was sitting in his living room writing letters and listening to music. He never heard a thing.

Atkins forgot her knife, but Watson had his compatriots dump most of the other evidence—including their clothing—in a ravine. When they got back to Spahn Ranch, they were on a high.

"Sadie was the first one out of the car," Manson said. "She was beaming with excitement as she ran up to me and threw her arms around my neck, saying, 'Oh, Charlie, we did it. . . . I took my life for you.'"

Watson filled Manson in on the details. Wanting to see for himself, Manson drove to 10500 Cielo Drive so he could do some final staging, to make it clear that the blacks were starting their war on whites. "My only concern was whether it resembled the Hinman killing," Manson said. Once he got to the Polanski-Tate residence, he was surprised how accurately his drug-fueled crew had described the killings. He wiped clean every place he figured his associates had touched, to make sure police would not get any clean fingerprints. He returned to the ranch after a little over an hour at the house on Cielo Drive.

When housekeeper Winifred Chapman arrived the next morning, she walked into a horrific scene in the living room. She screamed and ran from the house to where the bodies of Frykowski and Folger were on the lawn. Folger's white nightgown was so bloody it appeared to be another color.

When police arrived, they discovered Garretson in the guest house and took him in for questioning. His story was unbelievable. The driver of the car, the first person Watson killed, was a teenager named Steve Parent, who had the bad luck to visit Garretson on the night of a horrific murder.

Bugliosi called it "one of the most horror-filled, nightmarish nights of murder in the recorded annals of American crime. He [Manson] could get them to murder whoever he asked them to murder. Their credo was to kill as many people as they could."

As Susan Atkins said, they "wanted to do a crime that would shock the world, that the world would have to stand up and take notice."

News of the murders spread quickly, and Los Angeles responded with fear. There was a run on guns, security dogs, and alarm systems. All sorts of rumors spread, horrible stories about the victims, about Satan worship and black magic. The town was terrified.

Terry Melcher and Candice Bergen were walking on the sand at Malibu, where they were living in Doris Day's beach house. They were shaken, having learned what had happened at their former home. As they walked, they came across Lou Adler, the record producer and owner of a hot new label, Ode Records. He was with a young man, fairly new to town but making a lot of noise for his work with Neil Young and Joni Mitchell.

Melcher told Adler and his companion, David Geffen, about the near miss. They listened intently. Then Geffen asked if they planned to sell the beach house, because he wanted to buy it.

Manson wanted a repeat performance. "He said the murders the night before were too messy and he was going to show us how to do this," Kasabian said.

Manson loaded Watson, Atkins, Kasabian, Leslie Van Houten, and Clem Grogan into the car. Grogan was another rare male member of the Manson family and was, by all accounts, a drooling idiot. They drove around for a while until Manson selected a house on Waverly Drive, in the city's Los Feliz neighborhood. He'd once attended a party at the house next door. Once again, he had no idea who lived there.

He told the others to wait in the car while he scoped out the place. "I walked up a long driveway and looked in a window," he said. "The only person I could see was a heavy-set guy about forty-five years old who had fallen asleep while reading a newspaper." He went back to the car and got Watson, then returned to the house. Despite the dog—which, instead of growling, licked Manson's hand—Manson and Watson quietly sneaked into the house, where Manson nudged Leno LaBianca awake with the barrel of his gun.

"Who—who are you?" LaBianca asked. "What are you doing here? What do you want?"

"Just relax, pal," Manson said. "We're not going to hurt you, just be cool."

"That's easy enough for you to say," LaBianca said. "How can I help but be afraid when you've got a gun pointed at me?"

"It's all right, man," Manson reassured him. "All we want is your money. Is anyone else in the house?"

"My wife's in the bedroom. But don't bother her. I'll give you all I have."

Manson gave Watson a leather thong and told him to wrap up LaBianca. Back in the master bedroom, Manson found Rosemary LaBianca in bed. He pulled the covers off of her and said, "Wake up, lady, you've got company."

The LaBiancas had less than a hundred dollars in cash, which disappointed Manson. He went back out to the car and told Krenwinkel and Van Houten to go help Watson. "Do it good," he implored. "Make sure it's done so the pigs put it together with Hinman and that pad last night."

Krenwinkel and Van Houten went inside, where they found the LaBiancas tied up. Kasabian had been passed over and stayed behind. "I couldn't feel any relief," she said. "There was still that sense of dread. I knew some people were going to be killed."

Manson told Watson and the girls to hitchhike back to the ranch. He was taking the car so Atkins, Kasabian, and Grogan could find a house with other victims.

At the LaBianca house, the killers sought to create a scene that would again implicate the Black Panthers. They repeatedly stabbed the couple, leaving a fork protruding from Leno LaBianca's abdomen, onto which the word WAR was carved. Rosemary LaBianca was stabbed in the back. "Rosemary LaBianca had thirteen postmortem wounds," Bugliosi said. "She had already died and Leslie Van Houten continued to stab. That shows gusto, relish, enjoying what you're doing. Leslie Van Houten later said, 'The more I stabbed, the more fun it was.'"

The killers wrote DEATH TO PIGS and RISE on the wall in blood, and on the refrigerator, HEALTER SKELTER [sic]. The three of them showered, cleaned up, and made themselves dinner in the home where their victims lay, then hitchhiked back to Spahn Ranch.

Manson drove Atkins, Grogan, and Kasabian to a black neighborhood, where he asked Kasabian to leave the wallet they stole from Rosemary LaBianca in the women's room of a service station. He hoped a black customer would find the wallet and use the credit cards, making it clear that blacks had killed the LaBiancas. *Helter skelter.*

After ditching the wallet, Manson drove out to Venice Beach. Kasabian said she knew an actor with an apartment near the beach, and Manson dropped her off with Atkins and Grogan, with instructions to kill him, writing witchier, incriminating stuff on the wall. Kasabian walked up to the apartment door as Grogan and Atkins stood guard at the end of the hall. She purposely knocked on the wrong door, then told her companions that the target must've moved. They hitchhiked back to the ranch.

Kasabian decided she had to get away. "Innocent people were being murdered by this family that was supposed to be loving and caring and kind," she said. "They were basically little robots doing this killing that I didn't want to be a part of anymore."

It took a couple of days, but Kasabian concocted a ruse. She needed to take a car, she told Manson, to go see Bobby Beausoleil in jail. Though Manson didn't entirely trust her—Watson had told him of her hesitancy the night of the Tate murders—he let her drive off alone. She left her daughter, Tanya, but hoped she would be able to rescue her from the family.

Manson's plan backfired, due to the nature of police departments. Each case—Hinman, Tate, and LaBianca—was handled by detectives reluctant to share notes. Despite similarities, it took months for the murders to be linked. If springing Bobby Beausoleil was the goal, it didn't work.

"Bobby was still the prime suspect in the Hinman case," Manson said, "and we had not taken any of the heat off of him."

A week after the murders, police had Manson and most of the family in custody. Acting on a tip, they raided the ranch at 6 AM on Saturday, August 16. The cops thought they were coming down on a massive auto theft ring, so they were surprised by all of the guns at Spahn. A couple of days later, an attorney discovered that the search warrant for the ranch was misdated, and Manson and company were released.

Manson found Dennis Wilson at the apartment he'd rented from Gregg Jakobson after his hurried exit from the Sunset Boulevard estate. Wilson was playing the piano, and suddenly the door swung open and Manson was standing on the threshold. He demanded money. Making small talk, Wilson asked Manson where he'd been. "I been to the moon," Manson said. Wilson gave Manson the money he said he needed to fund the family's next move. Charlie showed up another time when Dennis was not home. He left a bullet with the houseguest, then asked about Dennis's beloved son, Scott. The implication was clear.

He also tracked down Terry Melcher at the beach house in Malibu. Melcher awoke one morning to find that a telescope had been moved from one side of the porch to another. He'd been creepy crawled.

Not long after the Spahn Ranch raid, Manson and his family migrated to Death Valley. One of the girls in the family provided entrée to the Myers Ranch, and Manson, with a select few of his followers, moved on to the nearby Barker Ranch, another location site for movies. Here, Manson told his followers they would find the bottomless pit, where they would wait out Helter Skelter before running to society in triumph, to rule the new world order.

Instead, police kept an eye on the family, even after the move to Death Valley. Stung by the misdated warrant fuckup, they shared information with the sheriff's office in Inyo County, where the family was living. Police raided the Barker Ranch on October 10 and found Manson hiding under a sink. In addition to auto theft, the police had additional charges against the family for defacing Death Valley National Park.

Now in police custody, one of the family members told authorities that Susan Atkins had been part of the Gary Hinman murder. She was charged and moved to a women's jail in Los Angeles, where she began bragging about the Tate killings to a fellow inmate, who soon told authorities. It took nearly two months of missed meetings and poor communication, but finally detectives learned that the Hinman, Tate, and LaBianca killings were all connected, and Charles Manson and members of his family were charged with murder.

The Manson news came as a shock to those who had met him. There was a mass sense of awareness—that crazy little dude, that whirling dervish, that appendage of Dennis Wilson . . . *that* was the guy? The guy with that freaky, crazy stare in all the newspapers?

And the community was struck. *It could've been me. It could've been us. He was in our house.*

Before long, the crimes were no longer referred to as the Tate-LaBianca murders. Instead, they became the Manson murders. As prosecutor Vincent Bugliosi said, "He upstaged the victims."

Manson changed Middle America's conception of hippies. They were hirsute but benign to many, the butt of Dean Martin jokes. But after Manson, hippies caused fear. "When Charlie was arrested, it had a devastating effect on the counterculture," said David Smith of the Haight-Ashbury Free Medical Clinic.

There was no doubt that the Manson murders drew a line of demarcation. "The historians in the United States, a lot of them, do attribute the demise of the generation of the sixties to the Tate-LaBianca murders and the Manson Family," said Steven Kay, who helped prosecute Manson and his followers. "Certainly, the hippies got terrible publicity from Manson and the Family and I think it did hasten their demise. Before, they were just kind of druggies, free spirits, throwing flowers around, taking their clothes off, free sex and stuff like that. But then after the Tate-LaBianca murders, people became genuinely afraid of hippies."

Thirty-five years after the murders, family member Sandra Good sat for an interview on a front porch in a Norman Rockwell neighborhood and defended Manson and the other murderers.

"My friends went all the way to the gas chamber for love of brother, to stop the war, for a lot of the causes that people were espousing in those times," she said. "We were for real and we did do it in the road. All the people who were saying they wanted to stop the war, and revolution, and all that—they turned their backs on us. They were fakes and frauds. In war, sometimes killing is needed."

Good did not participate in any of the Manson murders but served ten years in prison on charges of sending death threats through the mail.

Bruce Davis went to prison for his role assisting Manson with the Gary Hinman murder. He chose to explain, not to excuse, his actions. Drugs were partly responsible. Being vulnerable to the manipulations of a charismatic maniac also contributed. "You desensitize," Davis said. "It makes it easy to rationalize and to live with certain things that happen. When Tate-LaBianca happened, I refused to be in touch with how I felt. I succeeded in treating it as business as usual, another day at the farm."

At the same time, the extreme radicals embraced Manson. An underground magazine put him on the cover and proclaimed him man of the year. To some, Manson was a hero because he killed rich white people. Bernardine Dohrn of the Weather Underground, a rabid radical group of the time, spoke to a crowd not long after Manson and the family were arrested. "Dig it!" she shouted to the audience. "Manson killed those pigs, then they ate dinner in the same room with them, then they shoved a fork into a victim's stomach."

The week after the Manson murders, a half-million hippies gathered on a farm near Bethel, New York, for the Woodstock Music and Arts Festival, called "An Aquarian Exhibition." Promoters promised "Three Days of Peace and Music," which largely came true. One of the promoters was Artie Kornfeld, former songwriting partner of Jan Berry and Brian Wilson. He might win the award for the music career with the most twists and turns.

Getting to Woodstock was a mess. Fans driving to the festival abandoned their cars, blocking most access roads. Crosby, Stills, Nash and Young were to make only their second concert appearance, at Woodstock, in front of that sea of people.

Joni Mitchell wanted to go, but manager David Geffen said it was too chaotic and she might not be able to get back to New York City in time for a television appearance that Monday night. She watched reports of the festival on the television news and composed "Woodstock," which became the festival's anthem.

> *By the time we got to Woodstock*
> *We were half a million strong*

That fall, in an attempt to re-create Woodstock magic on the West Coast, members of Jefferson Airplane sought to stage a free concert in San Francisco's Golden Gate Park. Complications ensued, and the concert, now nicknamed Woodstock West, was rescheduled for the Altamont Speedway, an hour-and-a-half drive from San Francisco. The lineup was impressive: Jefferson Airplane (of course); Santana, a band that had made an indelible mark at Woodstock; the Flying Burrito Brothers, a country-rock band featuring former Byrds Gram Parsons, Chris Hillman, and Michael Clarke; the Grateful Dead; Crosby, Stills, Nash and Young; and, headlining—making their first American tour in three years—the Rolling Stones.

No one took credit for it, but *someone* hired the Hells Angels motorcycle club to provide security for the concert, paid with all the beer they could drink. One of the Angels punched Airplane singer Marty Balin during the performance, and the sense of dread was so overwhelming that the Grateful Dead refused to play. During the Rolling Stones' set, a man named Meredith Hunter was murdered in front of the stage by a Hells Angel with a knife.

A few weeks later, the sixties limped across the finish line.

Charles Manson never got that Warner Bros. recording contract, but he moved in the stratosphere of the Los Angeles music world at the end of the sixties. Neil Young and Dennis Wilson were only two upper-crusters of Los Angeles who knew Charlie. "A lot of pretty well-known musicians around L.A. knew Manson, though they'd probably deny it now," Young recalled.

Brian Wilson heard that when Manson was booked for the murders, in November 1969, he used his one phone call to try to reach Dennis Wilson. He wasn't home, and the friend who answered the phone wouldn't accept a collect call from Manson. "You're going to be fucking sorry!" Manson screamed.

Dennis gathered all of the music he'd recorded with Manson and destroyed the tapes. That music did not belong in this world, he said.

"The last time I spoke to Dennis about the Wizard," Brian said, "he had few words—just what a sick fuck Manson was. And what a lucky son of a bitch he was."

THE TAG

SUMMER'S GONE

Being called a musical genius was a cross to bear. Genius is a big word. But if you have to live up to something, you might as well live up to that.

—Brian Wilson

On January 13, 1971, Charles Manson, Susan Atkins, Leslie Van Houten, and Patricia Krenwinkel were found guilty of five counts of first-degree murder. They were sentenced to death. Charles "Tex" Watson was also found guilty of murder, in a separate trial in Texas.

All of their death sentences were commuted to life in prison. Susan Atkins claimed a religious conversion while behind bars and wrote a book about her turn to Christianity called *Child of Satan, Child of God*. She renounced Manson at every parole hearing and said she'd been brainwashed. She died at age sixty-one in 2009, having served forty years in California prisons.

While in prison, Tex Watson was ordained as a minister.

All of the Manson killers remain locked up, routinely denied parole. Leslie Van Houten was granted parole in summer 2016, but California governor Jerry Brown overturned the decision.

Family member Lynette "Squeaky" Fromme achieved notoriety in 1975 when she approached President Gerald Ford with a .45-caliber semiautomatic pistol. She was convicted of attempting to assassinate the president and sentenced to life in prison. She was paroled in 2009.

Several family members went into hiding. Linda Kasabian disappeared after testifying against Manson and the other killers. She was given immunity from prosecution. On the fortieth anniversary of the murders, she appeared in a documentary film but did not allow herself to be photographed clearly. After the film, she resumed her extremely private life.

Bobby Beausoleil was sentenced to death for the murder of Gary Hinman, but the sentence was commuted to life in prison. While in San Quentin in the early seventies, Beausoleil was interviewed by writer Truman Capote. Capote said that Beausoleil had continued his music career behind bars and was active in his local chapter of the Aryan Brotherhood.

Capote confronted Beausoleil with the accusation that the Tate and LaBianca murders would not have happened if Charles Manson had not been trying to cast blame for the Hinman murders on others. Capote reported that Beausoleil responded with silence. At other times, he seemed flip about it, with his self-described Zen approach of *It's all good*, including the murders.

"It's all right that Manson sent Tex Watson and those girls into that house to slaughter total strangers, innocent people—"

"Who says they were innocent?" Beausoleil interrupted. "They burned people on dope deals. Sharon Tate and that gang. They picked up kids on the Strip and took them home and whipped them. Made movies of it."

Referring to the murders committed in order to free Beausoleil, Capote asked, "And you don't regret that?"

"No," Beausoleil said. "If my brothers and sisters did it, then it's good. Everything in life is good. It all flows. It's all good. It's all music."

Capote served up a litany. "War. Starving children. Pain. Cruelty. Blindness. Prisons. Desperation. Indifference. All good?"

"What's that look you're giving me?" Beausoleil asked.

Capote's piece about the encounter, "Then It All Came Down," finally appeared in his 1980 book *Music for Chameleons*. Beausoleil immediately denied the impressions given by the interview and any association with the Aryan Brotherhood.

Beausoleil composed and recorded the soundtrack to Kenneth Anger's film *Lucifer Rising* in 1980.

The Beach Boys were resurrected in the seventies. Their albums *Sunflower* (1970) and *Surf's Up* (1971) were among the finest of their career. Brian Wilson was increasingly erratic and reclusive, staying in bed for months at a time while the touring band won raves for immaculate concert performances and took over songwriting and production duties in the recording studio.

The group moved to the Netherlands for much of 1972 and built a state-of-the-art studio, hoping the change of scenery would inspire Brian. It did not. His sole contribution was "Mount Vernon and Fairway," a fairy tale about a prince seeking the lost chord of God from a magic transistor radio. It took its name from the location of Mike Love's childhood home, where the boys harmonized when they were young. Warner Bros. executives were first baffled, then infuriated by the story-song. Realizing that rejecting the piece might destroy Brian, it was released on a separate seven-inch record packaged with the album. If the fairy tale had been recorded by anyone but Brian Wilson, it likely would never have been released.

As critic Jim Miller wrote in *Rolling Stone*, "In its recounting of an encounter with a glowing transistor radio playing divine rock, Brian's whimsy perhaps strikes an autobiographical note. His occasional music for the tale is quirky and inspired, while the snippets of several new songs included are both frustrating and tantalizing. It hopefully does the rest of the group no disservice to remark that Brian, even in such enigmatic expressions as 'Mount Vernon and Fairway,' remains the Beach Boys' most profound source of creative energy; it is Brian who sets the group's musical standards."

Brian collaborated on two other pieces for *Holland*, as the album was called, but one of those was an old song from the vaults. The move to the Netherlands was a financial debacle.

By 1976, the situation was intolerable. Brian was a lost soul, adrift in a sea of blankets and bedclothes. "Meals happened without me," he recalled. "Kids went to school and came back and I might still be in a bathrobe up in the bedroom or downstairs, sitting at the piano, still in the bathrobe."

Finally, Marilyn Wilson hired a round-the-clock psychologist, Eugene Landy, to help Brian reenter the world. Brian did come back, producing and writing two albums for the group. The record company launched a promotional campaign touting that Brian was back. He was, in a way. He had lost that wistful look and often looked like a chain-smoking grizzly, but physically, he was back. And so Dr. Landy was dismissed. Within a couple of years, Brian was worse off than he had ever been. By the early eighties, Brian was again in a drugged stupor, separated from Marilyn Wilson and their children, ballooning to 340 pounds, and living in sloth. The group asked Landy to return. Landy and his team brought Brian Wilson back to the living, but on Landy's terms. He became Brian's business partner, claiming composing and producing credits and looting Brian and his family.

While Landy took complete control of Brian's life, Dennis Wilson was careening toward death, at thirty-nine, in 1983. Although the band continued throughout the eighties and into the nineties, without Dennis and with only limited interest from Brian, the group went into a prolonged creative skid. The death of Carl Wilson from cancer in 1998 appeared to be the group's death knell.

The Beach Boys perfected the art of suing each other. Brian's 1991 autobiography, *Wouldn't It Be Nice*, pissed off nearly everyone in his world. Audree Wilson sued her eldest son, and Carl Wilson sued his big brother. Mike Love filed suit and also decided to sue for his unacknowledged contributions to songs credited solely to Brian. Brian sued to regain rights to the Sea of Tunes songs his father had sold cheap in 1969. This suit cited his mental incompetence and his father's forgeries. Brian won. The songs Murry Wilson sold for $700,000 in 1969 were valued at $65 million at the time Brian regained control.

The Beach Boys were inducted into the Rock and Roll Hall of Fame in 1988, in a class of inductees that included the Beatles, the Rolling Stones, and Bob Dylan. When it came his turn to speak, Mike Love delivered a rambling and deranged attack on nearly every other performer in the room, calling them wimps compared to the Beach Boys. During *his* induction speech, Bob Dylan said, "I'd like to thank Mike Love for not mentioning me."

Eventually Mike wrested control of the Beach Boys name and began touring with an aggregation under that banner—a group that included only himself and Bruce Johnston from the original Beach Boys. In response to the criticism that the Beach Boys without a Wilson cannot truly be the Beach Boys, Johnston defended his bandmate: "Everybody's kind of tried to dial Mike out and make Brian a deity. You get so swept away by Brian's incredible production abilities that people probably overlook the fact that they hear all this through Mike Love's words."

In the midnineties, Al Jardine formed a touring act called the Beach Boys Family and Friends. In addition to his sons, Jardine's group included longtime Beach Boys sidemen as well as Brian and Marilyn's daughters, Carnie and Wendy Wilson. The Wilson girls had found success, teamed with Chynna Phillips, daughter of John and Michelle Phillips, in the trio Wilson Phillips. The Jardine touring group also included Owen Elliot, Cass Elliot's only child.

Love sued, and Jardine was ordered to no longer tour under a name that referenced the Beach Boys. "Mike has his own vision of what the Beach Boys are," Jardine said, "and he doesn't need us anymore. It's like, 'Wow, that hurts.'"

In 1997, Capitol released a box set called *The Pet Sounds Sessions*, devoted to the recording of the album by then acknowledged as one of the greatest achievements of the rock 'n' roll era. In 2012, Capitol Records released a box set of Brian Wilson's 1966–1967 recordings called *The Smile Sessions*. It won a Grammy Award.

Hell froze over in 2013 when the surviving Beach Boys reunited. The revived group included David Marks, absent for four decades. He'd had a moderately successful music career interrupted by occasional drug and alcohol abuse. Clean and sober, he'd toured with the Love-Johnston–other guys Beach Boys group in the nineties.

The success of *The Smile Sessions* led the group to mount a fiftieth anniversary album and tour. Instead of an exercise in quick-cash nostalgia, *That's Why God Made the Radio* had the beautiful and heartbreaking melancholy Brian explored so well on *Today* and *Pet Sounds*. There were a few *remember when* crowd pleasers on the album, but the trilogy of songs at the conclusion—"From There to Back Again," "Pacific Coast Highway," and "Summer's Gone"—were magnificent in their grand despair. Despite their age and history, the Beach Boys rarely sounded as beautiful as they did on "Summer's Gone."

> *One day begins, another ends*
> *I live them all and back again*

If the Beach Boys ended up never recording another note, that song made a satisfying farewell.

The tour's nightly excellence astonished critics. When the tour concluded at the end of summer, Mike Love took his version of the Beach Boys back on the road, and the group returned to doing what it did so well: suing each other.

The estrangement deepened. "I have nothing but sympathy for Brian," Mike Love said. "When somebody in your family suffers from a mental illness, sometimes it's gone past the opportunity to have a normal relationship."

The Wilson hell house on 119th Street in Hawthorne no longer exists. It was torn down to make way for a freeway ramp. Scott Wilson, the son of Dennis Wilson who'd been threatened by Charles Manson, was a building contractor and erected a monument to the Beach Boys at the site of the Wilson home. He published a memoir called *Son of a Beach Boy* in 2015.

———

Van Dyke Parks released solo albums every presidential election cycle for many years and continued producing other artists and scoring films. Among his albums was a 1998 masterwork called *Orange Crate Art*, a collaboration with Brian Wilson.

He was, as always, happily removed from the mainstream—even more so as the old century died and the new one began.

"Rock became a corporate classification, just like the blues," Parks said. "They took off its sexual organs. Some people got paid a lot of money to bottle the rebellion of the sixties, and that's when it started to mean zero to me. To me, 1969 really suggested the death knell of the counter-culture revolution. The terrible event of Charles Manson showed the cultism of the period; I was always wary of crowds. I didn't go to Woodstock. I didn't want to be in a mudflat waiting to get into a portable toilet. I thought it was a terrible idea. So I stayed at my office at Warner Bros. . . . I don't even know what happened around then, for many reasons. One is I was working so hard and was too busy to really get totally turned around by what other people were doing."

When the Beach Boys' contract with Capitol expired in 1969, no suitors lined up to sign the veteran and apparently passé act. Parks was able to help.

"The Beach Boys were at a very low point in their career," he said. "They'd left Capitol Records, but they ended up at Warner Bros. because I personally begged Mo Ostin to sign them. And they were considered a problem at that time. They were an industry albatross, simply because there were so many egos involved.

Everyone at the label just wanted Brian Wilson to come over and write some songs."

Warner signed the Beach Boys and secured a significant participation from Brian for *Sunflower*, released in October 1970, complete with a thank-you note on the back cover from Ostin. He appreciated Warner being the new home of the Beach Boys.

A couple of years later, the relationship had soured, but Parks again came to the rescue of his old friend and his not so merry band, which had just spent buttloads of money moving to the Netherlands and recording there for a year. The resulting album was considered unreleasable by the record company, so Parks—then Warner's vice president for audio and visual—revived his collaboration with Brian Wilson.

"I still had a demo tape of 'Sail On, Sailor,'" Parks said. "I came up with that lyric when I was working with Brian, as well as the pitches those words reside on. I did nothing with that tape until I saw the Beach Boys crisis at the company where I was working, earning $350 a week. Well, they recorded the song, and it was a hit. . . . You could say I did the Beach Boys a nice turn there. It was just a nice thing to do."

Jan Berry learned to walk and talk again and, after a decade in the wilderness, returned to performing. He and Dean Torrence revived their career, mostly on the oldies circuit. They had a successful phase two (as they called it), and interest in the duo was reignited in 1978 by a television film about Berry's struggles called *Deadman's Curve*.

Jan Berry died on March 26, 2004, after suffering a seizure. He had endured years of dependency on painkillers.

In 2010, the experimental *Carnival of Sound* was finally released. This was the densely creative album Berry made after his accident, when he was relearning how to live.

Dean Torrence remains a successful and much-honored graphic designer, owner of Kittyhawk Graphics. His memoir is titled *Surf City*.

Barry Keenan, the inept kidnapper of Frank Sinatra Jr., was found by the court to be legally insane at the time he and his two hapless accomplices abducted the singer. This determination came four years into Keenan's sentence, which was soon commuted. He was judged to no longer be a threat to society and was released.

He started a new life after prison, becoming a real estate mogul. He also pushed hard to get Hollywood to make him famous by making a film about the kidnapping. *Stealing Sinatra* debuted on the Showtime cable network on January 24, 2003. David Arquette played Keenan, and William H. Macy played John Irwin.

Keenan's success as a mogul cast him into the social circle of Los Angeles celebrity. As he sipped martinis at high-end parties, he sometimes noticed above the rim of his glass Frank Sinatra Jr. across the room. They did not speak.

Frank Sinatra Jr. died March 16, 2016, while on concert tour. He was seventy-two.

The Mamas and the Papas made four albums, broke up, then released the pallid *People Like Us* in 1971, to fulfill contractual obligations.

John Phillips became one of the most prolific drug users of his generation. His intake was so staggering that witnessing him, Keith Richards of the Rolling Stones was said to be in awe. Substance abuse crippled his planned solo career, and he never achieved the success of the days with his quartet, though he cowrote the Beach Boys' number-one hit "Kokomo" with Mike Love and Terry Melcher in 1986. Busted for drug trafficking and in need of money, he revived the Mamas and the Papas with Denny Doherty, Spanky McFarlane (in the Cass Elliot role), and his daughter from his first marriage, Mackenzie Phillips, an actress mostly known for her role in *American Graffiti*. He died of heart failure in 2001 at age sixty-five. Soon after his death, Mackenzie published a memoir, *High on Arrival*, stating that her father raped her and that they had a decadelong incestuous relationship.

Cass Elliot had the greatest success apart from the group and moved away from rock music, becoming recognized as a versatile singer and all-around entertainer. She died in London at 33, of a heart attack. She was survived by her daughter, Owen Elliot.

Denny Doherty had a *take it or leave it* attitude toward his career after the Mamas and the Papas ended. He joined John Philips in revivals of the group. He died in 2007, back home in Canada, from an abdominal aortic aneurysm. He was sixty-six.

Michelle Phillips led the campaign to get the Mamas and the Papas into the Rock and Roll Hall of Fame. She succeeded in 1998. She acted in film and television and raised Chynna Phillips, her daughter with John.

Joni Mitchell became one of the most celebrated and respected singer-songwriters of her generation. She continued her musical growth and moved beyond folk rock and into the realm of jazz, collaborating with such great artists as Charles Mingus. Her string of albums in the early seventies, including *Blue* and *Court and Spark*, are among the most distinctive recordings of the modern era.

In the eighties, she was reunited with the daughter she'd left in foster care, of whom she'd mournfully sung in "Little Green" on *Blue*. Her daughter found her, and they inaugurated an adult and loving child-and-parent relationship.

After Mitchell suffered a brain aneurysm in 2015, she began a long road to recovery.

Dennis Hopper and Peter Fonda said they used David Crosby and Roger McGuinn as their models for their *Easy Rider* characters. Indeed, one of the film's best sequences was of the bikers roaring through the western desert while the Byrds' "Wasn't Born to Follow" played on the soundtrack.

The success of *Easy Rider* nearly killed Hopper. Drunk on his long-sought recognition after years in the film industry, he gorged at a buffet of drink and drugs. His next directorial effort, *The Last Movie*, was a cursed production almost brought down by Hopper's excesses. It flopped. His marriage to Michelle Phillips lasted eight days. His drug use could have supported the economy of a Central American country.

Eventually he sobered up, and a decade after *Easy Rider*, he began making several memorable films as an actor, including *Apocalypse Now* and *Blue Velvet*, as well as *Hoosiers*, for which he was nominated for an Academy Award. He died of prostate cancer in 2010, at age seventy-four.

Peter Fonda transcended the biker genre and won praise for several intelligent and restrained performances, including *The Hired Hand*, *Ninety-Two in the Shade*, and *Ulee's Gold*.

Jack Nicholson was famous after his performance in *Easy Rider* and became one of Hollywood's most enduring stars.

The musicians known as the Wrecking Crew finally achieved the fame they deserved, thanks to books and documentaries. Denny Tedesco, son of studio guitarist Tommy Tedesco, worked on his film *The Wrecking Crew* for nearly twenty years before it was finally released in 2015. Several of the musicians, including Hal Blaine, Carol Kaye, and Don Randi, wrote memoirs—Randi's was called *You Have Heard These Hands*—and others were recognized by the Musicians Hall of Fame. Blaine and Earl Palmer have been inducted into the Rock and Roll Hall of Fame.

Carol Kaye frequently pointed out that no one used the term the "Wrecking Crew" during the sixties and that the name was devised by Hal Blaine in order to market one of his books. Kaye said the only name she recalled being used to describe the session regulars was the Clique.

Several of the studio greats have died, including Palmer, Tedesco, Larry Knechtel, Mike Deasy, Ray Pohlman, Barney Kessel, Billy Strange, and Steve Douglas.

Leon Russell (real name Claude Russell Bridges) and Glen Campbell both had hugely successful solo careers when their studio days ended. Russell was part of the Mad Dogs and Englishmen aggregation behind Joe Cocker before launching his solo career. Campbell served a brief season as a stage replacement for Brian Wilson, then found his greatest success as a singer working with songwriter Jimmy Webb on "By the Time I Get to Phoenix," "Galveston," and "Wichita Lineman."

By the end of the sixties, P. F. Sloan disappeared. Sickened by his experience in the music business, he went into a long period of seclusion. During his absence, Jimmy Webb wrote a song about him.

> *I have been seeking P. F. Sloan*
> *But no one knows where he has gone*

In an odd twist, Brian Wilson's psychologist Eugene Landy said he was, in fact, P. F. Sloan, which gave him the right to exert influence over his damaged client's musical career. Landy, a pathological liar, claimed to have written all of the songs credited to Sloan.

Eventually, the real P. F. Sloan stood up, describing his missing years as "catatonia" and also alluding to a spiritual vision quest. He recorded once a decade or so but never again actively sought the spotlight. He published his autobiography not long before his death from pancreatic cancer in 2015.

Jim Morrison managed to make two fine albums with the Doors after the disappointing *Waiting for the Sun* and *The Soft Parade*.

The group explored blues and jazz on *Morrison Hotel* and *L.A. Woman*, both of which became staples of FM radio, and continued to sell well into the next century. Morrison died in 1971. Bloated from severe drinking, he suffered a heart attack at twenty-seven while living in Paris. He was buried in the City of Light, and his grave became a shrine.

The Doors continued without him and in later years performed with guest vocalists. The group was inducted into the Rock and Roll Hall of Fame in 1993.

Ray Manzarek died of cancer in 2013, at age seventy-four. Robby Krieger and John Densmore continued to be active in the music industry.

Phil Spector had often plucked singers from obscurity, made great records with them, then moved on. After three years of retirement, he wanted to prove he hadn't lost his touch and pulled Sonny Charles and the Checkmates, Ltd. from lounge act status and made an impeccable, soulful record of "Black Pearl," a song Spector coauthored. Having made his point, he dropped Mr. Charles and company.

The Beatles called on Spector to supervise the release of *Let It Be* in 1970. The tapes had been sitting around for nearly a year when Spector took over the project, undercutting the group's desire to create a "Beatles with their pants down" record. Spector added strings and female choirs to several of the tracks, tremendously irritating Paul McCartney. He then coproduced solo albums by John Lennon and George Harrison and did occasional productions with Leonard Cohen, Dion, and the Ramones. He had essentially retired (really) from the music business by 2002 when actress Lana Clarkson was found in his home, dead from a gunshot wound. Spector was found guilty of second-degree murder in 2009 and was sentenced to nineteen years to life in prison.

Bill Medley left the Righteous Brothers briefly at the end of the sixties but returned in time for "Rock and Roll Heaven," a massive hit in the early seventies. The group still played the supper club circuit until 1991, when "Unchained Melody," Phil Spector's payback to Bobby Hatfield, reached number one after being used in the film *Ghost*. Hatfield died in 2003 of a heart attack brought on by cocaine use. He was sixty-three.

Jackie DeShannon continued her recording career through the beginning of the eighties, then resumed her behind-the-scenes role as a songwriter. She is also a rock 'n' roll commentator for satellite radio. Her greatest success came with "Put a Little Love in Your Heart" in 1968.

Frank Sinatra had a long and hugely successful career in film, recording, and live performance. His recordings for Capitol in the fifties and for his own label, Reprise, in the sixties, are considered his greatest works—and some of the most sublime works in the history of recorded music. He never learned to like rock 'n' roll, though the record label he founded became a major force in popular music. He died at eighty-two after suffering a massive heart attack.

Morris Levy, the mob-connected owner of Roulette Records, sued John Lennon after the Beatles appropriated a line from Chuck Berry's "You Can't Catch Me," for which Levy controlled the copyright, in "Come Together" on *Abbey Road*, the last album the group recorded. As part of the settlement, Lennon promised to record three

Levy-owned songs on an album he was then making with Phil Spector. Those sessions collapsed, but Levy released the tapes anyway. Lennon then sued Levy and won.

In 1988, Levy was convicted of extortion after a three-year FBI investigation and died of cancer in prison in 1990.

After brother Bobby Fuller's death, Randy Fuller took over the band and renamed it after himself. It didn't last, and Fuller spent a fitful couple of years trying to go solo. Eventually he joined a reconstituted Buffalo Springfield, led by the group's drummer, Dewey Martin. The Springfield's other former members objected to the name New Buffalo Springfield, so Martin changed it to Blue Mountain Eagle before recording an album for ATCO Records. Fuller stayed with Martin through the run of his next group, Medicine Ball, and then returned to El Paso and maintained a career in music.

Boyd Elder, the El Paso friend who was one of the first to find the body of Bobby Fuller in 1966, later became an artist and created album covers for the Eagles, including *One of These Nights* and *Their Greatest Hits*, the bestselling album of the twentieth century.

David Crosby was nearly destroyed by prolific drug use, but an arrest in Texas in the eighties (followed by conviction and incarceration) saved his life. He remained sober after jail and resumed his career with Crosby, Stills and Nash (and sometimes Young). He is a two-time inductee into the Rock and Roll Hall of Fame, for the Byrds and Crosby, Stills and Nash.

Roger (formerly Jim) McGuinn kept the Byrds going for several years despite being its sole remaining original member. His latter-day version of the group—the brilliant Clarence White on guitar, Gene Parsons (no relation to Gram), and Skip Battin (songwriting partner of Kim Fowley) was together longer than the original group and earned a reputation for energetic and satisfying performances. They also produced excellent albums, such as *(Untitled)* and *Farther Along,* that stood alongside albums by the original members.

McGuinn owned the rights to the name but agreed to retire it after the original group reunited in 1973 on David Geffen's Asylum label. The reunion was short-lived.

In the late seventies, McGuinn formed a trio with Gene Clark and Chris Hillman, and in 1990, McGuinn, Hillman, and Crosby reunited to play a benefit as the Byrds (and were joined onstage by Bob Dylan). The five original members reunited for their induction to the Rock and Roll Hall of Fame in 1991. Within two years, Clark and Michael Clarke died. Gene Clark's death at forty-six was deemed due to natural causes. Michael Clarke died of liver failure at forty-seven.

———————

After leaving the Byrds, Gram Parsons formed the Flying Burrito Brothers with ex-Byrd Chris Hillman. After a year, former Byrd Michael Clarke joined the group. The Parsons-era Burrito Brothers released *The Gilded Palace of Sin* and *Burrito Deluxe.* Those two albums—along with the Byrds' *Sweetheart of the Rodeo* and Poco's *Pickin' Up the Pieces*—formed the sacred texts of country rock.

After leaving the Burritos, Parsons pursued a solo career on Reprise Records, with *GP* and *Grievous Angel,* his posthumous album that introduced the world to his protégé, Emmylou Harris. She went on to a long and excellent career, which began with her Reprise albums in the seventies.

Parsons died at twenty-six of a drug overdose in September 1973 while visiting Joshua Tree National Park. Charles Manson's old prison buddy, Phil Kaufman, a road manager for rock stars and one of Gram's close friends, abducted Parsons's body from Los Angeles International Airport, where it was to be loaded onto a flight to New Orleans for a family funeral. Kaufman drove the corpse to Joshua Tree and burned Parsons's body in the desert.

———————

The three surviving members of Buffalo Springfield, Stephen Stills, Neil Young, and Richie Furay, reunited for a benefit performance in 2010 and at the Bonnaroo Festival in 2011. Stills and Young had a second career together as part of Crosby, Stills, Nash and Young.

Stills continued to record solo in the early seventies but cut back considerably in the late eighties, spending most of his musical energy on the various derivations of Crosby, Stills, Nash and Young.

Young aggressively pursued a recording career that saw him work in country, blues, and electronic music, as well as rock 'n' roll (usually with his collaborators Crazy Horse). He was widely hailed for his willingness to experiment and change styles.

One of Young's most daring albums was his jittery and frightening *Tonight's the Night*, released in 1975. Written with fury and sadness in response to the drug-related deaths of two friends—Danny Whitten of Crazy Horse and roadie Bruce Berry (brother of Jan Berry)—the album was held back for two years because Reprise Records thought it was too bleak for release. When it was, it was praised by critics and was ranked by *Rolling Stone* as one of the five hundred greatest albums in rock history.

Furay was in Poco and the David Geffen–assembled supergroup Souther-Hillman-Furay Band, featuring former Byrd Chris Hillman and J. D. Souther, along with such stellar sidemen as drummer Jim Gordon of the Wrecking Crew and steel guitarist Al Perkins. The group failed to meet its expectations. Furay moved to Colorado, pursued a modest solo career, and served as pastor of Calvary Chapel in Broomfield, Colorado.

Buffalo Springfield was inducted to the Rock and Roll Hall of Fame in 1996. Bruce Palmer died of heart failure in 2004, at fifty-eight. Dewey Martin died in 2009, of natural causes, at sixty-eight. Palmer's replacement, Jim Messina, was an excellent producer and engineer in addition to being a fine musician. He joined Furay in Poco, then formed a hugely successful duo with one of his producing clients, Kenny Loggins. After five years of million-selling albums, Messina launched a solo career.

Despite producing such masterpieces as *Younger than Yesterday*, *The Notorious Byrd Brothers*, and *Sweetheart of the Rodeo*, Gary Usher was fired by Columbia Records in 1968 but recovered from that setback by starting his own label, Together Records, which released archival material. He collaborated with Brian Wilson again in the late eighties, though little came of their union. Usher died of cancer at age fifty-one in 1990.

Jim Gordon, the in-demand Wrecking Crew drummer who played on classic albums by the Beach Boys and the Byrds, later joined the Souther-Hillman-Furay Band, the British group Traffic, and Derek and the Dominos with Eric Clapton. His piano exercise was grafted onto a Clapton melody to become the classic-rock staple "Layla."

Gordon developed schizophrenia and by 1983 was so deeply disturbed that he beat his mother with a hammer, then stabbed her to death. He is in a psychiatric prison in Vacaville, California.

Murry Wilson died of a heart attack at age fifty-five in 1973. Neither Brian nor Dennis Wilson attended his funeral. Dennis named his last child Gage, which was Murry's middle name.

Dennis Wilson emerged as the most intriguing Beach Boys composer in the early seventies. His songs on *Sunflower* and *Holland* were highlights of those albums. But tension between Dennis and Mike Love caused Dennis's work to sometimes be pushed aside. Despite having several fine songs recorded, none of Dennis's compositions appeared on *Surf's Up*. He made a stab at a film career, costarring with James Taylor and Warren Oates in *Two-Lane Blacktop*. He nearly made the cut for the ensemble cast of *The Choirboys* but was passed over in the end. He never played another film role.

Wilson was volatile off stage, once shattering a sliding-glass door with a punch that severed tendons in his hand. For a couple of years he couldn't play drums but took to standing at the front of the stage with the Beach Boys, exhorting the audience to sing along.

His private life was also subject to change without notice. He was twice divorced when he married Karen Lamm, a midwestern beauty who had a semisuccessful modeling career before becoming the rock-star wife of Robert Lamm, keyboardist in the brass rock band Chicago. Wilson and Lamm began their romance when Chicago and the Beach Boys toured together in 1974. It was a passionate and explosive marriage, and they were married and divorced twice. Once, in a fit of anger, Dennis set Karen's Ferrari afire.

At a birthday party for keyboardist Billy Preston in 1974, Wilson presented Preston with a half-finished song called "You Are So Beautiful." Preston finished the song, and Wilson, intending it as a gift, refused composer credit and the song's significant royalties. The song became a huge hit for Joe Cocker, and for years, Dennis sang it solo as the first encore at Beach Boys concerts.

The band's infighting dispirited Dennis. Referring primarily to Mike Love, Dennis suggested to a journalist that it might be time for the group to call it quits. "If these people want to take this beautiful, happy, spiritual music we've made and all the things we stand for and throw it out the window just because of money, then there's something wrong with the whole thing and I don't want any part of it," he said.

In 1977, Dennis became the first member of his group to emerge from the family cocoon and launch a solo career. His album, *Pacific Ocean Blue*, was received with unanimous praise and midrange sales. "He was not only under-appreciated in the rock world," Al Jardine said, "he was under-appreciated in our band. We didn't know what we had."

But rather than build on the album's critical success, Dennis began to free-fall. A planned follow-up, *Bambu*, went unreleased. Dennis lost his creative home when the Beach Boys sold Brother Studios in Santa Monica. A chain-smoker, his always rough voice became painful to hear.

Dennis's alcoholism and cocaine use cost him his fortune and rock-star perks. Mike Love called him a "drugged-out no-talent parasite." He had a romance with Fleetwood Mac pianist Christine McVie, whose substance abuse paled next to Dennis's problems. He then married Shawn Love, a teenager who claimed she was Mike's illegitimate daughter. She and Dennis had a son, Gage.

Eventually Dennis's bank foreclosed on his beloved sailboat, the *Harmony*. In and out of treatment programs, he spent the last weeks of life homeless, wandering the coastal streets of Santa Monica, pulling from an ever-present jug of orange juice and vodka. The *Harmony* had been moved to another marina when it was repossessed, and Dennis often visited the empty slip his boat used to occupy. Still friends with dockside neighbors, he was diving off the pier one Sunday afternoon, finding artifacts thrown overboard during long-ago arguments with Karen. It was wintertime, cold, and Dennis was obviously drunk. Yet despite warnings from friends, he continued to dive.

When he didn't come up, friends called police. Dennis was found on the floor of the bay, curled into a fetal position. It was December 28, 1983.

President Ronald Reagan waived the restrictions on burials at sea, and the body of Dennis Wilson was committed to the waters off the Los Angeles coast.

Shawn Love died of cancer in 2003. Dennis is survived by his children, Scott, Jennifer, Carl, Michael, and Gage.

Carl Wilson, whose angelic voice framed "Good Vibrations," "God Only Knows," "I Can Hear Music," and so many other songs of divine beauty, died in 1998 from brain and lung cancer. He was fifty-one. He helped found the group when he was sixteen.

In the early eighties, with his brothers incapacitated by drugs, Carl challenged his bandmates to do better. He boycotted the group, recording two solo albums and touring with a soul-flavored band. He returned to the Beach Boys in time to lend his signature voice to "Kokomo," a number-one song in 1988. (The song was written by Mike Love, John Phillips, Scott McKenzie, and Terry Melcher. Brian Wilson did not participate in the recording.)

Carl's teenage marriage to Annie Hinsche endured nearly twenty years and produced two sons, Justyn and Jonah. The couple divorced in 1978, in part because of his relentless touring schedule. Annie's brother Billy Hinsche was part of Dino, Desi and Billy, a popular midsixties trio that included the sons of Dean Martin and Desi Arnaz. In 1987, Carl married Gina Martin, Dean Martin's daughter.

"The last time I saw Carl," Van Dyke Parks said, "I played 'Ave Maria' at his mother's funeral, and he embraced me afterwards. To be with him and Brian at Audree's funeral was a very big deal to me, personally."

A smoker since age thirteen, Carl continued to perform after receiving his diagnosis and while undergoing chemotherapy treatment.

Though few would have believed it back in the seventies, the only Wilson brother to survive into the twenty-first century was Brian.

Being married to him during his reclusive years was a trial, but Marilyn Wilson managed to do so for fifteen years. Their two daughters, Carnie and Wendy, followed their father into the music business.

His drug use was off the charts after his marriage to Marilyn ended, but once the group brought back psychologist Eugene Landy, Brian seemed, finally, settled. Eventually, after reclaiming his life in the late eighties and jettisoning the controlling and abusive Landy, he married Melinda Ledbetter, and together they raised five children—Dakota, Daria, Dylan, Dash, and Delanie.

Brian surprised the rock 'n' roll world by becoming a prolific recording and performing artist. He made his first solo album in 1988. In the nineties, his output became bountiful, and it has remained steady.

He worked with the urgency of a man about to burst into flame. He performed with a band of supremely talented acolytes who could quote chapter and verse on his music. Considering his emotional history, audiences would have been justified in expecting a train wreck onstage. Instead, the concerts were unflaggingly superb.

On his 2000 tour, he played *Pet Sounds* in its entirety. In 2002, he announced the debut of *Smile* forty-two years after he scrapped the project. After months of working with the archivists in his band, he assembled the *Smile* he recalled from 1966 and performed it live. At its London debut, audience members wept.

That fall, he recorded and released *Brian Wilson Presents Smile*. He continued to tour widely and released albums devoted to George Gershwin and the music from Disney films. In other collaborations, he worked with Bob Dylan and British guitar virtuoso Jeff Beck, as well as such younger artists as Kacey Musgraves, Zooey Deschanel, Sebu, and Nate Ruess. In 2016, he returned to playing *Pet Sounds* on stage in its entirety, to mark the fiftieth anniversary of the album's release.

Five decades into his career, Brian Wilson regularly accumulated accolades and was often proclaimed one of the great composers of his time. Rock 'n' roll scripture featured the narrative of the painfully shy boy who so effectively chronicled the hopes and dreams of America, then walked a torturous path through drugs and madness to eventually find joy and contentment on the other side of the abyss. The story was told in a biographical film called *Love and Mercy*, in which two actors shared the lead role. Paul Dano was Brian in the *Pet Sounds* years, and John Cusack played the damaged Brian of twenty years later, reeling from Dennis's death and tortured and manipulated by Eugene Landy. *New York Times* critic A. O. Scott called the film "smart, compassionate, [and] refreshingly unconventional."

Among Brian's many prizes was a Kennedy Center Honor in 2007. The proclamation read, "He is rock and roll's gentlest revolutionary, and the songs he wrote for the Beach Boys have been among the most joyfully influential and exhilarating vibrations in the history of music in our time. There is real humanity in his body of work, vulnerable and sincere, authentic and unmistakably American. . . . 'We wanted to bring some love to the world,' remembered Brian Wilson. 'I thought we were good at doing that.' God only knows, that's true."

Creating art allows us to beat the odds and find immortality, without having to do the whole Doctor Faustus thing. Though Brian Wilson and Mike Love no longer collaborate and Carl and Dennis Wilson are gone, they are all still together on the radio late at night, where they join voices and are young and golden and beautiful forever.

ACKNOWLEDGMENTS

Deepest appreciation to the Dana Farber Cancer Institute. Everyone there—nurses, surgeons, technicians, and receptionists—encouraged me as I labored on this book during my illness. Work was the best therapy.

Bottomless gratitude to my tribal council for suggestions, support, and patience. Thank you, Lisa Bassett, Mary Chapman, and Sarah Kess. I could not have made it through my illness or the writing of this book without you. Two dear friends freely offered their abundant kindness and wisdom. Thank you, Andrea Billups and Noelle Dinant Graves.

At Boston University, big props to my College of Communication colleagues Tobe Berkowitz, Barton Carter, Abigail Clement, Christopher Daly, Anne Donohue, Tom Fiedler, Allison Hoyt, Dick Lehr, Maureen Mahoney, Elizabeth Mehren, Charles O'Connor, R. D. Sahl, Nathaniel Taylor, Jennifer Underhill, Susan Walker, and Mitchell Zuckoff. They all helped, often without realizing they were helping. The university also houses the magnificent Howard Gotlieb Archival Research Center and the people who make it the grand place that it is: Sean Noel, Alex Rankin, and the glorious Vita Palladino. I worked daily in the Paul Pratt Memorial Library in Cohasset, Massachusetts, and I thank the staff for not calling the cops on me for loitering. It was also a swell place to take a nap.

Jeff Grossman and Joe Madden helped me talk through the story over countless beers. *Cheers, boys!* Other friends over the years helped forge and deepen my appreciation of the musicians in this book. Thank you, Neil, Wayne, Bill, John, and Steve.

Everlasting thanks to Jane and Miriam, the namesakes of Dystel and Goderich Literary Management. Nothing happens without them; everything happens because of them.

I've long admired the music books from Chicago Review Press, and so I'm thrilled to publish with this company. Standing ovation for senior editor Jerome Pohlen for his tolerance and dedication and for keeping me in line. Figurative high-fives also to Caitlin Eck, Geoff George, Jonathan Hahn, Mary Kravenas, Meaghan Miller, and Francesca Kritikos.

This book reflects the breathtaking professionalism of Lindsey Schauer. If there is a hall of fame for editors, she's there.

NOTES

INTRODUCTION

"been all around": Brian Wilson and Mike Love, "California Girls" (Sea of Tunes Publishing, 1965), appeared on *Summer Days (and Summer Nights!!)* (Capitol Records, 1965).

"Brian Wilson is the Beach Boys": Erik Hedegaard, "Mike Love's Cosmic Journey," *Rolling Stone*, February 25, 2016, 46.

"teenage symphony to God": Jules Siegel, *Record* (San Francisco: Straight Arrow Books, 1972), 93. This anthology of Siegel's writing includes "Goodbye Surfing, Hello God," the present-at-the-creation article describing *Smile*. For a long time, this sacred text was the only source for tales of the doomed album. Siegel's piece, commissioned by the *Saturday Evening Post*, was rejected by that magazine and appeared in *Cheetah* in October 1967.

"a bunt": Richard Harrington, "Brian Wilson and the Angry Vibrations," *Washington Post*, December 1, 1991.

"Don't fuck with": Peter Ames Carlin, *Catch a Wave: The Rise, Fall, and Redemption of the Beach Boys' Brian Wilson* (Philadelphia: Rodale, 2006), 84.

"He wanted a sandbox": David Felton, "The Healing of Brother Brian," *Rolling Stone*, November 4, 1976, www.rollingstone.com/music/news/the-healing-of -brother-brian-the-rolling-stone-interview-with-the-beach-boys-19761104.

patience to a time bomb: From the opening line of John Irving's novel *The 158-Pound Marriage* (New York: Random House, 1974): "My wife, Utchka (whose name I sometime ago shortened to Utch), could teach patience to a time bomb."

"That ear": Benjamin Hedin, editor, *Studio A: The Bob Dylan Reader* (New York: W. W. Norton, 2004), 236.

"This sounds like shit": Felton, "Healing of Brother Brian," *Rolling Stone*.

"primary architect": Ben Edmonds, "The Beach Boys: A Group for All Seasons," *Circus*, June 1971, retrieved from Rock's Back Pages, www.rocksback pages.com/Library/Article/the-beach-boys-a-group-for-all-seasons.

"Dennis was the bane": Jeff Guinn, *Manson: The Life and Times of Charles Manson* (New York: Simon and Schuster, 2013), 148.

"The ovaries": Scott Cohen, "Surfer Boy: The Dennis Wilson Interview," *Circus*, October 26, 1976, retrieved from Cinetropic, http://www.cinetropic .com/blacktop/circus.html.

"Are you going to hurt me": Vincent Bugliosi with Curt Gentry, *Helter Skel-ter: The True Story of the Manson Murders* (New York: W. W. Norton, 1974; twenty-fifth anniversary revised edition, 1994), 335.

"Who are you": Steven Gaines, *Heroes and Villains: The True Story of the Beach Boys* (New York: New American Library, 1986), 201.

CHAPTER 1

"the eighth wonder of the world": Paul Donnelley, *Fade to Black: A Book of Movie Obituaries* (London: Omnibus, 2000; revised edition, 2003), 151.

"abnormal, unnatural": Kieron Connolly, *Dark History of Hollywood: A Cen-tury of Greed, Corruption, and Scandal Behind the Movies* (New York: Metro Books, 2014), 28.

"There's no economic": *Annie Hall*, directed by Woody Allen (United Artists, 1977).

"They realize that they've": Nathanael West, *The Day of the Locust* (New York: Random House, 1939); from an edition featuring *Miss Lonelyhearts* and *Day of the Locust* (New York: New Directions, 2009), 178.

"There's this cat": Bumps Blackwell, "Up Against the Wall with Little Rich-ard," in William McKeen, ed., *Rock 'n' Roll Is Here to Stay: An Anthology* (New York: W. W. Norton, 2000), 100.

"The problem was": Ibid.

"I told him that": Ibid., 101.

"At first I was mad": *Chuck Berry: Hail! Hail! Rock 'n' Roll*, directed by Taylor Hackford (Universal Pictures, 1987).

"The only people for me": Jack Kerouac, *On the Road* (New York: Viking, 1957), 8.

CHAPTER 2

"Flying free of the wheel": Timothy White, *The Nearest Faraway Place: Brian Wilson, The Beach Boys, and the Southern California Experience* (New York: Henry Holt, 1994), 68–69.

"We had a shitty": Carlin, *Catch a Wave*, 12.

"You think the world": Ibid., 11.

"I saw a fistfight once": *Good Vibrations: The Life and Times of the Beach Boys*, directed by Johnny Baak (independent production, 2011).

"My father resented": Gaines, *Heroes and Villains*, 47.

"overbearing Cyclops": Ben Edmonds, "Dennis Wilson: The Lonely Sea," *Mojo*, November 2002, retrieved from Rock's Back Pages, www.rocksbackpages.com/Library/Article/dennis-wilson-the-lonely-sea.

"Murry had made him stand": Edmonds, "Dennis Wilson: Lonely Sea."

"He yelled so loud": *Good Vibrations*, directed by Baak.

"If you walked by": Brian Wilson and Ben Greenman, *I Am Brian Wilson: A Memoir* (Cambridge: Da Capo, 2016), 37.

"We used to sing": *Good Vibrations*, directed by Baak.

"Music was always": Geoffrey Himes, "High Times and Ebb Tides: Carl Wilson Recalls 20 Years With and Without Brian," *Musician*, September 1983.

"Weaving his voice together": Carlin, *Catch a Wave*, 7.

"The Wilson Boys have always": Tom Nolan, "The Beach Boys: A California Saga, Part II," *Rolling Stone*, November 11, 1971.

"My dad was an asshole": Gaines, *Heroes and Villains*, 50.

"By age 10": Himes, "High Times."

"I used to wish": *Good Vibrations*, directed by Baak.

"He was like our coach": Carlin, *Catch a Wave*, 12.

"Carl was born thirty": David Leaf, *The Beach Boys and the California Myth* (New York: Grosset and Dunlap, 1978), 56.

"My refuge from the uncertainty": Brian Wilson and Todd Gold, *Wouldn't It Be Nice: My Own Story* (New York: HarperCollins, 1991), 32.

"They were in varying": Ibid., 34.

"months at a time": Gaines, *Heroes and Villains*, 51.

"High school was confusing": Wilson and Gold, *Wouldn't It Be Nice*, 35.

"I really had no idea": Carlin, *Catch a Wave*, 16.

"Most of his classmates": Himes, "High Times."

"People confuse me": Wilson and Gold, *Wouldn't It Be Nice*, 39.

"Brian got Al's leg busted": Nolan, "Beach Boys: California Saga."

"He'd disappear every Saturday": Ibid.

"Dennis was really living": Himes, "High Times."

"Geography is key": William Weir, "Way Before the Beach Boys," *Boston Globe*, June 20, 2014, K3.

"the wet, splashy sound": Deuce of Clubs, "Dick Dale, King of the Surf Guitar," *Planet Magazine*, September 26, 1995, retrieved from Deuce of Clubs, http://deuceofclubs.com/write/dickdale.htm.

"When we left": Felton, "Healing of Brother Brian."

"We have something": Keith Badman, *The Beach Boys: The Definitive Diary of America's Greatest Band on Stage and in the Studio* (San Francisco: Backbeat Books, 2004), 16.

"Drop everything": Nolan, "Beach Boys: California Saga."

"It was my guitar": Himes, "High Times."

"We got so excited": Badman, *Beach Boys: Definitive Diary*, 17.

"Dennis was so thrilled": Himes, "High Times."

"Although we were still": Badman, *Beach Boys: Definitive Diary*, 17.

"I've heard you guys": Wilson and Gold, *Wouldn't It Be Nice*, 57.

"We became almost platonic": Gaines, *Heroes and Villains*, 72.

"Gary and I spent all": Wilson and Gold, *Wouldn't It Be Nice*, 57.

"Shit, we'll get killed": Gaines, *Heroes and Villains*, 73.

"That's old-fashioned": Ibid., 75.

Nick Venet: He was born Nikolas Kostantinos Venetoulis, shortening his name to Nick Venet. Later in his career, he changed his first name to Nik. I use the spelling he used when working with the Beach Boys.

"Before eight bars": Gaines, *Heroes and Villains*, 78.

"Little Miss America": Herb Alpert and Vincent Catalano copyrighted the song as "Little Girl (You're My Miss America)." It was released by Imperial Records in April 1962.

CHAPTER 3

"One night, while Jan and I": Dean Torrence, "The Four Car Garage Band: 1957–1958," in *Jan and Dean* (e-book), Jan and Dean's Website, www .jananddean.com/biochp01/biochp01.html.

"I had to accept": Torrence, "Four Car Garage Band."

"I am stunned": Dean Torrence, "Teen Idols: 1958–1962," in *Jan and Dean* (e-book), Jan and Dean's Website, www.jananddean.com/biochp02/biochp02.html.

"Anybody with soul": Daniel Wolff, S. R. Crain, Clifton White, and G. David Tenenbaum, *You Send Me: The Life and Times of Sam Cooke* (New York: William Morrow, 1995), 171.

"I was making more": Ibid.

"a couple of very talented guys": Torrence, "Teen Idols."

"We were determined": Dean Torrence, "A Personal Recollection," *Jan and Dean Anthology Album* (United Artists Records, 1971), liner notes.

"A new breed of young men": Torrence, "Teen Idols."

"Surfing music had just": Torrence, "A Personal Recollection."

"He said he": Badman, *Beach Boys: Definitive Diary*, 34.

"He said that he had": Torrence, "A Personal Recollection."

"Jan and Brian sang": Dean Torrence, "Surfer Boys: 1963–1964," in *Jan and Dean* (e-book), Jan and Dean's Website, www.jananddean.com/biochp03 /biochp03.html.

"You have recorded on": Murry Wilson to Brian Wilson, May 8, 1965, 3, from James B. Murphy, *Becoming the Beach Boys, 1961–1963* (Jefferson, NC: McFarland, 2015), 291.

"There's a real heart": Himes, "High Times."

"'In My Room' is a": Ibid.

"It brought peace": Badman, *Beach Boys: Definitive Diary*, 39.

"somewhere where you could": *Endless Harmony*, directed by Alan Boyd (VH1, 1998).

CHAPTER 4

"I got with a bunch": Earl Palmer, Oral History Program interview, National Association of Music Merchants, August 3, 2002, www.namm.org/library /oral-history/earl-palmer.

"Earl Palmer was really": Hal Blaine, Oral History Program interview, National Association of Music Merchants, August 24, 2002, www.namm .org/library/oral-history/hal-blaine.

"I was making more": *The Wrecking Crew*, directed by Denny Tedesco (Lunch Box Entertainment, 2015).

"I'm a producer": Kent Hartman, "The Hidden History of a Rock 'n' Roll Hitmaker," *Smithsonian*, February 28, 2012, www.smithsonianmag.com/arts -culture/the-hidden-history-of-a-rock-n-roll-hitmaker-109251370/?no-ist.

"had given birth to": Mick Brown, *Tearing Down the Wall of Sound: The Rise and Fall of Phil Spector* (New York: Alfred A. Knopf, 2007), 16.

"Do you think I have": Kent Hartman, *The Wrecking Crew: The Inside Story of Rock 'n' Roll's Best-Kept Secret* (New York: St. Martin's, 2012), 42.

"Phil was definitely": Brown, *Tearing Down the Wall of Sound*, 30.

"dreadful": Ibid., 37.

"'We bought your home,'" "All the Drifters": Jann S. Wenner and Joe Levy, eds., *The Rolling Stone Interviews* (New York: Back Bay Books, 2007), 24.

"Since then I've never": John Gilliland, "Show 14—Big Rock Candy Mountain: Rock 'n' Roll in the Late Fifties [Part 4], *Pop Chronicles* (1969), audio, University of North Texas Digital Library, last updated August 4, 2016, http://digital.library.unt.edu/ark:/67531/metadc19763/m1/#track/1.

"This man was more": McKeen, *Rock 'n' Roll Is Here to Stay*, 642.

"Phil had quirks": Brown, *Tearing Down the Wall of Sound*, 81.

"The pure tone of the echo": Gareth Murphy, *Cowboys and Indies: The Epic History of the Record Industry* (New York: St. Martin's, 2014), 120.

"Most regarded it as": Brown, *Tearing Down the Wall of Sound*, 110.

"I'm Phil": Hartman, *Wrecking Crew*, 51.

"sonic totalitarianism": Murphy, *Cowboys and Indies*, 120.

"The sound was all-consuming": Bob Stanley, *Yeah! Yeah! Yeah!: The Story of Pop Music from Bill Haley to Beyoncé* (New York: W. W. Norton, 2014), 62.

"The control room": Brown, *Tearing Down the Wall of Sound*, 115.

"He wanted to get": Mark Ribowsky, *He's a Rebel: Phil Spector—Rock 'n' Roll's Legendary Producer* (New York: Cooper Square, 2000), 131.

"I sold out": Ibid., 130.

"Philly was a user": Brown, *Tearing Down the Wall of Sound*, 81.

"The minute I heard": Ibid., 127.

"That's gold": Paul Du Noyer, *The Illustrated Encyclopedia of Music* (London: Flame Tree, 2003), 14.

"Oh my God": Wilson and Gold, *Wouldn't It Be Nice*, 82.

CHAPTER 5

"I combined that surf": Himes, "High Times."

"To expect love": P. F. Sloan and S. E. Feinberg, *What's Exactly the Matter?: Memoirs of a Life in Music* (London: Jawbone, 2014), 28.

"You'll have to explain": Ibid., 29.

"To not receive the love": Ibid.

"For the most part": Ibid., 34.

"I bet you'd like": Ibid., 43.

"Anybody can sign": Ibid., 44.

"Aladdin is all R&B": Ibid., 45.

"Do you write": Ibid., 46.

"I want you to know": Ibid.

"It was the first time": Ibid., 41.

"I started out with": Ken Sharp, "Brian Wilson: The Rhapsody of a Beach Boy," *Goldmine*, January 2011, 42.

"Spector walked in": Wilson and Gold, *Wouldn't It Be Nice*, 84.

"His aberrant personality": Ibid., 86.

"I quit": Jon Stebbins and David Marks, *The Lost Beach Boy: The True Story of David Marks, One of the Founding Members of the Beach Boys* (London: Virgin Books, 2007), 94.

"They're in the same key": Philip Lambert, *Inside the Music of Brian Wilson: The Songs, Sounds, and Influences of the Beach Boys' Founding Genius* (New York: Bloomsbury, 2007), 136.

"Just about everything": "Alan Jardine," *Mojo*, June 2012.

"I went into the": Brian Wilson, *Surfin' Safari/Surfin' USA* (Capitol Records, first compact disc issue, 1990), liner notes, 3.

"Brian would [make] all": Badman, *Beach Boys: Definitive Diary*, 25.

"Brian was really the one": Himes, "High Times."

"Brian did everything": Badman, *Beach Boys: Definitive Diary*, 25.

"I could get": Wilson and Gold, *Wouldn't It Be Nice*, 79.

"The concept was about": David Leaf, *Surfin' Safari/Surfin' USA* (Capitol Records, first compact disc issue, 1990), liner notes, 11.

"I realized that with": Wilson and Gold, *Wouldn't It Be Nice*, 79.

CHAPTER 6

This is the land where: A respectful reference to Alan Lomax's epic *The Land Where the Blues Began* (New York: Pantheon, 1993).

"Jook is a word for": Zora Neale Hurston, "Characteristics of Negro Expression," in *Within the Circle: An Anthology of African American Literary Criticism from the Harlem Renaissance to the Present*, ed. Angelyn Mitchell (Durham, NC: Duke University Press, 1994), 89. Hurston's essay first appeared in *Negro: An Anthology*, ed. Nancy Cunard (London: Wishart, 1934).

"Little Robert, he dead": Alan Lomax, *The Land Where the Blues Began* (New York: Pantheon, 1993), 14.

"Man, don't ever": Patricia R. Schroeder, *Robert Johnson: Mythmaking, and Contemporary American Culture* (Urbana: University of Illinois Press, 2004), 46.

"Well, I hope your": Philip Norman, *Rave On: The Biography of Buddy Holly* (New York: Simon and Schuster, 1996), 275.

Cooke was born: He was born Cook but altered the spelling when he began his secular career in 1957. I use the second spelling throughout.

"I gone just as": Wolff et al., *You Send Me*, 132.

"If . . . that's the way": Ibid., 146.

"I thought it was": Peter Guralnick, *Dream Boogie: The Triumph of Sam Cooke* (New York: Back Bay Books/Little, Brown, 2005), 173.

"I feel he was": Wolff et al., *You Send Me*, 165.

"fornication and bastardy": Guralnick, *Dream Boogie*, 229.

"Here was a guy": Wolff et al., *You Send Me*, 168.

"Sam just seemed": Guralnick, *Dream Boogie*, 235.

"Bumps was a teacher": Wolff et al., *You Send Me*, 236.

"Sam Cooke shared": Craig Werner, *A Change Is Gonna Come: Music, Race and the Soul of America* (New York: Plume, 1999), 40.

"This is my god": Wolff et al., *You Send Me*, 232.

"That man could mess": Ibid., 233.

"I was the one": Ibid., 184.

"A white boy writing": Ibid., 291.

"Sam Cooke!": Guralnick, *Dream Boogie*, 558–559.

"Mommy, Vincent's in": Guralnick, *Dream Boogie*, 500.

"He was not as quick," "starting to drink": Wolff et al., *You Send Me*, 278.

"When a woman start": Gurlanick, *Dream Boogie*, 606.

"Sam would say," "Now you get you": Ibid.

"I'm mad about you": Wolff et al., *You Send Me*, 3.

"We're just going" . . . "Lady, you shot": Ibid., 3–5.

CHAPTER 7

"He had mentioned": Priscilla Beaulieu Presley with Sandra Harmon, *Elvis and Me* (New York: Putnam, 1985), 259.

"She tried everything": Joel Williamson, *Elvis Presley: A Southern Life* (New York: Oxford University Press, 2015), 233.

"Dad, will you go": Badman, *Beach Boys: Definitive Diary*, 35.

"I don't want to tour," "My dad was so": Ibid.

"I was proud of": Ibid., 39.

"Sessions on the": Wilson and Gold, *Wouldn't It Be Nice*, 80.

"Everyone sensed their": Himes, "High Times."

"Our president is dead": Badman, *Beach Boys: Definitive Diary*, 44.

"It was a tragedy": Ibid.

"I suggested that we": Dan MacIntosh, "Mike Love of the Beach Boys," Songfacts, www.songfacts.com/blog/interviews/mike_love_of_the_beach_boys/.

"What I saw impressed": Wilson and Gold, *Wouldn't It Be Nice*, 89.

"Did you see the Beatles" . . . "You don't get it": Ibid.

"I hope you": Wilson and Gold, *Wouldn't It Be Nice*, 100.

"I need you": Ibid., 101.

"Before he got messed up": "Marilyn Wilson Comments," AlbumLinerNotes.com, http:// albumlinernotes.com/Marilyn_Wilson_Comments.html.

"the most solicitous": Wilson and Gold, *Wouldn't It Be Nice*, 81.

Mike Love's lyrics: "I Get Around" was originally credited only to Brian Wilson. In a 1994 lawsuit, Mike Love argued that many of his lyrics graced songs previously credited solely to Wilson. The song credits were then amended. "I Get Around" was one of the songs whose credit was changed to Brian Wilson and Mike Love.

"A sociologist might say": Brian Wilson, *All Summer Long* (Capitol Records, 1964), liner notes.

"Something in me": Jeffrey A. Kottler, *Divine Madness: Ten Stories of Creative Struggle* (San Francisco: Jossey-Bass, 2006), 255.

"Something has to give": Wilson and Gold, *Wouldn't It Be Nice*, 91.

"He has a goddam opinion": Ibid.

"OK now, hard and strong": The original compact disc version of *Smiley Smile* included a bonus track called "Good Vibrations (Various Sessions)," which featured Brian directing musicians on with this advice. This track of sessions excerpts, with Brian interrupting on the talkback to direct the musicians, was also featured on the five-disc retrospective *Good Vibrations: Thirty Years of the Beach Boys* (Capitol Records, 1993) and *The Smile Sessions* (Capitol Records, 2011).

"I broke just about": Vernon Scott, "Mel Blanc Scorns Injuries," *United Press International*, March 27, 1961.

"I thought someone": Bathroom Readers' Institute, *Uncle John's Bathroom Reader* (New York: Macmillan, 1988), 140.

"I always envied": Artie Wayne, "Artie Kornfeld and the True Story Behind 'Dead Man's Curve'," *Artie Wayne on the Web* (blog), November 14, 2009, https://artiewayne.wordpress.com/2009/11/14/artie-kornfeld-and-the-true-story-behind-dead-mans-curve/.

CHAPTER 8

"having sexual intercourse": exlrrp, "Frank Sinatra: Busted for Seduction," *Daily Kos*, July 20, 2008, www.dailykos.com/story/2008/7/20/554172/-.

"either his signature or": Mario Puzo, *The Godfather* (New York: G. P. Putnam's Sons, 1969), 43.

"For the first time": Peter Gilstrap, "Snatching Sinatra," *Washington Post*, March 8, 1998, www.washingtonpost.com/archive/lifestyle/1998/03/08/snatching-sinatra/5f406163-1d9d-4a81-b62e-9f312893d60b/.

"I was there to listen": Ibid.

"I went to University High": Associated Press, "Sinatra Jr. Kidnapper Goes from Inmate to Criminal Justice Advocate," *Amarillo Globe-News*, February 12, 2001, http://amarillo.com/stories/2001/02/12/usn_sinatra.shtml#.V6s7vUYrLcs.

"I decided on Junior": Gilstrap, "Snatching Sinatra."

"I don't think I ever": Ibid.

"I didn't think he'd": Ibid.

"He was my best friend": Mark A. Moore, "Mysterious Financier: Dean Torrence and the Kidnapping of Frank Sinatra Jr.," Jan and Dean—Jan Berry, August 8, 2010, www.jananddean-janberry.com/main/index.php/features/dean-kidnapping-story.

"That all sounds great": Gilstrap, "Snatching Sinatra."

"I always had a": Moore, "Mysterious Financier."

"You're not still thinking": Gilstrap, "Snatching Sinatra."

"Now, we had to kidnap": Ibid.

"Let's go back to L.A.": Ibid.

"Who is it?," "I have a delivery": Nancy Sinatra, *Frank Sinatra: My Father* (New York: Doubleday, 1985), 158.

"Come in" . . . "We'd all reassured": Gilstrap, "Snatching Sinatra."

"Just keep your mouth": Sinatra, *My Father*, 160.

"Jesus": Gilstrap, "Snatching Sinatra."

"Shoot me": Ibid.

"Is this Frank Sinatra?": Sinatra, *My Father*, 161.

"Dean was a little shaken," "I'm actually going": Gilstrap, "Snatching Sinatra."

"Is Frank Sinatra there?": Ibid.

"We got the money": Sinatra, *My Father*, 164.

"Suppose I get in": Ibid., 167.

"I'm sorry, Dad": Kara Kovalchik, "The Incompetent Kidnapping of Frank Sinatra Jr.," *Mental Floss,* August 20, 2008, http://mentalfloss.com/article/19395 /true-crime-incompetent-kidnapping-frank-sinatra-jr.

"We laid all the": Roger D. McGrath, "All-American Abduction," Free Library, December 1, 2011, www.thefreelibrary.com/All-American+abduction%3A +I+knew+Sinatra+Jr.'s+kidnapper--he+got+my...-a0281790371.

"We intend to show": Moore, "Mysterious Financier."

"Staged with consent": Ibid.

"This was a planned": Ibid.

"It's a terrible experience" . . . "When someone comes": Ibid.

"So obviously the word": Ibid.

CHAPTER 9

"The sixties called all": *Wrecking Crew,* directed by Tedesco.

"Everything I needed was": Judy Collins, *Sweet Judy Blue Eyes: My Life in Music* (New York: Three Rivers, 2011), 120.

old, weird America: I borrow this phrase from the title of a wonderful book called *The Old, Weird America* (New York: Picador, 2011) by Greil Marcus. It was originally published as *Invisible Republic: Bob Dylan's Basement Tapes* (New York: Henry Holt, 1997).

laments of the old: Obviously another nod to Greil Marcus, *The Old, Weird America* (New York: Picador, 2011), a revised and retitled version of his *Invisible Republic: Bob Dylan's Basement Tapes* (New York: Henry Holt, 1997).

"They ushered in": Collins, *Sweet Judy Blue Eyes,* 136.

"The influx of the": Barney Hoskyns, *Hotel California: The True-Life Adventures of Crosby, Stills, Nash, Young, Mitchell, Taylor, Browne, Ronstadt, Geffen, the Eagles and Their Many Friends* (Hoboken, NJ: John Wiley and Sons, 2006), 6.

"L.A. was less the promised": Ibid., 3.

"I remember her as a": Matthew Greenwald, *Go Where You Wanna Go: The Oral History of the Mamas and the Papas* (New York: Cooper Square, 2002), 1.

"I've been fat since," "I'm going to be": Eddi Fiegel, *Dream a Little Dream of Me: The Life of 'Mama' Cass Elliot* (London: Pan, 2006), 5.

"They were embarrassed": Ibid., 24.

"I was a cheerleader": Ibid., 25.

"There wasn't much call": Ibid., 45.

"At least Dad finally": Ibid., 47.

"I was *fascinated*": Ibid., 56.

"It was the greatest": Ibid, 59.

"I thought, *fucking awful*": Ibid., 65.

"Most of the values": David Crosby and Carl Gottlieb, *Long Time Gone: The Autobiography of David Crosby* (New York: Doubleday, 1988), 19.

"I followed my unit": Ibid., 37.

"I didn't like him": Ibid., 44.

"When I got to the": Ibid., 51.

"David was a bit": Hoskyns, *Hotel California,* 15.

"I don't think Cass": Fiegel, *Dream a Little Dream,* 3.

"Boy, what a *horrible*": Ibid., 90.

"Sometimes you meet people": Greenwald, *Go Where You Wanna Go*, 15–16.

"I wasn't going to turn": John Einarson, *Mr. Tambourine Man: The Life and Legacy of the Byrds' Gene Clark* (San Francisco: Backbeat Books, 2005), 31.

"I quit the Christies": Ibid., 38.

"I was unprepared": Collins, *Sweet Judy Blue Eyes*, 138.

"McGuinn was a dreamy guy": Ibid., 139.

"I liked Jim's friendly": Ibid., 139.

"lanky and smooth-moving": Ibid., 9.

"He sold funeral plots": Michelle Phillips, *California Dreamin': The True Story of the Mamas and the Papas* (New York: Warner Books, 1986), 26.

"At the very moment": Fiegel, *Dream a Little Dream*, 139.

"I might have been one of": Einarson, *Mr. Tambourine Man*, 40.

"They were mixing": Ibid., 40–41.

"I was really getting": Ibid., 41.

"Look. Do you mind": Ibid.

"They'd sit there with": Hoskyns, *Hotel California*, 5.

"The Beatles validated": Ibid., 4.

"This kid came out": Elijah Wald, *Dylan Goes Electric!: Newport, Seeger, Dylan and the Night That Split the Sixties* (New York: Dey Street Books, 2015), 175.

"The enthusiasm was". . . "Phil brought him": Brown, *Tearing Down the Wall of Sound*, 163–169.

"We learned faster": Christopher Hjort, *So You Want to Be a Rock 'n' Roll Star: The Byrds Day-by-Day 1965–1973* (London: Jawbone, 2008), 17.

"Playing bass and singing": Crosby and Gottlieb, *Long Time Gone*, 83.

"Chris told me he'd joined": Hoskyns, *Hotel California*, 5.

"Jac was open to all kinds": Collins, *Sweet Judy Blue Eyes*, 136.

"This is going to surprise": Bosley Crowther, "The Four Beatles in 'A Hard Day's Night'; British Singers Make Debut as Film Stars," *New York Times*, August 12, 1964, 41.

"I can remember coming": Crosby and Gottlieb, *Long Time Gone*, 83.

"How about 'Birds'": Ed Ward, "The *Rolling Stone* Interview: Roger McGuinn," *Rolling Stone*, October 29, 1970, www.rollingstone.com/music/news/the-rolling-stone-interview-roger-mcguinn-19701029.

"Oh no, you haven't" . . . "My mother and dad": David Kaufman, *Doris Day: The Untold Story of the Girl Next Door* (New York: Virgin Books, 2008), 299–300.

"The whole business": Ibid., 300.

"He was tall": Ibid., 317.

"Terry had pull": Crosby and Gottlieb, *Long Time Gone*, 89.

"We've got to have McGuinn": Ibid.

"I'd been a studio": *Wrecking Crew*, directed by Tedesco.

"You need a written request": Sloan and Feinberg, *What's Exactly the Matter?*, 93–94.

"a fateful moment": Clive Davis and Anthony DeCurtis, *The Soundtrack of My Life* (New York: Simon and Schuster, 2013), 50.

"The Byrds created": *Neil Young's Music Box: Here We Are in the Years*, directed by Alex Westbrook (Sexy Intellectual Studios, 2011).

CHAPTER 10

"pocket symphonies": David Cheal, "Beach Boys Maestro Confirms His
Genius," *Guardian*, January 28, 2002, www.telegraph.co.uk/culture/music
/rockandjazzmusic/3572378/Beach-Boys-maestro-confirms-his-genius.html.

He put the Wrecking Crew: The *Today!* version of "Help Me Rhonda" spells
the name "Ronda." The hit single version, later to appear on *Summer Days*,
spells it "Rhonda."

"Mike! God!": Badman, *Beach Boys: Definitive Diary*, 82.

"They wanted someone": Ibid., 89.

"In the beginning": Edmonds, "Dennis Wilson: Lonely Sea."

"Brian, you've got a wonderful" . . . "Don't ever forget": An audio recording
of the exchange is available on many YouTube posts, some of which contain a full half hour of uncomfortable arguing between Brian Wilson and
his father. The selection here includes a transcription from Badman, *Beach
Boys: Definitive Diary*, 84–85.

"I cannot believe": Wilson and Greenman, *I Am Brian Wilson*, 150.

"I could kill the guy": Felton, "Healing of Brother Brian."

"I read in the *Times*": Ibid.

"The song was a big": Badman, *Beach Boys: Definitive Diary*, 89.

"I wrote every last": Hedegaard, "Mike Love's Cosmic Journey," 45.

"The door starts to fly": Felton, "Healing of Brother Brian."

"I love the way," "We call fadeouts": Ibid.

"We had them all," "We made lines in": Crosby and Gottleib, *Long Time Gone*, 91.

Four hundred miles: Tom Wolfe, *The Electric Kool-Aid Acid Test* (New York: Far-
rar, Straus and Giroux, 1968).

"started the whole thing": David McGowan, *Weird Scenes Inside the Canyon:
Laurel Canyon, Covert Ops and the Dark Heart of the Hippie Dream* (London:
Headpress, 2014), 64.

"A band didn't have": Barney Hoskyns, *Waiting for the Sun: Strange Days, Weird
Scenes, and the Sound of Los Angeles* (New York: St. Martin's, 1996), 78.

twist-a-frug-jerk: This is a term coined by Tom Wolfe.

"Phil Sloan is down," "I like it, Phil": Sloan and Feinberg, *What's Exactly the
Matter?*, 95.

"You've got a hit": Ibid., 97.

"Man, this is awesome": Fiegel, *Dream a Little Dream*, 165.

"What do you think": Ibid., 166.

"a visual that was": Ibid., 167.

"I'll give you whatever": Ibid., 168.

"They were confused": Wilson and Gold, *Wouldn't It Be Nice*, 125.

"I was alone among": Ibid., 126.

"They put only": Ibid., 129–130.

"I just finished listening": Wilson and Gold, *Wouldn't It Be Nice*, 130.

CHAPTER 11

"The open and wild": Neil Young, *Special Deluxe: A Memoir of Life and Cars* (New York: Blue Rider Press, 2014), 1.

"There really wasn't anything": John Einarson and Richie Furay, *For What It's Worth: The Story of Buffalo Springfield* (New York: Cooper Square, 2004), 46.

"We were recording artists": Young, *Special Deluxe*, 64.

"My voice is a little": Einarson and Furay, *For What It's Worth*, 48.

"Some people would yell": Young, *Special Deluxe*, 77.

"We had the most original": Neil Young, *Waging Heavy Peace* (New York: Blue Rider, 2012), 60.

"I was writing a lot": Ibid.

"We started at five dollars": Ibid., 52.

"Somehow I started": Neil Young, "My Defining Moment," *AARP: The Magazine*, February/March 2016, 10.

"I thought a hearse": Young, *Special Deluxe*, 47.

"I loved the hearse": Cameron Crowe, "The Rebellious Neil Young," *Rolling Stone*, August 14, 1975, www.rollingstone.com/music/news/the-rebellious-neil-young-19750814.

"The crowd really went": Young, *Special Deluxe*, 85.

"I didn't die": Jimmy McDonough, *Shakey: Neil Young's Biography* (New York: Random House, 2002), 45.

"Neil was different": Einarson and Furay, *For What It's Worth*, 50.

"There was a guy singing": Young, *Waging Heavy Peace*, 64.

"We got on quite well": Einarson and Furay, *For What It's Worth*, 51.

"Neil really struck me": Ibid., 55.

"I met Neil walking": Ibid., 56.

"I had to eat": Ibid., 60.

"I had to go down": Ibid., 81.

"We had made it": Young, *Special Deluxe*, 92.

"We couldn't find Stills": Young, *Waging Heavy Peace*, 130.

"Bruce and I were just": Einarson and Furay, *For What It's Worth*, 83.

"We pulled off Sunset": Ibid., 84.

"I looked around out": Young, *Waging Heavy Peace*, 130.

"Everything just fell": Einarson and Furay, *For What It's Worth*, 85.

"She raised eleven children": Sheila Weller, *Girls Like Us: Carole King, Joni Mitchell, Carly Simon and the Journey of a Generation* (New York: Simon and Schuster, 2008), 50.

"If you can paint": Ibid., 72–73.

"I discovered I": Cameron Crowe, "Joni Mitchell Defends Herself," *Rolling Stone*, July 26, 1979, www.rollingstone.com/music/news/joni-mitchell-defends-herself-19790726.

"Thirty-six hours" . . . "Chuck said, 'Joni'": A. L. McClain, "Two Single Acts Survive a Marriage," *Detroit News*, February 6, 1966.

"Listen, I have to": Ken Sharp, "Interview with 'Pet Sounds' Lyricist Tony Asher," *Rock Cellar Magazine*, September 4, 2013, www.rockcellarmagazine.com/2013/09/04/beach-boys-pet-sounds-lyricist-tony-asher-interview-brian-wilson.

"The most difficult part": Wilson and Gold, *Wouldn't It Be Nice*, 132–133.

"I just wanted," "I want people": Ibid., 133.

"Why don't you": Sharp, "Tony Asher."

"The only times I actually": Nick Kent, *The Dark Stuff: Selected Writings on Rock Music* (Cambridge, MA: Da Capo, 1995; revised edition, 2002), 18.

"For the most part": Badman, *Beach Boys: Definitive Diary*, 104.

"He was a genius musician": Kent, *Dark Stuff*, 25.

"Did you see how beautiful": Wilson and Gold, *Wouldn't It Be Nice*, 135.

"I found Brian's lifestyle": Kent, *Dark Stuff*, 20.

"The general tenor": Ibid., 16.

"With 'God Only Knows'": Sharp, "Tony Asher."

"Hey, Brian," "Hey you guys": Badman, *Beach Boys: Definitive Diary*, 114–115.

"Love's main concerns": Ibid., 21.

"I was aware that Brian": Brad Elliott, "The Beach Boys *Pet Sounds* Track Notes," Beach Boys Fan Club, August 21, 1999, www.beachboysfanclub .com/ps-tracks.html.

"It was a whole new": Badman, *Beach Boys: Definitive Diary*, 115.

"We were standing": Elliott, "*Pet Sounds* Track Notes."

"That's how the album": Mike Love with James S. Hirsch, *Good Vibrations: My Life as a Beach Boy* (New York: Blue Rider, 2016), 133.

"Don't fuck with": This quote appears in a number of sources, perhaps first in Tom Nolan's two-part "California Saga" for *Rolling Stone* in 1971. It was repeated in most major articles and books about the Beach Boys that followed.

"Actually, the quote had": Love, *Good Vibrations*, 164.

"Throughout the whole" . . . "We went into the bedroom": Badman, *Beach Boys: Definitive Diary*, 130.

CHAPTER 12

"The show was just": Brown, *Tearing Down the Wall of Sound*, 200.

"When it wasn't": *Brian Wilson: I Just Wasn't Made for These Times*, directed by Don Was (Palomar Pictures, 1995).

"the Scheherazade of": Badman, *Definitive Diary*, 135.

"Artistic freedom in those": Wilson and Gold, *Wouldn't It Be Nice*, 78.

"My real intention": Ibid., 126.

"Write this!" . . . "He was a genius": Robert Farley, "Mary and Jim to the End," *St. Petersburg Times*, September 25, 2005, www.sptimes.com/2005/09/25 /Doors/Mary_and_Jim_to_the_e.shtml.

"He clammed up": Ibid.

"She was a great girl": Mick Wall, *Love Becomes a Funeral Pyre: A Biography of the Doors* (Chicago: Chicago Review Press, 2015), 50.

"She was Jim's": Farley, "Mary and Jim."

"My friend Judy": Eve Babitz, "The Second Coming of Jim Morrison," *Esquire*, March 1991, 88.

"I've been writing": Wall, *Love Becomes a Funeral Pyre*, 64.

"Jim just went": Ibid., 75.

"We don't want to": Ibid., 74.

"Like everyone back then": Babitz, "Second Coming of Jim Morrison," 88.

"He had the freshness": Ibid.

"that sexy motherfucker": Wall, *Love Becomes a Funeral Pyre*, 90.

"They appealed to the snob": Ibid., 83.

"You're talking about": Ibid., 102.

"They were totally": Ibid., 106.

"I always sat first": Van Dyke Parks, "The Lost Weekend—Last Piano/Vocal Performances by Van Dyke Parks with Very Special Guests," Largo website, www.largo-la.com/event/805127-lost-weekend-last-los-angeles/.

"I had lots of music-business": Badman, *Definitive Diary*, 114.

"Brian needs a lyricist": Ibid.

"He writes fantastic": Nolan, "Beach Boys: California Saga."

"Brian was the most": Danny Eccleston, "The Seldom Seen Kid," *Mojo*, August 2012, 54.

"That started with": *The Beach Boys: An American Band*, directed by Malcolm Leo (Malcolm Leo Productions, 1985).

"I told Brian that": Bill Holdship, "Heroes and Villians," *New Times Los Angeles*, April 6, 2000.

"It's still sticking pretty": Luis Sanchez, *The Beach Boys' Smile* (New York: Bloomsbury, 2014), 85.

"It's definitely a": Ibid.

"It's not a pleasant": William Overend, "When the Sun Set on the Strip," *Los Angeles Times*, November 4, 1981.

"We're going to be": Ibid.

"Riot is a ridiculous": Cecilia Rasmussen, "Closing of Club Ignited the 'Sunset Strip Riots,'" *Los Angeles Times*, August 5, 2007.

"I told them to be," "I had to skedaddle": Ibid.

"I have this song": Einarson and Furay, *For What It's Worth*, 127.

"It really affected me": Phil Alexander, "David Crosby: John Coltrane Blew My Mind," *Mojo*, November 1, 2013.

"I walked up to" . . . "Maybe the guilt": Hjort, *So You Want to Be*, 84.

"You could hear him": Greenwald, *Go Where You Wanna Go*, 123.

hotter than lightbulbs: An expression employed by the great Stan Cornyn of Warner Bros. Records.

"John was a really good": Greenwald, *Go Where You Wanna Go*, 119–120.

"I knew something was up": Ibid., 134.

"This letter is to," "I found out Michelle": Ibid., 137.

"The film was fairly": Bill Wyman with Ray Coleman, *Stone Alone: The Story of a Rock 'n' Roll Band* (New York: Viking, 1990), 271.

"Of course I'm the": Marc Spitz, *Jagger* (New York: Gotham Books, 2011), 53.

"During an incredible": Wyman, *Stone Alone*, 272.

"This work was not": Mark A. Moore, "'A Righteous Trip': In the Studio with Jan Berry, 1963–1966," *Dumb Angel Gazette No. 4: All Summer Long*, 2005, retrieved from Jan and Dean—Jan Berry, www.jananddean-janberry.com/main/index.php/jdhistory/1965-folk-n-roll.

"We soaked up": Graham Nash, *Wild Tales: A Rock and Roll Life* (New York: Crown Archetype, 2013), 73, 87–88.

"I had seen the album cover": Ibid., 88.

"Oh, it's a surprise": Greenwald, *Go Where You Wanna Go*, 157.

"Crosby intimidated": Nash, *Wild Tales*, 84.

"Without much" . . . "That small decision": Greenwald, *Go Where You Wanna Go*, 157.

"I thought, 'If that'": Badman, *Beach Boys: Definitive Diary*, 142.

"I'm not a genius": Nolan, "Beach Boys: California Saga."

"Brian, there's no place": Ibid.

"All right, let's go": Jules Siegel, *Cheetah*, October 1967, quoted in McKeen, *Rock and Roll Is Here to Stay*, 388–390.

"'Surf's Up' was the first": *American Band*, directed by Leo.

"Who the fuck": "Good Vibrations?: The Beach Boys' Mike Love Gets His Turn," *Goldmine*, September 18, 1992, retrieved from http://troun.tripod.com/mikelove.html.

"Mike Love made my": Eccleston, "Seldom Seen Kid," 56.

"Mike Love said to me": *American Band*, directed by Leo.

"It just got too": Dorian Lynskey, "Van Dyke Parks: 'I Was Victimised by Brian Wilson's Buffoonery,'" *Guardian*, May 9, 2013, www.theguardian.com/music/2013/may/09/van-dyke-parks-victimised-brian-wilson-buffoonery.

CHAPTER 13

"The height of the": John Blair and Stephen J. McParland, *The Illustrated Discography of Hot Rod Music 1961–1965* (Ann Arbor, MI: Popular Culture Ink, 1990), xvii.

"That song was just": Hjort, *So You Want to Be*, 113.

"Once Bobby got": Edna Gunderson, "Broken Melody: The Death of Bobby Fuller," *El Paso Times*, June 6, 1982, http://elpasotimes.typepad.com/morgue/2011/07/1982-broken-melody-the-death-of-bobby-fuller.html.

"He had incredible": John Ratliff, "L.A. Confidential," *Texas Monthly*, May 2000, 98.

"Bobby was a real": Gunderson, "Broken Melody."

"It was a sight to": Chris Campion, "The Short Life and Mysterious Death of Bobby Fuller, Rock 'n' Roll King of Texas," *Guardian*, July 16, 2015, www.theguardian.com/music/2015/jul/16/the-short-life-and-mysterious-death-of-bobby-fuller-rocknroll-king-of-texas.

"It's a border sound": Miriam Linna and Randell Fuller, *I Fought the Law: The Life and Strange Death of Bobby Fuller* (New York: Kicks Books, 2014), 283.

"never be able to do": Campion, "Bobby Fuller."

"The club became": Gunderson, "Broken Melody."

"England Has Beatles": Linna and Fuller, *I Fought the Law*, 117.

"I've got to talk to Randy": Gunderson, "Broken Melody."

"was found lying": Ibid.

"He was not self-destructive": Ibid.

"no evidence of foul": Eccleston, "Seldom Seen Kid," 56.

One of the more lunatic: Several sources mention the Manson theory, including Chis Campion in "Bobby Fuller."

"Motown and surf music": Tommy James with Martin Fitzpatrick, *Me, the Mob, and the Music: One Helluva Ride with Tommy James and the Shondells* (New York: Scribner, 2010), 29.

"One of them": James, *Me, the Mob, and the Music*, 58–59.

"We'd heard stories": Nash, *Wild Tales*, 72–73.

"Wonderful, I thought": James, *Me, the Mob, and the Music*, 62.

"In some ways": Ibid., 144.

"No, no, no": Linna and Fuller, *I Fought the Law*, 233.

"It sucks and you're": Karen O'Brien, *Joni Mitchell: Shadows and Light* (New York: Virgin Books, 2001), 44.

"One song especially": Al Kooper, *Backstage Passes and Backstabbing Bastards: Memoirs of a Rock 'n' Roll Survivor* (New York: Backbeat Books, 2008), 86.

"I have to get up soon": Ibid.

"As her blond hair": Collins, *Sweet Judy Blue Eyes*, 216.

"It was a crazy": Hedegaard, "Mike Love's Cosmic Journey," 46.

"If you take a bunch": Badman, *Beach Boys: Definitive Diary*, 175.

"Brian was afraid": McKeen, *Rock and Roll Is Here to Stay*, 398.

"They're shooting this": "The Byrds, 'He Was a Friend of Mine' (Live at 1967 Monterey Pop Festival) with David Crosby's Intro," YouTube video, posted by "whatmeworry," November 22, 2014, www.youtube.com/watch?v=TZqXP9z9xL0.

"were all trying": *It Was 20 Years Ago Today*, directed by John Sheppard (BBC, 1987).

as Jim McGuinn said: In 1967, Jim McGuinn changed his name to Roger McGuinn, after converting to Subud. His guru told him his new name must begin with the letter R. A longtime fan of science and science fiction, McGuinn delivered a list to his guru with suggestions such as Retro, Radio, and Rocket. He included Roger as the sign-off used by pilots to indicate affirmative. That was the name his guru chose.

"Michael?" . . . "What are you in the group for": The Byrds, *The Notorious Byrd Brothers* (Columbia Records, 1967; expanded edition, 2005). The bonus track "Universal Mind Decoder" features the Crosby-Clarke argument and Usher's attempts to mediate.

"They tossed me out": Crosby and Gottlieb, *Long Time Gone*, 118.

"I thought I'd been": Ibid.

"David was wonderful": Ibid., 130.

"It wasn't to replace": David Mikkelson, "Equinimity," Snopes.com, April 18, 2015, www.snopes.com/music/hidden/notoriousbyrds.asp.

"If we had intended": Uncredited, "The 100 Greatest Albums Ever Made," *Mojo*, 1995.

CHAPTER 14

"A *hippie* was sort": Michael Walker, *Laurel Canyon: The Inside Story of Rock and Roll's Legendary Neighborhood* (New York: Faber and Faber, 2006), 29.

"Charlie was in the yard": *Charles Manson: The Man Who Killed the Sixties*, directed by Peter Bate (XiveTV, 1995).

"I don't want to leave": Charles Manson with Nuel Emmons, *Manson in His Own Words: The Shocking Confessions of 'The Most Dangerous Man Alive'* (New York: Grove Press, 1986), 77–78.

"My guitar, my voice" . . . "The little broad": Ibid., 83–84.

"Peace and love": *Charles Manson*, directed by Bate.

"I'm not a child" . . . "Charlie didn't like": Ibid.

"Hi, I'm Brian Wilson": Nolan, "Beach Boys: California Saga."

"We are most human": Paul Williams, *Rock and Roll: The 100 Best Singles* (New York: Carroll and Graf, 1993), 121.

"I think the main": Domenic Priore, *Smile: The Story of Brian Wilson's Lost Masterpiece* (New York: Bobcat Books, 2005), 123.

"Most of *Smiley Smile*": Badman, *Beach Boys: Definitive Diary*, 189.

"They maneuvered Brian": Priore, *Smile*, 129.

"exuberant singing . . . and beautiful": Paul Williams, *Brian Wilson and the Beach Boys: How Deep Is the Ocean?* (New York: Omnibus, 1997), 33–35.

"If it's called *Song*" . . . "It was such a painful": Eccleston, "Seldom Seen Kid," 57.

"When Joni would": Weller, *Girls Like Us*, 274.

"David did me a": Crosby and Gottlieb, *Long Time Gone*, 130.

"At the time I": Crowe, "Joni Mitchell Defends Herself."

"There was a party": Crosby and Gottlieb, *Long Time Gone*, 138–139.

"I subscribed to": Ibid., 139.

"All these chicks": Walker, *Laurel Canyon*, 11.

"Whenever things weren't": Ibid., 166.

"No one knew": Greenwald, *Go Where You Wanna Go*, 185.

"She was very important": Walker, *Laurel Canyon*, 50.

"I always got a lot": Ibid., 49.

"Music happens in my": Ibid., 166.

"My original idea": Ward, "*Rolling Stone* Interview: Roger McGuinn."

"I was curious": Ibid.

"I didn't contribute": Ken Viola, "Incandescence: Memories of the Buffalo Springfield," Buffalo Springfield, *Box Set* (New York: ATCO Records, 2002), booklet, 39.

"These old studios": Young, *Waging Heavy Peace*, 111–112.

"David wanted to be": Einarson and Furay, *For What It's Worth*, 195–196.

"I admit wanting": Manson, *Manson in His Own Words*, 110.

"You look like you": Ibid., 106.

"He changed everybody's": *Charles Manson*, directed by Bate.

"We were alienated": Ibid.

"He gathers": Ibid.

"I had a lot of": Manson, *Manson in His Own Words*, 114.

"Spahn Ranch was": *Manson: 40 Years Later*, directed by Neil Rawles (History Channel, 2009).

"Manson would visit": Harold Schechter, ed., *True Crime: An American Anthology* (New York: The Library of America, 2008), 647.

"It was an isolated": *Manson: 40 Years Later*, directed by Rawles.

"There was flies": Bugliosi, *Helter Skelter*, 89–90.

"Self-destruction and": Wall, *Love Becomes a Funeral Pyre*, 141.

"The Doors seemed": McKeen, *Rock and Roll Is Here to Stay*, 400–402.

"It was a long while": Joan Didion, *The White Album* (New York: Simon and Schuster, 1979), 24.

"erotic politicians": Ibid.

"What do you want": Jerry Hopkins and Daniel Sugerman, *No One Here Gets Out Alive* (New York: Warner Books, 1980), 144.

"Mr. and Mrs. Rock 'n' roll," "Finally she broke": Ibid., 171.

"The Stones were": Lester Bangs, "The End Is Always Near," *Rock's Backpages Library*, 1975, www.rocksbackpages.com/Library/Article/the-end-is-always-near-dread-drunkenness-and-the-doors-pt-1.

"My house is," "That was a fascinating": Fiegel, *Dream a Little Dream*, 289–290.

"Dennis, get your" . . . "She did weigh": Ibid., 259.

"David and I were": Walker, *Laurel Canyon*, 53.

"Three times, the same": Nash, *Wild Tales*, 5–6.

"song-spewer": "'Revolution Blues' by Neil Young," Songfacts, www.songfacts.com/detail.php?id=3835.

"This guy is": Guinn, *Manson: Life and Times*, 155.

"The songs were fascinating": Young, *Waging Heavy Peace*, 104.

"I was finally": Ibid., 336.

"All during the evening": Collins, *Sweet Judy Blue Eyes*, 231.

yet another attempt: Inspired by Nietzsche's "It is the sad duty of governments to establish justice in a sinful world."

"I discovered him at": Linda Ronstadt, *Simple Dreams: A Musical Memoir* (New York: Simon and Schuster, 2013), 183.

"Brian worked really hard": Felton, "Healing of Brother Brian."

"Just chanting, fucking": Nolan, "Beach Boys: California Saga."

"Everything I heard": Gaines, *Heroes and Villains*, 181–182.

"We were in there," "Dennis is bringing": Ibid., 210–211.

"She was convicted": Love, *Good Vibrations*, 215.

"The Wizard was": Ibid., 182–183.

"Dennis Wilson was fascinated": *Manson: 40 Years Later*, directed by Rawles.

"Denis introduced": Ibid.

"Dennis was just": Nolan, "Beach Boys: California Saga."

"I found he had": David Griffiths, "Dennis Wilson: I Live with 17 Girls," *Record Mirror*, December 21, 1968.

"Dennis himself thought": Manson, *Manson in His Own Words*, 148.

"Dennis was a hell," "Dennis opened": Ibid., 187.

"They were sleeping": Gaines, *Heroes and Villains*, 205.

"Charlie was a very": Ibid., 207.

"Looking around": Guinn, *Manson: Life and Times*, 6–7.

"very un-Brian album": Leaf, *Beach Boys and the California Myth*, 128.

"Dennis ran up": Tom Nolan, "The Beach Boys: A California Saga, Part II," *Rolling Stone*, November 11, 1971.

"Manson's blending of": Love, *Good Vibrations*, 206.

"I remember that": *Manson: 40 Years Later*, directed by Rawles.

"Wilson was part": Guinn, *Manson: Life and Times*, 155.

"I saw six": Phillips, *California Dreamin'*, 172–173.

"I don't deny": Manson, *Manson in His Own Words*, 165.

"I went to see": Ibid., 184–185.

"One day, Charles Manson": Holdship, "Heroes and Villains."

"At that point": Guinn, *Manson: Life and Times*, 224.

CHAPTER 15

"Manson became a": *Manson: 40 Years Later*, directed by Rawles.

"He had this": Ibid.

"Manson was a racist": Ibid.

"They were anticipating": Ibid.

"When the Beatles": Ibid.

"You'd better get": Bugliosi, *Helter Skelter*, 102–103.

"Come on, Gary," "It's all your": Manson, *Manson in His Own Words*, 189.

"We ain't going" . . . "could hear": Bugliosi, *Helter Skelter*, 102–103.

"I'll talk to you": County of Los Angeles Sheriff's Department, Gary Hinman murder investigation police report, file no. 069-02378-1076-016, August 9, 1969, retrieved from "Gary Hinman Investigation," CieloDrive.com, http:// www.cielodrive.com/gary-hinman-homicide-report-08-09-69.php.

"They wanted to start": "Charles Manson: The Man Who Killed the 60s," *Pure History Specials*, 1995.

"On that night": Manson, *Manson in His Own Words*, 202.

"Wilson, always gracious": Ibid., 149.

"I immediately decided": "Linda Kasabian Was Part of the Manson Family. Then She Became the Star Witness Against Them" *Vox*, www.vox.com /sponsored/10829348/linda-kasabian-was-part-of-the-manson-family-then -she-became-the-star.

"Tex had told me": Ibid., 186.

"There was a magnetism": Annie Brown, "Charles Manson, the Monster Who Sent Followers on Orgy of Violence," *Daily Record*, August 8, 2009, www.dailyrecord. co.uk/news/uk-world-news/charles-manson-the-monster-who-sent-1033247.

"I felt special": *Manson: 40 Years Later*, directed by Rawles.

"Now is the time": Bugliosi, *Helter Skelter*, 319.

"What it meant": Ibid., 244–245.

"something witchy": Ibid., 260.

"A mother's intuition": Love, *Good Vibrations*, 219.

"The seclusion of": Ibid., 203.

"My body was": *Manson: 40 Years Later*, directed by Rawles.

"Manson, on the": Ibid.

"Sadie was the first": Manson, *Manson in His Own Words*, 203.

"My only concern": Ibid., 206.

"one of the most": *Manson: 40 Years Later*, directed by Rawles.

"wanted to do a crime": Bugliosi, *Helter Skelter*, 83.

"He said the murders": *Manson: 40 Years Later*, directed by Rawles.

"I walked up a": Manson, *Manson in His Own Words*, 209–211.

"I couldn't feel": *Manson: 40 Years Later*, directed by Rawles.

"Rosemary LaBianca had": Ibid.

"Innocent people were": Ibid.

"Bobby was still": Manson, *Manson in His Own Words*, 212.

"I been to the moon": Carlin, *Catch a Wave*, 143.

"He upstaged the": *Charles Manson*, directed by Bate.

"When Charlie was": Ibid.

"The historians in the": *Manson: 40 Years Later*, directed by Rawles.

"My friends went": *Charles Manson*, directed by Bate.

"You desensitize": Ibid.

"Dig it!": Gerard DeGroot, *The Sixties Unplugged: A Kaleidoscopic History of a Disorderly Decade* (Cambridge, MA: Harvard University Press, 2008), 433.

"A lot of pretty": Hoskyns, *Waiting for the Sun*, 180.

"You're going to be": Guinn, *Manson: Life and Times*, 341.

"The last time I spoke": Wilson, *Wouldn't It Be Nice*, 184.

THE TAG

The idea of calling the epilogue "The Tag" is borrowed from David Felton in his mammoth Beach Boys article in *Rolling Stone*, "The Healing of Brother Brian," November 4, 1976.

"It's all right that": Truman Capote, *Music for Chameleons* (New York: Random House, 1980), 219–220.

"In its recounting": Jim Miller, "The Beach Boys: Holland," *Rolling Stone*, March 1, 1973, www.rollingstone.com/music/albumreviews/holland-19730301.

"Meals happened without": Wilson and Greenman, *I Am Brian Wilson*, 194.

"I'd like to thank": Carlin, *Catch a Wave*, 253.

"Everybody's kind of": Hedegaard, "Mike Love's Cosmic Journey," 46.

"Mike has his own": Ibid.

"I have nothing": Ibid., 45.

"Rock became a corporate": Ryan Dombal, "5-10-15-20: Van Dyke Parks," *Pitchfork*, April 22, 2011, http://pitchfork.com/news/42269-5-10-15-20-van-dyke-parks/.

"The Beach Boys were" . . . "I still had": Holdship, "Heroes and Villains."

"Beatles with their pants down": Patrick Humphries, *The Complete Guide to the Music of the Beatles, Volume 2* (London: Omnibus, 1998), 149.

"If these people want": Adam Webb, "The Lonely One," *Guardian*, December 14, 2003, www.theguardian.com/music/2003/dec/14/popandrock.

"He was not only": *Endless Harmony*, directed by Boyd.

"drugged-out no-talent": Webb, "Lonely One."

"The last time I saw": Holdship, "Heroes and Villains."

"smart, compassionate": A. O. Scott, "Review: 'Love and Mercy' Gets Inside Brian Wilson's Head," *New York Times*, June 4, 2015, www.nytimes.com/2015/06/05/movies/review-love-mercy-gets-inside-brian-wilsons-head.html?_r=0.

"He is rock and roll's": "Brian Wilson: Biography," John F. Kennedy Center for the Performing Arts website, September 2007, www.kennedy-center.org/Artist/A18317.

BIBLIOGRAPHY

BOOKS

Altschuler, Glenn C. *All Shook Up: How Rock 'n' Roll Changed America*. New York: Oxford University Press, 2003.

Amburn, Ellis. *Pearl: The Obsessions and Passions of Janis Joplin*. New York: Warner Books, 1992.

———. *Buddy Holly: A Biography*. New York: St. Martin's, 1995.

Badman, Keith. *The Beach Boys: The Definitive Diary of America's Greatest Band on Stage and in the Studio*. San Francisco: Backbeat Books, 2004.

Bangs, Lester. *Psychotic Reactions and Carburetor Dung*. New York: Alfred A. Knopf, 1987.

Biskind, Peter. *Easy Riders, Raging Bulls: How the Sex-Drugs-and-Rock 'n' Roll Generation Saved Hollywood*. New York: Simon and Schuster, 1998.

Broven, John. *Record Makers and Breakers: Voices of the Independent Rock 'n' Roll Pioneers*. Urbana: University of Illinois Press, 2009.

Brown, Mick. *Tearing Down the Wall of Sound: The Rise and Fall of Phil Spector*. New York: Alfred A. Knopf, 2007.

Bugliosi, Vincent, and Curt Gentry. *Helter Skelter: The True Story of the Manson Murders*. New York: W. W. Norton, 1974.

Capote, Truman. *Music for Chameleons*. New York: Random House, 1980.

Carlin, Peter Ames. *Catch a Wave: The Rise, Fall, and Redemption of the Beach Boys' Brian Wilson*. Philadelphia: Rodale, 2006.

Cogan, Jim, and William Clark. *Temples of Sound: Inside the Great Recording Studios*. San Francisco: Chronicle Books, 2003.

Cohn, Nik. *Awopbopaloobop Alopbamboom: The Golden Age of Rock*. St. Albans, UK: Paladin, 1970.

Collins, Judy. *Sweet Judy Blue Eyes*. New York: Three Rivers, 2011.

Connolly, Kieron. *Dark History of Hollywood: A Century of Greed, Corruption, and Scandal Behind the Movies*. London: Amber Books, 2014.

Cornyn, Stan, and Paul Scanlon. *Exploding: The Highs, Hits, Hype, Heroes, and Hustlers of the Warner Music Group*. New York: HarperEntertainment, 2002.

Crosby, David, and Carl Gottlieb. *Long Time Gone: The Autobiography of David Crosby*. New York: Doubleday, 1988.

Dannen, Fredric. *Hit Men: Power Brokers and Fast Money Inside the Music Business*. New York: Times Books, 1990.

Davis, Clive, and Anthony DeCurtis. *The Soundtrack of My Life*. New York: Simon and Schuster Paperbacks, 2013.

DeGroot, Gerard J. *The Sixties Unplugged: A Kaleidoscopic History of a Disorderly Decade*. Cambridge, MA: Harvard University Press, 2010.

Doggett, Peter. *You Never Give Me Your Money: The Beatles After the Breakup*. New York: Harper, 2010.

Donnelley, Paul. *Fade to Black: A Book of Movie Obituaries*. London: Omnibus, 2000; revised edition, 2003.

Dylan, Bob, and Barry Feinstein. *Hollywood Foto-Rhetoric: The Lost Manuscript*. New York: Simon and Schuster, 2008.

Einarson, John. *Mr. Tambourine Man: The Life and Legacy of the Byrds' Gene Clark*. San Francisco: Backbeat Books, 2005.

Einarson, John, and Richie Furay. *For What It's Worth: The Story of Buffalo Springfield*. New York: Cooper Square, 2004.

Fiegel, Eddi. *Dream a Little Dream of Me: The Life of 'Mama' Cass Elliot*. London: Pan Books, 2006.

Fogerty, John, with Jimmy McDonough. *Fortunate Son: My Life, My Music*. New York: Little, Brown, 2015.

Fong-Torres, Ben. *Eagles: Taking It to the Limit*. Philadelphia: Running Press, 2011.

———. *Hickory Wind: The Life and Times of Gram Parsons*. New York: Pocket Books, 1991.

Gaines, Steven. *Heroes and Villains: The True Story of the Beach Boys*. New York: New American Library, 1986.

Gillett, Charlie. *The Sound of the City: The Rise of Rock and Roll*. Boston: Da Capo, 1996.

Goodman, Fred. *The Mansion on the Hill: Dylan, Young, Geffen, Springsteen, and the Head-On Collision of Rock and Commerce*. New York: Times Books, 1997.

Greenwald, Matthew. *Go Where You Wanna Go: The Oral History of the Mamas and the Papas*. New York: Cooper Square, 2002.

Guinn, Jeff. *Manson: The Life and Times of Charles Manson*. New York: Simon and Schuster Paperbacks, 2013.

Guralnick, Peter. *Dream Boogie: The Triumph of Sam Cooke*. New York: Little, Brown, 2005.

———. *Sam Phillips: The Man Who Invented Rock 'n' Roll*. New York: Little, Brown, 2015.

Hajdu, David. *Positively 4th Street: The Lives and Times of Joan Baez, Bob Dylan, Mimi Baez Fariña, and Richard Fariña*. New York: Picador, 2001.

Haring, Bruce. *Off the Charts: Ruthless Days and Reckless Nights Inside the Music Industry*. New York: Birch Lane, 1996.

Hartman, Kent. *The Wrecking Crew: The Inside Story of Rock and Roll's Best-Kept Secret*. New York: Thomas Dunne Books, 2012.

Hjort, Christopher. *So You Want to Be a Rock 'n' Roll Star: The Byrds Day-by-Day, 1965–1973*. London: Jawbone, 2008.

Hopkins, Jerry, and Danny Sugerman. *No One Here Gets Out Alive*. New York: Warner Books, 1980.

Hoskyns, Barney. *Hotel California: The True-Life Adventures of Crosby, Stills, Nash, Young, Mitchell, Taylor, Browne, Ronstadt, Geffen, the Eagles, and Their Many Friends*. Hoboken, NJ: John Wiley and Sons, 2006.

———. *Waiting for the Sun: Strange Days, Weird Scenes, and the Sound of Los Angeles*. New York: St. Martin's, 1996.

Huddleston, Judy. *Love Him Madly: An Intimate Memoir of Jim Morrison*. Chicago: Chicago Review Press, 2013.

Jackson, Andrew Grant. *1965: The Most Revolutionary Year in Music*. New York: Thomas Dunne Books, 2015.

James, Tommy, with Martin Fitzpatrick. *Me, the Mob, and the Music: One Helluva Ride with Tommy James and the Shondells*. New York: Scribner, 2010.

Jones, Quincy. *Q: The Autobiography of Quincy Jones*. New York: Doubleday, 2001.

Kaplan, James. *Sinatra: The Chairman*. New York: Doubleday, 2015.

Kaufman, David. *Doris Day: The Untold Story of the Girl Next Door*. New York: Virgin Books, 2008.

Kealing, Bob. *Calling Me Home: Gram Parsons and the Roots of Country Rock*. Gainesville: University Press of Florida, 2012.

Kent, Nick. *The Dark Stuff: Selected Writings on Rock Music*. Cambridge, MA: Da Capo, 1995; revised edition, 2002.

King, Carole. *A Natural Woman: A Memoir*. New York: Grand Central, 2012.

Knoedelseder, William. *Stiffed: A True Story of MCA, the Music Business, and the Mafia*. New York: HarperCollins, 1993.

Kooper, Al. *Backstage Passes and Backstabbing Bastards: Memoirs of a Rock 'n' Roll Survivor*. New York: Backbeat Books, 2008.

Leaf, David. *The Beach Boys and the California Myth*. New York: Grosset and Dunlap, 1978.

Lewis, Grover. *Academy All the Way*. San Francisco: Straight Arrow Books, 1974.

Lichtenstein, Grace, and Laura Dankner. *Musical Gumbo: The Music of New Orleans*. New York: W. W. Norton, 1993.

Linna, Miriam, and Randell Fuller. *I Fought the Law: The Life and Strange Death of Bobby Fuller*. New York: Kicks Books, 2014.

Lipton, Peggy, David Dalton, and Coco Dalton. *Breathing Out*. New York: St. Martin's, 2005.

Lomax, Alan. *The Land Where the Blues Began*. New York: Pantheon, 1993.

Love, Mike, with James S. Hirsch. *Good Vibrations: My Life as a Beach Boy*. New York: Blue Rider, 2016.

Manson, Charles, and Nuel Emmons. *Manson in His Own Words: The Shocking Confessions of "The Most Dangerous Man Alive."* New York: Grove, 1986.

Marcus, Greil. *The Doors: A Lifetime of Listening to Five Mean Years*. New York: PublicAffairs, 2011.

———. *Mystery Train: Images of America in Rock 'n' Roll Music*. New York: Plume, 2008.

———, ed. *Rock 'n' Roll Will Stand*. Boston: Beacon, 1969.

Marmorstein, Gary. *The Label: The Story of Columbia Records*. New York: Thunder's Mouth, 2007.

Marsh, Dave. *Fortunate Son: Criticism and Journalism by America's Best-Known Rock Writer*. New York: Random House, 1985.

———. *The Heart of Rock and Soul: The 1001 Greatest Singles Ever Made*. New York: Plume, 1989.

McDonough, Jimmy. *Shakey: Neil Young's Biography*. New York: Random House, 2002.

McGowan, David. *Weird Scenes Inside the Canyon: Laurel Canyon, Covert Ops, and the Dark Heart of the Hippie Dream*. London: World Headpress, 2014.

McKeen, William, ed. *Rock and Roll Is Here to Stay: An Anthology*. New York: W. W. Norton, 2000.

Merritt, Greg. *Room 1219: The Life of Fatty Arbuckle, the Mysterious Death of Virginia Rappe, and the Scandal That Changed Hollywood*. Chicago: Chicago Review Press, 2013.

Meyer, David N. *Twenty Thousand Roads: The Ballad of Gram Parsons and His Cosmic American Music*. New York: Villard Books, 2007.

Miller, James. *Flowers in the Dustbin: The Rise of Rock and Roll, 1947–1977*. New York: Simon and Schuster, 1999.

Monk, Katherine. *Joni: The Creative Odyssey of Joni Mitchell*. Vancouver: Greystone Books, 2012.

Murphy, Gareth. *Cowboys and Indies: The Epic History of the Record Industry*. New York: Thomas Dunne Books, 2014.

Nash, Graham. *Wild Tales: A Rock and Roll Life*. New York: Crown Archetype, 2013.

Norman, Philip. *Rave On: The Biography of Buddy Holly*. New York: Simon and Schuster, 1996.

O'Brien, Karen. *Joni Mitchell: Shadows and Light*. New York: Virgin Books, 2002.

Palmer, Robert. *Rock and Roll: An Unruly History*. New York: Harmony Books, 1995.

Phillips, Michelle. *California Dreamin': The True Story of the Mamas and the Papas*. New York: Warner Books, 1986.

Presley, Priscilla Beaulieu, with Sandra Harmon. *Elvis and Me*. New York: Putnam, 1985.

Priore, Domenic. *Riot on Sunset Strip: Rock 'n' Roll's Last Stand in Hollywood*. London: Jawbone, 2007.

———. *Smile: The Story of Brian Wilson's Lost Masterpiece*. New York: Bobcat Books, 2005.

Ronstadt, Linda. *Simple Dreams: A Musical Memoir*. New York: Simon and Schuster, 2013.

Sanders, Ed. *The Family: The Story of Charles Manson's Dune Buggy Attack Battalion*. New York: Dutton, 1971.

Schechter, Harold, ed. *True Crime: An American Anthology*. New York: Library of America, 2008.

Selvin, Joel. *Altamont: The Rolling Stones, the Hells Angels, and the Inside Story of Rock's Darkest Day*. New York: Dey Street Books, 2016.

———. *Here Comes the Night: The Dark Soul of Bert Berns and the Dirty Business of Rhythm and Blues*. Berkeley, CA: Counterpoint, 2014.

———. *Summer of Love: The Inside Story of LSD, Rock and Roll, Free Love, and High Times in the Wild West.* New York: Dutton, 1994.

Simmonds, Jeremy. *The Encyclopedia of Dead Rock Stars: Heroin, Handguns, and Ham Sandwiches.* Chicago: Chicago Review Press, 2008.

Sinatra, Nancy. *Frank Sinatra: My Father.* New York: Doubleday, 1985.

Sloan, P. F., and S. E. Feinberg. *What's Exactly the Matter with Me?: Memoirs of a Life in Music.* London: Jawbone, 2014.

Spector, Ronnie, and Vince Waldron. *Be My Baby: How I Survived Mascara, Miniskirts, and Madness.* New York: Harmony, 1990.

Spitz, Robert Stephen. *Barefoot in Babylon: The Creation of the Woodstock Music Festival, 1969.* New York: Viking Books, 1979.

Stanley, Bob. *Yeah! Yeah! Yeah!: The Story of Pop Music from Bill Haley to Beyoncé.* New York: W. W. Norton, 2014.

Stebbins, Jon. *Dennis Wilson: The Real Beach Boy.* Toronto: ECW, 2000.

Stebbins, Jon, and David Marks. *The Lost Beach Boy: The True Story of David Marks, One of the Founding Members of the Beach Boys.* London: Virgin Books, 2007.

Taylor, Derek. *As Time Goes By: Living in the Sixties with John Lennon, Paul McCartney, George Harrison, Ringo Starr, Brian Epstein, Allen Klein, Mae West, Brian Wilson, the Byrds, Danny Kaye, the Beach Boys, One Wife and Six Children in London, Los Angeles, New York City, and on the Road.* San Francisco: Straight Arrow Books, 1973.

———. *It Was Twenty Years Ago Today: An Anniversary Celebration of 1967.* New York: Simon and Schuster, 1987.

Torgoff, Martin. *Can't Find My Way Home: America in the Great Stoned Age, 1945–2000.* New York: Simon and Schuster Paperbacks, 2004.

Tosches, Nick. *Dino: Living High in the Dirty Business of Dreams.* New York: Doubleday, 1992.

Wald, Elijah. *Dylan Goes Electric!: Newport, Seeger, Dylan, and the Night That Split the Sixties.* New York: Dey Street Books, 2015.

Walker, Michael. *Laurel Canyon: The Inside Story of Rock and Roll's Legendary Neighborhood.* New York: Faber and Faber, 2006.

Wall, Mick. *Love Becomes a Funeral Pyre: A Biography of the Doors.* Chicago: Chicago Review Press, 2015.

Ward, Ed, Geoffrey Stokes, and Ken Tucker. *Rock of Ages: The Rolling Stone History of Rock and Roll.* New York: Rolling Stone/Prentice Hall, 1986.

Webb, Steve. *Looking for a Place to Fit.* Lakeland, FL: Textus, 2012.

Weller, Sheila. *Girls Like Us: Carole King, Joni Mitchell, Carly Simon—and the Journey of a Generation.* New York: Atria Books, 2008.

Werner, Craig. *A Change Is Gonna Come: Music, Race and the Soul of America.* New York: Plume, 1999.

White, Timothy. *The Nearest Far Away Place: Brian Wilson, the Beach Boys, and the Southern California Experience.* New York: Henry Holt, 1994.

Wilentz, Sean. *360 Sound: The Columbia Records Story.* San Francisco: Chronicle Books, 2012.

Williams, Paul. *Brian Wilson and the Beach Boys: How Deep Is the Ocean?* New York: Omnibus, 1997.

————. *Rock and Roll: The 100 Best Singles*. New York: Carroll and Graf, 1993.

Williamson, Joel. *Elvis Presley: A Southern Life*. New York: Oxford University Press, 2015.

Wilson, Brian, and Todd Gold. *Wouldn't It Be Nice: My Own Story*. New York: HarperCollins, 1991.

Wilson, Brian, and Ben Greeman. *I Am Brian Wilson: A Memoir*. Cambridge, MA: Da Capo, 2016.

Wolff, Daniel, S. R. Crain, Clifton White, and G. David Tenenbaum. *You Send Me: The Life and Times of Sam Cooke*. New York: William Morrow, 1995.

Wyman, Bill, and Ray Coleman. *Stone Alone: The Story of a Rock 'n' Roll Band*. New York: Viking Books, 1990.

Young, Neil. *Special Deluxe: A Memoir of Life and Cars*. New York: Blue Rider, 2014.

————. *Waging Heavy Peace*. New York: Blue Rider, 2012.

Zappa, Frank, and Peter Occhiogrosso. *The Real Frank Zappa Book*. New York: Poseidon, 1989.

Zollo, Paul. *Songwriters on Songwriting*. Boston: Da Capo, 2003.

ARTICLES

Carr, David. "Neil Young Comes Clean." *New York Times Magazine*, September 19, 2012. www.nytimes.com/2012/09/23/magazine/neil-young-comes-clean .html.

Chidester, Brian. "Brian Wilson's Secret Bedroom Tapes: A Track-by-Track Description." *LA Weekly*, March 5, 2014. www.laweekly.com/music/brian-wilsons-secret -bedroom-tapes-a-track-by-track-description-4479099.

Deitch, Charlie. "At 78 and with Myriad Health Issues, Surf-Rock Legend Dick Dale Plays Through the Pain." *Pittsburgh City Paper*, July 29, 2015. www .pghcitypaper.com/pittsburgh/at-78-and-with-a-myriad-of-health-issues -surf-rock-legend-dick-dale-plays-through-the-pain/Content?oid=1843341.

Eccleston, Danny. "The Seldom Scene Kid." *Mojo*, August 2012, 54–57.

Felton, David. "The Healing of Brother Brian." *Rolling Stone*, November 4, 1976. www.rollingstone.com/music/news/the-healing-of-brother-brian-the- rolling-stone-interview-with-the-beach-boys-19761104.

Fessier, Bruce. "Rock Hall of Famer Recalls Days in the Wrecking Crew." *Desert Sun*, April 2, 2015. www.desertsun.com/story/life/entertainment/music/2015/04/02 /hail-blaine-recalls-wrecking-crew/70816496.

Gilstrap, Peter. "Studio Musicians Who Played on Two Decades of Hits Finally Get Their Due." *LA Weekly*, March 3, 2015. www.laweekly.com/music/studio -musicians-who-played-on-two-decades-of-hits-finally-get-their-due-5414177.

Hedegaard, Erik. "Mike Love's Cosmic Journey." *Rolling Stone*, February 25, 2016.

Himes, Geoffrey. "High Times and Ebb Tides: Carl Wilson Recalls 20 Years with and Without Brian." *Musician*, September 1983.

Hinson, Mark. "Surf Is Still Up for Beach Boys' Bruce Johnston After 50 Years." *Tallahassee Democrat*, May 15, 2015.

Lewis, Randy. "'The Wrecking Crew!' Finally Sets the Records Straight." *Los Angeles Times*, March 7, 2015. www.latimes.com/entertainment/movies /la-et-ms-the-wrecking-crew-sound-explosion-20150308-story.html.

Marks, Scott. "Unsung Pros: Interview with *Wrecking Crew* Director Denny Tedesco." *San Diego Reader*, March 18, 2015. www.sandiegoreader.com /news/2015/mar/18/screen-wrecking-crew-director-denny-tedesco.

Martino, Alison. "How Dancing Took Off at the Whisky." *Los Angeles Magazine*, January 13, 2014. www.lamag.com/citythinkblog/vintage-los-angeles-how-go-go-dancing-took-off-at-the-whisky.

———. "The Tropicana Motel's Totally Rocking Heyday." *Los Angeles Magazine*, October 12, 2015. www.lamag.com/citythinkblog/the-tropicana-motels -totally-rocking-heyday.

McKay, Alistair. "Album by Album: Van Dyke Parks." *Uncut*, July 2010.

McKeen, William. "I Want the Beach Boys to Go On Forever." *Primo Times*, January 1977.

Nolan, Tom. "The Beach Boys: A California Saga." *Rolling Stone*, October 28, 1971. www.rollingstone.com/music/news/beach-boys-a-california-saga-19711028.

———. "The Beach Boys: A California Saga, Part II." *Rolling Stone*, November 11, 1971. www.rollingstone.com/music/news/beach-boys-a-california-saga -part-ii-19711111.

Peterycik, Rick. "Clarence White: A Byrd Who Truly Soared." *Guitar.com*. www .guitar.com/articles/clarence-white-byrd-who-truly-soared.

Rogers, Jude. "Joni Mitchell Has a Life Story that Reads Like a Tabloid Sensation." *Independent*, November 6, 2015. www.independent.co.uk/arts-entertainment /music/features/joni-mitchell-has-a-life-story-that-reads-like-a-tabloid -sensation-a6721081.html.

Ruggiero, Bob. "Carl Wilson: The Brother Who Kept the Beach Boys Together." *Houston Press*, December 15, 2015. www.houstonpress.com/music/carl-wilson -the-brother-who-kept-the-beach-boys-together-7853603.

Sharp, Ken. "Brian Wilson: The Rhapsody of a Beach Boy." *Goldmine*, January 2011.

———. "Interview with 'Pet Sounds' Lyricist Tony Asher." *Rock Cellar Magazine*, September 4, 2013. www.rockcellarmagazine.com/2013/09/04/beach-boys -pet-sounds-lyricist-tony-asher-interview-brian-wilson.

Smucker, Tom. "The Beach Boys: The Critics Kept a Knockin' But the Stars Kept a Rockin'." *Creem*, July 1972.

———. "The Beach Boys: A Sixties Epic, Part 2." *Creem*, August 1972.

Sullivan, John Jeremiah. "Seeking Jagger's Muse." *Paris Review*, September 28, 2015. www.theparisreview.org/blog/2015/09/28/seeking-jaggers-muse.

Sweeting, Adam. "Arthur Lee: Flower-Power Myth Maker Who Captured the Dark Side of the Summer of Love." *Guardian*, August 6, 2006. www .theguardian.com/news/2006/aug/07/guardianobituaries.usa.

Talese, Gay. "Charlie Manson's Home on the Range." *Esquire*, March 1970.

Webb, Adam. "The Lonely One." *Guardian*, December 14, 2003.

Weir, William. "Way Before the Beach Boys." *Boston Globe*, June 20, 2014.

Young, Neil. "My Defining Moment." *AARP: The Magazine*, February/March 2016.

FILMS

The Beach Boys: An American Band. Directed by Malcolm Leo. Malcolm Leo Productions, 1985.

The Big T.N.T. Show. Directed by Larry Peerce. American International Pictures, 1966.

Brian Wilson: I Just Wasn't Made for These Times. Directed by Don Was. Palomar Pictures, 1995.

The Doors. Directed by Oliver Stone. Lionsgate, 1991.

Endless Harmony: The Beach Boys Story. Directed by Alan Boyd. Capitol, 1998.

The Girls on the Beach. Directed by William Witney. Paramount, 1965.

Glenn Campbell: I'll Be Me. Directed by James Keach. Virgil Films, 2014.

Good Vibrations: The Life and Times of the Beach Boys. Directed by Jonny Baak. Independent production, California, 2011.

Head. Directed by Bob Rafelson. Paramount, 1968.

Love and Mercy. Directed by Bill Pohlad. Lionsgate, 2015.

Lucifer Rising. Directed by Kenneth Anger. New Cinema, 1972.

The Monkey's Uncle. Directed by Robert Stevenson. Walt Disney Productions, 1965.

Monterey Pop. Directed by D.A. Pennebaker. Leacock-Pennebaker, 1968.

Phil Spector. Directed by David Mamet. HBO Films, 2013.

Riot on Sunset Strip. Directed by Arthur Dreifuss. American International, 1967.

The T.A.M.I. Show. Directed by Steve Binder. Screen Entertainment Company, 1964.

The Trip. Directed by Roger Corman. American International, 1967.

Two-Lane Blacktop. Directed by Monte Hellman. Universal, 1971.

The Wrecking Crew. Directed by Denny Tedesco. Magnolia Pictures, 2015.

LINER NOTES

Blair, John. *Cowabunga: The Surf Box.* Rhino Records, 1996.

Peeples, Stephen K. *The Monterey International Pop Festival, June 16-17-18, 1967.* Rhino Records, 1997.

Torrence, Dean. *The Jan and Dean Anthology Album.* United Artists, 1971.

Viola, Ken. *Buffalo Springfield Box Set.* Rhino Records, 2001.

SELECTED DISCOGRAPHY

This discography is for the major Los Angeles artists and bands covered in the book and is generally limited to the timeframe of the sixties.

THE BAND

Music from Big Pink, Capitol Records, 1968.
The Band, Capitol Records, 1969.

THE BEACH BOYS

Surfin' Safari, Capitol Records, 1962.
Surfin' USA, Capitol Records, 1963.
Surfer Girl, Capitol Records, 1963.
Little Deuce Coupe, Capitol Records, 1963.
Shut Down Volume 2, Capitol Records, 1964.
All Summer Long, Capitol Records, 1964.
Concert, Capitol Records, 1964.
Christmas Album, Capitol Records, 1964.
Today!, Capitol Records, 1965.
Summer Days (and Summer Nights!!), Capitol Records, 1965.
Party!, Capitol Records, 1965.
Pet Sounds, Capitol Records, 1966.
Smiley Smile, Brother/Capitol Records, 1967.
Wild Honey, Capitol Records, 1967.
Friends, Capitol Records, 1968.
Stack-o-Tracks, Capitol Records, 1968.
20/20, Capitol Records, 1969.
Sunflower, Brother/Warner-Reprise Records, 1970.
Surf's Up, Brother/Warner-Reprise Records, 1971.
The Pet Sounds Sessions, Capitol Records, 1997; recorded 1965–1966.
The Smile Sessions, Capitol Records, 2011; recorded 1966–1967.
Beach Boys' Party! Uncovered and Unplugged, Capitol Records, 2015; recorded 1965.

Pet Sounds: Fiftieth Anniversary Edition, Capitol Records, 2016; recorded 1965–1966.

BLAINE, HAL

Deuces, "T's", Roadsters and Drums, RCA Records, 1963.
Drums! Drums! À Go Go, RCA Records, 1965.
Hal Blaine, RCA Records, 1965.
Psychedelic Percussion, Dunhill Records, 1967.

THE BOBBY FULLER FOUR

KRLA King of the Wheels, Mustang Records, 1966.
I Fought the Law, Mustang Records, 1966.

BUFFALO SPRINGFIELD

Buffalo Springfield, ATCO Records, 1966.
Buffalo Springfield Again, ATCO Records, 1967.
Last Time Around, ATCO Records, 1968.
Box Set, ATCO/Rhino Records, 2001.

THE BYRDS

Mr. Tambourine Man, Columbia Records, 1965.
Turn! Turn! Turn!, Columbia Records, 1965.
Fifth Dimension, Columbia Records, 1966.
Younger than Yesterday, Columbia Records, 1967.
The Notorious Byrd Brothers, Columbia Records, 1968.
Sweetheart of the Rodeo, Columbia Records, 1968.
Dr. Byrds and Mr. Hyde, Columbia Records, 1969.
Ballad of Easy Rider, Columbia Records, 1969.
(Untitled), Columbia Records, 1970.
Byrdmaniax, Columbia, 1971.

CAMPBELL, GLEN

Too Late to Worry—Too Blue to Cry, Capitol Records, 1963.
The Astounding 12-String Guitar of Glen Campbell, Capitol Records, 1964.
Burning Bridges, Capitol Records, 1967.
Gentle on My Mind, Capitol Records, 1967.
By the Time I Get to Phoenix, Capitol Records, 1967.
Hey, Little One, Capitol Records, 1968.
A New Place in the Sun, Capitol Records, 1968.
Wichita Lineman, Capitol Records, 1968.
Galveston, Capitol Records, 1969.

THE CITY

Now That Everything's Been Said, Ode Records, 1968.

CLARK, GENE

Gene Clark with the Gosdin Brothers, Columbia Records, 1967.
White Light, A&M Records, 1971.

COOKE, SAM

Songs by Sam Cooke, Keen Records, 1958.
Encore, Keen Records, 1958.
Tribute to the Lady, Keen Records, 1959.
The Wonderful World of Sam Cooke, Keen Records, 1960.
Cooke's Tour, RCA Records, 1960.
Hits of the '50s, RCA Records, 1960.
Swing Low, RCA Records, 1961.
My Kind of Blues, RCA Records, 1961.
Twistin' the Night Away, RCA Records, 1962.
Mr. Soul, RCA Records, 1963.
Night Beat, RCA Records, 1963.
Ain't That Good News, RCA Records, 1964.
Live at the Harlem Square Club, 1963, RCA Records, 1985.
The Man Who Invented Soul, RCA Records, 2000.

CROSBY, STILLS AND NASH

Crosby, Stills and Nash, Atlantic Records, 1969.

CROSBY, STILLS, NASH AND YOUNG

Deja Vu, Atlantic Records, 1970.
4 Way Street, Atlantic Records, 1971.

THE CRYSTALS

Twist Uptown, Philles Records, 1962.
He's a Rebel, Philles Records, 1963.

DESHANNON, JACKIE

Jackie DeShannon, Liberty Records, 1963.
Breakin' It Up on the Beatles Tour, Liberty Records, 1964.
Don't Turn Your Back on Me, Liberty Records, 1964.
You Won't Forget Me, Imperial Records, 1965.
This Is Jackie DeShannon, Imperial Records, 1965.
Me About You, Imperial Records, 1968
Put a Little Love in Your Heart, Imperial Records, 1969.

DICK DALE AND HIS DEL-TONES

Surfers' Choice, Deltone Records, 1962.
King of the Surf Guitar, Capitol Records, 1963.
Checkered Flag, Capitol Records, 1963.
Summer Surf, Capitol Records, 1964.
Mr. Eliminator, Capitol Records, 1964.

DILLARD AND CLARK

The Fantastic Expedition of Dillard and Clark, A&M Records, 1968.
Through the Morning, Through the Night, A&M Records, 1969.

THE DOORS

The Doors, Elektra Records, 1967.
Strange Days, Elektra Records, 1967.
Waiting for the Sun, Elektra Records, 1968.
The Soft Parade, Elektra Records, 1969.
Morrison Hotel, Elektra Records, 1970.

THE FANTASTIC BAGGYS

Tell 'Em I'm Surfin', Imperial Records, 1964.

THE FLYING BURRITO BROTHERS

The Gilded Palace of Sin, A&M Records, 1969.
Burrito Deluxe, A&M Records, 1970.

THE GRASS ROOTS

Where Were You When I Needed You, Dunhill Records, 1966.
Let's Live for Today, Dunhill Records, 1967.
Feelings, Dunhill Records, 1968.
Lovin' Things, Dunhill Records, 1969.

THE HONDELLS

Go Little Honda, Mercury Records, 1964.
The Hondells, Mercury Records, 1964.

THE IKE AND TINA TURNER REVUE

River Deep–Mountain High, Philles Records, 1966.

THE INTERNATIONAL SUBMARINE BAND

Safe at Home, LHI/ABC Records, 1968.

JAN AND DEAN

The Jan and Dean Sound, Doré Records, 1960.
Jan and Dean's Golden Hits, Liberty Records, 1962.
Surf City (and Other Swingin' Cities), Liberty Records, 1963.
Drag City, Liberty Records, 1963.
Dead Man's Curve/The New Girl in School, Liberty Records, 1964.
Ride the Wild Surf, Liberty Records, 1964.
The Little Old Lady from Pasadena, Liberty Records, 1964.
Command Performance, Liberty Records, 1965.
Folk 'n Roll, Liberty Records, 1965.
Jan and Dean Meet Batman, Liberty Records, 1966.
Filet of Soul, Liberty Records, 1966.
Popsicle, Liberty Records, 1966.
Jan and Dean Anthology Album, United Artists, 1971.
Save for a Rainy Day, Sundazed Records; recorded 1967, released 1996.
Carnival of Sound, Rhino Handmade Records; recorded 1968, released 2010.

JOHNSTON, BRUCE

Surfers' Pajama Party, Del-Fi Records, 1962.
Surfin' 'Round the World, Columbia Records, 1963.

KESSEL, BARNEY

Bossa Nova, Reprise Records, 1961.
Contemporary Latin Rhythms, Reprise Records, 1963.
On Fire, Emerald Records, 1965.

THE KICKSTANDS

Black Boots and Bikes, Capitol Records, 1964.

KING, CAROLE

Writer, Ode Records, 1970.
Tapestry, Ode Records, 1971.

LOVE

Love, Elektra Records, 1966.
Da Capo, Elektra Records, 1966.
Forever Changes, Elektra Records, 1967.
Out Here, Blue Thumb Records, 1969.

THE MAMAS AND THE PAPAS

If You Can Believe Your Eyes and Ears, Dunhill Records, 1966.
The Mamas and the Papas, Dunhill Records, 1966.

The Mamas and the Papas Deliver, Dunhill Records, 1967.
The Papas and the Mamas, Dunhill Records, 1968.
People Like Us, Dunhill Records, 1971.

THE MARKETTS

Out of Limits!, Warner Bros. Records, 1964.

MCGUIRE, BARRY

The Barry McGuire Album, Mira Records, 1963.
Eve of Destruction, Dunhill Records, 1965.
This Precious Time, Dunhill Records, 1965.
The World's Last Private Citizen, RCA Records, 1968.

MR. GASSER AND THE WEIRDOS

Surfink!, Capitol Records, 1964.

MITCHELL, JONI

Song to a Seagull, Reprise Records, 1968.
Clouds, Reprise Records, 1969.
Ladies of the Canyon, Reprise Records, 1970.
Blue, Reprise Records, 1971.

THE MONKEES

The Monkees, Colgems Records, 1966.
More of the Monkees, Colgems Records, 1967.
Headquarters, Colgems Records, 1967.
Pisces, Aquarius, Capricorn and Jones Ltd., Colgems Records, 1967.
The Birds, the Bees and the Monkees, Colgems Records, 1968.
Head, Colgems Records, 1968.

NELSON, RICKY, 1957–61; RICK, 1961–

Ricky, Imperial Records, 1957.
Ricky Nelson, Imperial Records, 1958.
Ricky Sings Again, Imperial Records, 1959.
Songs by Ricky, Imperial Records, 1959.
More Songs by Ricky, Imperial Records, 1960.
Rick Is 21, Imperial Records, 1961.
The Very Thought of You, Decca Records, 1964.
Bright Lights and Country Music, Decca Records, 1966.
Country Fever, Decca Records, 1967.
Another Side of Rick Nelson, Decca Records, 1967.
In Concert at the Troubadour, Decca Records, 1970.
Rick Sings Nelson, Decca Records, 1970.

PARKS, VAN DYKE

Song Cycle, Warner Bros. Records, 1968.
Discover America, Warner Bros. Records, 1972.
With Brian Wilson, *Orange Crate Art*, Warner Bros. Records, 1995.

PARSONS, GRAM

GP, Reprise Records, 1973.
Grievous Angel, Reprise Records, 1974.

PAUL REVERE AND THE RAIDERS

Like, Long Hair, Gardena Records, 1961.
Paul Revere and the Raiders, Sande Records, 1963.
Here They Come!, Columbia Records, 1965.
Just Like Us!, Columbia Records, 1966.
Midnight Ride, Columbia Records, 1966.
The Spirit of '67, Columbia Records, 1966.
Revolution!, Columbia Records, 1967.
Goin' to Memphis, Columbia Records, 1968.
Something Happening, Columbia Records, 1968.
Hard 'n' Heavy (with Marshmallow), Columbia Records, 1969.

THE RIGHTEOUS BROTHERS

Right Now!, Moonglow Records, 1963.
Some Blue-Eyed Soul, Moonglow Records, 1964.
This Is New!, Moonglow Records, 1965.
You've Lost That Lovin' Feelin', Philles Records, 1965.
Just Once in My Life, Philles Records, 1965.
Back to Back, Philles Records, 1965.
Soul and Inspiration, Verve Records, 1966.
Go Ahead and Cry, Verve Records, 1966.
Sayin' Somethin', Verve Records, 1967.
Souled Out, Verve Records, 1967.

THE RIP CHORDS

Hey Little Cobra and Other Hot Rod Hits, Columbia Records, 1964.
Three Window Coupe, Columbia Records, 1964.

THE RONETTES

Today's Hits, Philles Records, 1963.
Presenting the Fabulous Ronettes Featuring Veronica, Philles Records, 1964.

RONSTADT, LINDA

Hand Sown . . . Home Grown, Capitol Records, 1969.
Silk Purse, Capitol Records, 1970.

THE SILLY SURFERS

Music to Make Models By, Hairy Records, 1964.
The Sounds of the Silly Surfers, Mercury Records, 1964.

SLOAN, P.F.

Songs of Our Times, Dunhill Records, 1965.
Twelve More Times, Dunhill Records, 1966.
Measure of Pleasure, ATCO Records, 1968.

SPECTOR, PHIL

With various artists. *A Christmas Gift for You from Phil Spector*, Philles Records, 1963.

STILLS, STEPHEN

Stephen Stills, Atlantic Records, 1970.

THE STONE PONEYS

The Stone Poneys, Capitol Records, 1967.
Evergreen, Volume 2, Capitol Records, 1967.

THE SUPER STOCKS

Thunder Road, Capitol Records, 1964.
Surf Route 101, Capitol Records, 1964.
School Is a Drag, Capitol Records, 1964

THE SURFARIS

Hit City '64, Brunswick Records, 1963.
Wipe Out and Surfer Joe and Other Popular Selections by Other Instrumental Groups, Dot Records, 1963.
Play, Decca Records, 1963.
Fun City, U.S.A., Brunswick Records, 1964.
It Ain't Me, Babe, Decca Records, 1965.
Hit City '65, Decca Records, 1965.

THE TEDDY BEARS

Teddy Bears Sing, Imperial Records, 1959.

THE TURTLES

It Ain't Me Babe, White Whale Records, 1965.
You Baby, White Whale Records, 1966.

Happy Together, White Whale Records, 1967.
The Turtles Present the Battle of the Bands, White Whale Records, 1968.
Turtle Soup, White Whale Records, 1969.
Wooden Head, White Whale Records, 1970.

VARIOUS ARTISTS

Cowabunga! The Surf Box, Rhino Records, 1996.

THE VENTURES

Walk, Don't Run, Dolton Records, 1960.
The Ventures, Dolton Records, 1961.
Another Smash!!!, Dolton Records, 1961.
The Colorful Ventures, Dolton Records, 1961.
Twist with the Ventures, Dolton Records, 1962.
Twist Party, Volume 2, Dolton Records, 1962.
Mashed Potatoes and Gravy, Dolton Records, 1962.
The Ventures Play Telstar and the Lonely Bull, Dolton Records, 1963.
Surfing, Dolton Records, 1963.
Let's Go!, Dolton Records, 1963.
The Ventures in Space, Dolton Records, 1964.
The Ventures a Go-Go, Dolton Records, 1965.
Where the Action Is!, Dolton Records, 1966.

WILSON, MURRY

The Many Moods of Murry Wilson, Capitol Records, 1967.

YOUNG, NEIL

Neil Young, Reprise Records, 1968.
With Crazy Horse. *Everybody Knows This Is Nowhere*, Reprise Records, 1969.
After the Gold Rush, Reprise Records, 1970.

INDEX